TREK

Studies about the Mobility of the Pioneering Population at the Cape

PJ vd Merwe

Translated by Roger B Beck

SUN MeDIA

First edition 2022

ISBN 978-1-998951-14-7
ISBN 978-1-998951-15-4 (e-book)

Set in Times New Roman 12/16

Cover design, typesetting and production by African Sun Media
Cover image: © South African Library Archive, Cape Town

This publication can be ordered from:

orders@africansunmedia.co.za
Takealot: bit.ly/2monsfl
Google Books: bit.ly/2k1Uilm
Amazon Kindle: amzn.to/2ktL.pkL
JSTOR: https://bit.ly/3udc057
africansunmedia.store.it.si (e-books)

Visit africansunmedia.co.za for more information.

TABLE OF CONTENTS

TRANSLATOR'S INTRODUCTION

It has been more than 25 years since I published my translation of Dr. Petrus Johannes van der Merwe's *Die Trekboer in die Geskiedenis van die Kaapkolonie (1657-1842)*, as *The Migrant Farmer in the History of the Cape Colony, 1657-1842* (Ohio University Press, 1995). At the time I intended to translate and publish all three volumes of his classic trekboer trilogy—the other two studies being *TREK. Studies oor die Mobiliteit van die Pioniersbevolking aan die Kaap*, and *Die Noordwaartse Beweging van die Boere voor die Groot Trek*. With that in mind, I worked on all three volumes at the same time in the late 1980s and 1990s so I would not have to duplicate (triplicate?) my research for each volume. Thus, for example, I tried to check all of Dr. van der Merwe's sources, bibliographies, and footnotes in libraries and archives in the Netherlands and in South Africa for all three volumes at once, rather than making separate trips to do so. By the time I had *The Migrant Farmer* ready for publication, the majority of the translation of TREK was complete, as was more than half of *Die Noordwaartse Beweging* [*The Northward Movement*].[1]

Following the publication of *The Migrant Farmer*, however, Ohio University Press decided they did not want to publish the other two volumes. I tried for some years to find a publisher for these studies, and was told by some South African presses and scholars that translations were not needed because anyone who could read Afrikaans could understand these works. Of course, I did not agree that the works could just be picked up and read by anyone with a modicum of Afrikaans, and obviously not if one does not read Afrikaans, which is much of the international audience. Also, if one looks at them closely, particularly *Die Trekboer* and *Noordwaartse Beweging*, they will realize that besides the Afrikaans text, there are extensive, untranslated passages (sometimes a page or two or more) in Dutch, German, French, and English. I assume that Professor van der Merwe thought the scholarly reader in the Europe and South Africa of the 1930s and 40s would need no translations. Therefore, to understand the texts in their entirety, one must be capable of reading at least five (there are also a few brief passages in Latin) languages, many of them employing grammar, vocabulary, and spellings from the 17th, 18th, and 19th centuries. As I wrote in my "Translator's Introduction" to *The Migrant Farmer*, "Although some of the works from which these quotations are taken are now available in English editions, I have chosen to offer my own translation of the entire book and not to translate some here and borrow from others there. I hope this will make reading of the work more consistent throughout."[2] Likewise, all the translations in whatever language in TREK are mine.

Unable to find a publisher, I abandoned the project.

Over the last 15 years or so, Dr. van der Merwe's daughter, Margaretha Schäfer, has been busy organizing her father's archives and papers. She has gathered various of his writings,

---

[1] P.J. van der Merwe, *Die Noordwaartse Beweging van die Boere voor die Groot Trek (1770- 1842)* (The Hague: W.P. van Stockum & Son, 1937); *Die Trekboer in die Geskiedenis van die Kaapkolonie* (Cape Town: Nasionale Pers, Beperk, 1938); *TREK. Studies oor die Mobiliteit van die Pioniersbevolking aan die Kaap* (Cape Town: Nasionale Pers, Beperk, 1945). *P.J. van der Merwe, The Migrant Farmer in the History of the Cape Colony, 1657-1842*. Translated by Roger B. Beck (Athens, Ohio: Ohio University Press, 1995).

[2] van der Merwe, *The Migrant Farmer*, p. XI.

photos, and publications and published these collections both in the original Afrikaans and in her own translations into English. These works, published by African Sun Media at the University of Stellenbosch (Dr. van der Merwe's university where he was a student and then professor of history), include *Pioneers of the Dorsland, Reports from the Dorsland,* and *Meer oor P.J. van der Merwe.* I highly recommend Mrs. Schäfer's collections as they are excellent complements to Dr. van der Merwe's trilogy, and are beautifully illustrated with the photos he took on his travels across the Cape interior. African Sun Media, with Mrs. Schäfer's assistance, has also published new Afrikaans editions of *TREK, Die Trekboer,* and *Noordwaarste Beweging,* all three of which have been long out of print.

To make this as complete a collection as possible of her father's work, Mrs. Schäfer encouraged African Sun Media to publish the other two volumes of my translation of the trilogy. I am so very grateful for her assistance in this. She has also been extremely helpful as I worked to put the finishing touches on this present volume, particularly with a number of obscure and local words and phrases from the Karoo and other regions.

There were some reviewers who felt that I should have included in *The Migrant Farmer* a biography of Dr. van der Merwe to put his life and work in context. I agree that that would have been a useful addition but it would have put me over my word limit and could not be done. For such a biography I would recommend, for those who read Afrikaans, the extensive discussion of Dr. van der Merwe written by F.A. van Jaarsveld in 1981, "P.J. van der Merwe: Ondersoeker van die Afrikaner se landelike pioniersgeskiedenis," ("P.J. van der Merwe: Researcher of the Rural Afrikaner 's Pioneer History."). Much more recently, and in English, one of South Africa's leading historians, Hermann Giliomee, wrote a Foreword to Margaretha Schäfer's compilation of her father's work, *Reports from the Dorsland and other pioneering regions.* Dr. Giliomee was a student of Professor van der Merwe's at Stellenbosch University and brings both scholarly and personal insights to his essay.[3]

Although I did not write a comprehensive overview of Dr. van der Merwe's work for *The Migrant Farmer,* I did write a six page introduction that does do some of that. Rather than repeat what I said there, I will here just refer the reader to my "Translator 's Introduction" in that work, and to the two works cited above. What I will note here is that *TREK,* far more than either of the other two books in the trilogy, displays the extensive personal observation and interaction Dr. van der Merwe had with the trekboer volk of the 1930s and 40s. Travelling by car over 15,000 miles throughout the Karoo and Northwestern Cape, Dr. van der Merwe spoke with hundreds of people—women, men, children—from all classes, occupations, and races. This work in itself is a unique archive of the life of the trekboer that has long passed into history and can never be duplicated. Again, Mrs. Schäfer's publication of her father's articles, photos, and other, shorter publications are primarily concerned with this aspect of his work. In *Pioneers of the Dorsland,* Dr. van der Merwe set out to "share a few things about the Northwest that I

---

[3] F.A. van Jaarsveld, in *Wie en wat is die Afrikaner?* (Cape Town: Tafelberg, 1981), pp. 129-91. Hermann Giliomee, "FOREWORD. PJ van der Merwe: Trail-blazing historian of the Afrikaners' pioneering way of life," in P.J. van der Merwe, *Reports from the Dorsland and other pioneering regions.* Compiled and translated, Margaretha Schäfer; final edit, Franz Schäfer. (Stellenbosch: African Sun Media, 2020), pp. i-iv. This work appears in both Afrikaans and English editions.

won't be able to fit into the book." *Pioneers* is more of a very personal journal of his travels—a kind of "here is where I went, how I carried out my research, and what I found" account.[4]

Again, because my approach to all three of three volumes was the same—in terms of how I approached the translator's task—I devoted much space to this in my "Translator's Introduction" in *The Migrant Farmer*, and will again refer the interested reader to that writing. What is clearly different about this translation, however, from that of *The Migrant Farmer*, is that I have retained the term *trek* in all its various configurations, rather than change *trek* to "migrant." In my "Translator's Introduction" to *The Migrant Farmer*, I wrote:

> Some South African readers may find fault with me for translating such common terms as boer, trekboer,.... Although these terms are widely understood in South Africa, they would not be in the United States or among English readers in, say, Nigeria or India. As one example, trek and boer are recognized to some extent internationally, but in combination with other words—such as trekkos, trekpad, trekgees, boerwoning, veeboer and boerdery—they are not as familiar to non-South African readers and, I felt, had to be rendered in English.[5]

And indeed, some reviewers were critical of this change. Dr. Edwin Hees, retired faculty member from the Department of English, University of Stellenbosch, who did the final reading and editing of *The Migrant Farmer*, and I spent much time discussing whether the translation was appropriate and in the end decided it was. I still agree with this decision. Dr. van der Merwe himself, at the end of the first chapter in this volume, uses the term "migration" (*migrasie*) to describe the movement of these migrant farmers when he discusses the variety of migrations — "seasonal migrations," "temporary migrations," "incidental migrations," and "permanent migrations" (or "nomadism"). Nevertheless, for this translation I have used the term "migration" only where Dr. van der Merwe uses it, and in a few other cases where I believe it will be too confusing not to use it. Otherwise, I have retained the original terms.

Finally, once again I checked every one of Dr. van der Merwe's footnotes, published and unpublished. With many of the published sources, there were a number of errors, most of which were typos I suspect, such as incorrect page numbers, volume numbers, titles, and dates. One significant problem with much of the unpublished, primarily archival, sources in the Netherlands and South Africa, was that they had either not yet been catalogued at all when Dr. van der Merwe researched them, or their catalogue numbers have since been redone. So, I redid all of the footnotes, correcting where necessary, employing current catalogue numbers, and resetting them all in modern footnoting formats. For the first appearance of a name in the text, Dr. van der Merwe often only uses the last or family name — Barrow, Theal, Burchell. I have added in brackets the individual's first name where known at the first appearance. As with *The Migrant Farmer*, I have also constructed an Index, which was not done for any of the Afrikaans editions of the trilogy.

---

[4] P.J. van der Merwe, *Pioneers van die Dorsland*. Translated by Margaretha Schäfer. (Stellenbosch: African Sun Media under the Rapid Access Publishers imprint, 2017), p. i.
[5] van der Merwe, *The Migrant Farmer*, p. xi.

ACKNOWLEDGEMENTS

It is not entirely unusual for an author to be working on three books at a time, but perhaps this particular case is different because of the lapse of time between when I published the first volume and the publication of the second, and (forthcoming) third, volumes now. I have referred the reader above to the "Translator 's Introduction" in *The Migrant Farmer* for information about the translation because what I wrote then remains generally true today. The same is true for the "Acknowledgements" pages in *The Migrant Farmer* because the people I was grateful to for their help with that book are the same ones who, at the same time, were helping me in some way or another with TREK. To those friends, scholars, archivists and librarians acknowledged there I remain indebted.

After all the travel, research, discussions, and dusty shelves were behind me, however, there remained three people without whom I could not have completed this translation. First, Edwin Hees, retired professor of English at the University of Stellenbosch, who taught Afrikaans translation to English, and who Mrs. M.E. van der Merwe, Dr. van der Merwe's widow, personally asked to be the final editor for the *The Migrant Farmer* and *TREK*. He was a great pleasure to work with, a good friend, and saved me from making several egregious mistakes. Second, Mrs. van der Merwe, who had grave doubts when an American showed up on her doorstep and asked if he could translate her husband's works. With Dr. Hees' help, we convinced her that I was capable of doing the translation, and I made several lovely visits to her home in Stellenbosch, learning about her husband (who I never knew) and meeting her family. Third, and most recently, I have enjoyed knowing, and extensively corresponding with, Dr. van der Merwe's daughter, Margaretha, who is an excellent scholar and translator in her own right. As I mentioned, she has intervened to make it possible for me to publish TREK with African Sun Media, and also answered my many questions about local terms that are difficult to find in any text (including dictionaries) other than in Dr. van der Merwe's work. I am also very grateful to her brothers, Lieb (Gottlieb) and Joos, who contributed as well to getting TREK published.

Finally, infinite thanks to my wife, Ann, who has been hearing about these translations since we were married twenty-seven years ago. I suspect no one will be happier than she, even more than I, to see them finally come to fruition.

FOREWORD

It was originally my plan to write a trilogy about the pioneering history of the Cape colony *before* the Great Trek. The two parts that have already appeared, i.e., *Die Noordwaartse Beweging van die Boere voor die Groot Trek* [*The Northward Movement of the Farmers before the Great Trek*] and *Die Trekboer in die Geskiedenis van die Kaapkolone* [*The Migrant Farmer in the History of the Cape Colony*], cover the period 1657-1842. However, for the treatment of the phenomena described in this part, the Great Trek does not form a natural closing point. Therefore, I needed to continue my investigation up to the present time. This is one of the reasons why the book, which was first announced in 1937, is only now appearing. The original title, *Die Mobiliteit van die Pioniersbevolking aan die Kaap* [*The Mobility of the Pioneer Population at the Cape*], was changed at the insistence of the publisher.

This work is based primarily on research in various archives and libraries that are listed in the bibliography. However, I found it desirable to personally visit different areas that are written about with the intention of getting to know the country and the people better, as well as to gather oral tradition and personal information. In carrying out this fieldwork, I covered about 15,000 miles by car and questioned hundreds of people (old pioneers, farmers, teachers, magistrates, school inspectors, livestock inspectors, surveyors and police agents). This work was done in 1938 and 1939. Since then, many of the old pioneers who spoke to me have died. In particular, I visited areas where livestock are still trekked today (such as the Bokkeveld, the Roggeveld, Namaqualand and Bushmanland) as well as regions of younger settlements where pioneers still live who have witnessed the expansion process with their own eyes (such as Gordonia, Griqualand West, Bechuanaland and Southwest Africa). This investigation not only enabled me to better interpret the sometimes fragmentary data found in the archives and old travel descriptions, but also served to supplement it.

P.J. v.d. Merwe

Stellenbosch,
August 1944

CHAPTER I

Historical Preface

In older countries one often finds that the inhabitants live near to where they grew up. Large communities often consist of people who were born in the area. The territorial migration of individuals is rare, and where it occurs, is confined to a relatively small area around the place of birth. A good example of this is found in India where, according to the 1901 census, 90 percent of the population lived in the district in which they were born. Even people who did move away, moved only a relatively short distance from their birthplace.[1]

In the Cape Colony the situation was totally different.

One of the most notable phenomena in our pioneer history is the surprising rapidity with which our forefathers, in spite of geographical obstacles and resistance from the indigenous peoples, spread throughout the interior like oil upon water. By the beginning of the eighteenth century, when the Colony was a half century old, the limits of the settlement did not extend beyond the present magisterial districts of Cape Town, Stellenbosch and Paarl. Around 80 years later the expansion of whites eastward had reached the banks of the Fish River and the northerly colonists lived on lands along the line formed by the Kamiesberg, Kobiskow, and the Roggeveld, Nieuweveld and Sneeuberg mountain chains. When the Great Trek began (1836) there were already farmers living in what is today the southern Orange Free State. Less than a century later the Afrikaner vanguard had reached Angola along the west coast and the Tropic of Capricorn in the east.

1. The government and the expansion

The spread of the colonists into the interior was not the result of a progressive colonial policy. The Dutch East India Company, which had established a refreshment station at the Cape, was a trading company that originally had no plans for the expansion of territory. The Company's limited intentions in this respect are obvious from the fact that [Jan] Van Riebeeck considered the possibility of separating the Cape settlement from the interior by joining Table Bay and False Bay with a canal. Among other Company officials, like the Commissioners [Pieter] Van Rheede and Simon van der Stel, the ideal of colonization had emerged more consciously, but their influence was temporary, and that ideal was secondary to other ultimate goals.

The Company's decision to still allow free burgers, and to provide free passage to the Cape for emigrants from Europe for about a half century, did not stem from a desire to transplant a branch of the Dutch tree in South Africa. The Company began to colonize on a small scale simply in the interests of trade with the East Indies. The Cape settlement was intended primarily as a point of support for this trade. It had to produce enough food to support itself and supply the essential fresh meat and vegetables to the passing ships for combating scurvy. A secondary objective was for the settlement to be sufficiently populated to defend itself from outside attacks.

When this stage was reached, the Company lost interest in further colonization. This is evident from the fact that after 1707, when the production problem was solved, the Company was no longer willing to offer emigrants a free passage to the Cape on Company ships. From this time on population growth at the Cape was mainly dependent on natural increases, except for officials who asked for their discharge with the intention of remaining at the Cape as free burghers.[2]

The trek into the interior was initiated by the colonists. The Company was not at all pleased with this. Occasionally Company authorities voiced opposition to the rapid expansion of the colony and attempted without success to prohibit it. But each time the Company was simply compelled to extend its authority over a wider area to prevent the colonists in the interior from running wild and to ensure it did not lose income from the loan farms.[3]

The causes for the expansion of the pioneer population into the interior must thus be sought among the colonists themselves and their living conditions.

2. Agriculture versus Stock-breeding

Of primary importance in this connection is that by the beginning of the eighteenth century the Cape colonists had turned from land cultivation to stock-breeding.

During the seventeenth century agriculture was the basis for individual farming. The government also made a conscious effort to establish an agricultural settlement at the Cape. They met with little success, however. The colonists were obliged to sell all of their products at fixed prices to the Company, and these prices were set so low that there were no economic incentives for agricultural production at the Cape.

Those who lived in the rural districts began to devote themselves more to stock farming, which was much more profitable than agriculture. The work associated with it was much lighter, the operating costs were lower, it required less initial capital than agriculture, and there were no transportation problems. By the 1670s, when the demand for agricultural products was still unsatisfied, we come across farmers in the Cape colony who are already exclusively stock farmers. Before the end of the century stock farming was already an independent concern not connected with agriculture.[4]

At the beginning of the eighteenth century yet another heavy blow struck the languishing agricultural industry. The limited Cape market had become over-supplied. The production problem, which had caused the first commanders so many headaches, had developed into a chronic marketing problem. The first symptoms were already evident in the time of Simon van der Stel. During the term of office of his son and successor, the malady became acute. The farmers were left with an overabundance of agricultural products.

At first Cape Town itself qualified as a market. The Company had to buy grain, wine, and vegetables for the hospital, the garrison, and their passing ships. There were also a few city dwellers who required produce, and occasionally there were foreign ships calling at the Cape that had to be provided with victuals. But the Cape market was very limited and developed extremely slowly.

There was little possibility for the export of these agricultural products. There was little demand for Cape wine in foreign markets. The result was overproduction. When the wine farmers had one or two good harvests, they often had to sit with their product for two or three years. In the meantime the wine spoiled and, although the farmers could not make any money from it, they still had to pay the taxes on it. In this situation the wine farmers fell into debt, and so stood surety for one another, creating a fear that unsolvable difficulties would develop if fourteen or fifteen houses burned down.[5] By the end of the eighteenth century the farmers often had to open their wine vats and let the wine run out because they could not get it sold.[6]

The grain farmers were not in much better shape. Production costs were so high that Cape grain could not compete on the overseas markets. Grain prices at the Cape, impossibly low as they were, were still higher than the prevailing market prices in the Netherlands. What is more, the Company could not provide space on its heavily laden, homeward-bound ships for grain, which had such a limited value in relation to its weight and volume. Batavia was not dependent upon Cape grain. The requirements of the Dutch colonies in the east could be met more cheaply locally.[7] The Company had for a long time against its better judgment bought the Cape's surplus grain and exported it at a loss. But the farmers were not satisfied with the price the Company paid. They alleged that they were falling deeper into debt. Bankruptcy was a common occurrence.[8]

It is understandable then that in the eighteenth century the Company was not keen to encourage grain production. In 1717 the Cape government was forbidden from distributing land without permission for the cultivation of produce, "the overproduction of which principally rests in the final instance with the Company." At the same time the Cape authorities were notified that they should suggest some means of livelihood to the colonists whereby the Company would be released from the necessity of buying Cape products at high prices. In this connection the Lords Seventeen suggested that colonists devote themselves to the cultivation of tobacco, silk, indigo and olives. Between 1717 and 1743 little land for agriculture was allocated. Only persons who already possessed land could make use of the fifteen-year quit-rent system (1732). In 1743 [Gustaaf] Van Imhoff gave the colonists the opportunity to acquire ownership of land for agriculture, but few took advantage of this because most of the farms were too far from the market.[9]

As a result of weak marketing opportunities, mounting production costs, and constantly falling prices, agriculture at the Cape during the eighteenth century was not capable of great expansion.[10] The colony's population, however, was constantly increasing and the natural result was that, as the Cape Patriots declared in 1784, "the substantial poverty of a great part of the colonists, who could not make a living from agriculture, caused them to trek over the mountains in substantial numbers where they sought to support themselves by stock farming."[11]

3. The Desire for an Independent Existence

It is evident from this analysis that from the end of the seventeenth century agriculture could not offer to every white person at the Cape an *independent* existence. But it could provide many whites with a livelihood comparable to that experienced by millions of the poor in Europe, if they were ready to serve as laborers. The sons of farmers were not, however, willing to work for others. Even soldiers who had received their discharge to go and serve as farm workers, as well as other emigrants from Europe, never remained long as wage laborers, in spite of the chronic labor shortage about which there were still complaints.

This typical colonial phenomenon, which occurs in all young countries, must be explained by the fact that, throughout the pioneer period, it was possible for every white man to enjoy an independent existence by hunting and stock farming in the interior. Of great importance in this connection is the liberal land policy of the different Cape governments, whereby every person who possessed cattle was recognized as an independent farmer. The effect of this was that even the poorest colonist developed a strong sense of independence, which made them unwilling to hire themselves out to others.

4. Equality with Slaves and Hottentots

Apart from this state of affairs, there developed over time a strong prejudice against working for others in the colony. In the pioneer community, where there were no class differences and the gap between rich and poor was not as great and unbridgeable as in older countries, the whites regarded one another as equals. The effect of this was that it was seen as a debasement for a white person to hire himself out in the service of another. Furthermore, the people who most often worked for bosses were slaves and Hottentots. The idea therefore evolved that a white man who hired himself to another was behaving like a heathen and member of the inferior races. This acted as a strong counter to the development of a white worker class, which would have been an ideal solution for the overpopulation in the young colony. The fear of being regarded as equal with slaves was so strong that it even made whites fearful of taking positions as artisans since during the slave period the trades were generally practiced by slaves.[12] It sometimes happened that farmers' sons learned trades but it was an exception if they practiced this as their life calling. They abandoned their trades as soon as they had made enough capital to start a private farm.[13]

5. The Demand for Labor in the Nineteenth Century

The repeal of the slave trade and the economic development of the Cape Colony during the nineteenth century created a great need for white wage earners and artisans. A number of immigrants who came to the Cape after the second English occupation easily found work. [Benjamin] Moodie had no problem in successfully selling the contracts, in terms of which he had brought his laborers out, for twice the amount that it cost him to bring the immigrants here. The demand for labor was so great and wages in the colony so high, that most of the workers were soon able to buy their own freedom.[14] [George McCall] Theal tells of 700 to 800 soldiers who were discharged at the Cape and easily earned a living.[15] We also know that about two-thirds of the British immigrants who arrived at the Cape in 1820, mainly artisans and workers who had little success with farming, were able to find work at high wages with little difficulty.[16]

In spite of the extensive immigration, the demand for labor remained high. One of the greatest complaints of the British settlers was that they could not get enough workers. A few years after their arrival they made a fruitless attempt to persuade the imperial government to send workers to the Cape. A list was compiled of settlers who were ready to guarantee work for 780 workers at an average wage of £1 per month plus meals.[17] In 1827 [John] Ingram, who a few years before had had great success in bringing a group of immigrants to the Cape, stated that there was still room for many more in the Cape Colony: "I do not hesitate to say that from two to three thousand annually would be absorbed at wages sufficient to make a poor Irishman feel he was removed from poverty to affluence."[18]

Ingrams's optimism was perhaps a bit excessive, but in any case it is true that in the 1820s in the inhabited parts of the Cape Colony, there were opportunities for making a living other than being a self-supporting farmer that were attractive enough for the poorer classes from Great Britain to persuade them to leave their homeland and move to the Cape. In 1827 the sober-minded [George] Thompson wrote, "The number of these (mechanics and labourers) who might at once find profitable employment in the Colony it is difficult to estimate with accuracy; but from the speedy absorption of several importations of persons of this description that have recently taken place, without any diminution of the high price of labour, it may be pretty safely inferred, that a progressive influx of three to four hundred annually, for many years to come, would scarcely meet the demand."[19]

6. The Trekboer [Migrant Farmer] Treks Further Away

While thousands of foreign immigrants were streaming into the Cape Colony and were finding work in the older areas, the descendants of the original pioneers were trekking ever deeper into the wilderness, because in their opinion the colony was overpopulated. Just like the pioneers in the eighteenth century, they did not allow themselves to be turned round at the colonial borders fixed by the government. They simply trekked over the boundaries, laid out their farms, and the government was subsequently obliged to establish a new border, which it was required to do again every time in order not to lose its authority and control over its subjects.[20]

Farmers' sons in the stock districts were simply not prepared to consider job opportunities other than farming. Apart from their prejudice against servitude and trades, they were the descendants of generations of stock-farmers, and knew little about other callings. The average farm boy could do anything well enough to take care of himself, but not good enough to pass himself off as a craftsmen. He had not had the opportunity to train for anything other than farming. In his isolation he had also not learned to appreciate the worth of any other calling and consequently felt no attraction for it. Moreover, every farm boy was practically a farmer from birth because of the practice of setting aside livestock for children. The son received his inheritance in the form of cattle and married a young maid who owned livestock. So in the course of time a deeply rooted tradition developed that every farmer's son must also become a farmer.[21]

The stock-farmers in the interior, those pioneers who led the natural expansion of the colony into the unpopulated areas, form the subject of this study. The purpose here, however, is to look at the pioneer history of the Cape Colony from the viewpoint of mobility.

7. Definition of Concepts

Mobility in its widest sense refers to the phenomenon that an individual moves in space. It is self-evident that the historian cannot account for every movement that every pioneer made throughout the pioneer period. Many of these movements deserve no mention because they are of no historical significance. We are thus going to limit ourselves to those movements that played an important role in our pioneer history, more specifically to the phenomenon of the individual changing his place of residence more or less regularly and trekking.

This act of trekking sometimes took the form of a move, a change of residence whereby the person concerned abandoned the place where he lived with the intention of going elsewhere to settle. In some cases such a trek involved leaving the centers of civilization and journeying into the interior. This movement into the interior played a very important role in our pioneer history. For that reason it shall be dealt with at length—not from the perspective of trek routes, or the scale that it attained at specific times, but merely as a phenomenon of mobility—in other words, we are going to study the territorial expansion of the pioneer population, not as a sequence of events, but as a process.

Apart from the permanent moves, one also sees the phenomenon of an individual temporarily abandoning his residence with the intention of returning there again. In this connection we shall principally devote our attention to two forms of temporary migration, namely, the expeditions undertaken into the interior with an eye to exchanging livestock and hunting, and periodical migrations with livestock.

The trek with cattle did not always take place in the same way. Sometimes it took the form of regular seasonal migrations. Some of the migrants trekked back and forth between summer and winter farms; others wandered around within a greater or smaller region during the trek season.

Besides seasonal migrations we also find incidental migrations with livestock, which occurred suddenly and irregularly whenever the need arose. They occurred most often as a result of droughts, but were sometimes also due to locusts, migratory antelope, or livestock diseases.

Finally, it also happened that a trekker would change his residence so often that he would end up with no permanent home. Such permanent migrations will be called "nomadism" in this study.

The different forms of population movement that have been referred to will be discussed in the following chapters.

ENDNOTES

[1] P. Sorokin, *Social Mobility* (New York: 1927), p. 382.

[2] Cf. A.J.H. van der Walt, *Die Ausdehnung der Kolonie am Kap der Guten Hoffnung, 1770-1779* (Berlin: 1928), pp. 1-8.

[3] 1/STB 19/165, Overberg Affairs: Minutes of Heemraad meeting, Swellendam, 17 October 1744; C 148, Resolutions, 13 February 1770, p. 54; C 2285, Original Oridance Book, 16 June 1774, p. 474; a/STB 1/17 Resolutions, 7 August 1775, p. 351; C 2288, Original Ordinance Book, 19 July 1786, pp. 482-86; P.J. van der Merwe, *Die Trekboer in die Geskiedenis van die Kaapkolonie, 1657-1842* (Cape Town, 1938), pp. 53 and 155-68.

[4] Van der Merwe, *Trekboer*, pp. 23-5.

[5] C 36, Resolutions, 3 March 1716, p. 300.

[6] A.L. Geyer, *Das Wirtschaftliche System der Niederländischen Ostindischen Kompanie am Kap der guten Hoffnung, 1785-1795* (Munich and Berlin, 1923), pp. 74-5.

[7] Van der Walt, *Ausdehnung*, p. 31.

[8] C 36, Resolutions, 3 March 1716, p. 300; 1/STB 1/13, Resolutions, 27 January 1744, pp. 249-50; 1/STB 1/16, Resolutions, 15 August 1757, p. 59; C 174, Resolutions, 18 May 1787, pp. 413-15; C 177, Resolutions, 8 January 1788, pp. 23-5.

[9] C 428, Letters Rec., Lords XVII to Cape Government, 17 August, 1728, pp. 109-10; van der Walt, *Ausdehnung*, pp. 33-4.

[10] Van der Walt, *Ausdehnung*, pp. 37-41; Geyer, *Wirtschaftliche System*, p. 33.

[11] C 1283, Petitions, Reports, etc., Burgher Petition, Woeke, Bletterman, et al., 17 February 1784, p. 57. See also, C 171, Resolutions, 19 April 1786, pp. 426-8; A. Sparrman, *Reize naar de Kaap de Goede Hoop, de Landen van den Zuid Pool, en rondom de Waereld (Leiden, 1786)*, II: 681; van der Walt, *Ausdehnung, p. 37*.

[12] Van der Merwe, *Trekboer*, pp. 183-90.

[13] G. Thompson, *Travels and Adventures in Southern Africa* (London: 1827), II:132-35; J.W.D. Moodie, *Ten Years in Southern Africa* (London, 1835), II:28.

[14] Thompson, *Travels*, II:217-18; Sir George Cory, *The Rise of South Africa* (London, 1921 and 1926), II:54-5; George McCall Theal, *History of South Africa* (London: 1915), V:346.

[15] Theal, *History*, V:347.

[16] Ibid., V:373; Thompson, *Travels*, II:217-19.

[17] Thompson, *Travels*, II:220.

[18] J. Ingram to R.W. Horton, 5 October 1827, in George McCall Theal, *Records of the Cape Colony, 1793-1831 (Cape Town, 1897-1905)*, XXXIII:481.

[19] Thompson, *Travels*, II:217.

[20] P.J. van der Merwe, *Die Noordwaartse Beweging van die Boere voor die Groot Trek (1770-1842)* (The Hague, 1937), pp. 150, 336-58.

[21] Van der Merwe, *Trekboer*, p. 192; C 1483, Letters Disp., Cape Government to Lords XVII, 24 January 1730, p. 102; C 1265, Petitions, Reports, etc., P.A. Myburg to Landdrost, 1 May 1775, p. 457; C 1764, Letters Disp., J. van Plettenberg to Lords XVII, 1 March 1779, no. 23, p. 210; C.O. 2581, Letters Rec., Tulbagh, H. van de Graaff to Grey, 14 August 1811; Swellengrebel Family Archives, Hendrik Swellengrebel, Jr. to C. de Gyselaar, 26 June 1783. [Trans. Note: This last letter from Swellengrebel to Gyselaar may also be found in the collection of letters published by the Van Riebeeck Society (VRS), *Briefwisseling van Hendrik Swellengrebel Jr. oor Kaapse Sake, 1778-1792*, VRS, series II, vol. 13, pp. 151-62 in the original with a shortened English summary, pp. 348-52.]

CHAPTER II

Hunter-Stockfarmers

1. The Popularity of the Hunt

Two or three centuries ago South Africa was a true hunters paradise. In Jan van Riebeeck's time even the Cape was swarming with eland, hartebeest, steenbok, and other kinds of wild animals. Hippopotami were found in the Berg River. In 1702 a troop of elephants made an appearance in the vicinity of Cape Town.[1] Beasts of prey were also found in abundance. A resident of Cape Town at the time did not need to visit a zoo to see a lion. The Cape commander came across one in the Company's gardens, not far from where the parliament buildings stand today. At night the lions came prowling for livestock in the Company's pens. During the day tigers caught sheep under the herdsman's eye.[2]

In the early days, Van Riebeeck's Dutch compatriots could not hit a wild animal with their unwieldy weapons. In vain the commander had snare-pits dug and traps laid for a bit of venison. But he had to do without until one day the hounds caught a young hartebeest.[3]

It was not too long, however, before the pioneers learned how to shoot. In their constant struggle against wild animals and wild peoples our forefathers quickly learned how to handle a rifle. It was necessary for self-defense. During the hunt a poor shot could place a hunter's life in danger. Besides, powder and lead were scarce. It could not be wasted. When the shot rang out, the buck had to fall dead in its tracks or bear the presence of death within it in its flight.

So, in the crucible of the pioneer life, a nation of outstanding marksmen was born. To his surprise, Simon van der Stel found that during the militia exercises in 1687 at Stellenbosch, while shooting at the target and the wooden parrot, "of a hundred shots hardly one missed its mark."[4] According to him, many other observers expressed the opinion that the Afrikaners were good shots. [Otto] Mentzel mentions the three Botha brothers who—one day when they truly wanted to show what they could do—placed an egg on a pole and then shot at it from 400 or 500 paces. And—believe it or not—they seldom missed.[5] (± 1734). Around a century later a Dutch visitor wrote: "The Afrikaner possesses an inconceivable nimbleness in the handling of his mount and weapon. Should he accidentally miss, he will look at his weapon, and stand dumbfounded, as if to say: it wasn't my fault."[6] A few years after the Great Trek, Major [Samuel] Charters declared, "No country can produce better marksmen than the Dutch colonists of Southern Africa."[7]

In these circumstances it should come as no surprise that hunting for game became so popular. Simon van der Stel was already complaining by 1680 that not only was wild game systematically being killed off and driven away, but that many of the colonists "take time off from their daily work and play the slacker while simply abandoning their fields."[8] In 1823 [Johannes] Theunissen observed that "One finds a boundless passion for the hunt among everyone, from fourteen-year-old boys to sixty-year-old grey-beards."[9] This passion for the hunt among us Afrikaners survived until quite recently, above all in those parts of the country where there was still plentiful game.

There have been limitations on hunting from the beginning up to the present day.[10] In Van Riebeeck's time wild game hunting, except for predators, was totally forbidden. Not even the free burghers had the right to shoot wild game.[11] [Governor Jacob] Borghorst allowed the colonists to go hunting, provided they asked permission beforehand.[12] Later all kinds of regulations were passed to limit hunting to licensed hunters: a part of the year (lambing time and brooding time) the hunt was completely closed; even when the hunt was open, license holders could not go out every day to hunt—at the most twice per week; no one could give away or sell wild game without the permission of government.[13]

These hunting laws and many subsequent ones were violated unhesitatingly and shamelessly, however, from the earliest times until today.[14] This must not be viewed as a sign of criminality or lawlessness. In the old days everyone, from the savage with his bow and arrow to the itinerant judge on his circuit and the governor on expedition, considered wild game as everyone's property.[15] Likewise, the farmers viewed the shooting of game as a sort of natural right, especially when the game roamed about their own land or on unissued land. It is noteworthy that, while our poor whites of today consider a conflict with the government, crime, and imprisonment as a great disgrace, the illegal hunting of game is one of the few areas where they are strongly inclined to violate the laws of the land.[16] "This practice in particular," observed Dr. [Raymond] Wilcocks, "is not incompatible with their folk ethos and traditions, because these are people who are mostly hunters and the descendants of hunters, who lived from the hunt, and they consider it a self-evident right to be able to shoot wild game wherever it might be found."[17]

2. Sport and Recreation

Through the centuries the hunters of our civilization were always inclined to view the hunt as sport and recreation. Profit-seeking was often just a side-issue. The Afrikaner farmer also hunted, in very great measure, for his own pleasure. Simon van der Stel noticed this as well. He mentions the colonists going to shoot hippopotamus on the Olifants River and then observes irritably: "Their meat will cost them much more than if they stayed at home and remained at work; it is certain moreover that the shooting of wild animals is practiced more for recreation than for profits by the citizens."[18] Likewise, Theunissen described the hunt as one of the Afrikaners' chief pleasures.[19]

The existence of a non-material motive for the hunt appears quite evident as well from stories that old pioneers commonly told about it. They seldom refer to the money they made from the hunt, or to the profits a particular hunting trip fetched. If one listens closely to their stories, it is very clear that it was the sense of adventure of the hunt that caught their imagination, and not what they could earn. Many of the old hunters loved the hunt in itself and were truly interested in the wild game and open country. In very many cases this devotion to the adventurous hunter's life resulted in a neglect of their farming and this ultimately led to economic decline.

The popularity of hunting as an adventurous form of sport and recreation can be explained partially from the pioneers' living conditions. Rural farmers had little to draw their attention away from their daily work, which must have become quite monotonous in time. They seldom associated with other people. There was no cinema to provide a distraction. They did not have the forms of sport that we practice today. Thus, out of sheer necessity the pioneers had to direct their energies into other channels. The saddle horse and the rifle had to make up for everything. As a result the call of the wild had an irresistible fascination for so many.

3. Economic Significance of the Hunt

The comments above do not detract from the fact that hunting for game was of very great economical significance in our pioneer history. The hunt for game in the old days most certainly contributed very much towards the satisfaction of material needs. The hunt was also undoubtedly often undertaken precisely *in order* to satisfy such needs. Especially in the border districts, where game was plentiful, the yield from the hunt contributed in an important measure to meeting the pioneers' need for sustenance.

In his well-known travel account Pieter Kolbe furnishes very interesting information about the lifestyle of the farmers of the Heuningberge, a few miles east of the present-day Moorreesburg. At that time, by the beginning of the eighteenth century, they were living at the outpost of civilization. These first pioneers in the granary of the Cape Colony hardly ever ate bread. They were livestock farmers who did not even sow wheat and did not want to take the trouble to go and purchase meal from the wheat farmers of Stellenbosch or Paarl. Perhaps they also did not have the money to do this. "So they eat flesh with other flesh, that is, they take a piece of hamel or lamb meat, and eat in place of bread, dried deer or other wild game with it. This agrees with them so well that one very seldom hears of one of them becoming sick."[20]

We come across this phenomenon throughout the pioneer period in the frontier districts of the Cape Colony. Even in areas that were suitable for grain farming, the first pioneers did not immediately cultivate the land. And because of bad economic conditions or poverty they often could not purchase wheat. As a result, bread was a scarce commodity, for a certain period anyway, in every frontier district. Many of the interior farmers lived just on meat sometimes for weeks and months.[21]

In such cases the farmers ultimately became tired of mutton, and fresh venison or dried and cured meat was a tasty change. Mentzel assures us that even among wealthy farmers who counted their sheep by the thousands it was the custom in the eighteenth century to eat, in place of bread, lean venison together with fat mutton.[22] And, incidentally, it is interesting to note that in the official documents of that time this dish was also described as "meat to meat."[23]

The frontier farmers, however, certainly did not hunt in order to have a change in their diets. Wherever it was possible, they hunted for the pot with the intention of saving their livestock for the market. This was particularly the case among the poor and young beginners who were keen to enlarge their livestock herds. In the border districts the poor classes mainly lived on the meat of wild game.[24] But even for rich farmers the hunt for game was of great economic significance. In areas where little or no bread and vegetables were eaten, the consumption of meat was prodigious. Sometimes as many as three or four sheep were slaughtered per day if the family was large and the servants abundant.[25] As long as wild game was plentiful, large farmers could keep back many slaughter animals for the market, if they did not neglect hunting.

In 1786 the Cape government gave a very telling description of the economic development of the border districts and the prominent role the hunt played in that respect: "That although in the beginning, when the aforementioned livestock-breeding natives, and with them some Europeans, [who were] already concentrating on agriculture, set out to the far remote pastures, there were no dwellings or shelter to be found, and they had to make do with such huts as they could erect in a short time. And, having discovered the multitude of big game in the fields that had remained wild, they made use of them for the sake of economy in order thereby to spare many more of their tame livestock and to use these livestock for breeding purposes. Likewise, in a country where neither plow nor spade was known or had ever been used, no wheat for bread could be found, so that the inhabitants mostly found themselves forced to eat nothing but meat. However, at present these circumstances have changed to such an extent that their houses have by and large been changed into suitable farm houses. Also, due to the decrease of big game and the increase of tame livestock, the latter is being consumed more depending on the desires of every one among them, and through the cultivation of the ground, bread has once again become a daily food."[26]

Apart from fresh meat the hunt also yielded dried and cured meat, which in the old days was not considered as just a delicacy, but an important and popular food in every household in the country. One gets a good impression of the use that was made of dried and cured meat from a case reported by [Hinrich] Lichtenstein and [Jacob Abraham] De Mist. In 1803 the traveling party of the Commissioner-General met a farmer in the Hantam who had just returned from a hunting trip. Apart from the small game, which was routinely shot in the field for the pot, the hunting party had brought down seventeen large eland of between 700 and 800 pounds each. Each hunter received about 4,000 pounds of edible meat, which, as was customary practice on the hunt, was cut into pieces, packed into salted skins, and brought back home to be smoked and dried. This man was a well-to-do farmer who lived in a smart house, and owned 3,000 sheep, 450 goats, 200 horses, and a large number of cattle. But even for his household such a large store of meat must have been welcome.[27]

In areas of newer settlement, where marketing opportunities for farm products were minimal and wild game was abundant, the hunt occasionally furnished considerable cash income as well. There was always a market for ivory and the horn of a rhinoceros was also of some value. Hippopotamus bacon was in the old days a much sought-after delicacy, famous for its blood-purifying powers. Hunters often packed it in salt and even sold it in Cape Town. Sjamboks,* whip handles, and whips were made from hippopotamus and rhinoceros skins. Other large wild animals provided horns. From the skins, thongs and straps were braided and shoe soles and uppers were tanned. There was more or less always a demand for these things, and the farmers themselves could always find a good use for them.[28] Ostrich skins and good ostrich feathers could likewise always be sold.[29] Ostrich hunting, however, really only began to flourish during the second half of the nineteenth century, when fantastic prices were sometimes paid for feathers. Good white feathers were often sold for £50 and more the pound.[30]

By the beginning of the 1760s, when ostrich feather farming began, there were still thousands of wild birds in the Kalahari and south of the Orange as well. Agriculture had not displaced hunting. At the end of the nineteenth century ostrich hunting was still in full swing in Bushmanland. And when the birds gradually began to reach the point of extermination there, the hunters penetrated into the Kalahari. The birds were chased on horseback to exhaustion on hot

---

*Trans. note: a rhinoceros or hippopotamus hide whip.

days and then killed by being knocked over the head with a sjambok. Since they were lighter riders, bastards and natives were commonly used to "knock birds," as it's still referred to today in Bushmanland. Old pioneers still remember the good old days when they easily made £10 to £15 from a wild bird's feathers. Farmers also took part in illegal ostrich hunting, but those who made the most profits were the itinerant traders who bought the feathers from the bastards, and merchants who paid the local people to kill their birds. The sudden crash of the ostrich feather market as a result of the war [WWI]and the vagaries of capricious fashion, dealt the deathblow approximately thirty years ago to ostrich hunting as a significant source of income.[31]

4. Influence on Mobility

The hunt for wild game undoubtedly had a great influence on the pioneers' mobility.

The fact that there was always abundant wild game on and beyond the borders of the Cape Colony until well into the nineteenth century, made it possible for anyone who owned a rifle, a wagon and a team of oxen, to make an independent living in the interior. The hunt provided enough meat for daily use. In addition, it brought in enough money to purchase powder and lead—perhaps even to pay for clothes and household necessities. Furthermore, it was also possible in the border districts to build up a strong farm with the aid of hunting, because the pioneers did not have to slaughter many of their livestock animals. For this reason, the rich abundance of game in the interior was a great attraction to poor people and young beginners who did not yet have large farms.[32] The prospects that the hunt offered in border districts was often an important economic incentive to the indigent classes to migrate and settle there.[33]

The hunting era was normally only a temporary phase in the development of every border district—and likewise in the life of every frontier farmer. As soon as the wild game was wiped out or had moved away, the pioneers devoted more attention to their farming. At the same time, the expansion of their livestock herds and increased farm incomes in general made them more independent of hunting as a means of livelihood. Over the years the hunt became just a sideline, later even merely a pastime.[34]

One also came across another type of pioneer in South Africa, however, who remained devoted to the hunter's life and was not willing to abandon it. These obdurate old hunters usually had little farms. Some owned land, others were sharecroppers, a few merely wandered from place to place. All of them tended to neglect their farms for the sake of the hunt, and as soon as the numbers of wild game in one region declined and the hunting possibilities waned, they trekked farther to areas where wild game were still plentiful. Until recently one still met this type in the northern Transvaal, Rhodesia, and in East Africa.[35] In the written sources of the history of the Cape Colony one rarely finds references to this pioneer type.[36] Old people as well cannot relate many cases of farmers who always trekked farther after wild game. When the old people of today were children, the Cape Colony's wild game, especially the large animals, were already nearly exterminated. Based on this fact, one can surmise that the Cape Colony produced more such men long ago when wild game was still abundant here.

Apart from the fact that the presence of wild game in the border districts enticed the pioneers there, the hunt also contributed towards maintaining the population of a frontier district in a condition of high mobility for a certain time.[37] In 1753 the Swellendam landdrost complained, "that some of these inhabitants without the least forewarning go with their wagons and firearms for entire months into the wilderness beyond human settlement, under the bald excuse of shooting meat, etc; their livelihood, however, consists of livestock, and accordingly, no shortage of meat exists."[38] Here we are dealing, not with professional hunters, but with livestock farmers who wandered about after the wild game. The nomadic type of livestock farmer without a fixed dwelling place, which one found in the border districts from the end of the eighteenth century, trekked with their cattle not only in search of grazing land and water, but also after wild game.[39]

This phenomenon occurred not only in the Cape Colony. During the pioneer period one also came across it in other parts of South Africa. Listen, for example, to the striking description that L.C. de Klerk, one of the old Voortrekkers, gives of the appeal of the wandering hunter's life in Natal: "Some persons gradually turn to migrant or camp life, so that for years and years afterwards (1838) they still wander around about from one place to another. And this life then took on its own fascination. The world was open, the land belonged to no one, and wherever a man unhitched his horse, there, for that moment, he was at home. The life was carefree, and that was reason enough to attract many. They abandoned their old location only when the ground was exhausted, or the wild game scarce. The returns from the hunt were more than adequate not only to keep the pots on the boil, but also to provide for a family's necessities in clothes and other things, by exchanging horns, tusks, and hides with an itinerant trader. Or, when there were several hunters together, they often put together a large freight and traveled with it to the bay—to Durban or to Grahamstown, or one of the other frontier towns of the old colony, where it could be exchanged for money, ammunition, and clothes, and then they turned back to take up the same life again.

"Their journey usually brings them as closely as possible to the scene of the hunt, where they search for a suitable site, by a pretty stream and under the largest wild trees and set up a camp. For the livestock a corral is made from thornwood branches, one or more tents are set up, an anthill scooped out for a baking oven, and the journey comes temporarily to a halt, while the men go out on the hunt for days and perhaps weeks on end.

"But these were not the Voortrekkers. This was a small minority, mostly just the poorest people, who could for the moment make the most profitable or easiest living in this manner, and who either joined others on their own or perhaps also came together with others to help."[40]

By the end of the previous century a person still could come across this sort of nomadic livestock farmer who pursued wild game in the northern parts of the Transvaal. When the world around them began to become more populated, they headed out farther north. In 1905 Reverend J. N. Geldenhuis, at this time minister of the Dutch Reformed Church in Southern Rhodesia, met farmers of this class there who still trekked around, dwelling in tents, and who had never in their lives lived in a house.

ENDNOTES

[1] VC [Verbatim copy] 16, Logbook, 16 March 1702, p. 40.

[2] George McCall Theal, *History of South Africa* (London: 1915), III:23, 55, 57, 180.

[3] Ibid., III:23.

[4] C 1378, Letters Disp., Simon van der Stel to Patria, 18 April 1687, p. 650.

[5] O.F. Mentzel, *Lebens-Geschichte Heern Rudolph Siegfried Allemans* (Glogau, 1784), p. 158.

[6] J.B.N. Theunissen, *Aantekeningen van een reis door de Binnenlanden van Zuid-Afrika van Port Elizabeth naar de Kaapstad gedaan in 1823* (Oostende, 1824), p. 59.

[7] *Grahamstown Journal*, 19 December 1839.

[8] C 2270, Original Ordinance Book, 8 April 1680, p. 409.

[9] Theunissen, *Aantekeningen*, p. 58.

[10] Dr. Preller is mistaken when he states that the very first hunting law was enacted in 1837 in the Transvaal. See G.S. Preller, *Talana. Die Drie Generaals-slag by Dundee* (Cape Town, 1942), p. 75.

[11] Theal, *History*, III:58, 64.

[12] C 2269, Original Ordinance Book, 11 September 1668, p. 246; Theal, *History*, III:180.

[13] C 2271, Original Ordinance Book, 4 December 1690, pp. 74-81; C 23, Resolutions, 30 July 1698, p. 619.

[14] 1/SWM 1/1, Minutes from the Landdrost and Heemraden, 1 May 1753, p. 298 and 17 March 1753, pp. 293-95; C 2270, Original Ordinance Book, 8 April 1680, p. 409; C 2291, Original Ordinance Book, 1 September 1792, p. 125; B.O. 176, Original Ordinance Book, 15 July 1800, pp. 325-29; 1/WOC 17/8, Letters Disp., J.H. Fischer to all field cornets, 28 November 1818 (No. 934); Report of the Commissioners appointed to investigate certain charges against Sir George Yonge, 16 March 1802, in Theal, *Records of the Cape Colony, 1793-1831* (Cape Town, 1897-1905), IV:225.

[15] J.C. Chase, *The Cape of Good Hope and the Eastern Province of Algoa Bay* (London, 1843), p. 231.

[16] R.W. Wilcocks, *Die Armblanke* (Stellenbosch, 1932), pp. 83, 85, 86; J.R. Albertyn, *Die Armblanke en die Maatskappy* (Stellenbosch, 1932), pp. 41 and 69.

[17] Wilcocks, *Armblanke*, p. 86.

[18] C 1376, Letters Disp., Simon van der Stel to Patria, 12 April 1686, p. 2.

[19] Theunissen, *Aantekeningen*, pp. 58, 61; See also A.W. Drayson, *Tales at the Outspan or Adventures in the Wild Regions of Southern Africa* (London, 1865), p. 23: "...the Boer loves sport for its own sake."

[20] P. Kolbe, *Nauwkeurige en Uitvoerigne Beschrijving van de Kaap de Goede Hoop* (Amsterdam, 1726), I:125.

[21] P.J. van der Merwe, *Die Trekboer in die Geskiedenis van die Kaapkolonie, 1657-1842* (Cape Town, 1938), pp. 226-32.

[22] O.F. Mentzel, *Vollständige und Zuverläszige Geographische und topographische Beschreibung des Berühmten und in aller Betrachtung merkwürdigen Afrikanischen Vorgebirges des Guten Hoffnung* (Glogau, 1785, 1787), II:13, 95; See also, PSB, Mss. Germ. Fol. No. 879, Reisverhaal van De Mist (1803), pp. 294, 419, 430, 431; H. Lichtenstein, *Reisen im südlichen Africa in den Jahren 1803, 1804, 1805 und 1806* (Berlin, 1811-1812), I:154-6; G. Thompson, *Travels and Adventures in Southern Africa* (London, 1827), II:139.

[23] C 1814, Letters Disp., van de Graaff to Lords XVII, 19 April 1786, p. 528.

[24] C 171, Resolutions, 19 April 1786, p. 427; Report...against Yonge, 16 March 1802, in Theal, *Records*, IV:225; PSB, Mss. Germ. Fol. No. 879, Reisverhaal van De Mist (1803), p. 419; B.R. 61, Resolutions, 3 January 1805, p. 54; C.O. 49, Letters Rec. from Court of Justice, General Report of the Commissioners of Circuit, 1813; 1/GR 16/6, Letters Disp., Stockenström to Bird, 1 May 1817 (No. 690); C 1283, Petitions, Reports, etc., Burgher Petition, Woeke, Bletterman, et al., 17 February 1784, p. 58; J. Holman, *A Voyage round the World including Travels in Africa, etc. from 1827-1832* (London, 1834-35), II:309; Thompson, *Travels*, I:104 and II:139.

[25] Report of the Commission for Stock Raising and Agriculture, 20 November 1805, in George McCall Theal, *Belangrijke Historische Dokumenten over Zuid-Afrika* (Cape Town, 1896, 1911), III:359. Lichtenstein, *Reisen*, I:145, 602.

[26] C 171, Resolutions, 19 April 1786, pp. 426-8.

[27] PSB, Mss. Germ. Fol. No. 879, Reisverhaal van De Mist (1803), p. 340; Augusta Uitenhage de Mist, "Dagverhaal van een Reis naar de Kaap de Goede Hoop en in de Binnenlanden van Afrika door Jonkvr. Augusta Uitenhage de Mist in 1802 en 1803," *Penélopé* (Amsterdam), VIII(1835), pp. 94; Lichtenstein, *Reisen*, I:154-6.

[28] AR, Accession, 1900, XXII, 85, F.v.W., *Historische Nachrichten* (1789-91), p. 4; PSB, Mss. Germ. Fol. No. 879, Reisverhaal van De Mist (1803), p. 431; C.O. 4447, Sir R.S. Donkin's Collection of Missionary Complaints, 1820-1821, John Philip, Documents accompanying Tabular View; Lichtenstein, *Reisen*, I:157; Drayson, *Tales*, p. 23.

[29] E. Bergh, Petition, in Theal, *Belangrijke Historische Dokumenten*, III:60; T. Pringle, *African Sketches* (London, 1834), p. 299.

[30] F.A. Donnithorne, *Wonderful Africa* (London, 1925), p. 109; G. Nicholson, *Fifty Years in South Africa: Being some Recollections and Reflections of a Veteran Pioneer* (London, 1898), p. 111.

[31] 1/SBK 5/1/11, W.C. Scully to Assistant Commissioner of Crown Lands, 28 December 1891, p. 872; C.O. 3674, Civil Commissioners, W.C. Scully to Colonial Secretary, 18 December 1891; Nicholson, *Fifty Years*, pp. 110-12.

[32] C 1283, Petitions, Reports, etc., Burgher Petition, Woeke, Bletterman, et al., 17 February 1784, p. 58; Mentzel, *Beschreibung*, II:174; Holman, *Voyage*, II:309; Thompson, *Travels*, I:104; J.F.W. Grosskopf, *Plattelandsverarming en Plaasverlating* (Stellenbosch, 1932), p. 109. Albertyn, *Armblanke*, p. 8.

[33] C 1265, Petitions, Reports, etc., A.H. Krugel and twelve others to Governor van Plettenberg, Petition from Bruintjieshoogte, 10 November 1774, pp. 443-45.

[34] C 171, Resolutions, 19 April 1786, pp. 426-8.

[35] Cf. Albertyn, *Armblanke*, pp. 8-9.

[36] Lt. Col. E.E. Napier, *Excursions in Southern Africa, including a History of the Cape Colony, an Account of the Native Tribes, etc.*, (London, 1849), II: 358-59; Wilcocks, *Armblanke*, p. 8.

[37] Van der Merwe, *Trekboer*, p. 62.

[38] 1/SWM 1/1, Minutes from the Landdrost and Heemraden, 17 March 1753, p. 293.

[39] Lichtenstein, *Reisen*, I:34-5.

[40] G.S. Preller, *Voortrekkermense*, (Cape Town, 1920-25), I:236.

CHAPTER III

Traders in the Interior

I. CATTLE TRADERS

1. The Cattle Trade with the Khoikhoi

The Dutch who came to the Cape in 1652 in order to establish a colony brought no livestock with them. It was known at that time that the indigenous population possessed cattle, which they were prepared to trade for small items such as beads, copper wire, tobacco, mirrors, pocket knives and other items of a higher civilization that had such an irresistible attraction for them. The Company relied upon the cattle trade, which was hugely advantageous for the whites—and ultimately so disastrous for the natives—for its meat supplies.

The first free burgers received permission shortly after settling at the Cape to carry on trade with the natives, but they did not enjoy this privilege for long. In 1658 the cattle trade was forbidden. The Company had taken an interest in the cattle trade itself and was not willing to tolerate competition from its own subjects, who in its opinion paid much too much for Khoikhoi cattle.

In spite of all the ordinances, however, the cattle trade continued. Initially the colonial contraband trade was conducted with the Khoikhoi living near the settlement, and the tribes who now and then visited the Cape.[1] By the end of the seventeenth century, however, this type of cattle trade no longer produced very much. By then, there were not many Khoikhoi still living in the vicinity of the Cape. Sicknesses had decreased their numbers dramatically, and many had moved away to escape the diseases the white man had brought to the country. Those who remained behind were impoverished. By that time grazing land in the neighborhood of the Cape was poor as well, and in any event it was occupied by the farmers. Consequently the cattle-rich tribes deep in the interior remained where the grazing land was better and where the whole world was available for their own use.[2]

2. Trade Expeditions into the Interior

In these circumstances the colonists were obliged to equip trading expeditions, and send them over the mountains in search of tribes living in the interior, some of whom lived 400 to 500 miles from the Cape. The traders traveled out together in large parties and took with them considerable quantities of beads, copper, tobacco and other items for barter. To the governor's great annoyance they sometimes posed as Company servants, and even misappropriated the governor's name to coerce reluctant Khoikhoi to surrender their livestock.[3]

The government soon recognized that it did little good to forbid the cattle trade as long as the colonists were allowed to undertake expeditions into the interior. Accordingly in 1693 the free burgers were strictly prohibited from visiting the interior, alone or in the company of others, with or without wagons or livestock. Persons caught beyond the mountains would be fined and receive a year of hard labor. Moreover, everything found in their possession would be confiscated.[4]

3. Lifting the Ban on Cattle Trading

Shortly thereafter the Company decided it would no longer participate in the cattle trade. Trade expeditions into the interior had proven to be very costly and had produced very little indeed. Thus, one of the Company's chief grievances against private cattle trade fell away. About the same time the Company also decided to discontinue its livestock farming. In these circumstances it had become even more desirable to lift the cattle trade ban. The Company now was totally dependent on the colonists for its meat supply. Therefore it was to the Company's own advantage to give the colonists the opportunity to enlarge their livestock herds in all possible ways. The result was that the hated cattle trade ban was lifted in 1700 and the colonists were granted the right to trade with any Khoikhoi band for cattle. The only condition the Company set was that the burgers had to trade for the livestock and not just take them. They were also not to compel natives who were unwilling to surrender their livestock to do so by force.[5]

The colonists did not let the grass grow under their feet. In 1701 the new governor, Willem Adriaan van der Stel, reported that cattle traders in groups of twenty, thirty, and more men strong trekked into the interior toward far distant Khoikhoi tribes such as the Gri-griekwas, Houteniquas and Namaquas, some of whom lived some hundred miles from the Cape. According to rumours reaching the government, the cattle traders had robbed the natives of their livestock by force. But proving the truth of such stories would be very difficult. The Khoikhoi would not come complaining to the government about mistreatment. Many of them had never before been in the Cape and therefore were still apprehensive of whites. Others were afraid to undertake the journey, because they would then have to pass through the territory of their enemies, with whom they were continually at war. Moreover, they could also not speak Dutch. The governor was of the opinion that about half the colonists were engaged in the cattle trade, and he expected that in the future they would travel in increasingly larger parties still deeper into the interior.[6]

The following year Willem Adriaan van der Stel raised the question of mistreatment again in his general report. The ugly rumors of the cattle traders' violence, theft, and carnage grew more and more each day, he wrote, without the landdrost or fiscal being able to substantiate any of them.[7]

4. The Livestock Raid of 1702

Even as the governor was writing, just such an expedition was underway again. By chance we know a thing or two about this journey because the members of the party were later legally interrogated and made several confessions. The hunting party consisted of 45 whites and as many Khoikhoi. On 22 March 1702 they traveled in an easterly direction over the mountains, after promising one another in writing that they would not make public anything that happened on the journey. No one informed the government of the proposed expedition.

With the help of Khoikhoi guides, whom they found in the interior, the expedition members penetrated into Xhosaland. Here they were attacked by a large number of Xhosa. Thanks to the whites' firearms they warded off the attack fairly easily. They then took off after the Xhosa and shot a few dead. Only one white man lost his life in this skirmish.

The white traders then used this attack as an excuse to begin plundering on a grand scale. They made surprise attacks on several Khoikhoi kraals that had never done them any harm, seized large numbers of cattle, and shot and killed some Khoikhoi. After seven months the expedition returned home with a haul of over two thousand cattle, which were divided among the members of the hunting party. Some of them confessed that they had already obtained cattle in the same manner two or three times before.[8]

From the governor's report of this expedition one has to conclude that at the beginning of the eighteenth century similar expeditions were common. He explained that the members of the above-mentioned expedition did not receive their just punishment; because there were so many colonists who had taken part in similar practices, half of the colony would be ruined if everyone had to be punished. These mens' poor wives and innocent children would then be plunged into the greatest wretchedness. Moreover, the governor was afraid that, as soon as some of the offenders were arrested, others would flee into the interior where they would evade their deserved punishment. And so many fugitives in the interior could become a danger to the colony.[9]

The colonists then denied the governor's allegation. They stated that the cattle thieves were not being punished because Willem Adriaan lived in a glass house and therefore could not afford to throw stones. The governor himself was guilty of committing just such offences. If he now punished others for them, then perhaps his own crimes would be made public.[10]

The truth of the matter cannot now be easily established. But even if we assume that Willem Adriaan van der Stel did not give the real reason for his leniency toward the cattle thieves, it is still always possible that what he said about the popularity of the trade expeditions could be in keeping with the facts.

5. Types of Livestock Traders

The question now arises: what class of the society took part in these trade expeditions at the beginning of the eighteenth century?

From all the available evidence one must conclude that the greatest percentage of the cattle traders were "loners," that is to say, single males who "kept no home of their own or lived with their parents."[11] Many of them had no fixed residence, but roamed about from one place to the other. These men often belonged to the lowest class in society. Some were criminals. Others were fugitives on the run who were condemned to death but had been successful in evading the long arm of the law. They then hid in the mountains for safety or wandered about in the interior. Sometimes they received their weapons, ammunition, and provisions from "other mercenary inhabitants who did not accompany them, but like kidnappers in the fatherland equipped them to gain the filthy lucre."[12] They then had to go and barter livestock from the interior Khoikhoi tribes for their protectors. In other cases they exchanged cattle and sheep with the Khoikhoi for all kinds of small items on their own account that they then in turn bartered away with the settled colonists for a trifle. The farmers thus had an interest in fostering such livestock theft by these fugitives and for that reason were not going to inform on them.[13]

In his instructions to his son and successor, Simon van der Stel mentions another type of livestock exchange in 1699. He complains about people getting their dismissal from the service of the Company under the pretext that they want to practice agriculture, but who then do not go into farming. They simply roam, from one farmer to another, and are used by ill-intentioned farmers to drive the forbidden cattle trade with the Khoikhoi.[14]

The prominent, settled free burgers, whose attention to their farmsteads occupied all their time, did not personally take part in these expeditions into the interior, but they often had an interest in them. They organized trading expeditions or equipped those involved.[15]

The French historian [Henri] Dehérain, who studied the time of Willem Adriaan van der Stel thoroughly, arrived at the same conclusion. He discusses the expeditions and then declares: "These dangerous expeditions were carried out by adventurers, the unemployed, and military deserters. The wealthy and established colonists refrained from personal participation in them, but they were interested in them pecuniarily."[16]

6. The Cattle Trade Ban of 1727

Willem Adrian van der Stel used the raid of 1702 as an excuse to halt the cattle trade with the natives. The Lords Seventeen, however, were not happy with that. The cattle trade was again opened. From now on, the colonists only had to ask permission in advance if they wanted to make journeys into interior. This gave the government a certain measure of control over the cattle traders.

The colonists did not take any notice of this proviso, however. The single men in particular went out on expeditions again and again without permission. In many cases the government never even got wind of these expeditions. If the landdrost found out about them, the offenders were served a summons, sometimes in groups of ten or more at once, and each fined a few riksdollars. They did not, however, always respond to the summons. Often a second and even a third summons were sent out to no avail. Since many of them had no fixed place of residence and constantly roamed about from one place to an other, the messenger of the court did not know where to find them. Thus the livestock traders managed to evade the control of the government altogether.[17]

Complaints about the behavior of the members of the expeditions into the interior were received continually.[18] In 1723 the Church Council of Drakenstein, "because we could not remain silent, like mute dogs that could not bark," informed the governor of what they had heard "from reliable and devout people, lamenting over the flagrant sins of the country" about the latest expedition.

Jacobus van der Heiden, a very prominent burger, equipped the undertaking. According to the church council, members of the party never had the remotest intention not to steal livestock, since they did not take along enough goods for trading. The Khoikhoi who accompanied the expedition said that the traders killed in cold blood everyone they found among one particular Khoikhoi tribe, men as well as women, in the most barbarous manner, "until there was great consternation among the Khoikhoi who accompanied them, who had never seen so many dead." Furthermore, the white marauders then robbed the Khoikhoi of all their cattle and sheep and left behind those who had escaped death to starve. Later about 200 of the Khoikhoi followed the expedition and asked to be taken along or else be beaten to death as well, since they had been deprived of all their means of livelihood.[19]

The government carefully investigated this affair. The testimony that was collected, however, was so conflicting that the accused could not be prosecuted. The "reliable persons" upon whose information the church council based their complaints were also interrogated by the landdrost, but what they then related did not agree with their own testimony before the church council. And the Khoikhois' stories differed again from the information furnished by the "reliable persons." The landdrost thus concluded that the Drakenstein church council's complaints to the governor "had been a little too rash."[20] And that was the end of the story.

A few years later the Khoikhoi of the Zondereind River again complained about whites who stole their livestock or robbed them under the pretext of coming to trade. The Lords Seventeen decided that there must in fact be a fire where there was so much smoke. To avoid problems with the natives, the cattle trade was finally terminated in 1727. At the same time the colonists were forbidden from proceeding into the interior "to that end," in person or with wagons and trading goods, or to use anyone else for that purpose. Anyone who violated the prohibition would receive a flogging and everything he had in his possession when caught would be confiscated.[21]

With the cattle trade ban of 1727, however, the government did not forbid expeditions altogether. The colonists could still always visit the interior, provided that they not go to trade in livestock. And an excuse to visit the interior was always easy to find. They could go big game hunting. The expeditions therefore continued.

II. BIG GAME HUNTERS

7. The Hunt for Hippopotami

Apart from hunting for game in the immediate vicinity of the home or a temporary rest spot, the colonists undertook hunting trips into the interior throughout the pioneer period. By 1672 the colonists were already in the habit of journeying into the interior with their wagons to shoot large game to provide for their families and slaves.[22] At this time they had a particular interest in hippopotami, which one still came across in the Berg River.[23] When the hippopotami in the vicinity of the Cape had been exterminated and driven out, the hunters had to travel farther for their prey. By 1686 hippopotamus hunters had visited the Olifants River.[24] At the beginning of the eighteenth century (1712) the colonists had already crossed over the mountains and gone hunting along the Gourits and the Gamtoos rivers. This is clear from the hunting licenses that are registered in the Old Gamehunters Books.

When hippopotami started to become scarce in the vicinity of the Cape, the big game hunters began to focus mainly on elephants, because ivory will take one further than hippopotamus fat can!

8. The Elephant Hunt

The Company government was very sympathetic toward elephant hunters. Throughout the Company period there was a great demand for ivory in Batavia, much greater than the Cape could ever satisfy. The Cape government had a material interest in elephant hunting as well: the colonists were obliged to hand over a tenth penning of the money they made from the elephant tusks.

Since elephant hunting was thus a source of income for the Cape government, and the high authorities in Batavia kept on demanding a greater supply of ivory, the local government did not want to stand in the way of elephant hunting. On the contrary. It even encouraged this hunting and protested every time the Lords Seventeen tried to lower the price of ivory.[25] This is the reason why the Cape government did not prohibit all expeditions into the interior after the cattle trade was ended. It did not want to make elephant hunting impossible, even though the hunting expeditions allowed the colonists to carry on a contraband trade with the natives.

How much store the Company set by the elephant hunt will be evident from the following. In 1737 a rumor reached the Cape that some elephant hunters had been murdered by the Xhosa.[26] This gave the government a fright. To prevent further accidents of this sort, it decided not to allow anyone to shoot elephants in Xhosaland. A few months later, however, the government begin to fear that this prohibition would have a detrimental effect on the supply of ivory. The hunt in Great and Little Namaqualand no longer yielded much ivory. This meant that Xhosaland was about the only area where a considerable number of elephants were still to be found. And when the Cape government weighed the urgency of providing for Batavia's needs against the dangers of the Xhosa territories, the latter consideration became less important.

It was pointed out in the Council of Policy that since the most recent deaths, which had taken place some months before, the government had received no word of similar incidents. The government also suddenly began to doubt whether the natives would attack, unless they were "bothered or annoyed." It was therefore decided to permit elephant hunting again in the direction of Xhosaland. The hunters would be obliged only to take out a license, whereby they had to promise to sell all the elephant tusks they collected to the Company without exception or keeping any for themselves. Furthermore, the license prohibited the holder from exchanging any livestock with the natives, since this could lead to hostilities.[27]

Two years later a story reached the Cape that certain burgers, who were out shooting elephants, had traded with or stolen livestock from the Xhosa; that the Xhosa had followed them for seven days, and that in their flight they had left behind two flintlocks.[28] Even this news did not disturb the Cape government. Although the government was opposed to private individuals trading livestock, because this could provoke hostilities with the natives, it never prohibited elephant hunting, which could have given rise to the same fears, because the Company profited from it.

9. Description of an Expedition

The official documents of the eighteenth century do not contain many reports about expeditions. For that reason we can be very thankful that [Otto] Mentzel, who stayed at the Cape from around 1733 to 1741, informs us quite a lot about them. Thanks to Mentzel's splendid travelogue, we have a very vivid description of what took place on such an expedition.

Mentzel states that every year a number of young farmers equipped an expedition into the interior to go and shoot elephants. Usually they made up a party of fifteen or twenty, but smaller groups also went out. This was the case for example with the three Botha brothers, who were such good shots. These three often went elephant hunting with just one wagon and a few slaves.[29]

If a few farmers wanted to go out on an expedition, the undertaking was first discussed at length. After that they obtained permission from the government. It was likewise necessary to make careful preparations, because on such a long journey through the unknown, one could need many things. Outfitting such an expedition was obviously very costly. To begin with, a few good wagons were needed to transport the necessities of life (and goods for trade), and to bring back the elephant tusks and other products of the hunt. Furthermore, firearms, ammunition, provisions, tobacco, and other trading goods had to be provided for. The custom was that every member of the enterprise furnished something for the expedition. One man provided a wagon, another perhaps the oxen, and a third money. Moreover, each one brought along one or two Khoikhoi, or basters. The farmers generally did not have slaves accompany them on these expeditions, because these provided the slaves such a golden opportunity to run away.

After all the necessary preparations had been made, the expedition members decided on a day and place to meet. A seasoned person who had already taken part in one or two expeditions, and who already had experience and knowledge of the interior, was then chosen as leader. Everyone was bound to obey his commands without question. This was a matter of great urgency, since not only the success of the undertaking, but even the hunters' lives, depended on those commands.[30]

There was generally no prior discussion on how far the party would travel, and likewise nothing about when the hunters had to be back. Everything depended on when they had enough ivory. Once on the trail the party never hurried needlessly. Usually they rode only short stretches, because it was of paramount importance not to overwork the oxen. When the party reached an area where there was good pasture and plentiful water, it often camped there for a few days to let the oxen rest a bit. Meanwhile the hunters hunted at their leisure. But they never remained long in a specific area. They also never followed a fixed route, but travelled now in one direction and then in another. Everything depended on where the rivers could be crossed, and where the easiest routes over the mountains were.[31]

When the party came to a swollen river, they simply waited until the water had gone down. If the mountain was too steep, they found a way around it. In so doing they sometimes rode many days out of their way. "But this does not trouble them, for since they have no predetermined destination to reach, all places are alike if they can only find elephants and wild game there. One might liken them to beggars who wander aimlessly from here to there, looking for sustenance wherever they can find it."[32]

Most of the time the expedition members were not really in a hurry to return home. Generally they stayed away for months rather than weeks, and sometimes for more than a year, and as a result they traveled surprising distances. During this time they roamed about like Hungarian gipsies and lived more or less like them. They lived in or under their wagons and shot game for the pot. The meat from a hippopotamus they wrapped in its own hide and barbecued over glowing coals. If they ran out of bread and biscuits, they—like the first trekboers before them and generations of pioneers thereafter—ate dried beef jerky together with fat game meat.[33]

There was no danger that any of the party would die of hunger. They could never run out of food, because wild game was to be found everywhere. If necessary, they salted the fresh meat of wild game or made jerky. Their chief difficulty was the serious shortage of water that they sometimes experienced. It often happened that they rode for days in the blistering heat of the summer sun without finding water. Occasionally they were forced to ride back along their own trail to save themselves and their oxen.[34]

In Mentzel's time the expeditions concentrated first on the elephant hunt, because ivory was the most valuable product that the game hunt yielded. The hunters were usually not too fastidious in avoiding the unlawful cattle trade with the natives, however, because this sometimes yielded better profits than the elephant hunt, which was such a precarious business. The hunters could always sell livestock that had been exchanged for trifles in the colony, or use such stock to increase their own herds. The cattle trade was a sideline, however, and was generally postponed until the journey home. If the wagons were full of ivory—or the hunters had become tired of roaming—they would ride from one Khoikhoi kraal to another and trade for sheep and cattle. The livestock was divided equally among the members of the party when they arrived back in the colony. In case one of them had contributed more to the outfitting of the expedition than another, he was compensated for it. After that the hunters went home. After they had rested and visited a bit, the group came together again at a previously designated spot, from where they then undertook a short trip to the Cape to sell the elephant tusks to the Company.[35]

With the profits that the ivory provided they then perhaps bought wagons, ammunition, and other necessities for the following trip. But it also happened that the hunters—after they had been exposed for months to dangers, fatigue, hunger and thirst—squandered their hard-earned money within a short time. Particularly those who loved having a snort of liquor quickly lost their money. They were now suddenly rich and in the taverns they found many mates who, for a few drinks, were willing to listen patiently to their heroic, wondrous hunting adventures and believe it all. The true elephant hunter—just like some of the professional livestock traders in the time of Willem Adriaan van der Stel—was often a restless, unsettled chap who was little concerned with the long-term improvement of his economic position.[36] This mentality was likewise noticeable among many of the seasoned old elephant hunters that one came across at the end of the nineteenth century in the Transvaal and other northern areas. So long as the money held out, they lived a comfortable life. When it was gone, they went on the hunt again. Many of them made no effort at all to obtain land. Others let land, which they had acquired for next to nothing, slip out of their hands. They lived from hand to mouth, and when the elephants were all killed off, they were totally impoverished.

10. Lists of Expedition Members

Apart from the interesting information that Mentzel provides, we know very little indeed about the expeditions that were undertaken during the first half of the eighteenth century. Luckily, however, two lists have been preserved in the Stellenbosch archive that furnish very important data on the expeditions. The two lists, which complement each other, both bear the title:

"Alphabetical list of persons who have gone out on expeditions."[37] They cover the period from 1735 to 1744. Besides the name of the hunter, they also provide the date on which he gave notice of his going on an expedition, and the date on which he gave notice that he had returned again. In some cases the second date is missing. What follows now is a summary of the two lists:

Name	Departure	Return
Arentsdorp, Andries	05.05.1735	10.10.1735
	09.12.1735	23.08.1736
	10.10.1736	04.11.1737
	16.10.1738 ?	20.09.1739
Arentsdorp, Jan Andries	24.11.1736	?
	22.12.1738	?
Becker, Marthinus	24.02.1735	07.01.1736
Burgert, Jacobus	08.02.1736	01.09.1746
Burgert, Jan	28.02.1739	12.04.1740
Campfer, Cornelis	05.05.1735	08.10.1736
	08.10.1736	?
Campher, Elias	27.10.1738	21.08.1739
	23.10.1739	05.09.1740
	10.11.1741	?
Cloeten, Lowies	05.05.1735	?
	11.11.1737	?
Cnoetse, Koert	12.09.1736	?
Cnoetse, Gerrit	08.09.1735	12.09.1736
	12.09.1736	07.05.1737
	01.06.1737	31.03.1738
	19.07.1738	21.08.1739
Cok, Jan J.	10.08.1743	07.09.1744
Cordje, Gideon	16.06.1737	?
	23.11.1737	01.08.1738
de Bruyn, Nicolaas	18.03.1735	27.10.1735
	31.10.1736	12.08.1737
	05.12.1737	28.07.1738
de Bruyn, Pieter	26.03.1737	19.02.1738
de Jager, Christiaan	?	26.01.1736
	24.02.1736	?
	30.10.1736	24.11.1737
	12.08.1738	19.04.1739
	26.09.1740	24.02.1742
	05.03.1742	05.03.1743
de Jager, Christiaan	17.11.1736	24.11.1737
	06.01.1738	21.07.1738
de Jager, Louw	23.11.1737	?
du Weges, Gideon	28.02.1739	12.04.1740
Eksteen, Hendrik	26.11.1736	16.08.1737
Esterhuysen, Andries	02.11.1736	?
Esterhuysen, Christoffel	16.11.1737	25.08.1739
Geldenhuys, Jacobus	10.09.1736	13.12.1736

Greefde, Christoffel Hoog	18.05.1736	?
Hatting, Johannes J	18.11.1736	26.11.1737
Heppenaar, Fredrik	09.10.1736	?
la Grange, Jan	23.05.1739	?
	02.10.1742	20.10.1743
le Roux, Abraham	06.12.1735	23.08.1736
	13.12.1736	29.11.1737
le Roux, Jan. jr	11.10.1736	05.08.1737
Marks, Dirk	26.11.1736	?
Marrais, Lucas	11.10.1736	05.08.1737
Meyer, Willem	17.11.1736	24.11.1737
Minnaar, Philip, jr	21.12.1736	12.10.1737
Oelofsz, Roelof	11.11.1737	27.10.1738
Oosthuysen, Gerrit	31.12.1736	?
Oosthuysen, Marthinus	24.02.1735	07.01.1736
Potgieter, Hermanus	10.08.1743	07.09.1744
Potje, Anthony	09.10.1736	?
Redecker, Ernst	23.10.1739	?
Rik, Anthony, jr	21.12.1747	?
Roy, Jan	19.12.1737	28.10.1738
Saayman, Daniel	26.11.1738	15.10.1739
	25.11.1739	15.09.1740
	15.09.1740	03.10.1741
	01.11.1742	01.10.1743
	02.10.1743	07.09.1744
	08.02.1736	08.12.1736
Scheepers, Fredrik	08.12.1736	04.10.1737
	04.09.1740	12.06.1741
	10.08.1743	?
	16.10.1737	?
Scheepers, Fredrik	30.10.1736	29.11.1737
Senekal, Jakob	23.11.1737	?
	21.12.1736	29.10.1737
Senekal, Samuel	13.12.1736	24.11.1737
Stokviet, Hermanus	27.03.1737	13.02.1738
Swart, Jacob	27.03.1737	?
ter Blanche, Steven	16.10.1737	?
van Delve, Claas, Claasz	21.12.1736	15.08.1737
van de Venter, Jacob	04.09.1740	12.06.1741
van der Wat, Hendrik	24.10.1743	07.09.1744
	28.06.1737	?
van der Wy, Jan C.R	29.08.1736	04.01.1737
van Dyk, Sybrand	16.10.1736	15.08.1737
van Emmenes, Jan	06.01.1738	19.08.1738
	14.02.1736	19.11.1736
van Tongeren, Cornelis	22.12.1738	22.03.1739
	11.04.1740	12.06.1740
	14.06.1741	03.05.1742

	03.05.1742	25.09.1742
	07.10.1736	26.08.1737
van Vooren, Jan	11.11.1737	?
	27.03.1737	05.03.1738
van Wyk, Willem	01.10.1735	04.11.1736
Venter, Hendrik	04.11.1736	?
	28.11.1737	29.10.1738
Vermaak, Cornelis	26.11.1738	02.11.1739
	02.11.1739	?
	22.06.1737	20.05.1738
Willemsz, Matteus		

This list, undoubtedly, does not provide an exact indication of the extent of elephant hunting during the years 1735 to 1743. It has already been shown that single hunters went out on expeditions, often without the permission of government. We can therefore assume that during the period concerned many more persons participated in elephant hunts than those about whom the government knew. Nevertheless the list reveals a few very interesting facts.

In the first place it is clear that expeditions from the district of Stellenbosch into the interior were made every year between 1735 and 1743. It is also evident from the lists that such expeditions were substantial undertakings. The overwhelming majority of the hunters stayed away between nine months and a year. In some cases expeditions even lasted more than a year.

Another significant fact is that the majority of the persons whose names appear on the lists of hunters between 1735 and 1743 participated just once during this period in an expedition. Of the sixty persons about whom the lists give an account, thirty-eight went out only once in the nine-year period. Thirteen went out twice and three went three times. Only six persons took part in four or more expeditions.

In some cases, which were clearly exceptions, the hunters went out so often for a few years that during that time they could have devoted very little personal attention to their farms. Daniel Saayman, for example, participated in six expeditions between 19 December 1737 and 7 September 1744, a period of less than seven years, most of them lasting nearly a year. In most cases the time that passed between expeditions was just long enough to make preparations for the next trip. It even happened one time that Saayman reported on the same day that he had returned from one expedition and gave notice that he was going out the following day. In effect, then, he actually led the life of a professional hunter for a period of nearly seven years. We do not know how long he maintained this existence. Presumably he begin to concentrate more earnestly on farming by 1745, however, because on 16 March of that year he took a loan farm by ordinance, where he lived until his death in 1778.[38]

With the aid of the Gamehunters Books, in which are recorded the loan farm ordinances, it is possible to determine how many of the persons who owned farms at that time or later, went on expeditions between 1735 and 1743 with the foreknowledge of the government. Research reveals that about 65 percent of the hunters' names appear in the Gamehunters Books. One can safely assume, however, that a much higher percentage were farmers (or potential farmers), because even in the eighteenth century certainly not every farmer had a farm. Some of the traders farmed perhaps on undistributed crown land. Others were share croppers or died before their farming activities warranted their getting a farm. This was the case, for example, with Ernst Redecker, whose livestock grazed on Elias Campfer's farm, and who was trampled to death while hunting an elephant.[39]

11. Professional Hunters?

On the basis of this reasoning one must conclude that the great majority of persons who took part in elephant hunts during the eighteenth century were farmers. This supposition is supported by numerous references in the contemporary sources to farmers who undertook expeditions.[40] Apparently among these farmer-hunters there were some professional hunters, but they would have constituted only a minimal percentage of the total population. [Anders] Sparrman, who travelled in the Cape Colony between 1772 and 1776, states: "Some years ago, when elephants could still be found near the Cape, nine or ten people, several of whom were still alive in my time there, particularly excelled in the elephant hunt. Though they were away for several months and had to endure many dangers, hunger, and some of the greatest difficulties, they would, upon their return, in the same or even shorter amount of time, casually and freely spend everything they had earned on the expedition."[41] Here we are apparently dealing with professional hunters, but it is not clear at all that some of them were not involved in farming as well.

A factor that undoubtedly worked against the development of a class of professional hunters in the Company period was the fact that elephant hunting could not offer the colonists an ample livelihood. This was partly the result of the monopolistic policies of the Company. The colonists were obliged to deliver all their ivory at fixed prices to the Company. Throughout the eighteenth century the hunters received 16 stuiwers (about 1s. 4d.) per pound for the first type, 16 stuiwers per two pounds for the second type, and 16 stuiwers per three pounds for the third type of ivory. In 1747 the East India Company government granted its permission to raise the prices from 16 to 20 stuiwers per pound, but the Cape government never availed itself of this opportunity.[42] These prices were not attractive at all. Forty, fifty years ago hunters in the Transvaal and East Africa received 10s to £1 per pound for ivory and even at such prices elephant hunting was never a serious rival to farming.

12. Decline of the Elephant Hunt

During the first half of the eighteenth century, when elephants were still fairly plentiful in the Cape Colony, the colonists still devoted much of their attention to elephant hunting, in spite of the low prices. As a result of the constant hunting, however, the elephants were quickly exterminated. As time went on those that survived fled deeper into the interior toward the Tsitsikamma and thick bushy areas so that after a while it became more difficult to find the animals.[43] By the middle of the eighteenth century the hunters often had to remain out between eight months and a year to accumulate just a few wagon loads of tusks, with the result that the profits from such a trip were largely absorbed by the high costs incurred. The result of this, the Council of Policy declared in 1744, was "that all of the inhabitants that still do some of this work, though they are very few, have taken a greater dislike to it the longer they've been at it."[44]

The decline of elephant hunting during the first half of the eighteenth century is evident as well from the list of hunters above. In 1736 thirty-seven hunters from the Stellenbosch district journeyed into the interior with the foreknowledge of the government. The following year the total fell to twenty-three and the year after that to nine. During the years 1740 to 1743 there were never more than five hunters who went out on expeditions.

By the end of the eighteenth century elephants were already so scarce in the Cape Colony that hunters probably did not even always cover their expenses. This is evident from the case of Jacobus Coetsee, who became famous because, so far as is known, he was the first white man to cross over the Orange River. In 1760 Coetsee received written permission from the governor to shoot elephants in the interior. On 14 July he left his home in the Piketberge (the present-day village of Aurora) with two wagons and twelve Khoikhoi from Klipfontein. He crossed the Olifants, the Groen, and the Buffels rivers until he reached the Koperberge, which Simon van der Stel had visited in 1685. From there he traveled up to the Orange. He crossed the river and then moved into the land of the Great Namaquas up to Bunsenberg, about a day's ride north of Warmbad in present-day South-West Africa [Namibia]. According to his account, he travelled a distance of fifty days on horseback from his farm into the interior, but he shot only two elephants, the only ones he came across.[45]

For the hunters who went in the direction of Xhosaland, it probably went better, but there is no doubt in both cases that by the end of the eighteenth century elephant hunting in the Cape Colony no longer produced much. This is clear from the following official return of elephant tusks that were delivered to the Company between 1769 and 1779.[46]

Year	Weight in Pounds
1769 — 1770	537
1770 — 1771	104
1771 — 1772	555
1772 — 1773	2,347
1773 — 1774	724
1774 — 1775	590
1775 — 1776	790
1776 — 1777	898
1777 — 1778	1,299
1778 — 1779	1,045
Total	8, 889 pounds

The total for ten years consisted of 5,008 pounds of ivory of the first grade, 2,840 pounds of the second grade and 1,041 pounds of the third grade, which altogether was worth £451 13s. 0d. After the Company's tenth was deducted, this represented an amount of about £405 10s. 0d., that is, about £40 11s. 0d. per year

This return undoubtedly does not provide an accurate picture of the number of elephants that were shot in the Cape Colony during the relevant period, because there was also an illegal trade in ivory. Sparrman says that farmers often brought to the Cape smaller elephant tusks hidden in their butter casks and then sold them to private buyers at higher prices than the Company paid.[47]

There is no evidence that the illegal trade occurred on such a scale that one could make a profitable living from elephant hunting.

13. Expeditions Appealed to Young Men

An interesting fact in connection with the expeditions in Mentzel's time was that—just like the cattle trade expeditions in Willem Adriaan van der Stel's time—they were undertaken mainly by single men, that is, by unmarried men who no longer lived with their parents. This is clear if one compares the lists of hunters (1735-1745) with the lists of single persons from the same time. Around three quarters of the hunters' names appear on the "Alphabetical list of single individuals, their names and places of residence," which was compiled around the beginning of 1736.[48] And among the rest as well there would no doubt be unmarried sons who had not yet left their parent's homes.

From this list one can conclude that the hunters were usually fairly young. This is also evident from the numerous references to hunters in contemporary sources.[49] Sometimes the boys were still wet behind their ears when they went on an expedition for the first time. For example, on 31 October 1736, Pieter de Bruyn took his hunter's oath,[50] which establishes that he was then just sixteen years old, and in March 1737 he gave notice that he was going on an expedition. Elias Campfer and Jan la Grange were also not yet of age when they went out for the first time on an elephant hunt.[51]

The reason that expeditions were attractive to young men in particular is obvious. For a son without capital who wanted to stand on his own two feet, the big game hunt offered the opportunity to obtain a little ready money. Moreover, an expedition gave him a good chance to increase his livestock herd through the illegal cattle trade with the natives. It could open the way for him to independence. Besides, the young men usually did not have the same responsibilities as did the older men. They had no families. Generally they still did not have large farms that could not be neglected. Their farms were still small and their livestock usually grazed among the herds of others and therefore did not require their personal presence.[52]

What is more, in the eighteenth century it was considered as an essential element in the education of a young man that he take part in at least one proper hunting expedition. The boys of that time did not have the opportunity to be sent for a few years to the village school or to university to learn a little independence and to prepare them for life. They did not have the opportunity to round off their early manhood with a study tour. They could not measure their agility, physical strength, and endurance on the football field against others. They did not take public examinations through which they could obtain recognition for their ability.

The expedition was a part of their early education. It opened for them the door to the unknown. It had to satisfy their craving for adventure, which today's student can satisfy by travelling; their exploits on the hunt had to satisfy the urge to conquer, which is satisfied today on the sports field and athletics track. The expedition was a sort of examination as well. Until a farmer's son had shot a lion or elephant, he was not yet a man. And a young man who endured this test was particularly proud of his achievement. "A young Afrikaner," wrote Mentzel, "who has participated on such an expedition, is henceforth a brave fellow, someone who has proven himself in the world, and imagines that he has performed more and greater deeds than a veteran soldier who has been in ten campaigns, and twelve battles."[53]

14. Smaller Hunting Trips

The era of large expeditions in which twenty, thirty and more whites took part, and that lasted from eight months to a year occurred in the first half of the eighteenth century, while the natives still had a great deal of livestock to exchange and elephants were still relatively plentiful. Gradually after that the large expeditions gave way to hunting trips on a smaller scale,[54] which lasted perhaps only a few weeks and sometimes also involved illegal cattle trading. The following testimony of the Hottentot Piet, who had grown up on the farm of Klaas Prinsloo, gives one an impression of what happened on such a trip. He stated that together with his young master, two other burghers and a few boys he "rode far into the interior" to shoot elephants. First they travelled northwards toward "the great river," on the opposite bank of which they expected to find elephants. The river was flooded, however. They then headed southwards towards Xhosaland, where each of the burghers traded cattle for himself, "giving four bunches of beads and two copper plates for each head of cattle, and a string of beads for each calf." After they had traded for cattle "abundantly", they departed and on the other side of the Fish River, "at a wide place, where no one could see them," everyone separated out their cattle from the herd and took them with them. His young master then rode home alone, leaving his cattle behind with Piet and "giving him, as the lions were very bold there, a musket together with a horn of powder and some balls to set a spring gun." There a government commission surprised him. One morning when he was still asleep, the heemraad Johan Bernhard Hoffman came upon him. He recognized that they were Xhosa cattle hat he had with him. With that the heemraad took his rifle from him and brought him back to the drostdy along with the cattle....[55] And this chance meeting is responsible for our having the story. In the nineteenth century and even later hunting trips into the interior were often also undertaken by frontier farmers and other lovers of the hunt.[56]

15. Influence of the Expeditions

These expeditions had a great influence on our pioneer history, above all during the first years of the eighteenth century. In the time when agriculture was still the major occupation at the Cape, the expeditions gave an important boost to livestock farming. Furthermore, it was by way of these expeditions that young farmers learned to get to know the interior. They discovered where prime grazing land and good waters were, which they one day could obtain by ordinance, and where they could then farm to their hearts' desire. Their long peregrinations in the wilderness accustomed them to the loneliness and dangers of the interior and strengthened their love for the free life in the field. And depending on their own strength, they learned to be independent. Finally, the hunters who returned from the interior were living advertisements for the areas they had visited. They told all sorts of stories about fertile regions where the pasture was better and the game more plentiful—stories that were enticing enough to get others to decide whether to go there and hunt or to migrate there as well.

In this way the expeditions thus undoubtedly promoted trekking into the interior. But the pioneers who led the expansion into the interior were farmers. They took part in hunting and the cattle trade, but their first concern was livestock farming. Throughout the pioneer period travellers came upon farms or trekboers at the outposts of civilization—not trading stations or the temporary halting places of hunters. The cattle traders and the hunters were only the pathfinders of civilization, not the first wave of colonists.

ENDNOTES

[1] P.J. van der Merwe, *Die Trekboer in die Geskiedenis van die Kaapkolonie, 1657-1842* (Cape Town, 1838), pp. 35-42.

[2] C 1403, Letters Disp., Simon van der Stel to Patria, 1 August 1696, p. 75.

[3] Ibid.; C 22, Resolutions, 9 February 1696, p. 552.

[4] C 22, Resolutions, 20 July 1693, p. 475; C 2272, Original Ordinance Book, 20 July 1693, p. 177.

[5] C 2273, Original Ordinance Book, 28 February 1700, p. 320.

[6] C 1422, Letters Disp., W.A. van der Stel to Patria, 14 March 1701, p. 102; C 24, Resolutions, 27 October 1702, p. 80.

[7] C 1426, Letters Disp., W.A. van der Stel to Patria, 25 March 1702, p. 418.

[8] C 1428, Letters Disp., W.A. van der Stel to Patria, 1 April 1703, pp. 109-118; C 24, Resolutions, 27 October 1702, p. 81.

[9] C 1428, Letters Disp., W.A. van der Stel to Patria, 1 April 1703, p. 118.

[10] Leo Fouché, *Het Dagboek van Adam Tas, 1705-1706* (London, 1914), pp. 334-6; George McCall Theal, *History of South Africa* (London, 1915), III:416.

[11] 1/STB 19/25, Notices, 15 July 1709; C 1426, Letters Disp., W.A. van der Stel to Patria, 25 March 1702.

[12] C 24, Resolutions, 27 October 1702, p. 80.

[13] C 22, Resolutions, 2 February 1696, pp. 549-51; C 1426, Letters Disp., W.A. van der Stel to Patria, 25 March 1702, p. 418; BKR 1, Minute Book, Burgher Military Council, 3 September 1719, p. 19; C 24, Resolutions, 27 October 1702, p. 80.

[14] Instructions from Simon van der Stel to William Adriaan van der Stel, 30 March 1699, in Botha, *Collectanea*, Series 1, vol. 5, p. 14.

[15] C 1426, Letters Disp., W.A. van der Stel to Patria, 25 March 1702, p. 418; C 24, Resolutions, 27 October 1702, p. 80; Instructions from Simon van der Stel to William Adriaan van der Stel, 30 March 1699, in Botha, *Collectanea*, Series I, vol. 5, p. 14; H.C.V. Leibbrandt, *The Defence of W.A. v. d. Stel* (Cape Town, 1897), pp. 133-149.

[16] H. Dehérain, *Le Cap de Bonne-Espérance au XVIIe Siècle* (Paris, 1909), p. 179.

[17] 1/STB 19/25, Notices, 15 July 1709; BKR 1, Minute Book, Burgher Military Council, 3 September 1719, p. 19; 1/STB 1/8, Minutes from the Landdrost and Heemraden, 7 September 1722, p. 1; 1/STB 5/12, Minutes of the Civil Rolls, 1722-26.

[18] C 1447, Letters Disp., 18 April 1708, p. 10.

[19] C 64, Resolutions, 9 March 1723, pp. 601-603.

[20] C 71, Resolutions, 13 March 1725, p. 362; C 69, Resolutions, 11 January 1724, p. 585.

[21] C 2278, Original Ordinance Book, 9 April 1727, pp. 341-3; C 77, Resolutions, 4 April 1727, pp. 131-2.

[22] C 1341, Letters Disp., Government to Lords XVII, 19 April 1672, p. 5; C 8, Resolutions, 11 July 1673, p. 741.

[23] C 11, Resolutions, 29 July 1677, pp. 321-3; Theal, *History*, III:180.

[24] C 1376, Letters Disp., Simon van der Stel to Patria, 12 April 1686, p. 2.

[25] C 102, Resolutions, 15 February 1737, p. 102; C 126, Resolutions, 12 January 1748, p. 36.

[26] C 103, Resolutions, 2 July 1737, pp. 304-05 and 11 July 1737, p. 307.

[27] C 104, Resolutions, 15 October 1737, pp. 300-02.

[28] C 112, Resolutions, 31 October 1739, p. 372.

[29] O.F. Mentzel, *Lebens-Geschichte Heern Rudolph Siegfried Allemans* (Glogau, 1784), pp. 126, 156.

[30] O.F. Mentzel, *Vollständige und Zuverläszige Geographische und topographische Beschreibung des Berühmten und in aller Betrachtung merkwürdigen Afrikanischen Vorgebirges des Guten Hoffnung* (Glogau, 1785, 1787), II:195-6; Mentzel, Lebens-Geschichte, pp. 126-7.

[31] Mentzel, *Beschreibung*, I:9.

[32] Ibid., II:197.

[33] Ibid.

[34] Ibid.

[35] Ibid., II:194, 198-99.

[36] Ibid., II:199-200; A. Sparrman, *Reize naar de Kaap de Goede Hoop, de Landen van den Zuid Pool, en rondom de Waereld* (Leiden, 1786), I:374-5; C 24, Resolutions, 27 October 1702, p. 80.

[37] 1/STB 13/31, "Alphabetical lists."

[38] RLR 11/1, Old Gamehunters Book, 16 March 1745, p. 135.

[39] C 825, Enclosures, Account of E. Campfer, 5 September 1740, p. 509; See also, 1/STB 13/31, "Alphabetical lists."

[40] C 133, Resolutions, 5 December 1755, pp. 463-73; C 504, Letters Rec., Horak to Governor, 19 May 1761, p. 876; C 1655, Letters Disp., Ryk Tulbagh to Lords XVII, 1 March 1762, pp. 271, 276; C 112, Resolutions, 31 October 1739, p. 372; 1/GR 8/1, Letters Rec., Col. Secretary to Woeke, 20 June 1789; C.O. 4438, Papers of Col. Collins, Supplement, July, 1809; Mentzel, *Lebens-Geschichte*, p. 156; Sparrman, *Reize*, I:350, 359, 360-2, and II:580.

[41] Sparrman, *Reize*, I:374-5.

[42] C 126, Resolutions, 12 January 1748, p. 36; C 201, Resolutions, 7 February 1792, p. 379.

[43] Sparrman, *Reize*, I:374.

[44] C 122, Resolutions, 24 March 1744, pp. 122-23. See also C 102, Resolutions, 15 February 1737, p. 102 and C 126, Resolutions, 12 January 1748, p. 36.

[45] C 1655, Letters Disp., Ryk Tulbagh to Lords XVII, 1 March 1762, pp. 271-6. See also E.E. Mossop, ed., *The Journal of Hendrik Jacob Wikar (1779)... and the Journals of Jacobus Coetsé Jansz. (1760) and Willem van Reenen (1791)* (Cape Town: Van Riebeeck Society, 1935), Series I, vol. 15, p. 283, note 11.

[46] C 678, Enclosures, Report of Nederburg and Frijkenius, "Return of Elephant Tusks," 31 October 1792, No. 20, p. 775.

[47] Sparrman, *Reize*, I:374.

[48] 1/STB 13/31, "Aphabetical lists." This volume contains two lists of single persons. Both are undated, but from the names and residences, it is clear that the one list supersedes the other and immediately proceeds on from it. The oldest list must still have been in use in 1735, because the name of Elias Campfer, who took a burgher/milita oath on 31 October, 1835, appears on it. The newer list was already in use in 1736, because the address change for Jacobus Louw, for which notice is given in a letter from Johannes Louw dated 21 March 1736, is on it.

[49] 1/STB 3/9, Accounts and Declarations, 16 September 1740; C 825, Enclosures, Account of E. Campfer, 5 September 1740, pp. 509-11, and Account of Jantje and Dirk, 16 September 1740, pp. 513-19; 1/SWM 3/14, Testimony (1777-1783), testimony of Piet, 17 January 1778; Mentzel, *Lebens-Geschichte*, pp. 126, 156.

[50] C 2188, Logbooks, Stellenbosch, 31 October 1736, p. 803.

[51] 1/STB 13/31. According to a list that is contained in this volume, both Campfer and la Grange took their burgher/milita oaths on 31 October 1735.

[52] 1/STB 13/31, "Alphabetical lists." See also RLR 1 to 7, Old Gamehunters Books.

[53] Mentzel, *Beschreibung*, II:199.

[54] See C 504, Letters Rec., Horak to Governor, 19 May 1761, p. 876; A.W. Drayson, *Tales at the Outspan or Adventures in the Wild Regions of Southern Africa* (London, 1865), p. 23.

[55] 1/SWM 3/14, Testimony (1777-1783), testimony of Piet, 17 January 1778. See also 1/SWM 3/14, Testimony (1777-1783), testimony of Adam (the bastard son of J. Potgieter) and Ruijter (the servant of J. Erasmus), 17 January 1778.

[56] 1/WOC 10/2, Logbook, 20 February 1810; 1/WOC 10/5, Logbook, 8 November 1813; C.O. 4447, Sir R.S. Donkin's Collection of Missionary Complaints, 1820-1821, John Philip, Documents accompanying Tabular View; Drayson, *Tales*, p. 23; van der Merwe, *Trekboer*, p. 163; and P.J. van der Merwe, *Die Noordwaartse Beweging van die Boere voor die Groot Trek (1770-1842)* (The Hague, 1937), pp. 74-76.

CHAPTER IV

The Emigration of the Surplus Population

It has already been shown that as a result of the living conditions and traditions of the pioneer population at the Cape, nearly every farmer's son followed in the footsteps of his father and also became a farmer. Therefore, throughout the pioneer period the spread of livestock farming in the interior was in direct proportion to the population increase.

In the pioneer community households were usually large, with the result that a farmer's sons could seldom make a living on their father's land after his death. Many farmers did not even own land.[1] Thus only a small percentage of the next generation had a chance to make a living from inherited land. The overwhelming majority had to seek their livelihood elsewhere. So what were the possibilities for a young beginner without ground who wanted to become an independent livestock farmer?

1. The Possibilities for Becoming a Landowner

A son who wanted to farm on his own account could naturally purchase a farm near where he lived. There were always landowners who for one or another reason were keen to make a change. Indeed, one is sometimes inclined to think that during the pioneer period every farm had its price.[2] Apart from this, family farms often came on the market when an estate had to be divided.[3] As a result of the gradual increase of land prices that occurred over time in every region,[4] farms in older districts were usually beyond the reach of young beginners without capital. This group had a much better chance obtaining land in the border districts or regions of more recent settlement, where land prices were generally much lower.

By the end of the nineteenth century a person could purchase good farms in the northwestern parts of the Cape Colony from the first migrants for a few hundred pounds. In Griqualand West, Gordonia, and the Mierland the Basters traded their farms with white farmers for a wagon and a team of oxen, a small keg of brandy, a rifle, and a few cattle. A charming tale was told in Gordonia of a young Baster who bartered away his father's farm for sixty goats to a farmer. When the old man heard of it, he reprimanded the boy good-naturedly: "Good heavens, my boy, you cheated the Dutchman!" In Griqualand West I heard of a farmer who exchanged his farm for a new hat. Over the past few years, above all as a result of the present war,[*] land prices in all parts of the Cape Colony have risen appreciably, but fifteen, twenty years ago a person still could purchase land of good quality in the northern parts of the province, and likewise in Southwest Africa, for two shillings and two shillings six pence per morgen.

The cheapest way to become a landowner, however, was to try and obtain crown land. Under the loan-farm system, which was in use until 1813, a farmer paid nothing for a new or abandoned farm, apart from the yearly quitrent of 24 rixdollars, which was due for all loan-farms. If he took over a loan-farm from an ordinance holder, it carried with it, apart from the

---

[*]Trans. note: World War II

quitrent, a certain capital outlay. Officially a loan-farm could not be sold. All that the "owner" could lawfully turn over to someone else was the improvements that he had made on the land. Over time, however, when it became clear that the government usually never declined to grant to the buyer of the homestead the farm concerned in loan, it was not long before more was paid for a loan-farm than what the improvements were worth. Normally the purchase price was based on the value of the entire farm, including the improvements.[5]

Under the forms of land ownership that applied from 1813 onwards, higher demands were placed on the financial resources of the aspiring landowner. Usually he had to pay at least the surveying charges or a part of the purchase price in cash. Nevertheless, one generally paid much less for crown land than for distributed land. In addition, the government usually offered terms for the repayment of the capital sum that one could not get from any private landowner. Under the system of perpetual quitrent, for example, it was not necessary to pay off the entire capital amount. The buyer had only to pay the interest on the remainder in the form of perpetual quitrent. The settlers living in the Kalahari at that time had 65 years to pay for their farms, all the while paying their one percent interest for them.

Not only was undistributed land a bargain, until about a century ago it was still very easy to obtain government land. Under the loan-farm system it was the simplest thing in the world. The farmer sought out a piece of land for himself, erected a beacon on the spot where he wanted to establish his homestead, addressed a request to government to grant him the farm by ordinance, and went to live there in advance. Providing that the request did not conflict with previously granted grazing rights, the farmer could figure that his request would not be denied. Since the government did not have sufficient administrative power available to prevent the unlawful occupation of undistributed land, the farmer would use the land in any case and that simply meant that the government would lose the quitrent.

Under the form of land ownership that was introduced in 1813, which I have elsewhere called the "request farm system" to distinguish it from later forms of perpetual quitrent, the position was more or less the same. A farmer who wanted land in quitrent tenure, also picked out his farm himself, sent off a petition for it to the government and—in the expectation that the land would eventually be granted to him—immediately occupied it. And by the time that the land would one day be inspected and surveyed, and his petition had worked its way through government channels, he would already have such a strong claim to the land on the basis of prior occupation and cultivation, that his request could hardly be denied. Sometimes many years passed before a request farm was given out, and in the mean time the "occupier" had farmed it free of charge.[6]

In these circumstances one could expect that undistributed land held a great attraction for young beginners, who generally did not have the necessary capital available to purchase private "expensive" land.[7]

One can further state as a general rule that for persons who wanted to have undistributed land, there were always larger and more attractive possibilities in the border districts then in areas of older settlement. It goes without saying that there was more government land available in uninhabited and thinly populated areas than in older districts. For this reason those who wanted undistributed land already relied upon the border districts in the first place. The forms of land ownership that were in use in the Cape colony until the middle of the nineteenth century, however, provided additional incentives to farmers who wanted to have crown land to trek to uninhabited areas and areas of more recent settlement.

In this regard one can point out some aspects of the loan-farm system. Since under this system crown land was not systematically divided, but each person selected his own farm land, obviously the best land in a certain region would be the first to be taken by ordinance. After a time only ground of mediocre or poorer quality was left. It is for this reason that loan-farms never had a fixed or uniform size. The amount of grazing lands that the ordinance holder had available to him depended solely on the distance from his neighbors. Thus, in uninhabited and thinly inhabited parts, the loan-farm occupier had much more grazing land available to him—and likewise more seasonal trek pasture—than in areas of older settlements. The same quitrent was paid for all loan-farms, however, irrespective of size and quality. One can thus expect that a hand-picked farm in the border districts, where a farmer could make use of as much grazing land as he needed, must have had much more attraction for the aspiring landowner than patches of left-over land in an older district, where one had more neighbors than pasture.

As long as the possibility existed of trekking to still unoccupied land farther ahead, the loan-farm occupant was only prepared to take possession of the best land. Farms of average usefulness or poorer quality were ignored.[8] In 1775 the farmers who settled beyond Bruintjieshoogte against the orders of the government declared that it "absolutely had to be done from time to time because there was a shortage of good farms available, on which they could make a decent living, as with respect to pasture and water for their livestock."[9] It was no accident that the farmers spoke of "*good farms.*" There were still many farms available at this time between the Cape and Bruintjieshoogte, but not the sort of farms that the farmers really wanted to have.

2. Viability of Unoccupied Land

Apart from the possibilities for a young beginner to become a landowner, it was really not difficult during the pioneer period to obtain pasture for livestock for nothing or under easy conditions.

In the first place there was always undistributed land on and beyond the borders of settled areas on which farmers with no possessions could make a living, until the land came into the hands of private individuals. During the Company period a number of different laws were enacted forbidding the unauthorized use of undistributed land,[10] but these laws were never seriously enforced. Up until very recent times there were always still farmers who made free use of undistributed crown lands. In thinly populated areas of more recent settlement, farmers without farms settled as squatters on unoccupied land to which they had no legal right.[11] More common, however, was using the undistributed land in a more or less nomadic fashion, as they moved around with their livestock.[12]

3. Sharecroppers

In the old days it was likewise very easy for a farmer without land to assist landowners as a sharecropper. This was particularly the case in the border districts where land was vast and farm boundaries were still unfixed, so that the landowners could still use unoccupied land as their own. It is not possible on the basis of the fragmentary references to the sharecropper system,[13] that one finds in the eighteenth-century sources to form a clear impression of how this practice spread. Since the conditions on which the system were based were present at this time in a large measure, I am inclined to think that it was not uncommon in the eighteenth century for a farm owner to keep a sharecropper on his land. In any case, it is a fact that one comes across sharecroppers everywhere in areas of newer settlement during the nineteenth century. In 1817 Landdrost [Andries] Stockenstrom of Graaff-Reinet wrote to the colonial secretary: "A little nearer the frontier the proprietor of a place, is mostly obliged to get several other farmers to live with him for mutual protection against the savages and wild beasts....*bywooners*[†] as they are called....Also a farmer having several sons who have not enough to procure land of their own, must keep their flocks together with his own."[14]

According to the testimony of old pioneers there were always many sharecroppers sixty or seventy years ago in the sparsely inhabited livestock districts of the Cape colony. In areas of newer settlement nearly every farm had sharecroppers, sometimes five or six in places where there was water. Notwithstanding the insecurity of pioneer life, neighbors were very scarce in the border districts. The landowners therefore liked to have other people on their farms, not only for company, but also as help in times of sickness and need. The sharecroppers really did not have to beg. Many times the landowner invited—even "won over" or "persuaded"—him to come farm on his land. Later, when sharecroppers had already become something of a burden, the landowners who dearly wanted to keep going the small government-supported schools on their farms often helped poor people because they had children of school-going age.

In reality the sharecropper of the past obtained pasture for his livestock for nothing. There was also no expectation that he must work regularly for the master of the farm, but he usually lent a hand if there was special work to be done, such as digging wells, fetching water, repairing wind-pumps, or making paddocks. There was almost no social difference between farm owner and sharecropper. They treated each other as equals and often became intimate friends.[15]

The sharecropper system in its purest form was found mainly in those parts of the Cape Colony where the farms were permanently occupied. In the world of the migrants south of the Orange, a farmer without land was often an altogether nomadic migrant farmer. And between the nomadic migrant farmer and the sharecropper one comes across various transitional forms.

4. Reasons for Propertyless People Living in the Border Districts

As a general rule, then, we can say that for sons who wanted to lay out their own farms, there were greater possibilities in the border districts than in areas of older settlement. The chances of obtaining crown land or purchasing private land at a bargain were greater there. Moreover, the landowner in the border districts could usually have access to more land than he actually owned. And for those who did not immediately become landowners, it was much easier

---

[†] Translator's note: [sic]. i.e., sharecroppers or sub-farmers

to get pasture for livestock for nothing in the border districts than in older districts, where free land was already scarcer and sharecroppers less welcome.

Likewise, it did not require a large amount of capital to make an independent life in the interior, although living conditions were very poor and often full of hardships. Even if one possessed nothing but a wagon and oxen, a rifle and enough ammunition, one had all that was necessary to keep from starving. Thanks to the time-honored practice among livestock farmers to set aside lambs or calves for their children from an early age, however, the farmer's son possessed usually a handful of livestock (cattle)—sometimes even quite solid farming potential—by the time he left his parents house. Furthermore, a young man generally had his livestock holdings enlarged by marriage, since farmers' daughters as a rule also owned livestock. What the young couple was still lacking when they married, the parents or parents-in-law could usually provide. As long as there was still land available, it was apparently a common practice among farmers to give their sons—for whom they had no other way to make provision—a wagon, a team of oxen and a few cattle with which to go into the interior to seek their livelihood. Even the sons of landowners often began farming in this manner.[16]

Apart from a wagon, cattle, and a rifle and ammunition, the young couple had few needs. Life on the farm did not require much. Besides, there was not much space on the wagon for many household effects. A bed with removable legs in the wagon, a chest that could serve as a table, and a couple of foldable camp-stools, was quite enough furniture with which to begin. In addition to these basics, they carried with them perhaps a soap pot, a few smaller pots and a few tools—such as an ax, a hammer and a pair of tongs.[17]

The bridegroom did not have to worry too much about the necessity of having a house. During the pioneer period country girls were quite happy to begin their married lives under the wagon hood. As long as the young couple had no fixed residence, the wagon—and perhaps an extra tent—supplied all the needs of a house. When the trekking couple settled down in one place for a while, the man built a wattle-and-daub hut with his own hands, with material that cost him nothing. A few poles or stout reeds were planted in the ground, the ends fastened tightly together, and the openings in between smeared shut with clay. Upon these wattle-and-daub walls rested a roof of grass. If the couple decided later to settle somewhere permanently, they constructed their first house in no time. Four walls of stone or rocks were built, a few square cut beams set upon them, and the roof covered with reeds or shrub. "With that the dwelling is complete, including kitchen, cellar, loft, and other rooms, as well as living quarters for some Hottentots, which the young newlyweds hire as herders; for all of this is at first enclosed within four walls, until over time yet one or more rooms could be added on. Once there are also two or three pieces of land for the cattle, sheep, and horses, fenced in or encircled with limestone walls, then the entire homestead stands finished and ready."[18]

Young beginners who trekked into the interior in this manner had a good chance to improve their economic situation. With an unlimited expanse of unused grazing land—that still bore no signs of overgrazing or being trampled—available to them, they could quickly go ahead and farm. They could live on game and keep their livestock for the market. Likewise, the hunt furnished them with products for the market that supplemented their income from farming comfortably. Furthermore, landless farmers had excellent opportunities to become landowners under easy conditions. And the landowners could be quite sure that their farms, not even counting the improvements they made, would increase in value within the foreseeable future. If a young farmer without capital was to any degree hard working and went to work purposefully, the possibility existed in the border districts for him to accumulate a considerable fortune within a relatively short time and even, relative to the notions of his time and surroundings, to become rich.[19]

For sons in the older districts who did not inherit land and did not have the necessary capital to purchase land there, the obvious choice was to trek to the border districts. If he wanted to maintain his independence, this was the easiest—often the only—outlet left open to him.[20]

5. Farmers without land

One must not imagine, however, that all the young farmers who trekked into the frontier areas—or were born there—soon became landowners. Some of them never did well enough to own even a small little piece of land. Perhaps they managed pretty well for a few years, but then a drought or a livestock disease came along that so impoverished them that they had to begin from scratch again. And if the family was large, then it was very difficult after such a setback to get back on their feet again. Others perhaps did not have the necessary qualities to succeed in farming.

What is important to note in this connection as well is that in the old days there was a certain degree of casualness about land ownership among some of the pioneers. This mentality was not found only among poor farmers. Even wealthy people, who moved around with money in the box-seat of the wagon, or loaned out money and could easily have afforded to buy a farm, thought it unnecessary for a farmer to own his own land, because one could manage just as well without a farm of one's own. For this reason they were not willing to make the slightest sacrifice to obtain land. They were not prepared to spend money for land, or to sell any of their belongings to purchase a farm. Not only did they refuse to pay rents and taxes, but they even thought it a great sacrifice to travel a long distance once a year to the magistrate's office for that purpose. Many of them took the view that owning land was just too much of a bother. Some elderly people can even remember hearing others say: "I will not be a slave to land."[21]

One comes across this mentality in its most outspoken form in the dry northwestern Cape, where livestock farming was until recently still based entirely upon the system of trekking. Because of the limited and variable rainfall of that region, landowners in the old days, before farmers had conquered nature, had to wander about in search of water and grazing land just as much as landless farmers did. In 1938 I recorded the following case in Bushmanland. It concerned a farmer who, in 1932, at the age of forty-four acquired an application farm. He had never before owned land, but like many others had farmed on the move and now and then leased a field. The farm had received a little rain in the year that he acquired it, but not again since then. In the six years that he had the farm, he did not use it more than six months. He was obliged more or less to farm in the old way, as if he did not possess any land at all.

This case is certainly an exception. The majority of pioneers in the Dorsland[‡] had it better than this. But everyone had a similar experience to varying degrees. In such circumstances it is understandable that some of them questioned whether it was worth it to pay installments and taxes on a farm that you could not live on through the year; or worth it to own land if you were still obliged to wander about following the rain in any case. To the question as to why he had never tried to own land, an old inhabitant from Bushmanland answered: "I never wanted to have land. I always said that I would have a farm if I could get one on wheels, so that I could push it under the rain showers right where they dropped!"

This kind of farmer made the right decision for that time. As long as the opportunity still existed to make a living on undistributed land, or to be aided by landowners for nothing or under very favorable conditions, the trekboer was better off without land in certain respects than the owners of farms. He was not bound to a specific piece of land. There was nothing left behind that could become dilapidated if he trekked. He was thus freer to travel about in search of good grazing land. At the same time he was exempt from the financial burden that the landowner had to carry. The only mistake he made was that he predicted the future incorrectly. He supposed that, in some way or other, here or elsewhere, he would always be assisted for nothing or cheaply. He also believed that his children could make their living in the same way. When other farmers begin to buy up the dry farms in the Northwest, he figured that they were crazy. He did not expect to see the day when every bit of marshland would have its owner, and the landowner would need every inch of his farm for himself. "I supposed that money would run short, but never land," an old pioneer of this type assured me. Some foresaw the time when one would be obliged to pay for the grazing of his livestock, but even they never dreamed the day would come when it would be necessary to pay £2 10s. 0d. or £3 10s 0d. the hundred, or when a man would be prepared to pay a high rental but could find no land available to rent. So it happened that pioneers who had excellent opportunities to obtain land missed their chance to do so. When land was cheap and they could afford it, they thought it not necessary to own a farm. When they finally realized the necessity to buy, land was already so expensive that they could not pay for it.

One is sometimes inclined to think that the rise of a landless class of livestock farmer is a recent phenomenon.[22] But this is not in fact the case. Even in the eighteenth century there were already livestock farmers in the country who did not own farms. The researcher discovers this very quickly when he begins searching in the Old Gamehunters Books for the names of farmers he comes across in travel writings or official documents. One can establish the truth of this phenomenon by studying the yearly tax returns. For some years the tax returns are drawn up in such a way that one can determine on the basis of them the number of loan-farm owners in a certain district. If one compares this figure with the number of persons in the district who completed the tax return—or likewise with the number of married couples in the district—then it is quite evident that a large percentage of the farmers did not own farms. In 1809, for example, only 39 percent of the persons in Tulbagh completed a tax return, and only 75 percent of the married couples, owned farms. It is not possible to calculate precisely the percentage of landless farmers in the district, because one cannot determine on the basis of the tax returns how many *self-sufficient* farmers there were in the district. The persons who completed the tax return included not only self-sufficient farmers, but also sons over sixteen who were still dependent on

---

[‡]Trans. note: English "Thirstland" - an arid region in the northwestern Cape.

their parents, and widows who lived with their children. The figure for married couples also left out of account bachelors over the age of sixteen and widows who had thriving farms. We can thus assume that the number of independent farmers in the district surpassed the number of married couples, but that it was smaller than the number of persons who completed the returns. That is to say: in 1809 between 39 percent and 75 percent of the independent farmers in Tulbagh owned farms. During the following three years the percentage of landowners in the district declined markedly. In 1812, 36 percent of the persons who completed the returns and 70 percent of the married couples owned farms.[23] Unfortunately after 1812 it is not possible to make such a calculation on the basis of the yearly returns, because the returns did not take account of farmers who "owned" request farms.

In the district of Graaff-Reinet, which included more areas of newer settlement than Tulbagh, there were far fewer landowners. The following table gives the percentage of landowners in the two groups for different years.[24]

	1798	1800	1810	1812
Group I: Persons who completed tax returns	26%	25%	18%	18%
Group II: Married couples	39%	36%	29%	25%

It is clear from this table that in 1812 only between 18 percent and 25 percent of the independent farmers in Graaff-Reinet were landowners. It is also clear from other official documents that at the beginning of the nineteenth century there were many farmers without land in the Cape Colony.[25] The fieldwork done for this study revealed that a surprising number of the old pioneers acquired land for the first time only at an advanced age. Some farmed for their entire lives without owning their own land, either as a result of poverty or indifference. Some of them traveled around with their livestock on crown land until their deaths. Others spent a lifetime as sharecroppers, occasionally renting land here and there, or simply trekking. These types regularly changed their abodes. They often trekked from one district to the other, lived on twenty, thirty, and more different farms, and finally ended up old and weary someplace in a village or settlement, where they passed their last days in abject poverty, living only on an old age pension or the tender mercies of children.

6. Landless Farmers Are Forced Out From Older Districts

For landless farmers there were good reasons for living in the border districts just as long as the population of the area was still small. With the increasing density of population it became harder and harder for them to meet their needs. The farmer who roamed about on crown land and did not make sure that he got hold of a farm in good time was the first to be affected. As one farm after another was sold or leased out, free land diminished until after a while every little valley and each watering hole had its own master.

Because the opportunities for trekking had diminished, the nomadic livestock farmer was obliged to become a sharecropper, otherwise he was pushed out to unoccupied crown land farther into the interior, where he could continue his traditional existence and again have the chance to become a landowner. Sharecroppers could generally still make a living in the border districts even after all the crown land had been distributed. But it was also not long before they began to become a burden. As the neighbors came nearer, the need for sharecroppers diminished. In addition, in the course of time it became more difficult for the landowners to help other people on their land. As the amount of free land shrank, and surrounding farms were occupied, trekking opportunities for the landowner decreased as well, until finally everyone was obliged to farm just on his own land. Furthermore, as a result of subdivision, farms had continually become smaller, so that before long the farmers needed all their land for their own use. The landowners were obliged first to reduce the number of sharecroppers and later to rid themselves of them completely. Consequently, sharecroppers who were not able to purchase land were often obliged to trek away to newer districts, where they could make a living in the old way or acquire land cheaply.

Many cases that nicely illustrate this process came to my attention. It will be sufficient to describe one in particular. In 1898 a certain P.J. van der Merwe bought the farm Middelplaas near Griquatown in Griqualand West. He was not one of the first migrants, but it was still a new district and there was still much open space. Whites lived only here and there. Middleplaas was about 2,383 morgen in size and altogether too small for van der Merwe's own farming activities, but he had always kept on one or more sharecroppers. He could do this because there were various farms surrounding Middelplaas that he was free to use. He used the whole of Doradale (2,725 morgen) for grazing. It belonged to old man Meyer's daughter, but she could never lease it out because there was no water on the land yet. When she offered to lease it to van der Merwe, he told her that he had enough grazing land: if he could not use the farm for free, then she could keep it. Furthermore, he made use of the whole of the farm Onderplaas (2,500 morgen). This farm was also owned by someone else, but the water stream was weak and it had lain uninhabited for years. In addition, he let his livestock graze on the whole of Boorwater farm and parts of the farms Membie, Vaalpan, Taaibos, Pannetjie and Nouhoek. Some of these farms were already occupied, but the inhabitants had so few cattle—and so much grazing land in other directions—that they could not use all their fields. One can estimate that Van der Merwe had about 14,000 morgen at his disposal. The first few years that he lived on Middelplaas, he seldom saw his livestock. His sons almost constantly tended his flocks outside the boundaries of his farm.

From about 1906 the neighboring farms that he had used for free before for grazing were now one after the other inhabited by sharecroppers. This meant his grazing land diminished quickly. The process was completed when Middelplaas was entirely enclosed in 1912 and there was no longer any opportunity to graze over the boundary line. Before long Middelplaas could no longer support its owner's livestock. In 1907 he was obliged to lease the farm Doradale and in 1909 he bought it. This in turn meant that he incurred extra expenses and because of that he asked the one sharecropper he still had to pay a rent of £12 per year in the future. The sharecropper refused to pay this and moved away. He [i.e. the sharecropper] first roamed about aimlessly for a while in Griqualand West and then later went to South West Africa, where he eventually got hold of some land.

In a similar manner the majority of Griqualand West's sharecroppers have been squeezed out during the past thirty or forty years. When the world around them there had become "too narrow," they headed off toward areas of more recent settlement to the north, such as Betsjoeanaland, Gordonia and South West Africa.

This process occurred in all the more recent settlements, and many pioneers still living today can testify to this.

7. The Border Districts Had Little Attraction For Affluent Farmers

The opportunities offered by the border districts naturally existed for all classes of society. Landowners and wealthy farmers in the older settlements could use them to their advantage as well, if they were willing to move there. Trekking to distant parts, however, was accompanied by various sacrifices and hardships. It is always difficult to break up your home and to move. Without today's transportation facilities it must have been even more so in the old days. The pioneers had to leave their family members and friends behind and break various other ties that they had made in their neighborhood. They were obliged to give up many of the comforts of the 'civilized' life. Life was lonely in the wilderness. Their nearest neighbors sometimes lived miles away. There was often no security of life or property. They were inconveniently far from the church, the post office, the magistrate's office, and the doctor. There were few or no facilities for the education of their children, who had to grow up in ignorance in the wilderness. Sometimes it required great material and other sacrifices to give them an education. Afrikaners who today live at the foot of Mount Kilimanjaro are still obliged to send their children to schools and universities in the Union, if they want them to enjoy an advanced education in their mother tongue. As it happens, I know several such children who have traveled thousands of miles to Franschhoek and Stellenbosch to study. Because of the great distance and high travel expenses, it is sometimes six years before they can go home for vacation for the first time.

In the economic sphere as well the move to the border districts brought with it certain disadvantages. The distance to markets was great. Transport was bad and expensive. The result was that the pioneers at the outposts of civilization experienced great difficulties marketing their products and were often obliged to sell them locally far below the market value. The nearest stores were sometimes hundreds of miles away and even there one could not always obtain what he wanted. Besides, everything was expensive by the time it reached the border districts. This often obliged pioneers to live without many things to which they had grown accustomed. Lastly, they were usually obliged to build their farms from the ground up under difficult conditions, so that sometimes years passed before they had comfortable dwellings and workable lands and could really enjoy their farming.

There was also a considerable risk attached to the purchase of land in unknown areas. The suitability of the land for farming often still had to be ascertained. One did not always know beforehand what sort of livestock diseases and droughts this part of the world was subject to. In the drier parts of the Cape Colony, which had been occupied since the Great Trek, the pioneers often did not know how long it would take and how much it would cost them before they could get water on their farms. There was a possibility that one would have to spend two or three times as much on tapping into the underground water as what the land cost. And lastly, the future economic development of the regions settled by the pioneers, upon whom the increase in land values would depend, was not always clearly evident in advance.

For many such reasons land at bargain prices in the border districts usually had very little attraction for the class of farmer who could afford to purchase more expensive land in areas of older settlement or who already owned land there upon which he could make a living. For this type of farmer, the possibility of obtaining grazing sites for nothing in the border districts for his livestock and making a little profit from hunting did not compensate for the hardships, lowering of living standards, and economic drawbacks that this entailed. Among the poorer economic classes it was a different matter. They had sufficient reason to trek, in spite of the hardship and discomfort it would bring. Trekking to areas where land was cheap or where crown land could still be had, often offered the less wealthy buyer the only chance to become a landowner instantly. For the propertyless farmer, who was so fiercely independent and so opposed to subservience that it made him unwilling to hire himself out to someone else, trekking into the interior usually offered the only opportunity to work for himself.[26] Furthermore, for the poor, who were accustomed to having little, trekking to uninhabited areas did not entail a significant lowering of their living standards.

8. The Emigration Of The Surplus Population

In these circumstances one could thus expect that the trek to the border areas was mainly carried on by the lower economic classes. That this was indeed the case is clear from the petition of the farmers who, around 1770, went against government orders and trekked into Agterbruintjieshoogte. They stated emphatically that they had trekked over the border because they were "extremely poor." Many of the farmers who settled beyond Bruintjieshoogte with their livestock—they assured the government—owned not more than 100 sheep and 50 cattle: "that is why, we have come here to settle down, to live in peace with the Hottentots, where it is fertile for livestock and agriculture, and also much game to provide for our food."[27]

The same phenomenon can be observed in the nineteenth century as well. The migrant farmers who were responsible for the natural expansion of the Cape Colony toward the north, *before* the Great Trek, mainly consisted of the surplus population from already inhabited parts: young beginners and other poor people who could no longer obtain grazing there for their livestock for nothing or under easy terms; farmers without land, who could not get crown land in older districts and who were not wealthy enough to purchase farms there.[28]

It was also principally this class that always migrated further to the Northwest after the Great Trek. In 1879 J.H. Scott, the special commissioner for the northern border, wrote: "...it is the poorer class of farmers who, pressed out by their richer neighbours, move on in search of 'vrygrond'§."[29] This process is also clearly described by the resident-magistrate of Kenhardt in his annual report for 1910:

"Although a magistracy was established in this district as far back as 1869, it was until quite recent years regarded as a sort of 'No man's land.' For this reason it was only those people who found it impossible to make a living in more civilized portions of the Colony who immigrated hither. These people were naturally without capital, and to a great extent without education, with the result that this was one of the most

---

§Trans. note: [sic], i.e., "free land."

backward districts of the Colony. During the past six or seven years it has, however, made rapid progress."[30]

In areas of newer settlement such as the Bushmanland section of Namaqualand, Kenhardt, Prieska, Griqualand-West, Bechuanaland, Gordonia, the southern Kalahari and South West Africa, I questioned hundreds of the old inhabitants about the economic position of the first pioneers who had trekked into these parts. The information that they provided substantiates the conclusions that we made above on the basis of the written sources, namely, that the trek to uninhabited parts was chiefly carried on by the poorer economic classes, and more specifically, those who did not own land.[31] Some of these fellows already had thriving farms and often a little capital in ready money, but they were not strong enough financially to purchase land for cash in the vicinity that they left, and for these reasons decided to trek to areas where they could do just that. Not only were credit facilities for farmers in the old days much more poorly developed than today, but these old timers were very afraid of debt. They were not quite as readily prepared to take out a mortgage on their land as is the current generation.

When it is asserted that the greatest percentage of the first pioneers in a border district belonged to the poorer classes, this is not to claim that, from a psychological perspective, these people were poor whites in the modern sense of the word. During the pioneer period living conditions for the farmers in the interior—particularly in the border districts—were such that great wealth could seldom be accumulated. In addition, families were usually very large and the farmers had the practice of bequeathing their property to their children in equal portions. The inevitable result was that most farmers' sons began their careers somewhat impoverished.[32] During the pioneer period there were other causes of poverty as well that had nothing to do with the diligence or economic capacity of the victim, such as droughts, livestock diseases, war, livestock theft and other calamities. It ought to come as no surprise therefore that many of the poor from older districts who moved to the frontier areas made great economic progress and became distinguished members of their communities.[33] Even today it is still quite common to meet a prominent and prosperous farmer in areas of more recent settlement who originally trekked into the area penniless, sometimes even as a servant.

ENDNOTES

[1] I will return to this subject later.

[2] Edward Blount, *Notes on the Cape of Good Hope made during an Excursion in that Colony in the year 1820* (London, 1821), p. 43; W.W. Bird, *State of the Cape of Good Hope in 1822* (London, 1823), p. 104.

[3] J. Barrow, *Travels into the Interior of Southern Africa*, 2nd ed. (London, 1806), II:88: George McCall Theal, *History of South Africa* (London, 1915), V:265.

[4] Kenhardt Letter Book (D 16), *Letter Book of Resident Magistrate*, Annual Report for the Year 1911, p. 879; Kenhardt Letter Book (18), *Letter Book of Resident Magistrate*, Annual Report for the Year, 1912, p. 19; [Trans. Note: I could not locate these two documents in the Cape Archives.]

[5] P.J. van der Merwe, *Die Trekboer in die Geskiedenis van die Kaapkolonie, 1657-1842* (Cape Town: 1938), p. 114.

[6] P.J. van der Merwe, *Die Noordwaartse Beweging van die Boere voor die Groot Trek* (1770-1842) (The Hague, 1937), pp. 126-29.

[7] C 1283, Petitions, Reports, etc., Burgher Petition, Woeke, Bletterman, et al., 17 February 1784, p. 58; C.O. 2581, Letters Rec., Tulbagh, H. van de Graaff to Grey, 14 August 1811; G. Thompson, *Travels and Adventures in Southern Africa* (London, 1827), II: 132-35.

[8] C 1764, Letters Disp., J. van Plettenberg to Lords XVII, 1 March 1779, no. 23, p. 210.

[9] C 1265, Petitions, Reports, etc., P.A. Myburg to Landdrost, 1 May 1775, p. 455. See also C 153, Resolutions, 11 July 1775, p. 300.

[10] C 2285, Original Ordinance Book, 26 April 1770, p. 384 and 16 June 1774, p. 475; C 172, Resolutions, 19 July 1786, p. 881.

[11] B.R. 444, Minutes of van de Mist, Report of a conference over Land, 31 October 1803, p. 96; C.O. 2568, Letters Rec., Tulbagh, H. van de Graaff to Caledon, 7 January 1809; 1/GR 16/5, Letters Disp., Stockenström to P.A. Opperman, 17 June 1816; 1/GR 8/7, Letters Rec., Bird to Baird, Beaufort, 4 December 1818; T. Pringle, *African Sketches* (London, 1834), p. 162.

[12] Nomadism will be more fully discussed in a later chapter.

[13] 1/STB 13/31, "Alphabetical lists"; C 1265, Petitions, Reports, etc., P.A. Myburg to Landdrost, 1 May 1775, p. 457; 1/GR 13/2, Letters rec. from Private Individuals (1781-1800), Account of J. Slabbert, 10 October 1788, Petition of J.P. Hoffman, 21 November 1789, and L. Kotze, Sr. to Bresler, 27 November 1798.

[14] 1/GR 16/6, Letters Disp., Stockenström to Bird, 27 November 1817. See also, C.O. 4438, Papers of Col. Collins, Collins to Caledon, 6 August 1809; 1/B.W. 9/49, Field Cornet Letters, P.D. Jacobs to Baird, 21 September 1826; C.O. 4402, Arrears, Annexure B to No. 40: declaration of E.P. Nel, 10 November 1856; 1/WOC 14/12, Letters rec. from Private Individuals, Tax roll furnished by G.

52

Nieuwoudt, Hardeveld, 18 March 1828; A.W. Drayson, *Tales at the Outspan or Adventures in the Wild Regions of Southern Africa* (London, 1865), p. 22.

[15] Cf. J.F.W. Grosskopf, *Plattelandsverarming en Plaasverlating* (Stellenbosch, 1932), pp. 120-22; R.W. Wilcocks, *Die Armblanke* (Stellenbosch, 1932), p. 10.

[16] OPB 1/3, Evidence of W. Gisborne, 27 April 1836, in *Report of the Select Committee on Aborigines, Imperial Blue Book 538* (1836) (London: House of Commons, 1836), p. 361; J. Holman, *A Voyage round the World including Travels in Africa, etc. from 1827-1832* (London, 1834-35), II:309; O.F. Mentzel, *Vollständige und Zuverläszige Geographische und topographische Beschreibung des Berühmten und in aller Betrachtung merkwürdigen Afrikanischen Vorgebirges des Guten Hoffnung* (Glogau, 1785, 1787), II:170-74; Pringle, *African Sketches*, p. 182; van der Merwe, *Trekboer*, p. 179.

[17] Mentzel, *Beschreibung*, II:171; Barrow, *Travels*, I:401 and II:124; Holman, *Voyage*, II:309; Thompson, *Travels*, II:133-4.

[18] Mentzel, *Beschreibung*, II:172-73; Holman, *Voyage*, II:309; Barrow, *Travels*, II:124.

[19] PSB, Mss. Germ. Fol. No. 885, H.D. Campagne, *Considerations* (±1803); Thompson, *Travels*, II:129-36; Holman, *Voyage*, II:309; J. Philip, *Researches in South Africa* (London, 1828), II:267.

[20] C.O. 29, Letters Rec., Tulbagh, H. van de Graaff to Gray, 14 April 1811; Mentzel, *Beschreibung*, II:169-70; Barrow, *Travels*, I:410 and II:124; Thompson, *Travels*, II:134; J.W.D. Moodie, *Ten Years in Southern Africa* (London, 1835), II:27-28.

[21] Wilcocks, *Armblanke*, p. 10; Grosskopf, *Plattelandsverarming en Plaasverlating*, p. 36.

[22] Cf. Grosskopf, *Plattelandsverarming en Plaasverlating*, p. 134.

[23] J 376 (1809) and J 379 (1812), Tax rolls for Tulbagh

[24] J 115 (1798), J 119 (1800), J 133 (1810), J 138 (1812), Tax rolls for Graaff-Reinet.

[25] C.O. 4438, Papers of Col. Collins, Collins to Caledon, 6 August 1809; C.O. 2580, Letters Rec., Graaff-Reinet, A. Stockenström to Col. Secretary, 20 September 1810.

[26] Van der Merwe, *Trekboer*, pp. 171-93.

[27] C 1265, Petitions, Reports, etc., A.H. Krugel and twelve others to Governor van Plettenberg, Petition from Bruintjieshoogte, 10 November 1774, pp. 444, and P.A. Myburg to Landdrost, 1 May 1775, pp. 455-7. See also, C 1283, Petitions, Reports, etc., Burgher Petition, Woeke, Bletterman, et al., 17 February 1784, p. 58; PSB, Mss. Germ. Fol. No. 885, H.D. Campagne, *Considerations* (±1803); Swellengrebel Family Archives, Hendrik Swellengrebel, Jr. to C. de Gyselaar, 26 June 1783; Mentzel, *Beschreibung*, II:170. [Trans. Note: The letter from Swellengrebel to Gyselaar may also be found in the collection of letters published by the Van Riebeeck Society, *Briefwisseling van Hendrik Swellengrebel Jr. oor Kaapse Sake, 1778-1792*, VRS, series II, vol. 13, pp. 151-62 in the original with a shortened English summary, pp. 348-52.].

[28] Van der Merwe, *Noordwaartse Beweging*, pp. 328, 337, 342-3, 348, 364; C.O. 2581, Letters Rec., Tulbagh, H. van de Graaff to Grey, 14 August 1811; C.O. 3951, Memorials Rec., G.D. Joubert, Nu-Hantam, 15 August 1831, no. 148; L.G. 196, Letters Rec. from Colesberg, F. Rawstorne to Act.

Secretary to Government, 8 September 1840; Holman, *Voyage*, II:308-09; Thompson, *Travels*, I:101 and II:132-34; Barrow, *Travels*, I:410 and II:124; Philip, *Researches,* II:267.

[29] CCP 4/1/1/5, Papers connected with affairs on the Northern Border, J.H. Scott to Ayliff, 3 October 1879, no. 19, p. 17.

[30] Kenhardt Letter Book, (D 16), Letter Book of Resident Magistrate, Annual Report for the Year, 1910, p. 93. [Trans. Note: I could not locate this document in the Cape Archives.]

[31] P.J. van der Merwe, *Pioniers van die Dorsland* (Cape Town, 1941), pp. 132, 155-6.

[32] Van der Merwe, *Trekboer*, p. 184; Thompson, *Travels*, II:132.

[33] Thompson, *Travels*, II:133-36; Holman, *Voyage*, II:310; Philip, *Researches*, II:267.

CHAPTER V

THE EMIGRATION OF LANDOWNERS

1. Statement of the Phenomenon

It goes without saying that the expansion of livestock farming at the Cape made necessary the continuous occupation of still unoccupied land. And as soon as all the usable land in an inhabited area was occupied, those who still did not have land had to trek farther. The continual growth of the Cape population through natural increase (and in dribs and drabs through immigration in the eighteenth century), thus spontaneously promoted migration to uninhabited areas in the interior. The colony's expansion is often explained in this way.[1]

But the expansion process was not quite so simple. Throughout the pioneer period one encounters the phenomenon that not only farmers without land, but also landowners themselves joined the migration into the interior. That this was occurring in the eighteenth century is clearly evident from the Gamehunters Books. One repeatedly comes across cases of farmers who sell or simply leave their farms in areas of older settlement, trek into the interior, and take land again there by ordinance. Here one can refer to the case of Coert Grobbelaar, who will be discussed more fully later in another context.

There is still more evidence that landowners in the eighteenth century were drawn into the stream of emigration into the interior. In 1770 landdrost Faber wrote to Governor [Ryk] Tulbagh, "that for some years now along the Swartegebergte, and on this side of the Leeuwe River as well, there has been increasing drought, which has compelled those people living there to abandon their farms and to go in search of relief somewhere else, so they have gone higher up and landed here in the Camdebo."[2]

A few years later thirteen people, who had trekked across Bruintjieshoogte against the orders of the government, directed a petition to the governor in which they requested permission to remain there.[3] Examination of the Gamehunters Books has revealed that at least four of these people had previously possessed loan farms within the colonial borders. Seven of them later took farms on the other side of Bruintjieshoogte by ordinance. In 1775 Heemraad Myburg met 21 farmers, whose names he mentions, on and beyond the colonial borders.[4] From the Gamehunters Books it appears that at least six of these people previously owned land in older parts of the colony. Nine of them later had loan farms in their names.

In the nineteenth century as well, one comes across the phenomenon that landowners trekked into the interior together with the surplus population from the inhabited parts of the colony.[5] A considerable number of the trekboers who led the natural expansion of the colony to the north during the first half of the nineteenth century were people who had previously owned land.[6] This process continued until recent times. Many of the pioneers who live today in areas of newer settlement possessed land earlier in the older districts. Several farmers who trekked into Griqualand West after the Griqua War were landowners who were originally from the older districts south of the Orange River and from the Free State as well. It is also well known that many of the Afrikaners who trekked since the end of the nineteenth century into Angola, the Rhodesias and East Africa formerly had farms in the Transvaal and the Free State. Throughout the pioneer period the cheap land and good farming prospects in the border districts enticed not only farmers without land, but individual landowners as well.

Some of these landowners also not only migrated and then settled down, but they often moved on again later. Some of them never did settle down, but exchanged one farm after another, always for one farther ahead. In areas of newer settlement, I encountered various pioneers who moved with the emigration stream into the interior from one place to the other, and on the way had five, six, or more farms, building them up halfway, and then abandoning them. In one case the pioneer in question, who was born in Hopetown and who bought his first farm there, trekked farther and farther step for step, right through Griqualand West, until he finally landed up on a plot in Kuruman. In the meantime he owned ten different farms, one after the other, made a few improvements and then sold them.

It is not possible to give an account of all the particular reasons that motivated individual landowners to trek into the interior. We do not have the necessary information. In the following pages we shall, however, devote some attention to a few of the general factors that can serve to explain the phenomenon.

2. The Desire for Space

At the beginning of the eighteenth-century [Peter] Kolbe visited the farms of the French refugees at Drakenstein. He found that the majority of them lived well over a half hour and even further from each other, "and consequently it cannot be said that they stifle one another, although such is the universal complaint of these people, whilst they profess that they cannot possibly live so, because no one has enough pasture for his livestock."[7]

If we keep in mind that these people were farmers, then it is to be expected that the desire for space would find more deliberate expression among the extensive livestock farmers of the eighteenth and nineteenth century. This was in fact the case. No matter how far apart loan farms were located from each other—[Hendrik, Jr.] Swellengrebel stated in 1783—the farmers still complained that they did not have enough grazing land.[8]

It is often said that a farmer does not like it if he can see the smoke from his neighbor's chimney. From this one must not conclude that the old pioneers were anti-social and went to live as far as possible from one another to avoid associating with each other. It simply meant that the extensive livestock farmer was eager to have all the grazing land that he could see around him for his own use. He liked his neighbors well enough but did not like rivals for pasture. The truth of this saying is supported by the reports of the deputy heemraden who went out to investigate complaints over loan farms. From these reports it seems clear that the loan farm occupier wanted to keep his neighbor as far as possible away from his farmstead. With this goal in mind, various unsupported objections against the distribution of new loan farms were often voiced.[9]

Differences over farm boundaries and conflicts over grazing land and water in the eighteenth century were among the most fertile sources of disputes between neighbors and evidently occurred quite commonly.[10] At the end of the eighteenth century [John] Barrow wrote: "Though removed from each other to the distance of several miles and enjoying the benefit of many thousands acres of land under the rate of a farthing an acre, it is yet a singular fact, that scarcely any two neighbours are found to be on good terms with each other, but are embroiled perpetually in quarrels and disputes about the extent of their farms or the privilege of a spring or a watercourse."[11]

This assertion is supported by the testimony of [Hinrich] Lichtenstein, who traveled extensively through the interior a few years after Barrow. In the Roggeveld, he says, there were few colonists who were not involved in lawsuits with their nearest neighbors over grazing land. And in as much as the farmers lived far removed from the authorities who could resolve their differences, these often led to prolonged disputes.[12] In the Hantam, where farms were relatively far from each other and the farmers kept few cattle, quarrels over pastureland did not arise so often. But elsewhere, Lichtenstein assures us, they had assumed such proportions that for every ten neighbors, certainly nine of them were deadly enemies.[13]

On his journey through the colony Commissioner-General J.A. de Mist to his regret repeatedly came across this unpleasant phenomenon as well. On nearly every farm he came to various farmers awaited him in order to submit their disputes over boundaries to his judgement.[14] In many cases the dispute involved the use of undistributed land in the vicinity of the farms upon which, in the colonists' view, everyone had the same rights.[15]

These frequent disputes over pastureland were not just the result of cantankerousness, as Lichtenstein figured. Their cause must rather be sought in the nature of the loan farm system, under which the pioneers possessed their land.

Under this elastic system unsurveyed land without dimensions or boundaries was given to the farmers in loan. The license holder received unspecified grazing rights in the vicinity of a fixed point. The only restriction on his grazing rights was that he must not harm another ordinance holder. Therefore, if the occupant of a loan farm had no neighbors close by, he could use just as much pasture land as he needed. In thinly inhabited areas the ordinance holder was thus often undisputed lord and master of the whole world around him.[16]

In this connection [Otto] Mentzel, who was at the Cape during the first half of the eighteenth century, states: "These farmers, who live in mountain valleys over a hundred miles deep in the country, claim the entire valley as their own, and keep as much livestock as they believe it can support."[17]

About half a century later Lichtenstein mentioned the case of Field-Commander Abraham de Klerk, who lived at the source of the Gamka, sixty miles from his nearest neighbor.

The chief advantage of this farm—according to our informant—was that its owner had for his exclusive use the whole world for many miles around him. If his livestock grazed too much of one part of the field, they were simply moved to another part where the grass was more plentiful. So, De Klerk in his isolation ruled over a territory as large as many European princely states.[18]

There were many similar instances of the loan farm owner enjoying this luxury as long as no other ordinance holders lived in his immediate vicinity. As the neighbors came nearer, the boundaries for his farm were established as the pastureland was divided in one direction after another. Every time it happened, he had to forgo a piece of his original grazing area. After all the available land around his homestead was given out, he was left with a "farm," of which the shape and dimensions were determined by the local circumstances, but which in every case was much smaller than the grazing land that he had used before.[19]

The boundary line between adjoining loan farms was not designated by a surveyor or other government official. The license holders concerned divided the grazing land between their farmsteads themselves. If they could not come to an agreement, they could call for help from the landdrost and heemraden, who then sent a commission to resolve the problem. This brought with it a lot of trouble and expense, with the result that the farmers did not like to call on the government for help.

Under this system quarrels over loan farms boundaries were inevitable. The enforcement of boundaries, over which the parties concerned had already come to a clear understanding, also often led to problems. Loan farms were never fenced, with the result that it was very difficult in densely inhabited areas to keep your livestock off your neighbors' land.

From the above it is clear that the land an ordinance holder had at his disposal usually diminished in size with the increase in population density. Despite this, however, he still always paid 24 rixdollars quitrent for his loan farm. In these circumstances it is hardly surprising that farmers often got rid of loan farms in older districts and took land by ordinance in areas of newer settlement, where they had more space and fewer troubles with their neighbors.

Under the perpetual quitrent system land was first surveyed and mapped before it was distributed. Thus, quitrent farms, in contrast to loan farms—on paper at least—had fixed boundaries from the beginning. In practice, however, this did not make an immediate difference. At the beginning of the nineteenth century land was sometimes lived on for years as request farms, before it was surveyed and officially allocated. And even after farms were granted, the amount of grazing land that the farmer had at his disposal did not depend in the first place on what was marked on his map. Before farms were fenced – and that only happened in this century – the owner of a quitrent farm only worried about his neighbors, not about the imaginary boundaries of his land.

It often happened, particularly in the drier parts of the Cape Colony, that much undistributed crown land remained after the first farms had been granted to owners. Farms sometimes lay uninhabited for years because there was not enough water. Such dry farms could be used by adjoining landowners who had water. Indeed, this often happened.

The pioneers who settled on quitrent farms in the border districts therefore initially had more grazing land available to them than was indicated by the map of their farms. Sooner or later, however, the bordering crown land was allocated and the dry farms acquired owners. The pioneers were then obliged to manage with less land or to purchase additional land. But this could also provide a reason to sell the farm and to trek to newer districts where large farms were still to be had cheaply.

The phenomenon that the size of farms in the pioneering districts were reduced by population growth naturally affected only the first pioneers who had trekked into an area. As soon as all crown land was distributed and inhabited, this factor could no longer play a role. Before long, however, other influences began to emerge that prompted the desire for more land among some of the farmers. As a result of the subdivision of land some farmers acquired small pieces of land upon which they could not make a decent living. Other farmers prospered and in time their farms became too small for all their stock. Those who had enough capital available could naturally buy additional land in the vicinity. For the man who could not do this, there was an easy way out of the difficulty, providing he was ready to trek. Throughout the pioneer period there was always a great difference in the price of land in areas of older settlement, on the one hand, and areas of newer settlement and uninhabited areas, on the other. This enabled the small landowner who sold his farm to purchase bigger pieces of land farther ahead.

Thus did many small landowners in the Free State, for example, sell their little plots of land there after the English [Anglo-Boer] war, and with the money they received purchased larger pieces of land in Griqualand West and Bechuanaland. Many of the farmers who trekked into the Northwest, "because here there was more space, and as a result one could farm more enjoyably here," had previously owned farms in the older districts that were too small to make a living.

When farmers said that they trekked because the world in the neighborhood they left had "become a little cramped," they often meant that more pasture lands began to fall into private hands, which in turn meant that the possibilities to trek during droughts or during the stock trekking season had diminished. Particularly farmers who were accustomed to trekking regularly with their livestock often became anxious when free land was distributed to others. Revd. W.J. Conradie, who was a minister of the N.G. Church in Namaqualand at the end of the nineteenth century, mentioned that "Many Namaqualanders have said to me, 'When the farms in Bushmanland are all bought up, then we shall take off across the Great River, because then the world here will have become too cramped for us.'"[20] Some of them did, as a matter of fact, also migrate to South-West Africa, when the government began to distribute their traditional pasture lands to private individuals. The decline of possibilities for trekking in the colony was likewise one of the reasons why some of the landowners in the northeastern border field-cornetcies moved to the Trans-Orange during the 1820s and 1830s.[21]

3. Land for Children

In many cases farmers had enough land to live off of themselves, but they moved to areas of newer settlement for the sake of their children's future. In all areas of newer settlement—such as Kenhardt, Griqualand West, Gordonia, South-West Africa and even East Africa—one finds pioneers who trekked to these places because they felt they could more easily provide for their children there. This was also possible as a result of the great differences between the land prices in the older districts and in the districts of newer settlement. Until a few years ago it was often possible for farmers who sold their land in the older districts to purchase five or ten times as much uncultivated land of the same quality, if they were prepared to trek a few hundred miles farther and to do without the conveniences of civilization. I offer just a couple of examples as illustration.

Mr. J.J. Badenhorst of Burgersdam (106 miles north of Upington) told me the following. His father had farmed on a farm of 2,900 morgen in the district of Britstown. As the children grew up, the farming operation had become so extensive that the entire family could no longer live on the farm. In 1924 his father rented out the farm and leased a larger area of land in the district of

Prieska. There they lived for a year. After that they leased another farm for six months in Prieska. Finally in 1925 his father sold the land in Britstown for 17s. 6d. per morgen and bought the farm Vrouenspan in Gordonia (19,000 morgen) for 1s. 9d. per morgen. With the money that he received for the farm in Britstown, he paid for Vrouenspan and he still had quite a bit left over. Since then, the old man has died and the four sons have bought two additional farms. When I visited them in 1939, they owned altogether about 40,000 morgen of land of at least the same quality as the farm in Britstown. Mr. Badenhorst assured me that his father had trekked to Gordonia for no other reason than to make provision for his sons. And they have more than enough reason to be thankful for that.

Among the first pioneers who trekked into Griqualand West was a G.J. van der Merwe. He had formerly lived at Rooifontein (nearby the Potfontein stop) in the Philipstown district. The farm was around 6,000 morgen in size and he could make a good living off it. His land was not large enough, however, for his five sons also to farm on it. That led him to decide to move to Griqualand West. He felt he could get farms more easily there for his sons, who were already getting big. He sold his land in Philipstown and in 1884 bought Modderfontein (the present village of Niekerkshoop) for £2,200.

It was a high price for those days. Modderfontein was a good crop farm with plenty of water, but it was only about 3,500 morgen in size and it was far from the railway track and the market. But the move did have certain advantages. Around Modderfontein at this time there were a number of uninhabited (mostly dry) farms, all of which van der Merwe used for nothing. Besides Modderfontein, he also farmed Sandfontein (which had water), Klippoort, Mooipoort, Kameelpoort, Kromaar, Rooilaagte, Syferkrans, Droërivier and Nooitgedag. In fact, he thus had more land than he could use.

Apart from this, the sons could also easily obtain new land. It was possible then in Griqualand to purchase a farm of 3,000 morgen for £200 to £300. The land was nearly as good as in Philipstown and the underground water was near the surface, although the farmers often had to dig around all over the place to find the underground watercourse. It was therefore not long before all the older sons had land in the vicinity of Modderfontein. In Philipstown this would have been much more difficult.

According to the information that was kindly provided to me by Mr. H.J.C. Pieterse, some of the Afrikaners who trekked to East Africa after the gold war [South African War] were also mainly thinking about the future of their children. In this connection General Wynand Malan told me the following: "My father (Jacobus Malan) owned a few plots of land in Langlaagte, upon which he earned a living before the war. We were ten children—seven sons—of whom I was the oldest. I was 33 years old at the end of the war and still single. One of my younger brothers, Frans, was married. The youngest brother, Jan, would have been eight years old then. All the children lived at home, except one married sister.

"The older children all had to farm, because we had not learned any other trade or occupation. We also had to have land, because our family took pride in being independent. The idea of being a tenant or sharecropper was beneath us.

"In order for us children to get land, my father went to South-West Africa. There he bought two farms in 1903 near to Grootfontein. When the Herero rebellion broke out, he sold the land again, because he had had enough of war. After that he visited Griqualand-West, intending to purchase land there. That region pleased him, but he was afraid of the shortage of water and decided not to buy.

"My father then thought that it would not be possible for all his children to get land in South Africa and decided to trek to East Africa. He sold his plots for £3,000, and in spite of the expenses connected with the journey, we were much better off in East Africa than we would have been here. If my father did not have any children, he would not have trekked. I did not have land here, but all the same I saw a chance to survive. My mother, however, was terribly troubled at the thought of not being near her family. She could not even bear to think one of her children might remain behind. For that reason I went, but otherwise I would not have trekked."

Near Olifantshoek a farmer told me the following: "My deceased mother-in-law, three married sons and five other children farmed in Lindley, Orange Free State, on a farm of 1,800 morgen. We could not make a living from the land. We then sold the land there, bought 15,000 morgen here and are farming together again." There are multiple examples of this kind.

I do not want in any way to rule out the possibility that in some cases people were rationalizing, but this was certainly not always the case. It is the considered opinion of many pioneers who observed the expansion process in earlier times themselves that the desire to provide for the future of their children was an important stimulus for landowners in the older districts to move to the border areas.

4. The Tradition of Over-cropping and the Deterioration of the Land

In the documents of the last half of the eighteenth century one repeatedly comes across the allegation that grazing land at the Cape was deteriorating noticeably.

In 1750 the Cape government decided to sound out the opinions of the landdrosts and heemraden of the country districts about immigration. The government wanted to know if more colonists could earn a livelihood at the Cape.[22] To this question the landdrost and heemraden of Stellenbosch answered "No." In their opinion the colony was already overpopulated. Many farmers made only a meager living; others incurred such debt in the course of time that they would probably never be able to pay off their creditors "since many farms in the low-lying areas have in recent years deteriorated considerably." Many farmers from Stellenbosch, Drakenstein and elsewhere, who had kept livestock on their farms in the past, could not do so any longer, "since there is a scarcity of grazing land, and also because in some places the pasture has become sour and unhealthy, and in other areas where at one time the grazing land was quite good, it has now become overgrown with bushes and weeds."

To prevent loss, many farmers got rid of their livestock or sent them into the interior. This in turn affected agriculture adversely because the colonists could no longer get enough manure for their lands as a result. As a consequence some colonists, "seeing no chance of earning a living in any other manner, have likewise already determined, with the great risk that they will lose the little that they possess, to remove a considerable distance further inland to see if they will have better success there. This still occurs occasionally, or as soon as the slightest rumor reaches them that somewhere a small, suitable farm has been discovered."[23]

This remarkable letter, which gives such a somber picture of the economic condition of the farming population at the Cape, makes clear just how seriously grazing lands had deteriorated by the middle of the eighteenth century, as well as how this promoted the emigration of established colonists into the interior. In reading the piece, however, one is inclined to ask the question whether the patriarchs of the district, perhaps inflamed with an exclusive nationalism, were perhaps not exaggerating. Various other sources, however, support their contentions.

In 1758 sixty-one farmers from the Swellendam district approached their landdrost with a petition to reduce the quitrent: "Your Excellency is not unaware, that the only thing that matters to us is our livestock herds, we must report to our great regret the sorrowful condition of how little a cattle farmer can earn on account of the great transformation of the lands, which have become unhealthy for our cattle, as well as the lower price for which one must presently sell his livestock."[24] The landdrost and heemraden did not support the colonists' petition, but nevertheless confirmed what the farmers said about the "deterioration of the lands."[25] A few years later the same council [i.e., the landdrost and heemraden] again made reference to "the deterioration of the lands by which the income of these inhabitants is greatly diminished."[26] At about the same time the military council of Stellenbosch stated "that more and more because of the deterioration of the farms and grazing lands in the neighboring regions, our inhabitants on occasion are compelled to look for better farms in districts located farther into the interior."[27]

Travelers who visited the interior during the eighteenth century remarked on the same phenomenon and described it. In this connection, for example, [Anders] Sparrman says: "On the whole, the integrity of the soil and the fertility of the land has gradually declined here more and more. One can say with certainty that such farms, which had previously been uncommonly grassy, and were very productive in grain and the harvest for the kitchen, nowadays are considerably poorer, so that there is concern that in a short time they will be abandoned. The rhinoceros-bush, a sort of thistle bush that is dry and prickly, which normally grows well on infertile plots of land, gradually spreads out more and more robustly across the fertile and cultivated farms."[28]

The travel journal of [Hendrik, Jr.] Swellengrebel, a son of the governor with the same name, gives the same kind of information: "In the Camdebo there are about thirty farms, of which about twenty-five are inhabited. If people don't begin skillfully to conserve the pasture for their livestock, it is to be feared that the luxuriousness, which has already declined markedly since this region began to be populated seven to eight years ago, shall not last long and the land even laying nearer to the main towns shall wholly go to ruin. It has already gone so far that a certain Jac. Botha near to the Great Fish River had to move away, because he had no pasture for his livestock here, and one A. van den Berg said he wanted to trek somewhere else since he could not keep up his farm."[29]

Not only in the Camdebo, but also in various other parts of the colony (near to Riebeekkasteel, by the Duivenhoks River, in the Langkloof and on the eastern border) it was noticed that grassy pasture land, which had previously had plenty of grazing for the livestock, had become overrun with rhinoceros-bush and various other weeds in the course of time.[30] In connection with the grazing land along the Fish River, the following observation was made in the travel account: "On this outermost border there is plenty of good pasture for livestock, but to foresee that when the land becomes very overcrowded it shall decrease quickly as in Camdebo and other areas."[31] In a letter to [Cornelis] De Gyselaar* in 1783 Swellengrebel also mentioned the deterioration of the grasslands.[32]

At the beginning of the nineteenth century W.S. van Ryneveld, one of the best judges of farming conditions at the Cape, likewise reported on this phenomenon. "If one asks an old farmer about the state of the land," he wrote in 1804 to general [Jan] Janssens, "he will answer you that the land now is worse than before....In the district of the Camdebo the farmers previously had very good sheep farms—nowadays one finds it full everywhere there of so-called purslane trees and other useless shrubs." The drosdy of Graaff-Reinet, wrote van Ryneveld, had previously belonged to a farmer who kept 12,000 sheep on it; now one cannot farm with more than 1,500 on the land.[33]

This process continued without a break until very recent times. The alarming dimensions it has already assumed in some parts of the Cape today are clear from the Final Report of the Drought Investigation Commission (1923). "There are areas," one of the witnesses wrote, "where the rhinoceros-bush is absolutely dominating, and if one linked together such areas between Grahamstown and Uniondale, I would estimate it at not less than 600 square miles (over 190,000 morgen). That land which had previously been good pastureland is useless at present. It is impossible to make even a rough estimate of all the land that is relatively lightly overgrown with rhinoceros-bush, which makes it inferior, and that declines further in value from year to year."[34] In some districts large areas are made nearly worthless through jointed cactus and other weeds.

It is notable how often there are references in the sources of the eighteenth century to grasslands that have deteriorated. Likewise, in more recent times, it is repeatedly observed how easily grassland is crowded out by scrub. In this way large patches of grassland in different parts of the Cape have already nearly vanished altogether. To be sure, the grass is frequently superseded by edible scrub, which offers excellent grazing for sheep, but such a change must ultimately have affected the cattle farmer who needed grassland.

In areas where the deterioration of the land did not take the form of edible vegetation being supplanted by worthless weeds, the phenomenon was not always so striking. Nevertheless, it still happened, and usually took the form of plant growth being crowded out, which meant that the carrying capacity of the land declined. The destruction of the plant cover also exposed the land more to the wind and the rays of the sun, which promoted evaporation. At the same time, it facilitated accelerated water run-off and soil erosion. This all meant that the economic value of rainfall diminished and droughts increased. This in turn inclined the farmers to believe that the rainfall itself had declined.[35]

Any farmer can easily determine for himself how much the plant growth on his farm has deteriorated over time by simply fencing off a few morgen and letting it lie fallow for a few years.

---

*Trans. note: Cornelis "Kees" de Gijselaar (1751-1815) was a Dutch politician and a leader in the patriot rebellion against the House of Orange from around 1780 to 1787. Swellengrebel had frequent correspondence with de Gijselaaar and other Dutch politicians.

The majority who put up jackal-proof fencing,[†] and then applied sensible land management practices, noted that over time the plant growth of their land improved remarkably.

Farmers in the pioneer era did not always have a sound understanding of the causes of the land deterioration. Some ascribed it to the fact that the land had become "old."[36] Others believed it was a punishment from God imposed on the farmers because of their sins.[37] But there were also people at this time who recognized the root of the problem as the overstocking of farms and the consequent overgrazing of the land.[38] In this connection it is interesting to see how clearly Sparrman saw the matter. As result of the overgrazing of the land, he said, "the grasses and vegetation, which the livestock so relish, can only be prevented from taking root and growing; while on the contrary, the rhinoceros bush, which the livestock pass by without ever touching, spreads it roots freely and unhindered, and supplants the other plants and bushes."[39] Likewise, the drafters of the Burger Memorial of 1784 sought the cause of the deterioration of the pasture land in overgrazing: "That, no matter how far-flung the Colony may now be, experience has already shown that the natural fertility of the soil cannot be sufficient to feed so great a multitude of live-stock—as everybody must now apply themselves to maintain the greater quantity that is needed to make a living, to compensate for the small profit received due to the low price. The keeping of so much live-stock makes the proper upkeep of the grazing fields impracticable, and is the reason why people have already had to abandon numerous districts that, as a result of a lack of proper cultivation, have totally declined."[40]

It was sometimes very difficult to prevent the overstocking and overgrazing of the farms, even for farmers who seriously wanted to do so. This was especially true in dry parts of the Cape where the rainfall, and consequently the carrying capacity of the land, varied from year to year. In such circumstances it was impossible for a farmer to calculate beforehand how much livestock he could keep on his farm during a specific year, without harming his grazing land. On the other hand, however, it cannot be denied that among our farmers, especially during the pioneer era, there was a strong inclination to practice over-cropping for the sake of immediate profit.

Simon van der Stel had already noticed this tendency among the farmers. In his instructions to his successor he advised him to see that colonists not exhaust their land completely, "as some have already, even deliberately, begun to put into execution; not hesitating to abandon exhausted land and to look for other new fields in their place. They excuse themselves [by saying] that since they are not provided with sufficient livestock they cannot manure their fields, and hence cannot cultivate wheat. These are sinister tricks which, if Your Honour allows them, would mean that the whole of Africa would not be sufficient to accommodate and satisfy such people."[41]

A century later De Mist noted the same mentality in the loan farm owner, who had no interest in the improvement of the land but tried to get as much as possible out of it, then abandoned it and applied for a new farm.[42] This tendency to overgraze did not disappear – as De Mist expected – with the abrogation of the loan farm system. It was still noticeable in recent times, and even today is characteristic of the farming methods of a certain portion of our population.[43]

[†]Trans. note: This is wire fencing typically consisting of wire mesh or closely-spaced wire strands. It is used to protect against predators. Dr. van der Merwe has a more detailed discussion of its use in chapters X and XVII.

To summarize: there was a strong disposition to overgrazing among the pioneer population at the Cape. Among livestock farmers it took the form of the overstocking of farms with the consequent overgrazing of the land. This meant that the carrying capacity of the land was seriously diminished, and in some cases this prompted established farmers to relocate to other farms.

5. Lack of Economic Adaptability

During the pioneer period there was a strong inclination among our livestock farmers toward extensive farming. This was particularly the case in areas of newer settlement.

Land was cheap and readily obtainable. Labor was expensive in relation to land. Capital was very scarce. Not only was the possibility for capital formation limited in agriculture, but under the prevailing economic system it was nearly impossible for people without capital to become independent farmers and even to own land. The result was that the farming population in general, and particularly young beginners, had very little capital or credit available to them. In these circumstances the pioneers were prone to develop farming methods that depended on ownership of large areas of land and required a minimum of work and capital. Generally, the farmers were not inclined to increase the carrying capacity of the land through the application of labor and capital. Of all the production factors, the land, used in more or less its natural condition, had to play the most important role.

Another aspect of the extensive farming system was that the farmers concentrated more upon the quantity of their livestock than on the quality. The old ideal for a farmer was not to improve the quality of his livestock herds as he prospered, but rather to increase the total number.[44] This was perhaps the appropriate thing to do at a time when land was plentiful and cheap. Other circumstances also promoted the tradition of farming with large herds of livestock. During the eighteenth century the farmers still tried to compensate for the lower prices paid for livestock by increasing the size of their herds.[45] In addition, the precariousness of livestock farming, due to livestock diseases, droughts, and cold, which often decimated the livestock in large numbers, inclined the farmers during good years to allow their livestock herds to increase as much as possible, in order to enable them to cope with unexpected losses.[46]

This tradition, which developed during the pioneer period, persisted stubbornly until very recent times. In various progressive livestock districts of the Cape, one still found ten, twenty years ago the phenomenon that even large farmers kept a grade of sheep that was almost not worth the trouble of farming with. Their ambition was to have many sheep, regardless of the quality. Farmers whose sheep today produce ten to twelve pounds of wool per head still remember the time, not all that long ago, when the average yield per sheep was four pounds. As time went on, however, they realized that a bad sheep ate just as much as a good one, and cost just as much to take care of and keep healthy. This encouraged farmers to improve their flocks and many of them earn just as much today with 750 sheep as they earned before with 2,000. Different factors are responsible for this, but one of the chief reasons was undoubtedly the constant rise in land prices that made it increasingly difficult for a farmer to expand his farm.

Finally, during the pioneer period there was considerable backwardness in farming, and methods were often adopted that were not efficient.

This is clear from a letter by W[illem] S[tephanus] van Ryneveld, who was an outstanding judge of farming conditions. If one speaks to people who possess an intimate knowledge of livestock farming, he wrote in 1804 to General [Jan Willem] Janssens, they all complain about the carelessness and indifference of people toward their farming. They maintain such large livestock herds that they cannot look after them all. Some farmers possess 4,000 to 8,000 head of sheep and goats. Frequently, they do not employ enough herdsmen to care for the livestock properly. Instead of dividing the large number of cattle into proper herds and keeping the lambing ewes, barren ewes, wethers and weaners apart, they are all looked after in one herd. Some farmers do not even regulate the lambing time properly, but just let the rams remain among the ewes for the whole year. Many are negligent about removing the old ewes on time, keeping them from lambing and selling them.

During lambing time as well, wrote van Ryneveld, not enough care and attention was devoted to farming. "Many lambs are bred—nature never stands still—yet few, very few are raised." The ewes go out together with the flock to the fields and many lambs—on the very day that they are born—remain behind and perish. Others are crippled by the herder, who ties together the feet of the weak lambs and carries home as many as he can manage over a pole. Some of the lambs perish because proper, dry pens are not provided for them. Often not enough is done to keep the weak lambs with the ewes so long as necessary.

When one reads what experts write about sheep breeding, van Ryneveld concluded, "one must marvel, one must be astonished, that there are still sheep to be found in South Africa."[47]

Van Ryneveld perhaps exaggerates a little, but other observers have also remarked on things about which he complained. [John] Barrow mentions that farmers often sustained losses because they allowed lambing in wet, dirty pens, where the lambs suffocated in the manure.[48] And if one looks at the dung heaps that are like small mountains that are still to be seen today on older farms, one gets the impression that the old pioneers did not often clean out old pens, or build new ones.

The backwardness in farming in the old days is also evident in the fact that not enough precautions were taken against damage that could have been avoided. The Commission of Inquiry pointed this out.[49] There were not enough barns and pens built that could provide effective shelter against cold, rain and snow. Very little was done to prevent losses from drought. Not enough care was taken to ensure fodder during seasons when the grazing lands were poor and did not produce sufficient food. Recently an old farmer in the Ceres district, where livestock farming today is such an intensive occupation, told me that in his younger days he did not know that a sheep could be given fodder.

These farming methods were originally to a large extent justifiable for the conditions of the time. When they developed, the extensive farming system was undoubtedly the most economically effective. Unfortunately, however, it tended to be maintained stubbornly, even though it was no longer effective as a result of changing circumstances. It was a natural result of the living conditions in which our pioneer population found themselves.

In the patriarchal farming families, which remained together as long as possible, the son learned farming methods from his father and accepted that they were effective. Children had a great deal of respect for their parents and respected their opinions. Among the old farmers it was unheard of that a child could be "smarter than his father." Thus the same methods were passed down from generation to generation in the pioneer community, and it was very difficult to change a method once it had taken root.[50]

Aside from this, the farming families in the interior usually lived miles from each other. That limited the opportunities for association and exchange of ideas among them. There was a total lack of reading material on farming. There was no guidance or information from the government. There was no opportunity to become more familiar with more progressive farming methods or to observe their practical application with one's own eyes. All of this contributed towards making the farmers conservative and allowed a mentality to develop among them that was characterized by a devotion to tradition, a lack of initiative, the absence of a spirit of experimental inquiry, and a bias against anything that was new.[51]

The problems that the Commission for Agriculture and Stock Raising encountered at the beginning of the nineteenth century in trying to persuade the farmers to procure wool-bearing sheep, illustrates their conservatism nicely. More often than not the farmers' prejudice against wool-bearing sheep was based only on their novelty and the fact that their predecessors had never owned wool-bearing sheep.[52] The problems connected with sheering and transporting the wool to the Cape were cited as major reasons why they would rather farm with the fat-tailed Afrikaner sheep. Others said that the Merino sheep was too ugly, that its tail was too small, that its flesh was perhaps not so good and that the butchers perhaps would not purchase the sheep.[53]

In the Roggeveld the Commission interviewed an old gentleman named Jan Nel, of Kuilen. "The old man could not be absolved from prejudice. He thought that men in this land could do nothing with the big tails of the sheep; he especially seemed to have a tender spot for, as he called it, our old African landscape, with which our forefathers had made do well enough."[54]

W.S. van Ryneveld had a similar experience with a farmer on the Berg River. This man, Jacobus Laubscher, was the most prominent livestock farmer in the neighborhood, and owned four or five of the best farms along the river. "I tried," van Ryneveld wrote, "but I could not remove the prejudice, which this good man had against the Spanish sheep—they were ugly—he could not stand them—he continued the breeding of his livestock at the feet of his father—who had become very rich by it." To this van Ryneveld responded that wool farming is profitable and that several farmers had already achieved great success with it. But his argument made little impression on Laubscher. his answer was: "I am a wealthy man, and do not need anything—I would rather stick with my old ways—and what problems I would have in obtaining other rams again.

Van Ryneveld also observed to his surprise that Laubscher owned no native, crossbreed cattle. His wife would have liked very much to own a few of this sort of cow, since it gave more milk. "Yet Laubscher would never hear of cross-breeding his cattle—he had the same breed that his father had possessed for so long with blessing and profit and he did not like strange things."[55]

This devotion to tradition contributed a great deal towards the maintenance of extensive farming methods and to hinder adaptation to the already changing requirements of economic life. How then did this promote the trekking of landowners into the interior?

The first farmers who trekked into the interior during the pioneer era developed extensive farming methods based on extensive land ownership. It was not necessary at all to farm intensively. Farms were large and stock could generally graze beyond the farm's boundaries in all directions. The farmers could expand their livestock herds to their hearts' content and buy additional cheap land when necessary. Furthermore, there was plenty of grazing land in the vicinity. As a result, it was not necessary to improve the water supply on the land. When the water that was there deteriorated in quality or dried up, they could trek with their livestock.[56] It was also not necessary to save land for periods of drought. If the land began to deteriorate, they could look for grazing land somewhere else.

Before long, however, conditions began to change. As the population of the region grew and the neighbors got closer, the amount of free land decreased, and the landowners were increasingly obliged to farm their own land. In time the farms also became ever smaller through subdivision and the carrying capacity of the land begin to decline as a result of overgrazing and trampling. The result was that droughts had a greater influence at precisely the time that trekking opportunities were reduced.

These changes obliged the farmer to farm more intensively. He had to learn to make do with smaller pieces of land, and to increase its carrying capacity through the application of capital and labor. He had to improve the water supply on his farm. He had to fence his farm and use his grazing land as economically as possible, so that he could lessen the necessity to trek. He had to learn to farm with less livestock and compensate with quality what he lost in quantity. He had to ensure that more of the lambs grew to maturity. In short, his farming methods had to be increasingly adjusted to make sure that every morgen of land and every animal delivered the highest possible return. This inevitably meant that the burden of farming become continually greater. This in turn meant that higher demands were placed on the economic skills of the farmer. The more intensive farming methods required more deliberation and business insight, more regular and harder work.

Those who were incapable of adapting to the tougher requirements of economic life—or were prevented from doing so through their attachment to tradition—went downhill economically. Some farmers exhausted their farms and tried to obtain prime crown land further ahead or to get grazing land for their livestock under easy conditions. Others were crowded out gradually by farmers who had more capital or who were more capable and could get more out of the land through the implementation of progressive methods, and consequently could offer prices for their farms that the owners could not resist. For this class as well there often remained no other way out but to trek to new pioneer areas, where they could continue their traditional farming methods.

For those who could not adapt and those who constantly struggled, the trek to the borders throughout the pioneer period was always the easiest solution to economic difficulties. But it does not follow from this that it was only this class of landowner who was involved in the trek to the pioneer areas. Among the trekkers there were also farmers who could not cope in the older districts only because of their lack of capital to manage in the more intensive economic struggle, but who saw the farming possibilities in the newer districts and had the necessary initiative and expertise to grasp the opportunities available there.[57]

6. The Unearned Appreciation in the Value of Land

In all parts of the Cape Colony—for that matter in all young countries—one finds the striking phenomenon that the value of farmlands rises surprisingly quickly during a certain period, notwithstanding cyclical fluctuations. The owner naturally contributes directly to this if he makes improvements to the land. It often happens, however, that the appreciation is greater than the value of the improvements that were made, so these improvements cannot be exclusively the cause of the rise in value. It is even a quite common phenomenon that the land values rise, even in cases where no improvements have been made at all. This appreciation that occurs due to causes for which the owner is not responsible is called "unearned appreciation" by economists.

When it comes to farmlands, one finds this phenomenon in its most pronounced form in the pioneer areas. The first landowners in the pioneer areas usually acquired their farms dirt cheap or for nothing (apart from quitrent, leasehold, or long leasehold). Usually, however, this did not last long before the value of the land began to increase. As soon as the area had been tamed a little and people begin to trek there in larger numbers, the demand for land became greater and this pushed the prices up. This enabled the loan farm owner to sell his homestead for much more than it was worth. The tenant easily found someone who was ready to take over his lease by taking over the payment. The landowner sold his farm for a profit without any difficulty.

This still did not end the process. As the district developed, commercial traffic improved, and the suitability of the area for farming was demonstrated, it attracted wealthier and more capable farmers from the areas of older settlement. They were ready to purchase these farms for prices that made even the second or third owners of the land a good profit. As the train lines came nearer good local markets developed or market conditions generally improved; the result was perhaps a further increase in the value of the land. Even in old districts it sometimes happened that there was a sudden unearned appreciation of land if, for example, efficient farming methods were implemented with success, or if a profitable type of farming was introduced with success. This happened, for example, during the past quarter century in the Ceres district, when the suitability of the district for fruit farming became evident.

The unearned appreciation of land did not occur in all districts equally quickly nor did the process last equally long all over. But in the economic development of every pioneer district, it played an important role at one stage or another. In the more recent settlements such as Griqualand West, Bechuanaland, Gordonia, Kenhardt and parts of Namaqualand, where the present generation of farmers experienced the phenomenon, it repeatedly happened that the value of land (apart from improvements) doubled within a few years. In many cases landowners got the opportunity within ten years to get rid of their farms for four of five times the sum that the land plus improvements had cost them.

In his annual report for 1911 the Kenhardt magistrate wrote, for example: "Property is going up fast in price—farms that were sold from 6d. to 3s. 6d. per morgen some six years ago, are being sold to-day from 2s. to 10s. a morgen. This is due to the opening up of the district. Farmers have discovered the capabilities of the district and also that with average zeal and acumen, as good a living is to be made here as in any of the midland and northwestern districts. Men from other parts are purchasing property here."[58] The following year he wrote again: "There is a steady rise in the value of farm property in this district....land which could be bought for one shilling a morgen a few years ago, cannot be obtained now for less that four or five shillings. And if a property comes into the market, be it private or government property, there are many applicants."[59]

The unearned appreciation of land played an important role in our pioneer history. Again and again it placed farmers who for one reason or another wanted to make a change in the position of being able to sell their farms at a profit. Such people, however, could only derive the full benefit from doing so if they did not buy land again in the same area, but trekked farther up country to regions of newer settlement where land was still cheap. What made such a move still more attractive was the prospect that the new farm you purchased would within the foreseeable future also undergo unearned appreciation. The trek of landowners into the interior was encouraged in this way.

The permanent type of pioneer, who earnestly set himself to farming, was not a land speculator. He had made a profit perhaps once or twice from unearned appreciation, applied it in the interests of his farming and after that remained where he was. In some cases, however, the unearned appreciation gave rise to blatant land speculation, which led to repeated changes of residence, always farther into the interior. Some pioneers were quite prepared for the sake of immediate financial gain to take leave of their land again and again. This type of man obtained cheap land but did not cultivate it. Perhaps he built a pioneer home on it, dug a well, and perhaps erected a wind pump. After a few years he looked for someone to purchase the land, and he trekked farther into the interior, until he reached a place where he could again obtain cheap land. He again built a new farm, cultivated it just enough to attract a good buyer, and got rid of it as soon as he could make a profit of a couple of hundred pounds. Sometimes this process was repeated several times.

Such a mentality was often accompanied by a lack of spiritual steadiness, so that the profits that were made each time did not always lead to the long-term improvement of his economic position. The speculator lived well so long as the money lasted, and after that he began again from scratch. Sometimes it resulted in economic decline, the speculator loses all of his land and he dies a poor man. In general, those who obtained cheap land in time and held onto it, did better economically.

7. The Possibility of Trekking to Still Unoccupied Land

All the factors that we have mentioned in connection with the trek of landowners into the interior have a direct or indirect relation to the possibility of trekking to more still unoccupied land. The landowner could only improve his economic position by moving to the pioneer regions so long as he could still obtain undistributed land or cheap land there. This depended on the amount of crown land available, which at the same time also affected the price of private land in the pioneer areas.

During the era of free expansion (1700 to 1779) the available amount of undistributed land in the Cape Colony was nearly unlimited. In addition, grazing for livestock improved the farther the pioneers penetrated into the country. Every farmer who trekked into the interior could obtain a farm, an additional farm, or a different farm there just for the asking. During the 1770s, however, this expansion in all directions came up against certain obstacles. Between 1780 and 1800 no significant expansion took place, with the result that the available amount of undistributed land per capita of the population suddenly declined. At the beginning of the nineteenth century there was no still unoccupied crown land within the colonial borders that was regarded as useful according to the notions of the time. Shortly after 1800 the trek toward the north began along the Seekoei River. Under English rule large areas were added to the colony over and over every now and again, so that today it stretches up to the Molopo. Since Macartney's proclamation establishing the northern border in 1797 the Cape Colony's surface area has more than doubled. Thus, the possibility of getting hold of unoccupied crown land was repeatedly made available until into the twentieth century. The land that had been occupied since 1800, however, was mostly of poorer quality. Large parts of it were not inhabitable in their natural state because of the shortage of water. Moreover, the expansion into the interior—in relation to the growth of the population—did not occur as rapidly as it did in the eighteenth century. As a result, it was more difficult in the nineteenth century than before to obtain crown land in the Cape Colony. There were, however, different areas outside the Cape Colony where a landowner could improve his economic position. Since the Great Trek thousand of people from the Colony—drawn by the cheap land—have moved to the Free State, Transvaal, South-West Africa and other areas. Even those who did not personally take part in this emigration movement were indirectly affected by it. This is because it resulted in farms in the Cape Colony coming onto the market.

Since around 1910 the possibility of trekking to still unoccupied lands has diminished quickly, and today it no longer plays a significant role. As that possibility diminished, factors such as the unearned appreciation of land, the deterioration of the grazing land, the desire to acquire larger amounts of land, etc., would provide less and less incentive to move to the interior. These factors are still active today, in a similar or modified form, and in modern times it is often the cause of economic progress, but they seldom lead to the emigration of landowners to pioneer areas. Today there are, for example, many farmers who can make a profit from the unearned appreciation of land. But there is no longer any benefit to be gained from selling land here for a high price with the intention of buying a larger or better piece of land farther up country. Even if you find land to purchase in an area of newer settlement, you also have to pay a high price for it there today. For similar reasons the small landowner, who wants to enlarge his holdings, or the farmer who has a worn-out farm, no longer has the opportunity today to improve his economic position by moving to a region of newer settlement.

ENDNOTES

[1] C 1483, Letters Disp., Cape government to Lords XVII, 24 January 1730, p. 102; C 1265, Petitions, Reports, etc., P.A. Myburg to Landdrost, 1 May 1775, p. 457; C 1764, Letters Disp., J. van Plettenberg to Lords XVII, 1 March 1779, no. 23, p. 210; C.O. 2581, Letters Rec., Tulbagh, H. van de Graaff to Grey, 14 August 1811; Swellengrebel Family Archives, Hendrik Swellengrebel, Jr. to C. de Gyselaar, 26 June 1783. [Trans. Note: The letter from Swellengrebel to Gyselaar may also be found in the collection of letters published by the Van Riebeeck Society, *Briefwisseling van Hendrik Swellengrebel Jr. oor Kaapse Sake, 1778-1792*, VRS, series II, vol. 13, pp. 151-62 in the original with a shortened English summary, pp. 348-52.].

[2] 1/STB 20/2, Letters Rec., Landdrost Faber, Mintz., et al, to Tulbagh, 17 February 1770.

[3] C 1265, Petitions, Reports, etc., A.H. Krugel and twelve others to Governor van Plettenberg, Petition from Bruintjieshoogte, 10 November 1774, pp. 443-45.

[4] C 1265, Petitions, Reports, etc., P.A. Myburg to Landdrost, 1 May 1775, p. 455.

[5] W.M. Macmillan, *Bantu, Boer, and Briton* (London, 1929), p. 25.

[6] P.J. van der Merwe, *Die Noordwaartse Beweging van die Boere voor die Groot Trek (1770-1842)* (The Hague, 1937), pp. 243-4, 343-8, 364; L.G. 73, Letters Rec. from Colonial Office, J.J. Mienie to Rawstone, 16 November 1838 (Enclosure to 12 January 1839).

[7] P. Kolbe, *Nauwkeurige en Uitvoerigne Beschrijving van de Kaap de Goede Hoop* (Amsterdam, 1726), I:116.

[8] Swellengrebel Family Archives, Hendrik Swellengrebel, Jr. to C. de Gyselaar, 26 June 1783.

[9] C 495, Letters Rec., Horak to Governor, 26 July 1756, p. 415.

[10] C 1483, Letters Disp., Cape Government to Lords XVII, 24 January 1730, p. 102.

[11] J. Barrow, *Travels into the Interior of Southern Africa*, 2nd ed. (London, 1806), I:29.

[12] H. Lichtenstein, *Reisen im südlichen Africa in den Jahren 1803, 1804, 1805 und 1806 (Berlin, 1811-1812), I:171*.

[13] Lichtenstein, *Reisen*, I:149-50.

[14] Augusta Uitenhage de Mist, "Dagverhaal van een Reis naar de Kaap de Goede Hoop en in de Binnenlanden van Afrika door Jonkvr. Augusta Uitenhage de Mist in 1802 en 1803," *Pénélopé* (Amsterdam), VIII (1835), pp. 95; Lichtenstein, *Reisen*, I:149, 171-2.

[15] Lichtenstein, *Reisen*, 1:171 (Note **, which begins on page 170, but continues at the bottom of 171, where this information is found.); W.J. Burchell, *Travels in the Interior of Southern Africa* (London, 1822), I:222-23.

[16] Van der Merwe, *Trekboer*, p. 96.

[17] O.F. Mentzel, *Vollständige und Zuverläszige Geographische und topographische Beschreibung des Berühmten und in aller Betrachtung merkwürdigen Afrikanischen Vorgebirges des Guten Hoffnung* (Glogau, 1785, 1787), I:55.

[18] Lichtenstein, *Reisen*, II:54-9.

[19] P.J. van der Merwe, *Die Trekboer in die Geskiedenis van die Kaapkolonie, 1657-1842* (Cape Town, 1938), p. 95.

[20] Ds. W.J. Conradie, *Ondervindingen van een Jonge Predikant in Namaqualand* (London, 1909), p. 43.

[21] Van der Merwe, *Noordwaartse Beweging*, pp. 343-7.

[22] C 128, Resolutions, 1 December 1750, pp. 242-3.

[23] Landdrost and Heemraden to Governor, 11 January 1751, in *Reports of De Chavonnes and His Council, and of Van Imhoff, on the Cape* (Cape Town: Van Riebeeck Society, 1918), Series 1, vol. 1, p. 81.

[24] C 1244, Petitions, Reports, etc., January-February 1758, p. 27.

[25] 1/SWM 1/1, Minutes from the Landdrost and Heemraden, 25 January 1758, p. 431.

[26] C 2208, Logbooks for Stellenbosch and Drakenstein, 15 July 1771, p. 65.

[27] 1/STB 13/8, Military Council Resolutions, 7 May 1776.

[28] A. Sparrman, *Reize naar de Kaap de Goede Hoop, de Landen van den Zuid Pool, en rondom de Waereld* (Leiden, 1786), I:287.

[29] Swellengrebel Family Archives, Travel journal of Swellengrebel, 1776, p. 28.

[30] Ibid., pp. 2, 74, 85, 94, 98, etc.

[31] Ibid., p. 23.

[32] Swellengrebel Family Archives, Hendrik Swellengrebel, Jr. to C. de Gyselaar, 26 June 1783.

[33] AR, Colonial Accession 157, W.S. van Ryneveld to J.W. Janssens, 4 September 1804.

[34] SRP 1/2/106, U.G. 49 of 1923, Final Report of the Drought Investigation Commission, Appendix 6, Report of S. Schönland, p. 103

[35] Van der Merwe, *Noordwaartse Beweging*, pp. 186-96.

[36] AR, Colonial Accession 157, W.S. van Ryneveld to J.W. Janssens, 4 September 1804.

[37] Sparrman, *Reize*, I:288.

[38] AR, Colonial Accession 157, W.S. van Ryneveld to J.W. Janssens, 4 September 1804; Swellengrebel Family Archives, Travel journal of Swellengrebel, 1776, p. 2; D.G. van Rennen, Reisverhaal, p. 13 (MS); C 1283, Petitions, Reports, etc., Burgher Petition, Woeke, Bletterman, et al., 17 February 1784, p. 57; PSB, Mss. Germ. Fol. No. 857, J.W. Janssens, Memorandum on Loan farms, 30 January 1805, p. 58. [Trans. Note: Dr. van der Merwe does not include in the *TREK* bibliography a reference to the van Rennen document above. In *Noordwaartse Beweging*, however, it

is included in the bibliography on p. 390 as follows: "*Van Reenen, D.G.*, Dag-verhaal eener Reize naar de Binnenlanden van Afrika Beoosten de Kaap de Goede Hoop geleegen, in den Jaare 1803, gedaan door Z.E. den Gouverneur en Generaal en Chef, J.W. Janssens, ens. (In Ms. Gelees [Read in Ms].")]

39 Sparrman, *Reize*, I:288.

40 C 1283, Petitions, Reports, etc., Burger Petition, Woeke, Bletterman, et al., 17 February 1784, p. 57.

41 Instructions from Simon van der Stel to William Adriaan van der Stel, 30 March 1699, in C.G. Botha, *Collectanea* (Cape Town: Van Riebeeck Society, 1924), Series I, vol. 5, p. 13.

42 AR, Asiatic Council, 301, De Mist to Janssens, 10 October 1803.

43 R.W. Wilcocks, *Die Armblanke* (Stellenbosch, 1932), pp. 26-9; J.F.W. Grosskopf, *Plattelandsverarming en Plaasverlating* (Stellenbosch, 1932), pp. 82-4.

44 AR, Colonial Accession 157, W.S. van Ryneveld to J.W. Janssens, 4 September 1804; C. d'Escury, Memorandum, 20 December 1822, in George McCall Theal, *Records of the Cape Colony, 1792-1831* (Cape Town, 1897-1905), XV:170.

45 C 1283, Petitions, Reports, etc., Burgher Petition, Woeke, Bletterman, et al., 17 February 1784, p. 57; Swellengrebel Family Archives, Hendrik Swellengrebel, Jr. to C. de Gyselaar, 26 June 1783.

46 Lieut. T.C. White to Commissioners of Inquiry, 14 November 1823, in Theal, *Records*, XVI:431.

47 AR, Colonial Accession 157, W.S. van Ryneveld to J.W. Janssens, 4 September 1804.

48 Barrow, *Travels*, (first edition, 1804), II:403. [Trans. note: In his other references to Barrow, and in his bibliography, Dr. van der Merwe cites Barrow's second edition published in 1806. Here he appears to be particularly referencing the first edition, the second volume of which was published in 1804.]

49 Bigge and Colebrooke to Bathurst, 30 September 1825, in Theal, *Records*, XXIII:195-6.

50 Lichtenstein, *Reisen*, II:56; J.W.D. Moodie, *Ten Years in Southern Africa* (London, 1835), I:73-74; G. Nicholson, *Fifty Years in Southern Africa:Being some Recollections and Reflections of a Veteran Pioneer* (London, 1898), p. 62; G.A. Robertson, *Notes on Africa – to which is added an appendix, containing a Compendius Account of the Cape of Good Hope, its Productions and Resources with a variety of important information very necessary to be known by persons about to emigrate to that Colony* (London, 1819), p. 408. [Trans. note: In the reference to Lichtenstein, *Reisen*, the quotation in the text, "smarter than his father" is not in Lichtenstein but is simply a local saying Dr. van der Merwe is relating. In this footnote, Dr. van der Merwe has Robinson instead of Robertson. It is correct in his Bibliography, however.]

51 PRO (London), C.O. 48/143, Bell, Report on the Cape, 4 July 1831; Report of the Commission for Stock Raising and Agriculture, 20 November 1805, in George McCall Theal, *Belangrijke Historische Dokumenten* (Cape Town, 1896, 1911), III:405; C. d'Escury, Memorandum, 20 December 1822, in Theal, *Records*, XV:170; Bigge and Colebrooke to Bathurst, 30 September 1825, in Theal, *Records*, XXIII:195; J.B.N. Theunissen, *Aantekeningen van een reis door de Binnenlanden van Zuid-Afrika van Port Elizabeth naar de Kaapstad gedaan in 1823* (Oostende, 1824), pp. 48-9; William Mackenzie, *Outlines of Education; or, Remarks on the Development of Mind, and*

Improvement of Manners (Edinburgh: Archibald constable & Co., 1824), p. 305. [Trans. note: Dr. van der Merwe has: "Mackenzie: Sketches (In Outlines of Education or Remarks on the Development of the Mind, p. 305)" and in his Bibliography, he has "Mackenzie, W.: Sketches of Travels in Southern Africa, Edinburgh, 1824. (In "Outlines of Education.")." In Mackenzie's book, *Outlines*, pp. 247-298 are titled "Sketches of Travels in Southern Africa," and pp. 299-314 are titled "Sketch of the Boor."]

52 C.O. 9, Letters Rec. from the Grain committee, etc., W.S. van Ryneveld to Caledon, 19 January 1808.

53 Report of the Commission for Stock Raising and Agriculture, 20 November 1805, in George McCall Theal, *Belangrijke Historische Dokumenten over Zuid-Afrika* (Cape Town, 1896, 1911), III:362, 369, 374, 386.

54 Ibid., III: 369.

55 B.R. 406, W.S. van Ryneveld, Improvement of the Livestock, 16 April 1804, pp. 33, 34, 62. [Trans. note: The Van Riebeeck Society published this long document, edited by H.B. Thom, in 1942. See W.S. van Ryneveld, *Aanmerkingen over de Verbetering van het Vee aan de Kaap de Goede Hoop, 1804* (Cape Town: Van Riebeeck Society, 1942), Series I, vol. 23. The reference here is on p. 111 of that volume.]

56 Cf. J.C. Chase, *The Cape of Good Hope and the Eastern Province of Algoa Bay* (London, 1843), p. 16.

57 Cf. Grosskopf, *Plattelandsverarming en Plaasverlating*, pp. 106-7.

58 Kenhardt Letter Book (D 16), Letter Book of Resident Magistrate, Annual Report for the Year 1811, p. 904. [Trans. note: I was not able to locate this volume in the Cape Archives.]

59 Kenhardt Letter Book (D 18), Letter Book of Resident Magistrate, Annual Report for the Year 1811, p. 19. [Trans. note: I was not able to locate this volume in the Cape Archives.]

CHAPTER VI

The Psychological Basis of The Trek Away From Civilization

It is clear from the previous chapters that the principal causes of the trek away from the centers of civilization were economic. All classes of the pioneer community (landowners, tenants, young beginners, nomadic trekboers and hunter/stock farmers) moved to the border districts in order to improve their economic circumstances. Some were enticed there through undistributed land or cheap farms; others by the prospects of getting grazing land for their livestock for nothing or under easy terms; a small minority by the presence of wild game. A purely economic interpretation of the process of expansion, however, would be decidedly one-sided. From the establishment of the colony onward there were psychological factors at work that had an influence on the movement.

1. Becoming Afrikaans

A factor of great importance in connection with the trek into the interior is that at the Cape a settler population developed relatively quickly that threw in its lot wholeheartedly with South Africa. Although a large percentage of the original immigrants fled back home over the sea, and not all those who remained behind were happy with the Cape, before long the settlement developed into a genuine colonial population. The second and third generation of pioneers in particular, no longer considered returning to Europe. Willem Adriaan van der Stel formulated the difference between immigrants from overseas and colonists who were born at the Cape strikingly: "These people also know no other fatherland, unlike most of those who come out, who are sent to us, who, as soon as they have managed to scrape together something, once again depart from here."[1]

In the crucible of the pioneers' lives in a strange country, the colonists and their children gradually lost their sense of being Dutch. Dependent upon their own strength in their unceasing struggle against nature, against wild animals and wild peoples, they got the feeling that they had been forgotten by the old world and, in turn, they forgot the old world. As they learned to adapt to their new environment and to stand on their own two legs, their sense of independence grew. This was accompanied by the gradual awakening of a national consciousness. During the dispute between the colonists and Willem Adriaan van der Stel, a young boy, who had come in conflict with the landdrost, declared publicly: "I am an Afrikaner."[2] Proud of their colonial descent, later generations of pioneers called themselves "Afrikaners" as well.[3]

As far as the Afrikanerizaton of the colonists at the Cape was concerned, the composition of the population was likewise of very great importance. During the seventeenth century, which must be viewed as the era of immigration, the white population of the colony was a motley hodge-podge of heterogeneous population elements. The basis of the population was Dutch, but the immigrants came from different provinces and cities and their languages, manners, and customs often differed considerably from each other. Furthermore, there were many foreigners: Germans from Switzerland, Swabians and Saxons, Prussians, Pomeranians, Westphalians, Brandenburgers, and other German states; a considerable number of French people as well as people from Portugal, Poland, Sweden, Savoy, Denmark, Italy, England, Hungary and other European countries.

Chiefly as a result of the language policy of the government, all these foreigners became Dutchified relatively quickly. The facts are well-known. German died a painless, and French a very painful, death. Soon everyone at the Cape knew only Dutch. These Dutchified foreigners, however, were not Dutch in spirit. Nor were the children born from mixed marriages. As a result of the denationalization of foreigners and the fusion of different foreign population groups, a new product came into existence on South African soil that was not Dutch, and also not German or French, but Afrikaans.

It was a very long time before a united nation developed in Dutch South Africa, but when the spread of livestock farmers into the interior began, the greatest part of the farming population already felt that they were children of South Africa, and that their future lay here. When these people became dissatisfied with the possibilities for making a living that the settlement at the foot of Table Mountain offered, they did not take flight across the sea, but into the wilderness. During the difficult early years after the establishment of the settlement many who could not make a success in agriculture requested that they be taken into service again as a soldier or sailor in the Company. As the descendants of the first immigrants put down their roots ever more deeply in their new fatherland, the seaman's life, from which many of the colonists' ancestors had come, lost all attraction for them. All attempts to recruit soldiers and sailors at the Cape for service in the Indian service were fruitless. Cape–born Afrikaners chose the free life of the veld over the dangers and hardships of the sea.[4]

2. The Break between the Back Country and the City

When the trek into the interior first began, a split soon also developed between the farmers of the back country and the capital city and harbor, the seat of civilization and the doorway to Europe. The sand-flats between Cape Town and Stellenbosch had already done much to bring about the isolation of the countryside. The mountains cutting off the interior from the coast completed it. Before the passes through the mountains were made late in the nineteenth century, it was a difficult and dangerous thing to cross the mountains, even with an empty wagon.[5]

Soon distance also begins to be a factor. In the days of ox-wagon traffic, a person undertaking a long journey could not cover more than 25 miles per day on a regular basis. Furthermore, an ox wagon could not carry much. As the farmers moved farther away from the Cape, it became all the harder to maintain contact with the civilized areas. In 1726 the military council of Stellenbosch declared that well over two thirds of the farmers of that "colony" had to travel such a great distance into the interior "because of scarcity of pasture and death among the livestock" that it took fourteen days and longer for some of them to come from their livestock posts to Stellenbosch. They preferred to pay the fines and miss the militia exercises than to undertake a trip to the drosdy for this purpose. They visited the Cape only once a year to take care of their most essential business. Otherwise, they lived apart from the capital city.[6]

Visits to the Cape became less frequent in the course of time. A journey from Graaff-Reinet to Cape Town and back lasted from two to three months. Farmers who lived farther inland, were sometimes absent from their farms for four to five months when they visited the capital, which they did only once every two, three, or even four years. Many colonists saw the Cape only once in their lives, namely, when they went there to be married.[7]

During the Company period it was still necessary to visit the Cape now and then, even if it was very seldom. Marriages had to be performed in the Cape. Farmers had to go to the Cape for loan-farm business and to purchase necessities such as ammunition, textiles, and groceries. The need for this journey gradually diminished in the nineteenth century, after it became possible to be married in the country, and to pay quitrent at the magistrate's office. Furthermore, small towns arose at various places in the interior, where merchants set up business. In time, the itinerant trader made his appearance as well (hawking had been prohibited in the eighteenth century,[8]) and delivered what the farmers needed to their doorstep. In these circumstances the journeys of frontier farmers to the Cape died out altogether.

Cape Town, the tavern of the seas, remained a cosmopolitan harbor city for years. After the conquest of the country by the English, it quickly became Anglicized and radiated a non-Afrikaans influence. For the new, true Afrikaner, who had come into existence in the rural areas, the center of civilization soon became something quite alien, a place where they did not feel at home. For the rest, the farmers of the back country associated the city with government officials, the representatives of a foreign government, who impeded the possibilities for the local inhabitants of this country to earn a living, imposed taxes on them, and who were little concerned about the lot of the farmers.[9]

In this way, the ties that bound the farmers of the interior to the center of civilization weakened over time. This situation did not directly promote the spreading of the colonists into the interior, but it unleashed the centrifugal forces that drove the livestock farmers deeper into the country during the pioneer period.

3. Government Control and Taxes

One sometimes comes across the view that the trek into the interior was an attempt to escape government control. As the government expanded its authority, the malcontents who did not want to be subjected to that authority went in search of unrestrained freedom in the wilderness.[10]

This representation of events, which is not borne out by historical evidence, is unquestionably incorrect. From all the available evidence about the natural expansion of the colony (the Great Trek was altogether something else), the exact opposite appears to be true. The trekboers who stood on the outposts of civilization never paid much attention to the proclamations forbidding the expansion of the colony, and they trekked not as a result of political discontent, or to try and avoid government authority.

This seems very clear, for example, from the petition of some farmers who settled beyond Bruintjieshoogte in the 1770s, contrary to government orders. This remarkable document contains sufficient important information to justify full quotation. It was addressed to Governor [Joachim] van Plettenberg [and the Council]:

"We come in all respect and subservience, to request that Your Honors will accept our humble petition, and extend to us mercy and indulgence:

Great Sirs:

Whereas we understand with great sadness that numerous complaints against us have been made by our fellow burghers to Your Honors, and that these have aroused much anger against us among Your Honors, to our greatest concern and sorrow. That we are accused of being obstinate and rebellious against Your Great Honors' proclamation and also against Your prohibition of trade with the Caffers. And yet we are not, and we do not, but through our great poverty, for we possess little, should we go to live upon the Sneeuberg, and should the Bushman Hottentots take from us one head of cattle or a sheep, so we would suffer more than the Sneeuberg inhabitants who lost ten sheep and cattle. Because many of these inhabitants living beyond Bruintjieshoogte are people who do not own a hundred sheep or fifty cattle. Therefore, as there is peace and quiet here now with the Hottentots, and as it is fruitful for raising livestock and for cultivation, and as there is also plenty of wild game here to meet our food needs, we have come here to live.

"We request, entreat, and pray for Your Great Honors' forgiveness if we have committed an offense by migrating over here. Your Revered Honors, we beseech, in all humility, respect, and obedience, that Your Honors will have mercy on us and permit us to remain here, and to pay rent to the Honorable Company for this land. Then we shall, as obedient burghers and faithful servants, so far as the Company is concerned, take good care that such disturbing complaints are never again brought before Your Great Honors to provoke your wrath.

"Moreover, we humbly request that in that event, Your Honors would see fit to appoint a qualified person residing beyond Bruintjieshoogte as Field Commandant, and place under his authority the settlement of petty disputes, such as disputes between neighbors, and that he might report to the Council of Policy those who might trade or barter with the Caffris [sic] so that such transgressors might be punished as an example to others.

"To this we pray that the Lord will bestow his grace upon Your Honors to the desired result. Meanwhile, we will not cease to pray to God Almighty that he will keep you for many years under his holy protection, and that we remain with all imaginable respect..."[11]

Not only the contents of this document, but also the spirit that radiates from it attests to a childlike reverence for government and a desire to live under its authority. Van Plettenberg found evidence of a similar attitude a few years later on his cross-country journey. The inhabitants of the Sneeuberge, who were also at the vanguard of civilization, requested that he give them a minister. "They wished similarly that over their widespread district a landdrost or other representative official of government, might be appointed in order that they might be governed from nearby for the common good."[12]

By the end of the eighteenth century there was much dissatisfaction in the interior with the government, but not among the trekboers who lived on the outposts of civilization. The inhabitants of the Sneeuberge and other northern parts of Graaff-Reinet did not participate in the revolutionary movement that was brewing in that district. While their fellow countrymen nearer to the Cape repudiated the authority of the government, the farmers on the northern border remained loyal.[13]

Even during the Great Trek there was little dissatisfaction with the government among the trekboers who led the quiet expansion to the north. Precious few of the people from the frontier field-cornetcies south of the Orange River took part in the Great Trek. The overwhelming majority of these farmers, who normally trekked every summer with their livestock to the southern Free State, wanted nothing to do with the Voortrekkers.[14]

Between 1830 and 1840 many trekboers from the northeastern part of the colony trekked for good over the Orange River and established themselves in what is today the Free State. About the same time several colonists settled east of the Stormbergspruit, thus outside the colonial boundaries as well. But these emigrants did not leave the colony in order to get away from the authority of the English government, as was the case with the Voortrekkers. They had no desire to establish an independent government. All that they wanted was land.

They trekked with the expectation that the government would later extend the colonial boundaries and include them, as the Dutch East India Company's government had done since time immemorial. They repeatedly entreated the colonial government to recognize them as British subjects and to annex the territory on which they lived. Furthermore, both groups of expatriate trekboers, even after they had already settled beyond the colonial borders, regularly came into the colony to pay their taxes, until the government refused to accept them.[15] The desire to evade taxes therefore could not have served as an incentive to trek over the colonial boundaries.

4. Lack of Group Solidarity and Local Patriotism

In the Cape Colony the expansion into the interior occurred quite spontaneously and naturally. The government or private companies never recruited colonists, relocated them in groups to the interior, and based on previously worked out plans formed settlements on undistributed crown land. The expansion was led by individuals and patriarchal families with perhaps a sharecropper or two, who together followed one after the other, each one in his own good time. Apart from cases where family members or friends followed each other into the interior, trekkers usually had had very little contact with each other before they left. In the typical pioneer district people from various regions converged together quite by chance.

The manner of settlement took on the same individualistic character as the trek into the interior. They each settled down on their own and where they wished, usually at a fairly good distance from their neighbors. The fact that the trek did not take place in an organized fashion, as well as the needs of livestock farming, inevitably meant that the pioneers in the interior did not form organized communities. The individual with his family, not a group of colonists, was the colonizing unit based on which the interior became inhabited.

The consequence of this individualistic manner of trek and settlement was that from the beginning the pioneers in the interior were somewhat detached from the environment in which they coincidentally found themselves.

The economic organization of the pioneer community strengthened its independent character.

Aside from the limited market for agricultural products (especially in the eighteenth century), transport difficulties made it nearly impossible for the inland farmers to produce for the Cape market, and there were no local markets of any importance until well into the nineteenth century. The farmers in remote areas loaded their wagons full of products (butter, soap, hides, leather thongs, whips, horns, and perhaps ivory) when they occasionally had to go into town, but they could not make a special effort to transport their products to market. Throughout the pioneer era slaughter-stock, which were bought on the farms and delivered themselves to the market, were the staple product of the farmers at the outposts of civilization. The result was that the farmers had no need to worry unduly about the distance from the market.

Even for their slaughter-stock the farmers could not always count on good prices and a regular market. This meant that the cash income and the purchasing power of the pioneer family were small. In addition, the farmers did not always get an opportunity to purchase store goods. Under these circumstances the pioneers were obliged to provide for their own needs as far as possible. The farmer produced nearly all his own food, he tanned his own leather, and made shoes for himself and his family. His wife molded candles, prepared soap, and made clothes for the whole household from cured skins or material purchased by the roll. Pioneers were thrown back on their own resources as well to satisfy their needs in matters concerning housing. Good building material was difficult to obtain. Craftsmen were scarce and the average farmer could in any event not afford to hire them. Every person thus had to build his own house to the best of his ability with the material that could be found in his surroundings.[16]

Isolated in the interior, the pioneer family thus became in very great measure self-sufficient, and formed a more or less closed economic unit, in which products for the market were less important than products for their own use.

In contrast with modern society in which people, by applying the principle of division of labor according to occupation and production for the market, are dependent on each other, the pioneer family during the time period of the closed family household was fairly detached economically from its surroundings.

The social living conditions in the country were also not as conducive to the development of a feeling of group solidarity as among colonists who lived in the same neighborhood. In the pioneer community the organized social institutions that bind people in modern communities together into a group were almost completely absent. Membership of the same church certainly contributed to the notion among farmers that they formed a unit. But congregations were so large, and their members came together so seldom, that for them the church tower did not mean as much as it did to a little community that lived in the shadows of the church and constantly associated with each other on church matters.

The presence of a common danger from the natives, and the development of a sharply drawn distinction between white and black, Christian and heathen, were certainly consolidating factors in the development of a national awareness. More than anything else they gave the farmers the feeling that they formed *one* nation. But more than anything else it also strengthened the consciousness of a feeling of national solidarity, without thereby giving rise to local group solidarity. In connection with the Great Trek Dr. Theal remarked: "In one respect the Dutch colonists were very unlike their kindred in Europe. In the Netherlands men were strongly attached to the locality of their birth and to their own little province, but in South Africa beyond the first range of mountains, owing to the old land tenure, the people had lost all feeling of this kind. Their affection was for the country as a whole, and it was very strong, but whether they lived in one part or in another a great distance away, was a matter of little concern to them. It was thus not a cause of much regret in itself for these men and women to tear themselves away from the part of South Africa termed the Cape Colony and make new homes in a part bearing another name."[17]

The Afrikaans pioneer on his lonely farm was thus much more detached from his environment than, for example, a modern city-dweller, who is surrounded by his friends, belongs to a smaller congregation, is an ardent member of one or another sports club, takes part in social life, and has a number of other interests in the city. All such links bind the individual to the community and can bring considerable influence to bear when the question under consideration is whether he is going to move from the neighborhood.

5. Individualism

Finally, the whole organization of the pioneer community fostered individualism, which had a favorable effect in many respects, but often also tended to allow anti-social behavior to develop among the pioneers.[18]

The pioneer in the wilderness had to construct an existence for himself and his family, while confronted with numerous dangers and hardships. He was left nearly entirely to his own devices. He had to rely mainly on himself for the protection of his life and property and the satisfaction of his principal needs. The necessity for self-defense and self-sufficiency made him independent, versatile, and resourceful. He learned to get by with little, and to be satisfied with that. As he learned to stand on his own two feet, his self-confidence grew, and he developed a strong sense of independence toward the outside world. This sense of independence was strengthened by the fact that during the pioneer period there were equal chances for everyone. Advancement did not depend upon the class into which you were coincidentally born, but on your ability. In the pioneer communities, where class differences did not exist, the greatest emphasis was placed upon the personal qualities of the individual, and a man felt that his future depended upon his own actions. This strengthened his self-esteem.

Together with these qualities that made of our ancestors such able pioneers and equipped them so well for the task of opening up the interior, other qualities often developed, however, which impeded the social adaptation required in a more settled community. Pioneers usually allowed people to do as they wished and manage in their own way. This often made them self-willed and intolerant and quarrelsome, and led to a distorted sense of personal freedom, which made them unwilling to adapt to the interests of the community, towards which they felt independent.[19] The result was that the most typical pioneers, who coped best with all the difficult requirements of the pioneer life, often did not put down strong roots in the society that was developing. They remained individuals who stood apart from the community, as is often the case with children who grow up alone. Some of them became completely alienated from the ways of the world. When the pioneering work is over and the demand for their special talents begins to decline; as the population increases and society begins to make all sorts of demands of them, they feel oppressed and suffocated. They were not afraid to brave the loneliness, danger, and discomfort of the wilderness, but they found it disagreeable to live in very close contact with their fellow man. This type of person was inclined to trek continually further into the interior as civilization came nearer and to flee, as it were, from civilization. When he was asked why he trekked, he gave an evasive answer such as, "Sir, I could stand it no longer—the world had begun to press in on me too much." To a question as to why his father moved away from a relatively new young district in the past, an old pioneer confided: "When the people began to increase, my father said, 'I am a nomadic, not a domesticated, creature.'"

There were undoubtedly very few pioneers who belonged to this class. But in different degrees all members of the pioneer community—as a result of the formative influence of the social milieu—stood relatively apart from the community and the environment. This did not give rise to the trek in a direct way, but it certainly made it easier for it to occur.[20]

ENDNOTES

[1] C 1422, Letters Disp., W.A. van der Stel to Patria, 14 March 1701, p. 71.

[2] J.L.M Franken, "Hendrik Bibault of Die Opkoms van 'n Volk," in *Die Huisgenoot*, 21 September 1928, pp. 9, 11,13.

[3] C 1283, Petitions, Reports, etc., Burgher Petition, Woeke, Bletterman, et al., 17 February 1784, p. 59; O.F. Mentzel, *Vollständige und Zuverläszige Geographische und topographische Beschreibung des Berühmten und in aller Betrachtung merkwürdigen Afrikanischen Vorgebirges des Guten Hoffnung* (Glogau, 1785, 1787), II:199; G.A. Robertson, *Notes on Africa – to which is added an appendix, containing a Compendius Account of the Cape of Good Hope, its Productions and Resources with a variety of important information very necessary to be known by persons about to emigrate to that Colony* (London, 1819), p. 382; N. Polson, *Subaltern's Sick Leave; or, Rough Notes on a visit in Search of Health to China and the Cape of Good Hope* (Calcutta, 1837), p. 80; W. von Meyer, *Reisen in Süd-Afrika wärend der Jahre 1840 und 1841* (Hamburg, 1843), p. 179..

[4] C 1283, Petitions, Reports, etc., Burgher Petition, Woeke, Bletterman, et al., 17 February 1784; Swellengrebel Family Archives, Hendrik Swellengrebel, Jr. to C. de Gyselaar, 26 June 1783.

[5] P.J. van der Merwe, *Die Trekboer in die Geskiedenis van die Kaapkolonie, 1657-1842* (Cape Town, 1938), pp. 195-6.

[6] 1/STB 13/2, Minutes of the Military Council, 23 April 1726.

[7] Van der Merwe, *Trekboer*, p. 198.

[8] C 2285, Original Ordinance Book, 16 June 1774, pp. 478-9.

[9] E.A. Walker, *The Frontier Tradition in South Africa* (London, 1930), p. 8.

[10] A. Wilmot and J.C. Chase, *History of the Colony of the Cape of Good Hope from Its Discovery to the Year 1819* (Cape Town, 1869), pp. 176-7; E.B. Watermeyer, *Three Lectures on the Cape of Good Hope under the Government of the Dutch East India Company* (Cape Town, 1857), pp. 52-3.

[11] C 1265, Petitions, Reports, etc., A.H. Krugel and twelve others to Governor van Plettenberg, Petition from Bruintjieshoogte, 10 November 1774, pp. 443-45.

[12] Journey of Governor van Plettenberg (1778), in George McCall Theal, *Belangrijke Historische Dokumenten over Zuid-Afrika* (Cape Town, 1896, 1911), I:12.

[13] AR, Colonial Accessions (1900), XX, Account of Governor Janssens's Journey (1803); J. Barrow, *Travels into the Interior of Southern Africa, 2nd ed.* (London, 1806), I:206; Pietronella Anna Catharina Wieringa, *De Oudste Boeren Republieken. Graaff-Reinet en Zwellendam van 1775 tot 1806* ('s-Gravenhage: Martinus Nijhoff, 1921), p. 50.

[14] P.J. van der Merwe, *Die Noordwaartse Beweging van die Boere voor die Groot Trek (1770-1842)* (The Hague, 1937), pp. 367-76.

[15] Van der Merwe, *Noordwaartse Beweging*. Pp. 337-75.

[16] Van der Merwe, *Trekboer*, pp. 195-224.

[17] George McCall Theal, *History of South Africa* (London: 1915), VI: 273.

[18] Swellengrebel Family Archives, Van Plettenberg to Swellengrebel, 7 March 1780; J.B.N. Theunissen, *Aantekeningen van een reis door de Binnenlanden van Zuid-Afrika van Port Elizabeth naar de Kaapstad gedaan in 1823* (Oostende, 1824), p. 48; R.W. Wilcocks, *Die Armblanke* (Stellenbosch, 1932), p. 37; J.F.W. Grosskopf, *Plattelandsverarming en Plaasverlating* (Stellenbosch, 1932), pp. 29, 48, 105; SRP 1/2/106, U.G. 49 of 1923, Final Report of the Drought Investigation Commission, Appendix 6, Report of Dr. Holloway, "The Origin of the Poor White Problem," pp. 208-09.

[19] H. Lichtenstein, *Reisen im südlichen Africa in den Jahren 1803, 1804, 1805 und 1806* (Berlin, 1811-1812), I:624; B.R. 286, Letters, Janssens to De Mist, 7 July 1803, pp. 353-4; Wilcocks, *Armblanke*, p. 37.

[20] The roll that the trek spirit played in connection with the trek into the interior will be discussed in the last chapter.

CHAPTER VII

Typical Features of The Expansion Process

1. Rapid Expansion

One of the most striking characteristics of the expansion process from the point of view of geographical mobility is the surprising tempo at which the territorial dispersion of the colonists occurred. It is a fact that the carrying capacity of the land, especially in pioneering conditions, did not allow a dense population, but this still does not fully explain the phenomenon. Long before the already occupied land had reached its full productive capacity, there were already people who migrated again farther and colonized new areas. Of course the colony had to expand as the population increased, but it is difficult to escape the notion that the expansion of the colony was out of all proportion to the increase in population.

Baron [Gustaaf] van Imhoff was already complaining about this rapid expansion in 1743. The most distant stock farmers at that time lived about 120 hours from Cape Town, "where perhaps half the land is still not cultivated, as could be done."[1] The following year the deputy landdrost of Swellendam found it impossible to send someone specially to the farmers who had migrated to the Gamtoos River with their livestock. They were well over twenty days' ride from the sub-drosdy, "and most of that time one passed no dwellings or people."[2]

In 1804 W.S. van Ryneveld expressed his views on the same phenomenon: "anyone who carefully observes the Colony at the Cape of Good Hope must be amazed at the extensiveness of the Colony and the smallness of its population. The size of the occupied land, or land taken into possession, is out of all proportion to the number of colonists, and there is surely no similar example of a colony with so few Inhabitants, so irregularly spread out."[3]

When one looks at land issuance documents in the nineteenth century in the deeds office, one finds that years after new districts were already occupied, crown land was still continually being distributed in the older districts.

2. Unorganized Trek

Another feature of the natural expansion of the colony was that it occurred in an entirely spontaneous and unorganized fashion. It did not take the form of organized migrations in which large numbers of pioneers trekked to new living areas in groups under recognized leaders. The expansion into the interior was, with few exceptions, led by individuals and households who trekked on their own and they stopped or settled where they wanted, without having much contact with other individual pioneers who trekked before or after them. This was not a matter of large areas in the interior being colonized systematically piece by piece. In this way the population stream flowed unobserved, little by little, like water running over uneven ground and following the easiest path. A new pioneer area was slowly populated, the world was tamed, its environs domesticated, and the primitive pioneer conditions faded, but the stream of expansion flowed on, and the same process was repeated farther on. Conditions that gradually disappeared in one pioneer area recurred in nearly the same form a little farther along.

3. Pathfinders

As the expansion into the interior advanced, the economic and social structure of each subsequent pioneer area typically went through the following stages more or less. Before permanent colonization took place, the area first received temporary visitors from inhabited areas. The first to come were farmers who came there to hunt or to barter livestock from the natives. During the first years of the eighteenth century hunters and cattle traders undertook large expeditions. They penetrated into the unknown interior for hundreds of miles and criss-crossed it from one side to the other. Later these large expeditions made way for hunting trips and trading expeditions on a smaller scale that were occasionally undertaken by only one or two people. These people were the pathfinders of civilization, who disseminated information about uninhabited areas to the populations of inhabited areas.

4. Periodic Migrations with Livestock

Along the wagon trails laid by the great expeditions came the trekboers in search of water and pasture for their livestock. They too came and went back again. In nearly every pioneer area the trekboer was the vanguard of the pioneers and preceded the permanent settlements with his periodic migrations with livestock.

Periodic migrations with livestock into the interior are as old as livestock farming itself.[4] It is clear from the Old Gamehunters Books that the farmers from the inhabited areas were occasionally already going into the interior looking for relief for their livestock since the beginning of the eighteenth century. The duration of the permits (three, four, six, or nine months) proves that we are dealing here with temporary migrations, which satisfied temporary needs. After the stock farmers settled permanently along outposts in the interior, the trek with livestock still continued. In the official documents of the eighteenth century one repeatedly finds suggestions that the inland farmers now and then moved into uninhabited areas with their livestock and even laid out pasture farms for grazing there.[5]

Since the beginning of the nineteenth century periodic migrations with livestock stand out as the most prominent forerunner of permanent colonization. In connection with the northward movement of the farmers before the Great Trek I have shown elsewhere in detail how uninhabited areas were first used as temporary pastures, before the first pioneers settled there.[6] The trek to the east during the eighteenth century as well as the expansion from the Sneeuberge to the Orange River during the first years of the nineteenth century happened so quickly that uninhabited areas over the border were never used as pastures for long. In the northwestern section of the Cape Colony, however, the period of using temporary pastures was very long and drawn out in the evolution of the pioneer areas. Here the farmers from the winter rainfall areas (Namaqualand, the Onder-Bokkeveld, the Hantam and the Roggeveld) for a century and even longer used the summer rainfall areas to the east and the north (Bushmanland, the Agterveld and the Sak River area) as periodical pastures, before the first pioneers settled there permanently.[7]

5. The First Pioneers

The first pioneers followed later along the wagon trails laid by the trekboers, and they came to stay. Frequently these pioneers were trekboers who had visited the area periodically in the past and in time decided to remain behind in the pasture lands there.

The highest percentage of the first wave of colonists in a new pioneer area generally came not from the older and more densely inhabited areas of the colony, but from the border districts. This phenomenon has recently been observed repeatedly in the areas of newer settlement. The first colonists who moved into the southern portion of Bechuanaland mostly came from adjoining areas. A high percentage of the colonists came from Griqualand West. Recently an elderly farmer, who had lived his entire life nearby Griquatown, told me: "As I ride through Betsjoeanaland, I know the farmers who I meet there. They are mostly farmers who lived here before, or children of Griqualanders." The pioneers who settled in Griqualand West before 1900 for the most part came from districts just south of the Orange, such as Prieska, Philipstown, Hopetown and Hanover, although there were also a good many farmers from the Roggeveld and a handful of Namaqualanders among them. The first pioneers of Bushmanland were also usually farmers who came from adjoining areas such as Namaqualand, the Onder-Bokkeveld, the Hantam, Fraserburg, Carnarvon and Prieska.

Among the first settlers in new areas, however, there usually was also a small percentage of people from older, more distant districts. So, for example, among the pioneers of Mierland (in Gordonia) there were a few people who came from far away. Spangenberg was born in Malmesbury and moved into the area from there after he had undertaken a couple of trading expeditions into the area north of the Orange. The Rautenbachs came from Humansdorp, although they first lived for a long time in Kimberley before they trekked to Mierland. Le Riche was born near Simonstown and arrived in Mierland via the Free State. The vast majority of the pioneers of Gordonia, however, were people from the Northwest.[8]

This phenomenon could also be observed in the nineteenth century.[9] Dr. [John] Philip at that time used an attractive image to illustrate the migration to uninhabited areas: "(Nor is this practice) confined to those on the Colonial boundary. Like the breaking out of water, although that nearest the break runs out first, that behind, even to the extremity of the dam, soon follows. Allured by the prospects of an estate in the new territory, such as have interest with those that have it in their gift soon swell the tide of emigration, and others who are poor sell their estates to their next neighbours who want them for their sons and daughters, and with the price they receive stock their new farms."[10]

In connection with the natural expansion of the colony during the first half of the nineteenth century we coincidentally have a few statistics that nicely illuminate this phenomenon. There is a list signed by 108 farmers in 1842 who at that time lived along the Riet and the Kaffer rivers in Transorangia. Their colonial origins are recorded on the list. The vast majority of the farmers (78) came from the district of Colesberg, just south of the Orange. Sixteen came from the district of Graaff-Reinet and eight from Beaufort West. Furthermore, there were two farmers from Worcester, two from George and one from Paarl.[11]

It is easy to understand why the frontier farmers and their children were the first to settle down in new pioneer areas. They were the most familiar with the area and its potential. They did not have to travel far to get there. They were accustomed to pioneer life and the dangers and hardships that accompanied it. Another contributing factor was the fact that treks to uninhabited areas for the frontier farmers, whose living standards were already low, did not entail such a great lowering of living standards as it would have for farmers from older districts.

6. Unfavorable Economic Selection

During the first stages of its development a pioneer district usually did not place high demands on the industriousness and economic competence of its population. The pioneers had to have great courage and powers of endurance, but it was comparatively easy to make an independent living for all classes of society. Farmers with little livestock could supplement their income through hunting. Farmers without land could be assisted on crown land or by land owners for nothing. Land owners had plenty of grazing land and could farm extensively.

Over time, however, living conditions begin to change. The numbers of wild game quickly diminished, resulting in a decline in income from hunting. There was less free land as more farms were allocated, making it much more difficult for squatters and nomadic stock farmers to make a living on crown land. Even the land owners soon began increasingly to feel the pressure from the growing population density, which made them all the more unwilling to help the sharecroppers. Seasonal trek pasture had diminished, farms had become smaller, and the quality of grazing land had deteriorated. In these conditions land owners who wanted to farm in the old way soon found it difficult to keep their heads above water.

A certain portion of the pioneer population adapted successfully to the changed conditions and made economic progress. As the economic importance of the hunt declined, most of the hunters concentrated more on farming. Some of the nomadic stock farmers and sharecroppers, who had meanwhile built up quite robust farms, became land owners. Many land owners improved their farms or bought additional land and managed increasingly to farm successfully without seasonal trek pasture.

Those who were unable or unwilling to adapt to the changing living conditions became impoverished or were obliged to trek to new pioneer areas where the more carefree spirit of the good old times still prevailed. The seasoned hunters followed the wild game into the interior. The farmers who possessed no land trekked into areas where there was still free land, or where they could feed their livestock more easily on another man's land. Some land owners sold their farms and trekked to areas where there was more space and inexpensive ground still to be had.

7. Different Waves of Pioneers

So, as time passed, each pioneer district shook off a portion of its original settlers. But it never happened that such an area ever became "migrant-free." As quickly as the lower-income and less capable economic classes moved away, "because the world began to close in" on them and land was too "expensive," farmers from older districts trekked there on account of the "space" and "inexpensive" land. They were able to pay prices for the land that the original settlers were not able to resist, perhaps because in the older districts from where they came, they had sold their land "dearly," or because more progressive farming methods had been introduced.

This process was not completed in one big push. Even the second, third, or fourth owners of farms in the pioneer area later often trekked farther into the interior. They had perhaps exhausted their farms and began afresh further on, or they were able to sell their farms at a profit because of the constant rise in land prices and purchase a larger plot of land up ahead. And as the possibilities for farming in the region became evident, the area became domesticated, and social and economic conditions improved, people continually trekked in from behind to take the place of those who had left. This meant that it sometimes took years before such a pioneer district got a more or less permanent population.

The expansion into the interior thus did not assume the form of a surplus population from inhabited areas trekking into the interior, while the established population remained where they were. Over and over again, whenever the migratory stream began to flow into the interior, members of the already established society were torn away and were carried along with it. The expansion process also did not just assume the form of a migration out of the inhabited areas and into the uninhabited areas. There was an accompanying migration from areas of older settlement to areas of newer settlement. The farmers in areas of newer settlement settled in the uninhabited regions, but farmers from the older districts usually did not trek all the way to the outer limits of settlement. They also wanted to have abundant and inexpensive ground, but they did not want to have totally uncultivated land (even if water had only just been found), and they did not want to trek to the ends of the earth. They were thus entirely at ease with the prospects that areas of newer settlement offered.

The pioneers who took part in the expansion also did not always trek just once and have done with it. Just as different waves of pioneers passed over a pioneer area before it was finally colonized, many of the old pioneers packed up and trekked several times before they settled down for good. In 1826 Andries Stockenström, wrote the following in connection with the gradual expansion into the interior: "The encroachments on the aborigines began at Cape Town, and never ceased to extend by degrees until the Colonists had got to where they now are; as the leading adventurers advanced, their countrymen followed and as a tract of country became what they called 'full,' the more enterprizing again set forward and were followed as before."[12]

The forces behind the expansion can be compared with a stream that flowed into the interior. It continually dislodged objects in its path, picked them up, carried them a distance and then set them down again. At the same time it now and then—sometimes repeatedly—wrenched out deeply rooted trees, dragged them along in the same way, and then left them lying again somewhere along the path.

ENDNOTES

[1] C 2357, Instructions of Van Imhoff, 1743, p. 29.

[2] 1/STB 19/165, Overberg Affairs: Minutes of Landdrost and Heemraad meeting, Swellendam, 27 October 1744.

[3] B.R. 406, W.S. van Ryneveld, Improvement of the Livestock, 16 April 1804, p. 1. See also, A. Steedman, *Wanderings and Adventures in the Interior of Southern Africa* (London, 1835), I:105; J. Howison, *European Colonies in Various parts of the World* (London, 1834), I:202-03; J. Barrow, *Travels into the Interior of Southern Africa*, 2nd ed. (London, 1806), II: 295; J.F.W. Grosskopf, *Plattelandsverarming en Plaasverlating* (Stellenbosch, 1932), p. 31.

[4] A. Bogaerts, *Historische Reizen door d'Oostersche Deelen van Azie* (Amsterdam, 1711), p. 569; P.J. van der Merwe, *Die Trekboer in die Geskiedenis van die Kaapkolonie, 1657-1842* (Cape Town, 1938), p. 53; P. Kolbe, *Nauwkeurige en Uitvoerigne Beschrijving van de Kaap de Goede Hoop* (Amsterdam, 1726), I:130.

[5] 1/STB 20/2, Letters Rec., Landdrost Faber to Tulbagh, 7 February 1770, enclosed with Faber, Mintz, et al to Tulbagh, 17 February 1770; C 2285, Original Ordinance Book, 26 April 1770; P.J. van der Merwe, *Die Kafferoorlog van 1793* (Cape Town, 1940), pp. 14-15.

[6] P.J. van der Merwe, *The Noordwaartse Beweging van die Boere voor die Groot Trek (1770-1842)* (The Hague, 1937), pp. 205-07, 219-23, 279-91, 336, 344-458.

[7] I will return to this subject in later chapters.

[8] P.J. van der Merwe, *Pioniers van die Dorsland* (Cape Town, 1941), pp. 99-113.

[9] J.W.D. Moodie, *Ten Years in Southern Africa* (London, 1835), II:28.

[10] Cited by W.M. Macmillan, *Bantu, Boer, and Briton* (London, 1929), p. 25.

[11] G.H. 8/10, Dispatches rec., Annexure to J. Hare to Napier, 28 September 1842, pp. 536-539. [Trans. note: On the cover letter by Joubert to this list it says "signed by 107 persons." At the end of the list is written, "Total 109 Signatures." I (RBB) counted 108 signatures—108 is correct.]

[12] 1/GR 16/16, Letters Disp., Stockenström to Commissioners of Inquiry, 9 August 1826 (No. 4359).

CHAPTER VIII

Change of Residence Among Landowners

1. Statement of the Phenomenon

In the mother countries of Europe, from where our ancestors came, the farming population is very sedentary. It is common for a farmer to spend his entire life on the land on which he began to farm. Furthermore, after the farmer's death, the ownership of the land usually passes to one of his children, so that farms often remain for generations in the possession of the same family. There are also exceptions to this in practice, of course, but long-term occupation of land by individuals and families is a normal occurrence in countries like the Netherlands and Germany.

In the Cape Colony one finds the opposite phenomenon during the pioneer period. There was no such thing as being rooted in one place. Not only landless sharecroppers and other farmers, but landowners as well, displayed a remarkably strong tendency to change residences repeatedly. There were few farmers who died on the first farms they had ever owned, especially in areas of newer settlement. Even today our farming population is not quite as solidly rooted in the land as are the farmers of Europe.

The phenomenon of landowners wandering about a great deal during the period of Company rule is clearly evident from the Old Gamehunters Books, in which the old loan farm ordinances are registered. In the eighteenth century it was an exception if a loan farm occupier remained living at the same place for twenty or thirty years. In the great majority of cases ordinance holders repeatedly trekked from one farm to another. Often the ordinance holder simply abandoned the farmstead if he could not sell it.

It is very difficult, and in many cases altogether impossible, to track the history of a specific farm over a long period of time in the Old Gamehunters Books. It often happened that the same farm was held in loan under different names by a succession of ordinance holders. It also seems that different farms had the same name, so that one is not always certain with which farm one is dealing, except naturally when the previous occupier of the farm is mentioned incidentally in the license. Furthermore, all sorts of irregularities occurred in the registration of loan farms. Farms were often occupied without having been properly registered by ordinance, or after they had already been discarded. On the other hand, it also happened that farms were taken in loan, but never occupied, and then abandoned without first legally relinquishing rights to the land.

Similar difficulties make it impossible to provide an accurate, quantitative representation of the degree of mobility of loan farm occupants. One can only illustrate the phenomenon with examples. The following examples show how often the loan farms concerned changed occupants, in so far as this can be determined from the Old Gamehunters Books:

1. BACKELEY FARM (on the Olifants River)

Ordinance Holder	Previous Owner	Date of the ordinance	Date upon which the farm was let	Source
J. A. Meyer	?	09.12.1750	02.04.1756	S.G. 12, p. 419
J. Koekemoer, sr.	J.A. Meyer	12.04.1756	10.03.1762	S.G. 14, p. 325
J. Koekemoer, sr	J. Koekemoer, sr	04.11.1762	before 24.10.1776	S.G. 17. p. 263
G. van Zyl, P.sn.[1]	J. Koekemoer	24.10.1776	19.12.1780	S.G. 24. p. 413
J. Joubert, J.sn.	G. van Zyl	19.12.1780	13.12.1785	S.G. 27, p. 343
P. van Zyl, P.sn.	J. Joubert	13.12.1785	?	S.G. 34, p. 249

2. BIDOUW (across Olifants River):

Ordinance Holder	Previous Owner	Date of the ordinance	Date upon which the farm was let	Source
L. v. d. Byl	?	25.11.1750	23.11.1753	S.G. 12, p. 397
J. Louw, J. Sn	L. v.d. Byl	08.10.1755	30.09.1757	S.G. 14, p. 199
H. Engelbrecht	J. Louw, J.sn.	13.03.1759	13.03.1761	S.G. 15, p. 303(B)
C. v. d. Westhuizen	H. Engelbrecht	13.03.1761	before 29.03.1782	S.G. 16, p. 287

3. RIETFONTEIN (behind Piketberg):

Ordinance Holder	Previous Owner	Date of the ordinance	Date upon which the farm was let	Source
Andries Grove	?	27.02.1731	19.11.1732	S.G. 09, p. 317
C. H. Hardmansdorf and G. van Wyk	Andries Grove	15.11.1732	17.06.1735	S.G. 09, p. 747(a)
		21.01.1733	17.06.1735	S.G. 09, p. 785
S. ten Holder	C.H. Hardmansdorf	19.11.1735	20.02.1762	S.G. 98, p. 387
J. Spengelaar	Widow S. ten Holder	25.11.1762	13.12.1764	S.G. 17, p. 287
O. Mostert	J. Spengelaar	13.12.1764	17.03.1766	S.G. 18, p. 435
W. Eens	O. Mostert	11.02.1772	11.09.1777	S.G. 22, p. 81
P. Jourdaan, P.sn.	W. Eens	11.09.1777	01.08.1780	S.G. 25, p. 231
D. Jourdaan, L.sn.	P. Jourdaan, P.sn.	20.03.1780	08.07.1789	S.G. 27, p. 113
H. N Kotzé	D. Jourdaan, L.sn	08.07.1789	?	S.G. 36, p. 245

[1]Trans. note: These abbreviations — "P.sn." "J.sn." — refer to this person being someone's son (Afrikaans, *seun*). Thus G. van Zyl is the son of "P," which might be "Pieter." "J" might be Johannes.

4. BACKLEY FARM (along the Buffelsjagt River):

Ordinance Holder	Previous Owner	Date of the ordinance	Date upon which the farm was let	Source
T. Botha	?	02.07.1731	10.01.1749	S.G. 09, p. 459
J. Potgieter	Widow T. Botha	10.01.1749	19.04.1758	S.G. 12, p. 161
J.A. de Necker	J. Potgieter	19.04.1758	04.12.1764	S.G. 15, p. 199
L. de Jager	J.A. de Necker	04.12.1764	10.12.1766	S.G. 18, p. 425
J.A. Horak	L. de Jager	10.12.1766	22.07.1776	S.G. 19, p. 327
E.F. du Toit	J.A. Horak	27.04.1779	08.02.1786	S.G. 26, p. 151
A. Louw	E.F. du Toit	08.02.1786	?	S.G. 34, p. 287

5. GROENE VALLEY (BEHIND PIKETBERG):

Ordinance Holder	Previous Owner	Date of the ordinance	Date upon which the farm was let	Source
N. Blommert		19.10.1730	21.10.1740	S.G. 09, p. 87
J. Gildenhuyzen	N. Blommert	18.10.1740	20.09.1762	S.G. 10, p. 253
Widow J.A. Meyer	J. Gildenhuyzen	09.05.1764	07.02 1767	S.G. 18, p. 257
J. Carnspek	Widow J.A. Meyer	31.03.1767	17.12.1778	S.G. 19, p. 407
J.F. Kock	J. Carnspek	10.12.1778	11.03.1780	S.G. 26, p. 09
P.J. Moller	J.F. Kock	11.3.1780	Paid to 24.05.1786	S.G. 27, p. 99

6. KRUYSPAD (OTHER SIDE OF COGMANSKLOOF):

Ordinance Holder	Previous Owner	Date of the ordinance	Date upon which the farm was let	Source
Hendrik Schoeman		11.11.1745	03.01.1757	S.G. 11, p. 215
J. van Rhenen	Hendrik Schoeman	17.10.1758	15.12.1761	S.G. 15, p. 271
F.W. Botha	J. van Rhenen	15.12.1761	24.01.1766	S.G. 16, p. 433
J.van Zyl	F.W. Botha	24.01.1766	Paid to 24.11.1786	S.G. 19, p. 175

7. KRUYSRIVIER (BY PIKETBERG):

Ordinance Holder	Previous Owner	Date of the ordinance	Date upon which the farm was let	Source
N. Brommert	?	21.02.1731	23.09.1744	S.G. 09, p. 313
Frans Cruger	N. Blommert	23.09.1744	22.09.1745	S.G. 11, p. 79
J. v.d. Wey		10.02.1750	03.05.1756	S.G. 12, p. 295
J.M. Scheffers	J. v.d. Wey	19.05.1758	08.05.1759	S.G. 15, p. 217
J. Gildenhuyzen	J.M. Scheffers	24.11.1759	Paid to 09.05.1764	S.G. 15, p. 467
Widow J.A. Meyer	J. Gildenhuyzen	09.05.1764	01.12.1767	S.G. 18, p. 277
N. Laubscher	Widow J.A. Meyer	01.12.1767	07.12.1771	S.G. 18, p. 277
J. Koekemoer	N. Laubscher	31.07.1772	21.10.1780	S.G. 22, p. 223
H. Smit	J. Koekemoer	21.10.1780	25.09.1787	S.G. 27, p. 291
E.J. Laubscher	H. Smit	25.09.1787	Paid to 26.04.1792	S.G. 35, p. 351

8. DRIEVADERLANDSCHERIETVALLEY (ROGGELVELD):

Ordinance Holder	Previous Owner	Date of the ordinance	Date upon which the farm was let	Source
P.E. Kruger		25.02.1756	12.04.1757	S.G. 14, p. 279
J.F. Kruger	P.E. Kruger	29.01.1761	01.04.1767	S.G. 16, p. 235
F. Brand	J.F. Kruger	16.01.1769	11.01.1771	S.G. 20, p. 259
G. van Schalkwyk	F. Brand	13.06.1781	08.06.1782	S.G. 28, p. 109
G.D. Fiktor	G. van Schalkwyk	15.11. 1785	Paid to 07.02.1791	S.G. 34, p. 203

9. HENDRIK VAN DER WALTS GAT (ON OLIFANTS RIVER)

Ordinance Holder	Previous Owner	Date of the ordinance	Date upon which the farm was let	Source
J. Koekemoer	?	14.11.1730	22.10.1750	S.G. 09, p. 129
M. Mouton	J. Koekemoer	22.10.1750	14.11.1761	S.G. 12, p. 385
J. Visagie	M. Mouton	14.11.1761	19.11.1779	S.G. 16, p. 413
J. Liebenberg	L. Visagie	19.11.1779	16.01.1787	S.G. 26, p. 295
J. van Schoor	J. Liebenberg	04.04.1787	Extended on 30.7.1790	S.G. 35, p. 243

In the cases dealt with above more than half of the farms concerned remained in the possession of the same person from only one to five years. Only about twenty percent of the farms were held by the same person for ten years or longer. The average duration of the ordinance, in cases where it could be calculated precisely, was about six years. In choosing the examples, which easily could be multiplied, no special search was made for farms that had a frequent change of occupants. The most important objective was to find farms whose histories could be traced over a long period of time in the Old Gamehunters Books.

The rapidity with which farms changed occupants is not an altogether accurate indication of the degree of mobility manifested by the loan farm occupant. The occupant would not have trekked every time he sold a farm or given up ownership to it. Occasionally his widow or children abandoned the farm at this death. Sometimes a farmer possessed several farms and then discarded or sold one of more of them that he had never occupied. The termination of an ordinance, therefore, did not go hand in hand every time with a change of residence.

If one made a study of the names of people who appear in the Old Gamehunters books, this would also furnish evidence for the phenomenon that some farmers repeatedly changed residences. This type of investigation, however, raises certain difficulties as well. If you come across the same name in the Old Gamehunters Books repeatedly, you cannot always assume with certainty that you are dealing with the same person. Furthermore, one must also take into consideration that a farmer who owned more than one farm, did not necessarily move every time he sold a farm. The following examples must be examined in light of these observations. They indicate the loan farms that the persons concerned had in their names:

1. GOERT GROBBELAAR:

Name of Farm	Date of Issue	Expiration of ordinance	Source
Middelburg behind Hex River	10.06.1755	06.03.1756	S.G. 14, p. 189
Kwartelfontein over Hex River	03.09.1756	01.03.1760	S.G. 14, pp. 379-80
Postrivier in Houteniquasland	31.01.1760	23.01.1762	S.G. 15, p. 511
De Fontein over the Thou	01.12.1761	21.03.1775	S.G. 16, pp. 425-26
Camnasieloop (Mouth of the Doren River)	15.01.1772	16.04.1773	S.G. 22, p. 53
Allemansfontein (West of Bruintjieshoogte)	09.06.1775	10.12.1786	S.G. 24, p. 27
Bosheuvel (West of Bruintjieshoogte)	08.04.1779	02.11.1787	S.G. 26, p. 125
Blyde River (over the Camdebo)	12.11.1786	Before 08.10.1789	S.G. 35, p. 163
Niegennamd (along Swarthey)	24.02.1787	05.09.17(??)	S.G. 35, p. 207

2. JAN ALBERT VENTER:

Name of Farm	Date of Issue	Expiration of ordinance	Source
Eselsfontein (Roggeveld)	03.05.1768	22.11.1769	S .G. 20, p. 95
Kruisrivier (Roggeveld)	30.07.1768	24.10.1769	S.G. 20, p. 129
Ossefontein (on Sneeuberg)	29.10.1773	± 1782	S.G. 23, p. 73
De Rust (on Sneeuberg)	25.03.1772	?	S.G. 22, p. 149
Plattedrift (on Swart River)	25.01.1777	01.03.1782	S.G. 25, p. 55
Baviaanskrans (on Sondags River)	19.12.1782	22.02.1787	S.G. 29, p. 159
Eylandsfontein (on Sondags River)	22.09.1783	22.02.1787	S.G. 30, p. 201
Hooningskrans (on Groot Brak River)	04.09.1787	?	S.G. 35, p. 329

3. ALBERT VAN JAARSVELD:

Name of Farm	Date of Issue	Expiration of ordinance	Source
De Uytkomst (near Camdebo)	09.11.1775	03.11.1780	S.G. 24, p. 105
De Vondeling (behind Swartberg)	10.11.1780	16.11.1786	S.G. 27, p. 311
De Eensaamheid (near Camdebosberg)	02. 07.1773	15.01.1781	S.G. 22, p. 417
De Overschot (over Zondags River)	26.11.1773	04.10.1780	S.G. 23, p. 95
Hogas (behind Swartberg)	14.11.1786	12.10.1792(?)	S.G. 27, p. 313
De Rietkuil (Koup)	03.04.1782	12.10.1791	S.G. 28, p. 303
De Gunsteling (behind Sneeuberg)	19.03.1788	?	S.G. 36, p. 57

4. W. BOTHA (F.sn.)

Name of Farm	Date of Issue	Expiration of ordinance	Source
Welgevonde (behind Cogmanskloof)	22.01.1766	14.03.1774	S.G. 19, p. 173
Klyfontein (Swartruggens)	23.03.1781	26.09.1789	S.G. 28, p. 65
Gelegen on Little Fish River	30.12.1783	14.01.1785	S.G. 31, p. 109
Sak la Pontskraal (Great Fish River)	14.01.1785	10.04.1790	S.G. 33, p. 117B
Rietfontein (Great Fish River)	03.04.1790	?	S.G. 36, p. 411

5. ANDRIES VAN DER WALT:

Name of Farm	Date of Issue	Expiration of ordinance	Source
Eendekuil (Roggeveld)	07.01.1766	18.04.1769	S.G. 19, p. 163
Elandsberg	07.01.1766	18.04.1769	S.G. 19, p. 161
Uitkyk on Sneeuberg	11.07.1770	04.11.1782	S.G. 21, p. 71
Blauwkrans (behind Sneeuberg)	01.04.1774	11.10.1787	S.G. 23, p. 177

In the cases dealt with above the average duration of the ordinances was coincidentally around six years as well. It is not evident from the ordinances precisely how many times the persons concerned trekked, but in most cases it is clear that a change of residence must also have occurred. Coert Grobbelaar, for example, had to have lived on at least five different farms between 1755 and 1787 Albert van Jaarsveld, W. Botha, and Andries van der Walt each had to have possessed consecutively at least three different farms.

The phenomenon of land frequently passing from one occupant to another is not limited to loan farms. At the beginning of the nineteenth century [John] Barrow wrote: "There are, perhaps, few countries where property so frequently changes hands as at the Cape of Good Hope. Not only do estates go out of a family at the death of the parents, when they are sure to be sold in order to make a division of the property among the children, but there seems to be a universal propensity to buy, sell and exchange. Of this the Government has taken the advantage, and imposed a duty of 4 per cent on all immovable property that is transferred from one person to another. Two-thirds of the property, disposed of at the Cape, is by public auction, on which the vendue master charges 2 per cent, 1¾ per cent goes to the Government and ¼ per cent for himself; so that the duty on transferring an estate amounts to 6 per cent upon the value. In fifteen sales, therefore, by adding the expense of stamps and writings, Government runs away with the whole capital; and I have been informed, there are instances, within the memory of many persons, of estates being sold this number of times. I myself purchased a small estate that, within the last eight years, has changed hands six times; paying thrice a duty to Government of 6 per cent, and thrice of 4 per cent, making a tax of 30 per cent. on the value of the property. It may be observed that this rage for buying and selling makes the transfer and the public vendue duties two of the most productive branches of the public revenue."[1]

Research in the Deeds Office in Cape Town reveals that farmland, even after the introduction of the perpetual quitrent system at the beginning of the nineteenth century, still changed owners surprisingly often. A number of examples can be found of farms that changed owners six or seven times within a half century. If a person pages through the transfer books for any year, one is struck by the number of farms that were transferred again within ten years after the previous transfer.

Most of us who know the rural areas will have observed this phenomenon personally. The farm upon which I passed my early childhood changed owners seven times between 1906 and 1929. An adjoining farm, which was allocated in 1884, has had not less than eleven owners up to the present (1943). Many of the other farms in the region where I grew up changed owners one or more times during the past 25 years.

My personal experience is not exceptional. In most districts of newer settlement that were investigated in connection with this research, one can observe the same phenomenon. Many of the old inhabitants in different parts of the Northwest were asked: "How many of the farms in the region are still in the possession of the persons (or families) who lived on them when you were a child?" In most cases the answer was: "Very few." Many of the farms already had their second, third or fourth owners. In nearly every district one can find farms that have been in the possession of the same family for many years, sometimes for generations, but usually this is the exception and you are informed about it as a very noteworthy fact. All over the Cape one meets landowners who have owned and occupied three, four or more other farms previously. I am thinking incidentally just now about an old pioneer (born in 1850) whom I knew as a child, who, before he was sixty years old, had bought and sold farms ten times. He never owned more than one farm at a time, and in between he also farmed leased land several times.

Here and there, however, one comes across in smaller or larger areas, exceptions to the rule. In Namaqualand there are many farms in the possession of old settled families who hold on tightly to their land. It seldom happens that a farm comes onto the market. A family farm was a sacred heritage that must not be sold. Land speculation among farmers is almost unknown. In this region there are also a remarkable number of old farms that have been in the possession of the same family for generations. This was the state of affairs everywhere in Namaqualand until the discovery of diamonds along the west coast led to a general disruption in the Sandveld, which also had a remarkable effect in other parts of Namaqualand. Furthermore, increasing poverty has recently forced people to surrender their family land, which in the old days—inhabitants assured me—was unheard of.

2. Difficulties in Connection with Colonization

To form an accurate idea of the causes for the change of residence by landowners, one would have to know the reasons that led landowners, in every individual case, to decide to trek. That information is not available to us. The most that is possible is to indicate a few general factors that are connected with the phenomenon.

In many cases farmers left their farms because they had to struggle with serious difficulties over which they had no control. In this connection the chronic insecurity of life and property in the border districts during the pioneer period was of great importance. Until the nineteenth century, farmers along the entire northern frontier had to fight with the Bushmen, who stole their livestock (or stabbed them to death in heaps), murdered their herders, and sometimes even burned down their houses. Under these conditions farmers were not able to live on their farms with peace of mind. Mainly between 1770 and 1810 it appears that farmers were repeatedly driven from their farms by the Bushmen or abandoned their farms out of fear of the Bushmen.[2]

Similar conditions prevailed on the eastern frontier as a result of repeated Xhosa attacks. The facts are well-known. I cite just one letter, from which the reader can form an impression of the influence that the Xhosa attacks had on the mobility of the pioneer population. In 1803 Governor [Jan Willem] Janssens wrote to commissioner-general [Jacob] De Mist: "I wish to give you an impression of this currently unfortunate land: everywhere farms are burned down and abandoned; the inhabitants roaming from one place to another, as the cultivation of their little piece of land or the grazing of their livestock necessitates this. They already seem to be used to this, and it is for them and for the government, a great vexation; one no longer asks here: where does so and so live? but: where is so and so currently staying over? Is that group of people still sojourning here or there?"[3]

The pioneers who trekked into the dry parts of the Cape Colony, attracted by cheap land, often struggled a great deal to get water. Some lost heart before they could procure a satisfactory amount of water, and they decided to move to land that was better supplied with water. Others ran out of money before they got water and went bankrupt on the land for this reason.

Disasters for which the people were not responsible likewise often obliged the pioneers to leave their homesteads. It is a well-known fact that droughts have already ruined many farmers in the Cape and driven them from their farms. Livestock diseases (such as the rinderpest, wireworm, etc.) have forced many of them out of farming as well. Finally, it can be demonstrated that many farmers lost their land as a result of financial difficulties. The causes for this were occasionally of a personal nature, but the precariousness of farming contributed greatly to this as well. Often farmers took on heavier debts than they could carry for the sake of improvements to their land or in order to expand their farms, and in this way ran into difficulties.

3. Voluntary Moves

In cases where farmers voluntarily changed residences, this was usually done with the possibility, or supposed possibility, of making a change for the better. A farmer often left his home and trekked because he could obtain a better farm: a farm that had better grazing land, was healthier to live on, received more rain, had a better water supply, had more arable land, or perhaps was nearer to the market or to the railway line. Often a farmer wanted to enlarge his land, but he could not purchase additional land in the immediate vicinity of his farm and purchased more land elsewhere then. Occasionally a move was the result of more personal causes that were not related to farming. The farmer trekked, for example, to be nearer to his family or friends, or for the sake of his health or that of one of his family members. All such causes sometimes impel farmers today to move. One can therefore presume that during the pioneer period this would have been the case as well.

4. Lack of Attachment to the Land

An important cause for the change of residence by landowners must be sought undoubtedly in the spiritual attitude of the colonists toward the land that they occupied. Attachment to the land, which in the motherlands from which our ancestors came was so strongly developed, was almost non-existent among the pioneers of the Cape Colony. The Afrikaans colonist did not feel as strong a sentimental devotion as his ancestors did in Europe for the region in which he grew up, for the place where his cradle stood, and where the graves of his loved ones lay. Many foreigners from overseas who visited our country remarked on this.

"There is in the Colony," [William] Bird wrote in 1822, "none of that strong innate feeling of regard for a native spot, which obtains in England; no attachment to the place, where the years of boyhood were played away. Such a sensation could not be understood or felt by a Cape-Dutchman. So much land, of such a quality, will produce so much corn; so much veldt, or field, will feed so many oxen, cows and horses; no matter where."[4]

Around the same time another writer said with reference to the Cape colonists: "They have no local attachments; there is no pride of ancestry, no traditionary legends, no improvements in building or planting, to endear them to the spot of their nativity; so that it is commonly said, and I believe with truth, that a Dutchman will sell anything, his wife not excepted."[5]

Despite the exaggeration and the lack of sympathetic understanding, both these quotations emphasize the materialistic relationship of the colonists with the soil, as well as the typical lack of appreciation of irrational and traditional values that one usually finds in a young country. During the pioneer period land for the average colonist evidently had value or worth only as a factor of production. Even today for many of our farmers land still has no other value than that which can be expressed in terms of money. They will sell the land on which they live and then move, just as easily as they would trade in an old motor car for a new one. This phenomenon, which is often found among our farmers – that at an advanced age they say farewell to their homestead and spend their last years in town – is also an indication of limited attachment to the land.[6] Finally, in South Africa one is also often astonished at how easily children sell inherited land, as if it were a common commodity.

Nineteenth-century officials, who were usually not very up to date on farming conditions, often sought the cause for the limited attachment to the land in the temporary nature of the rental regulations under the loan farm system, which made for uncertainty of ownership.[7]

One of the sharpest critics of this system of land ownership was J.A. de Mist. He alleged that "the Inhabitants are not attached to a piece of land which they do not own, and which they cannot leave to their children as a freehold, with all rights to it, and they are therefore often deterred from making any possible improvements to lands when they know not whether it will be taken from them or their children again."[8]

Elsewhere the Commissioner-General states: "It is unthinkable that one will ever see improvement of land, of which the user, tenant, or leaseholder is not sure in one degree or another that he or his children will one day enjoy the fruits of his improvements. We should abandon then, in my humble opinion, that harmful practice of giving out the lands under all kinds of unintelligible titles, for a short time as a loan. In this one point the titles all agree, that they are all precarious, and do not instill in the user that respect and affection for the land, which he does not own—which he may never split up or divide between his children—and which can be taken away from him every day. He is therefore not interested in improving it, but only in getting everything out of it, and then abandoning it, and asking for a new place."[9]

The thinking of De Mist and other contemporaries of his was in short that: uncertainty of ownership under the loan farm system made the farmers less attached to the land; it also stood in the way of cultivation of the land, which would otherwise increase as a result of attachment to the soil. Theal was also of the opinion that the loan farm system was responsible for the Cape colonists having lost their attachment to their places of birth.[10] Dr. [Johannes] Grosskopf expressed the opinion that, "under this system attachment to the land becomes weaker, and people move away more easily, especially where livestock farming was the principal preoccupation."[11]

I cannot agree with this point of view. In the first place it is based on an error. Land ownership under the loan farm system was not quite as insecure as it is sometimes made out to be. Ordinance holders could count on the fact that the government would not bother them in the undisturbed use of their land without well-founded reasons and satisfactory compensation. Despite their true situation, which the farmers usually did not understand, in practice they themselves felt no insecurity about the possession of their farms. The farmers in De Mist's time did not have any doubt about the permanency of their ordinances. The theoretically temporary nature of the rental regulations under the loan farm system could therefore not have made the farmers hesitant to improve their farms through the employment of capital and labor. And indeed, it also made no difference to the cultivation and tillage of the land.[12]

Apart from these points, supporters of De Mist's standpoint must demonstrate that attachment to the land increased after the perpetual quitrent system replaced the loan farm system at the beginning of the nineteenth century. That will be very difficult. Even if one could establish that farms in the nineteenth century did not change owners as often as in the eighteenth century, you still must prove that this resulted from the change in the system of land ownership.

The lack of attachment to the land is sometimes related to the fact that in the old days the family farm usually passed into the hands of strangers at the death of the parents: "Loan places could not be divided among heirs. According to the law of the Colony, all the children shared equally in the inheritance of a dead parent, consequently when a man died, his farm—if a loan place—was necessarily sold, in order that the proceeds might be distributed. This system prevented the growth of that attachment to the soil which arises from long residence...."[13]

Land that was distributed under the perpetual quitrent system could in fact be divided among the heirs, and this did indeed often happen. A similar division among heirs was impractical, however, in the case of large families. There was naturally nothing that prevented one of the children from purchasing the family farm and buying out the others. But, as [George] Thompson correctly shows, farming families were generally large and the share of the inheritance that each child received was consequently very small. By the time the estate was divided, the older sons usually already owned land, and not one of the younger children perhaps had enough capital available to buy out the others.[14] And understandably a younger son would not be eager to go into debt in order to obtain a farm. In the old days, when crown land was still available on such easy terms, there was too little economic motive for doing so.

The fact that during the pioneer period land passed into strange hands so often at the death of the parents actually had important consequences. The farm came into the possession of people for whom it represented nothing more than a residence and a certain number of morgen of land. The children of the former owner were obliged to settle on land for which they felt no sentimental connection. In this way circumstances arose that were unfavorable for the development of a feeling of sentimental attachment to the soil. At the same time, a chance for a family to be firmly rooted in the land was lost.

The influence of this factor, however, must not be overestimated, because it affected only a small percentage of the farming population. In a society where families were large and nearly every farmer's son followed his father's occupation, [15] a large percentage of the population in any case would have had to begin with farms where there was no family tradition or association with the past, although it also happened in every case that land passed into the possession of one of the children at the death of the parents.

Limited attachment to the land is not a specifically South African phenomenon. It is something that is found in all young countries. In this connection one can accordingly refer to the findings of Wilhelm Roscher and Robert Jannasch, who have made a special study of colonial problems. "All colonists," they write, "lack the ancient traditions, family ties, etc., which otherwise probably tie man to the soil. The land is not regarded by them as the mother of men, the hearth of the gods, the grave of the fathers, but only as a tool of enrichment."[16]

In this respect one finds many striking similarities between our pioneer history and that of the United States. Lack of attachment to the land and the constant change of residence that went hand in hand with it were among the most notable characteristics in the pioneer lives of the American west.[17] European observers comment on this phenomenon among the present generation of farmers in the United States as well. Even today the farming population of North America, like that of our country, is still not as rooted in the soil as the farmers of old Europe.

5. Possibilities for Making a Change

The question as to whether a farmer would respond to an impulse to sell a farm would depend in a very large measure on the chances of obtaining other land advantageously. During the pioneer period such chances were great, particularly in the thinly populated parts where there was still a great deal of crown land. The opportunity to obtain other farms often arose as well when farmers in the vicinity, attracted by crown land or inexpensive land farther into the interior, moved away. Thus, a farmer was not bound to his land by necessity in the old days. If he really wanted to make a change for one or another reason, he had abundant opportunities to do so.

The result was that landowners during the pioneer period responded much more readily to the impulse to move than our farmers do today. If a man's farm did not please him—the pasture was perhaps poorer than what he thought, or the water supply was not satisfactory—he went in search of a better farm and moved. If his livestock began to die, he became dissatisfied and tried to get his hands on a healthier farm. If there were a couple of droughts, he became disappointed and moved to a farm where he felt it would rain more. The old timers constantly traveled about, and sometimes visited and hunted for weeks and months at a time. In this way they learned about other areas and often saw farms that they took a liking to. There was also not a great risk connected with moving. If the farmer was also not happy with the new farm, he was certain that he would soon get a chance again to make a change.

Today conditions are different. The farmer who owns land, or the propertyless man who has had the good fortune to have access to a piece of crown land—of whatever quality—has to be satisfied with that. No matter what kinds of difficulties he experiences in trying to make his farm livable, he must simply surmount these problems, because he realizes there is no relief elsewhere.

Namaqualand was one of the border districts where this state of affairs first arose. When the inhabitable crown land was distributed there, the farmers could not trek any farther. The territory was bordered on the west by the sea and on the east by a dry area that was not livable under pioneer circumstances. To the north the Orange River formed a substantial obstacle to traffic, and what is more the region to the north of the river was under a foreign flag. The result was that the landowners of Namaqualand quickly realized that they must keep what they had.

For the same reason the farmers who have obtained farms in Bushmanland since about 1907 have held fast to their land. These Dorsland pioneers have fought a bitter battle against droughts: they have often toiled for years and paid much blood money to get water, but the vast majority of them have refused to give up their farms, because there was no chance of assistance elsewhere. This is also the reason why the settlers along the Kuruman River are ready to scoop water for their livestock with tipping buckets from miserable boreholes a couple of hundred feet deep from dawn to dusk. They have toiled and sweated in an unrivaled way to make the hard and cruel desert inhabitable, but very few of them have returned their farms to the Department of Lands. The Kalahari is their last refuge, and they know it!

Changes of residence still occur today, but less now than earlier, since the possibilities for making an advantageous change have declined. Even the man who is apt to flounder will think twice today before he makes a change. If he perhaps makes a mistake, he will not quickly get a chance again to rectify it.

ENDNOTES

[1] J. Barrow, *Travels into the Interior of Southern Africa*, 2nd ed. (London, 1806), II:89; See also, W.W. Bird, *State of the Cape of Good Hope in 1822* (London, 1823), p. 104.

[2] P.J. van der Merwe, *Die Noordwaartse Beweging van die Boere voor die Groot Trek (1770-1842)* (The Hague, 1937), pp. 7-24, 66, 84, 110, 113.

[3] J.W. Janssens to J.A. de Mist, Algoa Bay, 12 May 1803, in George McCall Theal, *Belangrijke Historische Dokementen over Zuid-Afrika* (Cape Town, 1896, 1911), III:218. See also in the same, p. 179.

[4] Bird, *State of the Cape*, p. 104.

[5] Edward Blount, *Notes on the Cape of Good Hope made during an Excursion in that Colony in the Year 1820* (London, 1821), p. 43.

[6] C.O. 41, Letters Rec. from the Court of Justice, General Report, Commission of Circuit, 1811-1812, No. 16.

[7] P.J. van der Merwe, *Die Trekboer in die Geskiedenis van die Kaapkolonie, 1657-1842* (Cape Town, 1838), p. 107.

[8] AR, Asiatic Council, 298, Minutes of J.A. de Mist, J.A. de Mist to Janssens, 30 May 1803, p. 172.

[9] AR, Asiatic Council, 301, J.A. de Mist to Janssens, 10 October 1803.

[10] George McCall Theal, *History of South Africa* (London: 1915), VI: 273.

[11] J.F.W. Grosskopf, *Plattelandsverarming en Plaasverlating* (Stellenbosch, 1932), p. 30.

[12] Van der Merwe, *Trekboer*, pp. 107-23.

[13] Theal, *History*, V:265. See also Bird, *State of the Cape*, p. 104 and Barrow, *Travels*, II:88.

[14] G. Thompson, *Travels and Adventures in Southern Africa* (London, 1827), II:131-32.

[15] Van der Merwe, *Trekboer*, p. 192.

[16] W. Roscher and R. Jannasch, *Kolonien, Kolonialpolitik und Auswanderung* (Leipzig, 1885), pp. 77-8.

[17] Ibid., p. 78.

CHAPTER IX

The Winter Migration to The Karoo

1. The Karoo

Between the border of the Roggeveld and the Cold Bokkeveld lies a desolate and inhospitable strip of land that the farmers of that part of the world call "the Karoo." In the southeast it is bordered by the mountains of the Little Roggeveld. In the northwest it extends gradually into the South Bokkeveld and the Hantam. The area is about 100 to 120 miles long and 60 to 70 miles wide. The main road from Ceres to Calvinia runs diagonally through the "Karoo"; the main road from Ceres to Sutherland passes right through the southeastern part of the "Karoo."

There is considerable confusion in connection with the use of the term "Karoo." Originally the word was used to indicate an area with an arid climate. Today it is often used to describe a certain type of plant growth. Finally, it is used as a topographical designation for a whole number of different areas in the Cape. We speak of the Great Karoo, the Little Karoo, the Bo-Karoo, the Moordenaarskaroo, the Klipkaroo, etc. For the farmers in the vicinity, however, all these areas are simply "the Karoo." If five farmers in different parts of the colony say: "It rained in the Karoo," or "I'm going to the Karoo next week," then is it quite likely that each one of them is thinking of a different region. It is necessary, therefore, to state precisely what is meant in this chapter when we refer to "the Karoo." We mean by this that piece of Karoo veld between the Cold Bokkeveld and the Roggeveld.

At the beginning of the nineteenth century a distinction was normally made between the Bokkeveld Karoo and the Roggeveld Karoo. The Grootrivier (Dweka) was regarded at this time as the boundary between the two areas.[1] These designations, however, fell into disuse in the course of time. That part of the Karoo that the farmers of the Bokkeveld use today extends up to the Koedoesberg. It is usually called the Ceres Karoo, after the magistracy in which it lies. The rest of the Karoo is divided between Calvinia and Sutherland. Every piece is named after the district under whose jurisdiction it falls.

Topographically the Karoo offers great contrasts. If the traveler enters the Karoo from the Ceres side, there lies directly before him an outstretched plain of about 33 miles wide. On his left hand lies the Swartrug, which separates the Karoo from the Cold Bokkeveld. Farther to the northwest, in a direct line with Swartrug, lies the Cederberg, eerily jagged. Parallel with this range lie the pale blue Koedoesberg in the distance, on the far side of the plain. He would not yet be able to see the Roggeveld Mountains.

Up to the Koedoesberg the road to Sutherland runs through a flat plain. From there on to Verlatekloof, where the traveler climbs out of the Roggeveldsberg, he always remains between mountains for about 44 miles. From Karoopoort, where the Ceres road enters the Karoo, to Calvinia, the world remains flat for the first part of the journey. The plain, however, gradually changes into low hills, with here and there an isolated mountain to break the monotony of the landscape. Up ahead the landscape becomes entirely mountainous and finally the traveler ascends the Roggeveldsrand at Bloukrans.

The Ceres Karoo consists almost exclusively of steppes. The Sutherland Karoo is mountainous and the Calvinia Karoo has a mixed landscape: plains and hills and mountains.

From a farming viewpoint, the Karoo is undoubtedly one of the poorest parts of the Union. Large parts of it fall more or less into the same class as the Knechtsvlakte at Vanrhynsdorp. But there are great differences in the quality and carrying capacity of the pasture in the Karoo. In the rainy season the flat plains of the Karoo are much more accessible than the mountainous parts of the Karoo. The mountain pastures, however, are better than the plains, because the grazing land is more permanent and offers more acceptable summer grazing. In general, the grazing lands of the Karoo improve notably to the northwestern side. The Calvinia Karoo is already much better than the Ceres and Sutherland Karoo, although it is poor compared with the mountainous country surrounding the Karoo.

2. The Bokkeveld

For many understandable reasons, the first pioneers did not find the Karoo attractive enough to settle there permanently. They built their homes in the mountainous country around the Karoo. By 1728 the first farmers already had settled between the mountains to the southwest of the Karoo[2] (that they named the "Bokkeveld" because there were so many springbok there at this time.)[3] The area that was given this name lies between the Hex River Mountains in the south and the Elandskloof in the north.[4]

A part of the Bokkeveld lies considerably lower than the rest and is accordingly also warmer. It was therefore called the "Warm Bokkeveld," in contrast to the more high-lying parts that were given the name "Cold Bokkeveld." The Warm Bokkeveld, in which the pretty little village of Ceres is situated, divides the Cold Bokkeveld in two. The southeastern section of the Cold Bokkeveld, which lies on the line between Swaarmoed and Worcester, is today called the "Bokveld." The northern section, from Geido up to the Middelberg, is these days usually indicated by means of the suggestive names of the old fieldcornetcies dating from the Company period: Skotland and Friesland. In this chapter when we speak of the *Cold Bokkeveld*, then we include Skotland, Friesland and the area "Bokveld." When using the term the *Bokkeveld* we mean the Cold and the Warm Bokkeveld.

The Bokkeveld is excellently suitable for agriculture and has long been famous for its fertility and the diversity of its agricultural products. Grain thrived very well there; wine and brandy were abundant; and the Bokkevelders produced fresh and dried fruits, peas, beans and other greens in abundance. Transporting products to Cape Town, however, which until late in the nineteenth century was the Bokkevelders' only significant market, was accompanied by serious problems.

The Bokkeveld is cut off from the coast by high mountains. There were different passes over the mountains, but all were extremely dangerous. With a loaded wagon the mountain trail was completely impassable. Even with an empty wagon a person could cover only a few miles per day, and then you were lucky if you escaped without injury. The farmers who wanted to bring their products to the Cape were obliged to take their wagons empty over the mountains and to transport the freight for that portion of the journey on packhorse. Once across the mountains the wagons

Map 1: The Winter Trek to the Karoo

could be loaded again, but their difficulties were not over yet, because the sandy Cape flats still lay before them.

The slow rate of transport, the abnormal wear and tear on the wagons, draught-animals and gear, and the toll charges made transport costs very high. This worked against the development of agriculture in the Bokkeveld. Wheat was produced only for local consumption. Only products such as dried fruit and leguminous plants, which had a high value in relation to their weight, could—when prices were good—be transported to the Cape market. Under these circumstances the colonists were obliged to concentrate on livestock, which could walk to the market themselves.[5]

3. The Roggeveld

The colonization of the Roggeveld had begun by the middle of the eighteenth century. The first pioneers had settled all along the ridge of the Roggeveld mountains, where the rainfall was good and where there was plenty of permanent water. Even toward the end of the eighteenth century only a comparatively thin strip along the top of the mountains was inhabited. The region towards the Sak River first got permanent inhabitants in the nineteenth century.[6]

The Roggeveld consisted of three parts at the beginning of the nineteenth century. The northern part, which today falls under the Calvinia district, was known at this time as the "Under Roggeveld." These days the farmers usually speak of the "Calvinia Roggeveld" or the "North Roggeveld." The southern half of the Roggeveld, between Aapenberg and Komsberg, which today comes under Sutherland, was called the "Middle Roggeveld" in the old days. Today it is called the "Sutherland Roggeveld" or "South Roggeveld." The Little Roggeveld, which has retained its old name, is formed by the mountains that shoot out like a pair of bent fingers in the Karoo at Komsberg, where the outer edge of the central highland of the Cape suddenly turns upwards to the northeast.[7] The Little Roggeveld also falls into the Sutherland magisterial district.

The Roggeveld was always known as a good livestock district, but it did not offer as many possibilities for agriculture as the Cold Bokkeveld. Consequently the first pioneers concentrated almost exclusively on stock breeding.[8] Even today the Roggeveld is still primarily a livestock district.

4. Accounts of the Trek with Livestock to the Karoo

Since time immemorial, presumably since the first pioneers settled in these regions,[9] the farmers of the Bokkeveld and the Roggeveld have trekked in the winter with their livestock to the Karoo. The archival materials of the eighteenth century make no mention of these movements. The landdrost of Stellenbosch, under whose jurisdiction these distant districts fell, did not know what took place beyond the high mountains. Other government officials almost never went there. Only in the nineteenth century, when various questions arose in connection with land ownership in the Karoo, is there correspondence about the trek with livestock.

The earliest contemporary accounts about the winter trek are found in old travel accounts. [Carl Peter] Thunberg, [Andreas] Sparrman, [William] Paterson, and [Francis] Masson, who had visited these parts by the 1770s, all refer to it. And from what the travelers report, it seems clear that the trek at this time was not a new phenomenon, but was already well established.[10] Later reporters, such as [John] Barrow, [Willliam] Burchell, [Hinrich] Lichtenstein and [W.] Von Meyer, all tell of yearly migrations to the Karoo as well.[11] From that time to the present the farmers have trekked without a break. There are numerous references in archival documents from the nineteenth century that attest to this, as well as oral traditions from more recent times.

Contemporary sources provide very little information about the trek to the Karoo. The old travelers never gave any special thought to the matter. They only communicated facts that came to their attention by chance. The evidence that one finds in archival documents is likewise scanty. The government was interested in the trek only in so far as it gave rise to certain problems in the use of crown land in the Karoo. In the many letters and petitions that deal with the winter trek, the farmers are always only defending their claims to crown land. From their point of view, there was little reason to communicate any more about the trek than that it was absolutely necessary and that they could not manage without Karoo land. The government never questioned this. Therefore it was not even necessary to justify the argument too forcefully.

Consequently, the available information in the sources of the time about the trek with livestock to the Karoo is disappointing to the researcher. It leaves unanswered many questions that one might ask about the trek as a historical and sociological phenomenon. Therefore, it is very fortunate that the phenomenon still survives today, although in a slightly different form, and especially that there are still people alive today who observed the trek in its original form and even participated in it. The information that is provided by such persons is a valuable supplement to the fragmentary, historical accounts on the subject. And a careful study of the trek in its modern form, as well as of the environment in which it occurred, enables one to interpret those accounts more knowledgeably, and to construct a more intelligible representation from them. It is often asserted that we study the past in order to better understand the present. In many cases, however, one can come to a better understanding of the past by studying the present.

5. The Extent of the Winter Trek

It is clear from eighteenth and nineteenth century sources that the entire Cold Bokkeveld took part in the winter trek. Even where this is not expressly mentioned, matters are usually presented in such a way that one can conclude that this was the case.[12] In connection with the Warm Bokkeveld the Commission for Stock Raising and Agriculture stated in 1805: "People do not trek away, but keep their livestock there winters and summers."[13] The archival data from that time furnish proof, however, that at this time there were nevertheless livestock farmers in the Warm Bokkeveld who made use of the Karoo in the winter.[14] Even today the livestock farmers of the Warm Bokkeveld still take part in the trek to the Karoo. And according to oral tradition this has been the case since time immemorial. In view of this evidence one is therefore inclined to doubt the statement of the Commission for Stock Raising. There is no doubt, however, that the farmers of the Warm Bokkeveld did not trek so generally and so regularly as those who lived in the colder parts of the Bokkeveld.

The farmers of the Roggeveld did not all trek to the Karoo. In this regard Paterson stated: "This practice is not, however, general; several of them remain in their habitations, exposed to all the inclemencies of the weather."[15] Thunberg, who visited the Roggeveld around the same time, provides a clearer account of the matter: "The settlers in the lowermost Roggeveld, who are in possession of good houses," he said, "sometimes pass the winter there; but those who live in the Middle Roggeveld, always remove from thence."[16] The Commission for Stock Raising and Agriculture supported this statement. The farmers of the Middle Roggeveld trek to the Karoo during the winter, but in the Lower Roggeveld "some trek to the Karoo, while others journey to the east to the low lying places."[17]

With respect to the trek out of the Middle Roggeveld, however, the facts are less clear. In Thunberg's time only the ridge of the Roggeveldsberg was inhabited.[18] He was obviously only thinking of this part of the Roggeveld when he spoke of the "Middle Roggeveld." Over time, however, an expansion in the direction of the Sak River occurred. In the nineteenth century the area between the Roggeveld Mountains and the Sak River was vaguely called "the Agterveld." It formed part of the old frontier border field cornetcy of "Middle Roggeveld," but as topographic concepts the designations Middle Roggeveld and Agterveld were used in contrast with each other. From the sources of the nineteenth century it is clear that the farmers of the "Middle Roggeveld" still always trekked to the Karoo, but it is not clear whether this included the Agterveld.

It seems improbable to me, however, that the farmers of the Agterveld would trek regularly to the Karoo. On the Sak River side the land slopes down gradually and it becomes appreciably warmer. The cold of the winters is not at all so intense that the farmers would be obliged to trek. In addition, the winters are dry, which means the cold does not affect the livestock as much as it does on the ridge of the Roggeveld Mountains, which does receive winter rains. The distance from the Karoo is inconveniently far, in any event. This supposition is supported by oral tradition. According to the old people there is no question that the Agterveld farmers did not trek regularly to the Karoo in winter. Now and then they trekked in different directions in the winter because of drought, even toward the Karoo if there was relief to be found there, but the trek took the form of an incidental migration. A regular seasonal migration was out of the question.

The reports about the trek to the Karoo make few references to the Little Roggeveld. There is conclusive evidence, however, that the farmers who were settled here also trekked in the old days to the Karoo in winter and that the trek was just as extensive as in the Middle Roggeveld.[19]

It therefore appears that the farmers of the Cold Bokkeveld, the Middle Roggeveld and the Little Roggeveld generally took part in the winter trek to the Karoo. The farmers of the Under Roggeveld and the Warm Bokkeveld evidently did not trek as commonly, while the inhabitants of the Agterveld visited the Karoo only now and then.

6. Causes for the Trek

The causes for the winter trek to the Karoo must be sought in the first place in the geographic nature of the regions concerned.

Because of their high elevation, the mountainous regions that encircle the Karoo are very cold. Sutherland is the coldest place in the Union. It often happens that there is still frost there at Christmas. A Roggeveld farmer recently told me that on one occasion on New Year's Day 80 of his goats died in the snow. If something like this can happen in the summer, one can easily imagine how cold it must be in the winter. According to Mr. W. Steenkamp, one winter his father's herdsman and 500 animals froze to death. A farmer who spends the winter in the Roggeveld can expect similar losses at any time. The Cold Bokkeveld is a little warmer than Sutherland, but the winter there is still exceptionally severe. In cold weather the farmers often sustain great losses during the winter. Moreover, the cold is very harmful to the livestock. They could perhaps endure the low temperature as such, but the winter is also the rainy season, and the wetness together with the cold spells the death for the sheep. The Cold Bokkeveld in particular is very wet in the winter. It often happens that it rains for eight days on end, and this is usually accompanied by cold weather. In such weather it is desirable to keep the livestock in shelters, otherwise they easily freeze to death. This means that they cannot go to graze. Furthermore, most farms lie between the mountains and consequently receive little sunshine in the winter and do not dry out quickly. The pens then remain wet and messy for a long time and after a while the hoofs of the livestock fester from the wetness. In such circumstances it is also very inconvenient to work with the livestock.

Furthermore, there is severe frost in the winter. In the Cold Bokkeveld, where the farms get the sun late, the frost often lies white on the fields until eleven o'clock in the morning. When the livestock are chased from their warm pens out onto the frost-covered fields, they easily get dikkop* They therefore have to be kept in the pens until the frost melts, and before they have had a chance to graze sufficiently, they have to come back to their pens again.

During the winter the farmers of the Cold Bokkeveld and Middle Roggeveld can also expect a heavy snowfall at any time. Occasionally the ground is so covered by the snow that the livestock cannot go out to graze at all for eight or ten days. Admittedly, this does not happen very often and also not every winter, but the farmers do not know beforehand whether there will be a heavy snowfall the following winter and they have to make allowance for it happening. Apart from the fact that the snow often limits the livestocks' grazing opportunities, it usually goes hand in hand with extreme cold. Because of the biting cold it is very dangerous to remain in the Cold Bokkeveld or Middle Roggeveld with livestock during the winter. This was particularly the case before the farmers had barns that could provide effective shelter for the livestock.

In the Onder-Roggeveld the winters are not as severe as in the Middle Roggeveld and the Cold Bokkeveld. The closer one gets to the Hantam, the warmer the winter climate of the Roggeveldsrand becomes. On some farms, which lie very high up, the livestock farmer is also subject to cold rains and snow, but other parts are inhabitable throughout the year. The Little Roggeveld has a relatively mild climate as well. It lies a little lower than the Roggeveldsrand and consequently is considerably warmer. There is less frost there and the snowfall is not significant, except in exceptionally cold years. The same applies to the Warm Bokkeveld. In the Onder-Roggeveld, the Little Roggeveld and above all in the Warm Bokkeveld, however, the winters are wet as well and it is still very cold in any case for sheep and goats. The farmer who wants to over-winter there can also easily suffer damage from livestock perishing in the cold.

The old travelers, as well as the archival documents of the nineteenth century, usually only mention the severity of the mountain winters—with their cold, snow and foggy weather—as the cause for the trek to the Karoo, without once elaborating upon that point in detail.[20] The farmers

---

*Trans. note: Literally "thickhead", also known as "Geeldikkop" or "yellow thick head." A disease primarily affecting sheep, but also cattle and horses.

who participate in the trek today, however, also mention various other causes for it. These causes had to have been at work in the old days as well. The fact that they are not referred to in contemporary sources can be explained as follows: no other reasons were given then as the farmers had to trek with their livestock anyway because of the cold in the winter. That is why they declared that this was the reason for the trek. Once they began to find effective protection against the cold in modern times, which enabled them to isolate that as a factor, they became more clearly aware of other circumstances that made the trek desirable. What is more, the older generations of pioneers appear to have accepted the winter trek as an established institution without bringing its effectiveness into question. Consequently they did not always give such an accurate account of precisely why it was necessary. In addition, the authorities never questioned the need to make use of land in the Karoo. Hence the farmers did not have to explain in detail all the circumstances that made the trek desirable. It was quite sufficient to mention the primary cause, which was at the same time the most conspicuous as well.

The coldness of the winter does not provide, however, a sufficient explanation for the trek to the Karoo. Another factor of great importance was seasonal differences in the carrying capacity of the pasture land. In the mountainous country around the Karoo the land is poor during the winter months. This is especially the case in the Cold Bokkeveld. Until the beginning of the winter the grazing lands remain relatively good and there is plenty of food for the livestock. Then the frost kills the fields. As soon as the first frost comes, the grazing land quickly deteriorates. Furthermore the first winter rains leave the dry grass of the previous summer moldy and rotted.

During the months of May, June and July it is so cold in the Bokkeveld that the grass cannot even grow, so no new grass appears as well. Everything is dead and all of nature is in a winter's sleep. Only toward August does a change begin to take place slowly. In September the grass grows quickly: by the beginning of October it is again fully grown out. This means that in winter a farmer does not have enough pasture for his livestock in the Bokkeveld. Apart from the fact that snow and cold rains occasionally interfere with grazing opportunities for the livestock, during the winter his farm cannot support all his livestock, and the condition of the livestock that is kept there deteriorates. The Bokkeveld farmer, therefore, not only needs additional pasture land for the winter, but it is even necessary for him to get better pasture for his livestock than his homestead could offer.

The Roggeveld, with its permanent scrubland, is in this respect much better for grazing than the Bokkeveld. The land also displays seasonal differences in carrying capacity. In the spring the Roggeveld's pasture is at its best. From January on it gradually deteriorates and just before the winter it is at its poorest. Then come the rains. Because of the cold the grass grows very, very slowly during the winter months, but there is nevertheless some growth to be observed. What is more, the rains are not as detrimental for the scrublands as they are for the Bokkeveld. Consequently, in normal years the Roggeveld has reasonably good winter grazing. The quality of the grass is admittedly poorer than in the spring and the summer, but it is not so poor that this alone would have obliged the farmers to trek.

One sometimes hears the view today among Roggeveld farmers that they ought to let their farms rest during the winter. The grass is so wet then, they say, that the livestock completely trample it underfoot. What they stress even more, however, is that the farmer who does not trek to the Karoo in the winter, finds it difficult in the summer to manage on his homestead. They say that the farms in the Roggeveld have become too small to farm throughout the year. At the same time they concede that, as far as grazing land is concerned, they themselves could easily survive during the winter in the Roggeveld if they had bigger areas of land there or were prepared to keep fewer livestock.

From this it is clear that the Roggeveld farmers did not trek to the Karoo because their farms did not have suitable winter grazing, but rather to find additional pasture land. Those who trekked to the Karoo for the sake of grazing land, kept more livestock than they could support on their Roggeveld farms through the year, with the intention of making use of the Karoo for a part of the year. There was, however, nothing in particular that obligated them to go looking in the Karoo for the extra pasture that they needed so that they could keep more livestock. The question of pasture land could also theoretically have been resolved in the Roggeveld or elsewhere. This factor can therefore not be viewed as a primary cause for the winter trek out of the Roggeveld. It could not have been the original cause for the trek, because when the winter trek originated, there was still plenty of room and opportunities for trek in the Roggeveld itself. Over time, however, livestock farming and land ownership in the Roggeveld came to revolve entirely around the winter trek, with the result today that the Roggeveld is dependent upon the Karoo pasture.

The necessity for the winter trek to the Karoo would not have been quite so great, if the farmers of the mountain country did not have lambs born during the winter. Weak lambs are much less resistant against the cold than are ewes. Especially lambs that are born at night, or during cold weather, die very easily. Apart from the losses that the farmers suffered from the cold, having lambs born in the winter in the Roggeveld or Cold Bokkeveld also caused many more worries. The farmer had to get up constantly during the night to see if perhaps more lambs had been born that would freeze to death. In the cold weather he continually had to drive the lambs from the fields to the house during the day to care for them. The cold of the mountain country, therefore, made it very difficult to have lambs born there in the winter. This was especially the case in the old days when no one had shelters for their sheep.

Moreover, a farmer has to have good grazing land during lambing time. The ewes need green grass, otherwise they do not have milk for the lambs and their condition deteriorates too much. Furthermore, the lambs also need soft, young grass when they begin to graze. In this part of the Roggeveld, which formed part of the trek to the Karoo, the winter grazing was entirely suitable for the ewes to lamb on. There were even farmers who claimed that the ewes' milk did not run out as quickly in the Roggeveld as in the Karoo. The winter pasture of the Bokkeveld, however, was not suitable at all for lambing ewes. There was not only too little food for the livestock, but the little that there was was dry, killed by frost and without any potency.

It would have been much easier to spend the winter with livestock in the Roggeveld and Bokkeveld, if the farmers could have had the lambing time during another season of the year. The experience of nearly two centuries, however, has demonstrated that the winter, particularly June and July, in these regions is the best lambing time. This was especially the case during the pioneer period, when these farmers were dependent exclusively on natural pasture.

In the summer the land is too dry and lacking in nourishment for lambing ewes. If the farmers allowed the lambs to be born just before the winter—say in April—then the lambs are all strong enough to survive the worst cold. The Cold Bokkeveld's farmers then still had to trek in any case, since they did not have suitable winter grazing. And even then they were taking a big risk, because if the rains in the Karoo stayed away, they lost their season's fall of lambs. The Roggeveld farmers were also in a poor position if they had lambs in April, no matter whether they trek or not. Just before winter the Roggeveld is at its poorest and the Karoo land is useless. If the winter rains come in time, the farmers have enough grazing land. If the rains are late, they can suffer great losses. To have lambing time just after winter is also risky. The land is then at its finest, and for the first couple of months things go well, but before the lambs have been weaned, the land has already deteriorated again. Then not only the ewes, but the lambs as well, have difficulty surviving through the summer. The late lambs in particular suffer in the summer. They cannot manage when the land becomes dry.

The Bokkevelders and Roggevelders were thus obliged to have their lambs in the winter, and since their farms were not suitable for this, they chose to have the lambs in the Karoo.

The Karoo is an excellent place for lambs in the winter. It lies considerably lower than the surrounding mountain country and consequently has a much more moderate climate. The thermometer sometimes drops quite low at night and the greatest part of the Karoo experiences heavy frost. During the day, however, the sunshine is usually wonderfully warm. Moreover, the rainfall is negligible and the dry cold of the Karoo does not harm the livestock as much as the wet, foggy cold of the mountain country. In the Karoo the farmers did not have a difficult time at all with lambs that arrived in the night, or with livestock freezing to death in the cold weather.

What is more, the grazing land of the Karoo is at its best in the winter. This poor region, dealt with so niggardly by nature, then gets the little rain that it is promised. As soon as the first soaking rains have penetrated the earth's dry crust, plants appear with magical rapidity. Within a few weeks the gray landscape gives ways to the first tints of green and the inhospitable desert is transformed into a flower garden. In its best years the Karoo—just like Namaqualand and the Hantam—is bedecked with layers and layers of flowers, which cover the soil like a multi-colored carpet. The young grass and wild shoots, bidou bush, and lye-bush, fatten the livestock quickly and the ewes have an abundance of milk for the lambs.

When the livestock return after the winter from the Karoo, the pasture land in the Bokkeveld and Roggeveld is excellent for lambing ewes. And by the time that the land there begins to become dry and lose its potency, the lambs are strong and the ewes in good condition and they can easily make it through the summer. Because of its milder climate and excellent winter grazing, the Karoo is therefore an ideal retreat for the livestock farmers of the wintry mountains.

Today the farmers of the Cold Bokkeveld still mention other reasons why they find the trek to the Karoo desirable, if not essential. They explain that the sour grass of the Bokkeveld does not contain enough lime to build healthy bones. Furthermore, the grazing land of the Bokkeveld does not always contain all the nutritional components that the livestock need for healthy development and normal growth. The new shoots and scrub bush vegetation of the Karoo, however, provide everything that is lacking in the pasturage of the Bokkeveld. Therefore, the change of vegetation is good for the livestock.

The farmers feel they can confirm this on the basis of their own experience. In the Karoo, they claim, the livestock grow splendidly during the winter. Livestock that remain behind in the

Bokkeveld, first grow around August. In summer one can also never find livestock that spent the winter in the Bokkeveld in such fine condition as livestock that were in the Karoo. And in difficult years they have a much more difficult time surviving the summer. Livestock that were in the Karoo, the farmers declare unanimously, surpass those that remained behind in every respect. Some even claim that, if their livestock do not trek to the Karoo one year, the lambing season the following year is poorer and the wool production markedly lower. The bones of the livestock degenerate as well. If one keeps the livestock in the Bokkeveld a few years in succession, the bones become more and more brittle and eventually break like glass. Some of the Ceres farmers firmly believe that their livestock will degenerate physically unless they trek to the Karoo regularly. They maintain that the livestock will gradually become small and weak and stunted if they constantly graze on the sour grass, even though they are kept in condition with forage through the year.

Another cause that the farmers suggest today for the winter trek is that the Bokkeveld becomes unhealthy in the winter for sheep and goats. A few claim in vague terms that the small livestock become sickly and full of ailments if they continuously remain in the Bokkeveld and that the Karoo veld is like a medicine against all these illnesses. There is nothing quite as good as the Karoo, they swear, to keep the livestock healthy. The only sickness to which the farmers specifically referred is the (distended) loco disease.[†] Between March and November, but above all during the winter months, the entire Bokkeveld experiences this disease. Behind the Skurweberg it is a plague. In the Karoo the livestock do not get loco disease during the winter, and for many farmers this is a strong consideration in favor of the trek to the Karoo.

7. Trek Time[21]

The amount of time the farmers spent in the Karoo depended entirely on circumstances that were not the same from year to year. Usually the farmers trekked as soon as the first rains had fallen. Before that, there was neither pasture nor water.

If the winter rains fell uncommonly early one year, then the first farmers trekked as early as April. Others waited anyway until they had finished sowing in May. If the rains stayed away for the entire year, the farmers sometimes had to wait until June before they could trek. In most cases the livestock were moved to the Karoo between 15 May and 15 June. By the middle of June the farmer had to be at his destination, since by then the ewes had begun to lamb. After that time he could not really trek.

In normal years the farmers spent three to four months in the Karoo. They could not subsist there much longer. The Karoo's plant growth is not exclusively based on winter rains. If it rains in the spring and summer, the vegetation grows as well. But this almost never happens. Generally the Karoo gets rain only a few times during the winter months and then the plant growth has to live on that for the rest of the year. As a result, it never retains its wealth of flowers for long. The beauty of the desert is short-lived. As soon as the days begin to lengthen and the heat of the sun intensifies, the flowers wilt and the young shoots wither. When the summer arrives, the grazing land deteriorates quickly. The fig tree, which is excellent fodder in the winter, becomes altogether

---

[†]Trans. note: A nervous disease of cattle, sheep, and horses characterized by paralysis, impaired vision, and weakness, caused by eating the locoweed. Also see ch. X, p. 140.

worthless. It shrivels and becomes tart and no animal will eat it any longer. The yellow bush,[‡] which the livestock like to eat in the winter, gives them dropsy in the summer. In fact, most plants that can outlive the drought once the first flush of growth is over in the summer become relatively worthless, or poisonous. In the mountainous parts of the Karoo the fields are often covered with scrub, while the livestock die miserably. In the flat plains of the Karoo the plant growth vanishes almost entirely in the summer. The Karoo therefore has nearly no summer pasture. During this season it is difficult to keep the livestock alive. Livestock that are used to the Karoo, do surprisingly well. But in the mountainous areas livestock do not do well at all in the summer and quickly begin to decline. Moreover, certain parts of the Karoo become unhealthy in the summer. The loco disease is particularly troublesome. It also becomes too hot for the livestock that are not used to it, and they are plagued by horseflies.

When the winter rains have passed, the water soon begins to become scarce as well. The temporary streams and springs of the Karoo, which can block travelers when they are in flood, become dry beds in the summer. Standing water, in pools and pans, becomes brackish and dries up. Small springs and sluggish streams disappear. Lost travelers must dig behind embankments in the riverbeds to get drinking water. Thus the paradise gradually transforms into an inhospitable desert. The earth's crust dries out and becomes dusty. The scorching rays of the sun heat the air until the wind burns your face. And the fine dust coils like snakes in the air when it is gripped by the whirlwinds, which race one another over the plains. When one travels on a warm summer day from Sutherland to Ceres, you see a desert—as it were, in the shadows of the water-rich mountains of the more richly blessed Boland.

By September, occasionally even in August already, the lack of pasture and water generally obliges the farmers of the Bokkeveld and Roggeveld to return to their farms on the mountains. In good years, when late rains have fallen there, they can remain till October. Then they trek away one after the other. The Karoo becomes more lonely by the day and by the beginning of November it is altogether deserted. If the time to trek approaches, and the farmers perhaps still linger a while, the livestock begin to stray away.[22]

8. The Family Trek Together

In the Little and Middle Roggeveld it was common for the farm family to accompany the livestock to the Karoo.[23] In this connection [William] Burchell wrote: "The colonists of the Roggeveld quit their houses during the winter to reside in the Karoo. On these occasions, they carry with them all their furniture, and every thing that is moveable; giving themselves no concern about the fate of their house, which they entirely desert and leave even unfastened."[24]

Reports about the Cold Bokkeveld contradict each other. In his well-known travelogue [John] Barrow says: "The Cold in winter obliges the inhabitants to drive their cattle upon the Karroo plains, but not to quit their houses, as is the case with those of the Roggeveld."[25] This

---

[‡]Trans. note: "geelbos," or "sunshine conebush" in English. Scientific name leucadendron salignum, the most widespread species of the Protea (Proteaceae) family.

account does not agree with the known facts. There is absolutely no doubt that farm families from the Cold Bokkeveld trek to the Karoo. The question is only whether it was a common phenomenon.

According to the report of the Commission for Stock Raising and Agriculture it was not at all common. In the winter, the report states, the farmers of the Cold Bokkeveld had to "make use of the Karoo for their sheep and cattle, without trekking themselves from their farms, with the exception of any who live in the so-called Friesland, who do not remain there for this time."[26]

[Hinrich] Lichtenstein, who visited the interior about the same time, wrote in 1811 that the farmers of Friesland (the northern most part of the Cold Bokkeveld) move down into the Karoo in the winter together with their livestock. "In the southern part, where most of the colonists have settled in the valleys, only the herds are driven down to the *Karoo* and the family remains behind on the farm."[27] For his travel account, however, Lichtenstein made substantial use of the report by the Commission for Stock Raising and Agriculture. It is perhaps risky therefore to view him as an independent witness on this point.

The archival documents of the nineteenth century do not shed much light on this question. Nonetheless, one now and then comes across references in the fieldcornets' letters from which it appears that the trek of families to the Karoo happened more commonly then what one would conclude from the Commission for Stock Raising and Agriculture report and Lichtenstein's account. For example, on 27 July 1819 fieldcornet Hugo wrote of the Cold Bokkeveld to the Tulbagh landdrost: "As all the people under my jurisdiction have trekked to the Karoo....I am the only one at home in my district....while only one or two servants are left behind on all the farms."[28]

Similar evidence is supported by oral tradition. According to various old trekboers, whose personal memories go back to about 1880, in their younger days it was a common practice in the Bokkeveld to shut up the house towards the beginning of the winter, to leave the farm behind just as it was, and trek to the Karoo with the family. Perhaps only a coloured servant was left behind, who was given food for three months, to look after the farm. Not all the families trekked every year, but the vast majority of them did. This was the case until about twenty, twenty-five years ago.

It ought to come as no surprise that the farmers of the Bokkeveld and Roggeveld trekked with their livestock to the Karoo. They knew the value of personal supervision. And especially during the lambing season, when livestock farming needed the most attention, the farmers wanted to be there personally with their livestock, with everyone who could help. Besides, there was not exactly much work to do on the farmstead in the winter. Most Roggevelders were exclusively livestock farmers. When the livestock were away from the farms, they had nothing to do. The Bokkevelders had quite a lot to do in cultivating the land, but even among them livestock farming was more important than anything else. Until comparatively recently they received the greatest portion of their income from livestock. The importance of livestock farming therefore had the highest priority. Moreover, there was really no urgent need for the Bokkevelders to be present at their homesteads in the winter. They had finished sowing before the winter and gardening came to a standstill as a result of the cold, frost and wetness. Livestock farming in the Karoo, therefore, demanded much more attention than the farm did.

Apart from the fact that the importance of farming under the then prevailing system promoted the family trek to the Karoo, the farmers enjoyed being there very much. "One would think," W. von Meyer wrote in 1840, "that the privations and discomforts connected with nomadic life must be burdensome to them; it is, however, exactly the opposite. Wife and children waited impatiently for this yearly journey to the Karoo, as if they were going to a great festival, and everyone appears to love this Bedouin life."[29]

Those who participated in the Karoo trek in its original form, all speak about it in the same vein. The children were always happy when the time arrived to trek to the Karoo. They looked forward to it with great expectation. Likewise to the journey back. Children love change. But for the adults too the yearly sojourn in the Karoo was particularly pleasant. The Karoo was their vacation spot, their beach. When one talks today to the old people about life in the Karoo in the old days, their faces immediately brighten up and their eyes gleam. An old man from Ceres, who at the time had not farmed for many years and has since died, once told me: "Even as old as I am now, I can simply not contain myself. If the Karoo got rain today, I would run for it like a horse."

The Karoo must truly have been an inviting winter resort for the farmers of the Bokkeveld and Roggeveld. It gets cold in the Karoo during the night, but during the day the sun shines nice and warm. In the mountain regions it is wet then and rainy and unbearably cold. And this sort of weather must have been particularly unpleasant in the old days, when a decent, cozy house was an exception and even the best of them were not properly heated.

I would have fled to the Karoo in the winter as well, if I had to live in Sutherland. If one has spent a winter's day there and the next morning gone down Verlatekloof and driven through the Karoo, no one need explain to you why the old-timers trekked so eagerly to the Karoo. One would have to have urgent work to do in the mountain regions to spend a miserable, dreary winter there, particularly when the sun is shining just a little distance ahead of you.

9. Migration Trails

It was not difficult for the farmers of the Roggeveld to get their livestock to the Karoo. Those who trekked lived all along a strip on the ridge of the Roggeveldsberg. They therefore simply had to go down the mountain and they were in the Karoo. And one could go down the mountain with livestock at so many different places that it was not necessary for any farmer to travel in a roundabout way to get to the Karoo.

The recognized trails, which had been used for a very long time, went down the side of the Roggeveld at Oliviersberg, Vloksberg, Ouberg, Verlatekloof and Komsberg. The farmers whose homesteads bordered on their Karoo land did not even make use of the trails. In the summer they and their friends simply drove their livestock down the slope of the mountain. In such cases the livestock traveled only a few miles. But even those who were not in such a lucky position seldom traveled more than fifty miles before they were on their Karoo land.

Today Verlatekloof is the only trail out of the Roggeveld that is used by vehicles. Along the others the farmers only go down the mountain with livestock and pack animals. In the old days, however, the farmers also trekked over Vloksberg with ox wagons. This was a difficult and extremely dangerous trail. Old people say that, when they were children, an old gentleman named

Vlok lived at Klipfontein, just on top of Vloksberg, and hired relays of oxen to people who were stuck on the mountain. But even with relays of oxen it was still always a struggle to make it through the Vloksberg—and likewise to come down the mountain.

The Bokkevelders had to trek a longer distance than the Roggevelders to get to the Karoo. Many of them, especially those who lived beyond Skurweberg, were far from the boundary between the Bokkeveld and the Karoo. And once they had crossed the boundary, they were still by no means at their destination. Some of their Karoo land lay 80 to 100 miles from their farmsteads. And distance was by no means their only difficulty. High mountains separated them from the Karoo.

There were only two trails out of the Bokkeveld to the Karoo. Most farmers made use of the old main road to the north, which went through Karoopoort, since it was early negotiable by vehicles. This route is today still the one most used. All the Bokkeveld's vehicles, as well as the livestock from the wards of Bokveld, Warm Bokkeveld, and the greatest portion of Friesland go through Karoopoort.

The other trail passes over Swartrug. It starts at the mountain at Katbakkies and goes down the other side in Skitterykloof. This trail, which farmers from Skotland and a part of Friesland have used since time immemorial, was exclusively a livestock path until about 1905. The farmers preferred to start their trek with their livestock at Katbakkies, because the Riet River runs wide there and so it was easy to get the livestock across the water. They could not get through the mountain there with vehicles, however, before the wagon path over Katbakkies was made. The wagons had to make a detour over the Riet River. Their passage was just above the *Potte*.[§] Their vehicles could pass through, but the river was so narrow that it often proved very difficult to get the wagons through the ford. Occasionally the farmers were obliged to harness two or even three teams of oxen one behind the other to a wagon, and even then it was still a struggle. Sometimes the wagons could not cross the river at all. As a consequence, the Bokkevelders were not eager to take their wagons over Swartrug. Those who made use of the trail often first took their livestock to the Karoo with pack animals and then came back to fetch the family. The wagons then went through Karoopoort. Once a wagon trail over Katbakkies had been constructed, where the Riet River flows wide, it was no longer such a great problem to get the wagons across the water. But the trail was always rather bad. From Katbakkies on it was not very secure, stony, and arduous. Down the Skitterykloof it was full of twists and turns and very slippery when it rained. This trail was never very popular. And particularly in recent years—now that the ox-wagon has been replaced by motorcars—nearly all the vehicles go through Karoopoort.

The Ceres farmers who lived beyond the Skurweberg, had to go over two mountain ranges before they were in the Karoo. There is only one motor route over the Skurweberg. All the vehicles and a portion of the livestock make use of it, and then go farther through Ceres and Karoopoort. A few farmers, however, send their livestock on a footpath (over Rocklands) across the Skurweberg, and then further on the Katbakkies trail over the Swartrug.

[§]Trans. note: "*Die Potte*" is a mountain summit in the Northern Cape. It is today situated northwest of Sutherland in the Tankwa Karoo National Park.

10. Enjoying the Trek

The trek to the Karoo and back was in itself a great event in the old days. Making the preparations beforehand took up a lot of time and energy. There was baking and slaughtering and coffee roasting. By the time the wagon was hitched up to the oxen, the family was completely at home in their temporary residence. For the sake of company and also to able to help each other if there was trouble, the farmers usually traveled together in small parties. Sometimes there were fifteen or twenty wagons stationed at one spot along the way. There was no hurry to get to the Karoo. Therefore the farmers moved at a leisurely pace and hunted along the way. And wherever they outspanned to rest, they made coffee, barbecued some meat and chatted pleasantly around the fire.

When it was time to trek, a few young men rode all over the Roggeveld and informed everyone that they had to be at Vloksberg by a certain time. On the evening of the appointed day there was usually an entire encampment on the mountain. The next morning the farmers rose early and helped each get the wagons down the mountain one after the other. That evening they all came together again at the foot of the mountain and then there was much merriment. The old people chatted around the wagons and the young people soon hauled out a fiddle or concertina and began to dance. The following morning one of the oldest members conducted a religious service and after that they parted, everyone to his own grazing area. After the winter, when the Roggevelders trekked back again, it was the same thing over again. They came together below Vloksberg and the following morning helped get the wagons up the mountain, usually with two teams of oxen pulling in front.

The trek undoubtedly had its pleasurable side, but it was often accompanied by hardships as well. Often the trekkers got stuck at Swartrug and Vloksberg. The gear of the draught animals sometimes broke at the most inconvenient moments. Wagons at times got bogged down in swollen rivers. It was often a great struggle to lead the livestock through the ice cold water with harness in hand. Occasionally the trekkers experienced rain and cold again along the route. If the wagon tents started to leak and the children began to cry, then all the merriment was over.

But when the old people think back to those days, the past becomes a beautiful, romantic, idealized memory. The difficulties are pushed into the background, the enjoyable reminiscences are tenderly cherished, and they feel a wistful longing for the good old times when the long string of tent-wagons journeyed into the fair Karoo.

11. Karoo Life

Life in the Karoo in the old days, when more families trekked there with the livestock than today, must have been very sociable. One met family and friends there whom one had not seen for a long time. On occasion you had the privilege of having them as your neighbors for a few months.[30] There was not much farm work. It was exceptional for a farmer to have a garden in the Karoo. There was no problem with lambs freezing to death. The goats and sheep required attention only in the mornings and evenings. During the day they were under the care of the herders in the field. The large animals, such as cattle, horses, and oxen, roamed freely and were only brought together once every eight to fourteen days and counted.[31] There were thus plenty of opportunities to visit. What is more, the wild game, attracted by the rich vegetation and the mild climate, also came down to the Karoo in the winter.[32] In Lichtenstein's time there were still flocks of elegant ostriches and probably other game species as well.[33] The wild animals have all become scarcer over time, but about fifty years ago springbok, steenbok, duiker, rietbok and other small game were still abundant in the Karoo. Everyone could hunt to their heart's content, and this was certainly not one of the more limited attractions of life in the Karoo.

The few months in the Karoo were not passed altogether idly, however. The farmers took care of an important part of their normal business each year in the Karoo. The children and slaves, Lichtenstein says, were sent out to collect young shoots of the lye-bush. These were burned and lye was made from the ashes, which the women used to make soap from the fat that they had gathered during the summer. In this way they not only obtained soap for their own use, but also to sell when the wagon went to the Cape again. In addition, the women prepared the hides from which clothes were made. By the beginning of the nineteenth century rawhide clothes were in general use. "The young people and slaves wear hardly anything else than such prepared hides," Lichtenstein assures us.[34]

The men dressed thongs, and tanned the leather soles and vamps. For this they used the bark of a tree that grew in the Karoo.[35] This was essential work in the old days. The farmers performed all their work with horses and oxen and therefore always had need of thongs. Likewise, a farmer could never have too many vamps and soles, since the everyday shoes for the entire family were made on the farm. Today the farmers no longer go to the Karoo to tan, but old people still remember well how their parents always traveled with the bark vat under the wagon.

The winter residence in the Karoo involved other economic activities as well. It brought together the inhabitants of two different areas who desired each other's products. The Roggeveld was famous for its good horses and fat sheep. The Bokkevelders had grain, liquor, dried fruit, tobacco, beans and peas to barter. It was much more convenient for them to transport these products to the Karoo than to the Cape. They therefore took with them to the Karoo whatever they had too much of in order to exchange it there for livestock, or to sell it to those who possibly had some money. They often got higher prices there than in the Cape.[36]

By the middle of the nineteenth century the government tried to organize yearly markets in the Karoo, where the farmers could offer their products for sale. The expectation was that stock buyers would also attend these markets. But these efforts did not produce the desired results. It is not known how many times these markets were held, but it seems that they must have quickly died out again.[37]

12. Winter and Summer Farms

The winter migration to the Karoo differed in one significant respect from the seasonal migrations that we find in other parts of the Northwest: it took the form of a regular trek between summer and winter farms.

It is possible, but just so difficult to prove, that the farmers originally wandered about in the Karoo during the winter and used the land communally. This is what one can expect, but the sources for the earliest period of the trek provide no information about this question. Be that as it may, in time the practice developed of a farmer returning every year to the same place in the Karoo, which then was called a "winter farm." We find the first traces of this system of private grazing land already in the documents of the final years of the eighteenth century.[38] At the beginning of the nineteenth century the winter farm system was in general use in the Karoo,[39] and the farmers have maintained it ever since.

Naturally this does not mean that there was no roaming about freely in the Karoo and that the farmers did not mutually help each other. That happened. Many of the old trekkers can testify to this. But the farmers did not wander around like the trekboers in Bushmanland, where there were no fixed grazing farms. In the Karoo every independent farmer had his own winter farm.

The winter farm system evolved completely spontaneously. Through repeated occupation the farmers developed claims to the winter farms, which they recognized among each other. Only later, when disputes over winter farms arose that the farmers could not settle among themselves, was the government called in to help. One after the other then the farmers petitioned the government to attach** their winter farms to their loan farms, which is what indeed happened. This meant that the government gave the owner of the loan farm the right to use the winter farm as well with a license. The farmer paid nothing extra for this privilege, considering that his loan farm, for which he paid a full yearly quitrent, could not be occupied right through the year. Through the formal registration of the winter farms, which occurred at the beginning of the nineteenth century, the government granted official approval to the system that the farmers developed on their own.

Up to 1831 the farmers used their winter farms at no cost. After that they had to pay 12s (later £1) per year for this privilege. The system of yearly licenses continued until 1870. After that the winter farms, like other undistributed crown land, was leased out at public auctions for periods that ranged from one to twenty years. By the end of the nineteenth century crown land was sold to the farmers and they received proprietary rights for farms that their forefathers had used for about a century and a half under different temporary and uncertain forms of land ownership. I hope to return elsewhere to the development of the different forms of land ownership in the Karoo.

13. Karoo Dwellings

As long as the farms in the Karoo were still crown land, and the farmers had little security in connection with the ownership rights of the land, they hesitated in making permanent improvements to them. In addition, the farmers spent only a few months each year in the Karoo, so that was reason enough to believe it was not worth the trouble to build houses there. Besides, the mild climate of the region did not require high standards for their winter homes. In these circumstances farmers of the Roggeveld and Bokkeveld initially managed with temporary huts in the Karoo.

In 1778 Paterson wrote: "As this desart [sic] part of the country is inhabited only during a short part of the year, very few houses are to be found in it. Most of the inhabitants live in huts

---

**Trans. note: Dr. van der Merwe used the Dutch word here, within quotation marks, "accrocheer," which translates into English as "attach."

similar to those of the Khoikhoi, some dwell in the tent that covers their waggon; and, even in this situation the boors have the appearance of being the happiest of all human beings."[40]

A quarter century later Barrow described the winter abodes of the farmers in the Karoo as "temporary dwellings of rushes or straw."[41] The Commission for Stock Raising and Agriculture stated in 1805: "The families who trek together mostly live in straw huts."[42] About the same time at Smidswinkel in the Karoo Lichtenstein came across "a few miserable mud huts," which he described as the winter abode of a farm family.[43] Burchell (1811) speaks of "temporary huts,"[44] and [James] Holman (1829) reports: "They occupy their wagons, and slight huts formed for the occasion."[45]

From these accounts and many others,[46] it seems clear that during the last years of the eighteenth century and the first years of the nineteenth century the farmers usually spent the winter in temporary huts of one sort or another. Nowhere are tents mentioned in the sources of that time. Over time, however, the tent also made its appearance in the Karoo. In 1840 W. von Meyer, the German traveler, came across farmers from Friesland in the Karoo "where they have no other shelter than their wagon and a tent."[47]

From that time on the tent quickly prevailed. When the old people of today were children, tents were common in the Karoo. To be sure, one also finds here and there a wattle-and-daub house, a round stone hut covered with reeds, or a simple clay house with a roof made of brackish mud, but by 1880 the tent was in general use. Simple pens made from branches usually held the livestock.[48]

ENDNOTES

[1] W.J. Burchell, *Travels in the Interior of Southern Africa* (London, 1822), I:207, 216; Commission for Stock Raising and Agriculture, 20 November 1805, in George McCall Theal, *Belangrijke Historische Dokumenten over Zuid-Afrika* (Cape Town, 1896, 1911), III:354.

[2] A.J.H. van der Walt, *Die Ausdehnung der Kolonie am Kap der Guten Hoffnung, 1700-1779* (Berlin, 1928), p. 65.

[3] J.Barrow, *Travels into the Interior of Southern Africa*, 2nd ed. (London, 1806), II:62.

[4] Commission for Stock Raising and Agriculture, 20 November 1805, in Theal, *Belangrijke Historische Dokumenten*, III:344.

[5] 1/WOC 11/5, Letters Rec., Petition from the Cold Bokkeveld, 22 December 1818, enclosed with 82 January 1819; 1/WOC 1/6, Minutes of the Heemraad, 5 February 1827; C.O. 374, Letters Rec. from Land Board, Civil Commissioner Truter for Worcester to Land Board, 8 November 1830; H. Lichtenstein, *Reisen im südlichen Africa in den Jahren 1803, 1804, 1805 und 1806* (Berlin, 1811-1812), I:207-08; Commission for Stock Raising and Agriculture, 20 November 1805, in Theal, *Belangrijke Historische Dokumenten*, III:345.

[6] Van der Walt, *Ausdehnung*, p. 69; K.P. Thunberg, *Travels in Europe, Africa and Asia performed within the years 1770 and 1779* (London, 1793), II:169.

[7] Commission for Stock Raising and Agriculture, 20 November 1805, in Theal, *Belangrijke Historische Dokumenten*, III:358-71.

[8] Ibid., III:359.

[9] C.O. 2723, Letters Rec., Worcester, Truter to Bell, 14 September 1830, No. 77.

[10] A. Sparrman, *Reize naar de Kaap de Goede Hoop, de Landen van den Zuid Pool, en rondom de Waereld* (Leiden, 1786), I:284; Thunberg, *Travels*, II:22, 23, 176; Wm. Paterson, *A Narrative of Four Journeys into the Country of the Hottentots and Caffraria in the Years 1777, 1778 and 1779* (London, 1779), p. 47; P. Masson, "An Account of Three Journeys from Cape Town into the Southern Parts of Africa," in *Philosophical Transactions of the Royal Society* (London, 1776), 66:314.

[11] Barrow, *Travels*, I:359; Burchell, *Travels*, I:207, 210; Lichtenstein, *Reisen*, I:167, 198, 206-09; W. von Meyer, *Reisen in Süd-Afrika wärend der Jahre 1840 und 1841* (Hamburg, 1843), p. 163.

[12] Commission for Stock Raising and Agriculture, 20 November 1805, in Theal, *Belangrijke Historische Dokumenten*, III:344; B.R. 451, Minutes of De Mist, De Waal and Faure to Van der Riet, 15 May 1805, p. 268; 1/WOC 13/12, Letters Rec. from Field Cornets, Hugo (Cold Bokkeveld) to Landdrost Vischer, 27 July 1819; 1/WOC 13/14, Letters Rec. from Field Cornets, Hugo (Cold Bokkeveld) to Landdrost Vischer, 25 June 1821; C.O. 2962, Letters Rec., Worcester, Civil Commissioner to Col. Secretary, 5 October 1858.

[13] Commission for Stock Raising and Agriculture, 20 November 1805, in Theal, *Belangrijke Historische Dokumenten*, III:347.

[14] 1/WOC 17/5, Letters Disp. to Field Cornets, B. Pienaar to Field Cornet Naude, 24 April 1810; 1/WOC 1/3, Minutes of the Heemraad, 6 June 1814, p. 22.

[15] Paterson, *Narrative*, p. 47.

[16] Thunberg, *Travels*, II:168. See also 1/WOC 17/25, Letters Disp., P.J. Truter to Col. Secretary, 2 September 1837.

[17] Commission for Stock Raising and Agriculture, 20 November 1805, in Theal, *Belangrijke Historische Dokumenten*, III:360. Cf. C.O. 2962, Letters Rec., Worcester, Civil Commissioner to Col. Secretary, 5 October 1858.

[18] Thunberg, *Travels*, II:169.

[19] 1/WOC 17/25, Letters Disp., P.J. Truter to Col. Secretary, 8 August 1837; C.O. 759, Letters Rec. from Divisional Councils, Worcester, Civil Commissioner to Col. Secretary, 20 June 1860; C.O. 2962, Letters Rec., Worcester, Civil Commissioner to Col. Secretary, 5 October 1858.

[20] F. Masson, "Account of Three Journeys," 66:314; Thunberg, *Travels*, II:176; Paterson, *Narrative*, p. 45; Lichtenstein, *Reisen*, I:158, 167, 206; P.B. Borcherds, *An Auto-Biographical Memoir* (Cape Town, 1861), p. 52; Barrow, *Travels*, II:64; Commission for Stock Raising and Agriculture, 20 November 1805, in Theal, *Belangrijke Historische Dokumenten*, III:360; C.O. 2609, Letters Rec., Tulbagh, J.H. Fischer to Bird, 13 August 1817; C.O. 374, Letters Rec. from Land Board, Civil Commissioner Truter for Worcester to Land Board, 8 November 1830; C.O. 2962, Letters Rec., Worcester, Civil Commissioner to Col. Secretary, 5 October 1858; C.O. 2962, Memorials, C.P. van der Merwe, et al, 8 November 1872, No. 119; CCP 1/2/2/1/7, A16 of 1860, Worcester, Report of Select Committee on Crown Lands.

[21] Thunberg, *Travels*, II:22, 176; Barrow, *Travels*, II:64; Lichtenstein, *Reisen*, I:158, 167, 200; Masson, "Account of Three Journeys," p. 314; Burchell, *Travels*, I:207; Commission for Stock Raising and Agriculture, 20 November 1805, in Theal, *Belangrijke Historische Dokumenten*, III:360; Von Meyer, *Reisen*, p. 213; C.O. 374, Letters Rec. from Land Board, Civil Commissioner Truter for Worcester to Land Board, 8 November 1830.

[22] Commission for Stock Raising and Agriculture, 20 November 1805, in Theal, *Belangrijke Historische Dokumenten*, III:355.

[23] Thunberg, *Travels*, I:176; Barrow, *Travels*, I:359; Burchell, *Travels*, I:207, 258; Lichtenstein, *Reisen*, I:158; Borcherds, *Memoir*, p. 52; J. Holman, *A Voyage round the World including Travels in Africa, etc. from 1827-1832* (London, 1834-35), II:361; 1/WOC 17/25, Letters Disp., P.J. Truter to Col. Secretary, 8 August 1837; 1/WOC 12/30, Letters Rec., George Glaeser to P.J. Truter, 17 September 1838.

[24] Burchell, *Travels*, I:258.

[25] Barrow, *Travels*, I:359.

[26] Commission for Stock Raising and Agriculture, 20 November 1805, in Theal, *Belangrijke Historische Dokumenten*, III:344.

[27] Lichtenstein, *Reisen*, I:206-07.

[28] 1/WOC 13/12, Letters Rec. from Field Cornets, Hugo (Cold Bokkeveld) to Landdrost Vischer, 27 July 1819. See also 1/WOC 13/12, 1/August 1819, and further; 1/WOC 13/14, Letters rec. from Field Cornets, Field Cornet Hugo (Cold Bokkeveld) to Landdrost Vischer, 25 June 1821; Von Meyer, *Reisen*, p. 83.

[29] Von Meyer, *Reisen*, p. 84.

[30] Lichtenstein, *Reisen*, I:198-99.

[31] Ibid.; B.R. 549, Ships and other journals, H. Lichtenstein, "Trip to the Karoo, 19 August 1805-9 September 1805, pp. 764 and 787, enclosed with letter of 10 September 1805 from Lichtenstein to the Council of Policy.

[32] Sparrman, *Reize*, I:284.

[33] Lichtenstein, *Reisen*, I:198.

[34] BR 549, Ships and other journals, H. Lichtenstein, "Trip to the Karoo, 19 August 1805-9 September 1805, p. 787, enclosed with letter of 10 September 1805 from Lichtenstein to the Council of Policy; Borcherds, *Memoir*, p. 52.

[35] Lichtenstein, *Reisen*, I:199.

[36] 1/WOC 1/6, Minutes of the Landdrost and Heemraden, Worcester, 5 February 1827; E.C. Godée Molsbergen, *Reisen in Zuid-Afrika* (The Hague, 1932), II:266.

[37] C.O. 2867, Letters Rec., Worcester, Civil Commissioner to Col. Secretary Montagu, 3 October 1850; C.O. 4939, Letter Book, Col. Secretary Montagu to Civil Commissioner, Worcester, 14 October 1850, p. 149.

[38] RLR 34/1, Old Gamehunters Books, Permit for Petrus Johannes Naude, 3 August 1785, p. 85.

[39] See, among others, Commission for Stock Raising and Agriculture, 20 November 1805, in Theal, *Belangrijke Historische Dokumenten*, III:354.

[40] Paterson, *Narrative*, pp. 47, 48.

[41] Barrow, *Travels*, I:356.

[42] Commission for Stock Raising and Agriculture, 20 November 1805, in Theal, *Belangrijke Historische Dokumenten*, III:354.

[43] Lichtenstein, *Reisen*, I:202.

[44] Burchell, *Travels*, I:207.

[45] Holman, *Voyage*, II:361.

[46] C.O. 374, Letters Rec. from Land Board, Civil Commissioner Truter for Worcester to Land Board, 8 November 1830; 1/WOC 10/7, Logbook, 10 October 1818, p. 188.

[47] Von Meyer, *Reisen*, p. 84.

[48] 1/WOC 10/7, Logbook, 30 October 1818, p. 188.

CHAPTER X

The Winter Trek in Modern Times

1. Extent

The winter trek to the Karoo continues to the present, although in a somewhat altered form. In the Bokkeveld the winter trek plays a very important role even today. From Worcester's border in the southeast to the Citrusdal line in the northwest, everyone who owns some measure of livestock treks to the Karoo without exception. There is no question of the trek to the Karoo abating in recent times in the Ceres district, in the sense that stock farmers who formerly took part in it have subsequently stopped doing so entirely.

It is a fact, however, that stock farming in Ceres over the past twenty years has declined a good deal. This has affected the winter trek. In the Warm Bokkeveld farmers today make their living mostly from fruit-growing and crop farming. There are not many stock farmers left. As a consequence, the winter trek in this part of the Ceres district is much diminished in the sense that a smaller percentage of the farmers today trek than in the past. There are still only some half a dozen farmers in the Warm Bokkeveld who have enough livestock to trek to the Karoo. Some of the farmers have already sold their land in the Karoo. Others still have farms in the Karoo, but no longer have any livestock with which to trek.

In the Cold Bokkeveld stock farming today likewise plays a much smaller role than it did twenty years ago. The farmers, however, all still have livestock, and with a few exceptions they all still trek to the Karoo. Here and there, as very rare exceptions, one comes across a farmer who usually does not make use of land in the Karoo, but these are people who hardly farm with cattle any longer. They own perhaps only 300 or 400 animals and do not find it worth the trouble to trek with so few livestock to the Karoo. For such farmers it is also relatively easy to produce the feed that is needed for the winter and to provide shelter for the ewes and lambs.

In 1938 I estimated that there were about 100 to 120 Ceres farmers involved in the winter trek and that every year around 100,000 head of livestock trekked to the Karoo.

In the Roggeveld there has been little change in the trek to the Karoo. Almost all the Little Roggeveld farmers trek. As far as I know, in this region there is only one farmer who spends the winter on his farm. The farmers of the actual Roggeveld do not take part in the trek to the Karoo. Only those farmers who live along the ridge of the Roggeveld Mountains go down to the Karoo in the winter. The road from Sutherland via Middelpos to Calvinia more or less forms the boundary between the Roggeveld farmers who trek to the Karoo and those who do not trek. Almost all the farmers who live to the south of the road trek, while those who live to the north of the road generally do not.

Furthermore, the percentage of farmers who trek declines the nearer one gets to Calvinia. From Komsberg up to the Calvinia line more or less all the farmers who live along the ridge of the Roggeveld Mountains trek. From Calvinia's boundary up to Blauwkrans only a small percentage of the farmers still trek today. The vast majority spend the winter on their farms or trek "backwards," that is, in the direction of the Riet, Fish and Renoster rivers.

In the Sutherland-Roggeveld, that is, in the Little Roggeveld and old Middel Roggeveld, the trek to the Karoo has therefore not diminished. But in the Calvinia-Roggeveld it has decreased significantly since about 1933, especially after the farmers began spanning jackal-proof wire. Since then quite a number of farmers who had regularly trekked to the Karoo have given up trekking altogether. According to information supplied by the livestock inspector of Sutherland around 50 land owners from his district take part annually in the trek to the Karoo. Then there are also a number of renters from the Roggeveld who still trek. Altogether there should be around 100,000 head of livestock in the Roggeveld that are still involved in the trek to the Karoo. Far fewer trek from the Calvinia district, on average perhaps around 50,000 animals per year.

The Sutherland farmers who make use of the Karoo still always trek regularly. In a given year when the Karoo is in particularly poor condition, it happens that perhaps here and there someone does not trek. But these are exceptions. Normally the farmers trek every year. The Calvinia farmers who have land in the Karoo trek there every year as well. The others trek only in the years when the Karoo is particularly fine.

Until recently the Bokkeveld farmers also invariably trekked to the Karoo. Old-timers report that in their childhood there was never such a thing as occasionally passing the winter in the Bokkeveld. They trekked every winter. They did not even go to see if the Karoo had received rain. When the time came to trek, they packed up and moved the livestock out on the trail. Among these old trekkers I came across people who had trekked for thirty or forty years on end to the Karoo, without skipping a single year.

In this respect, however, a significant change has occurred during the last few years in the Ceres district. Since about 1922 the farmers have increasingly spent the winter in the Bokkeveld, if conditions in the Karoo were bad. I have not come across any Ceres farmers who had regularly trekked every year to the Karoo since 1922, without missing one year. But on the other hand, it appears that even the man who seldom trekked to the Karoo, trekked more often during the winter than he spent in the Bokkeveld. On average, a Bokkeveld farmer treks to the Karoo about seven to eight years out of every ten. Everyone does not trek equally regularly, however, because some have poorer land in the Karoo than others.

The farmers are unanimous in declaring that they would trek every year that the Karoo allowed it, but that recently it had often not been possible. Some years the Karoo is in such poor condition that they cannot trek, and then they are obliged to spend the winter in the mountain country, or make other plans. Many of the old timers ascribe this to the fact that rainfall in the Karoo has progressively diminished during the past thirty, forty years and become more and more irregular.

The farmers did not arrive at this conclusion on the basis of rainfall statistics, because these figures are not available to them. Their assertions are based on general impressions based on memories. For that reason one cannot attach too much value to them. Every reader can easily determine for himself just how risky it is to try and ascertain a change in the average yearly rainfall over a long stretch of years based on memory, by carrying out a simple test. Write down on a piece of paper what, in your opinion, the average yearly rainfall for the previous ten or twenty years was in the place where you live. Then compare this with the actual rainfall figures.

It is a fact, however, that the usefulness of the Karoo for the stock farmer gradually diminished with the passage of time. On this point there is general agreement among the Ceres farmers. But this phenomenon does not necessarily have to be related to the decline in yearly rainfall. It could just as well be explained by the deterioration of the plant growth as the result of overgrazing and fields being tramped bare.

At the same time, however, one must point out that in the old days the Ceres farmers were not in a position to spend the winter in the Bokkeveld. Several old farmers told me that they had not known when they were children that one could give the sheep feed. They simply had to trek to the Karoo every winter, no matter how bad conditions were there as well. The result was that the farmers trekked to the Karoo at that time under circumstances in which they would not dream of trekking today, and that they often suffered great losses by doing so.

Over time, however, farming methods became more intensive. Among other things, the farmers cut back their livestock herds and greatly improved the quality of their livestock. This made them all the more unwilling to take the risks connected with trekking to the Karoo in bad years. They reasoned that they could not afford to let their good livestock die if the Karoo failed them. Moreover, the current expenses related to stock farming had gradually become so high that the farmers could no longer afford to lose a season's fall of lambs.

In these circumstances the Ceres farmers eventually began to make provision to spend the winter on their own farmsteads when there was drought during the year in the Karoo. There is still a farmer here and there today who believes it is better all the same to trek in bad years to the Karoo, and then to provide feed there if it is necessary. They claim that in any case one uses less feed in the Karoo than in the Bokkeveld and that the livestock do not trample one's own wet fields so badly. Increasingly there is a tendency today, however, especially among farmers who farm with a better grade of sheep, to prefer to spend the winter in the Bokkeveld in bad years, and they increasingly organise themselves accordingly.

2. The Trek in New Forms

During the past twenty or thirty years the manner of trekking has changed significantly. The neighborly joint trek of the old days is something of the past. There is not much pleasure associated with the trek anymore. It has become a serious business—a bothersome activity that no one looks forward to. The trek trails today are so narrow and trampled over that there is not much more for the livestock to forage. As a result, everyone who treks is in a hurry and tries to get to his destination as quickly as possible.

The farmers also no longer trek with ox wagons. They generally make use of motor cars and trucks. If the family goes along, the farmer often takes his livestock with the motor car first and then comes to get his family and belongings with the truck. The motor car has greatly expedited the trek. A few hours after a farmer leaves his home, he unloads his people and goods at his farm in the Karoo. With the ox wagon the trek lasted for days.

An interesting development that arose a few years before the present war is that the farmers used trucks to transport their livestock instead of driving them on foot.

Sometimes it happened that the pasture in the Karoo gave out before it was time to trek back. The lambs were then still too weak to travel. Moreover, it was dangerous to trek with livestock over the Swartrug in August, when the resin bush blooms. The livestock die if they eat it. When the Karoo fails them, the farmers prefer to take the ewes and lambs back to the Bokkeveld in trucks. Some farmers prefer to transport their lambing ewes in trucks in any event. The trek is usually very bad for the ewes and lambs. For that reason the farmers prefer to pay the extra costs for trucks rather than to allow a loss of conditioning among the lambing ewes. Furthermore, this type of trek has other advantages as well. It completely eliminates the need to feed the animals along the trail. It also avoids the losses the farmer often suffers when trekking because of cold weather or because the livestock have grazed on poisonous plants.

Once the trek with trucks was commonly in use, a further development occurred. Instead of having lambing time in the winter in the Karoo, some farmers now arranged for lambing time about April in the Bokkeveld. Then they transported their ewes and lambs with trucks to the Karoo as soon as it had rained enough there. The lambs then arrived in the Karoo less dependent upon their mothers, and the ewes as well as the lambs thus survived the winter more easily if the Karoo pasture was poor. What is more, by shearing time in October or November, the early lambs already had six or seven pounds of wool, which amply made up for the expenses of the truck transport.

The problems experienced at the moment of getting gasoline and tires because of war conditions will doubtless hamper this sort of trek temporarily and impede its further development.

The trucks that are used for the transport of livestock are usually equipped in such a way that they have two levels. The ewes and lambs are placed in sacks and tied up so that just their heads stick out. Then they are packed into the truck like sardines in a can. The reason for the sacks is to force the livestock to lie down. If they stand, they constantly stumble about while the truck is moving and they can easily be injured.

Another development that has occurred over time is that the families do not go along on the trek to the Karoo as commonly as in the past.

The Sutherland-Roggeveld is the only area where the old practice of trekking together with the livestock is still strongly maintained. The children mostly remain behind today in hostels, but until recently there were still schools in Sutherland that accompanied the trek to the Karoo in the winter. In the Calvinia-Roggeveld, which has a more pleasant winter climate, the families do not accompany the livestock as often as they did in the old days. Farmers from the Little Roggeveld these days also mostly only move their livestock to the Karoo. The cold is less of a problem for them than for the farmers who live along the top of the Roggeveld Mountains. Moreover, their Karoo land usually borders on their farmsteads, so that they can easily keep an eye on their livestock without having to move themselves. As far as I could determine, there is only one farmer in the Little Roggeveld who treks with his livestock. His Karoo farm is a considerable distance from his homestead.

Until about 1920 the Bokkeveld farmers usually still trekked with their entire families. Since then, however, great changes have taken place in this region. The farmers have all begun to concentrate more and more on grains, vegetables, potatoes, and especially on fruit growing. Most Bokkeveld farms today have 10,000 to 15,000 fruit trees. On some there are as many as 50,000 and the planting continues on a daily basis. (1938). As a result of these new developments there is now much work to do on the homestead in the winter that requires the presence of the farmer and his family. The trees must be pruned and sprayed, the garden soil must be tilled; and then there is still general farm work that had been put aside in the summer and has to be done in the winter out of sheer necessity. As the farming has become more intensive, the farm work has increased enormously. What is more, the Bokkeveld has now reached the stage at which stock farming has become only a sideline activity and no longer makes the greatest claim to the farmer's time.

The farmstead now requires so much attention in the winter that the farmer today can hardly travel together with his livestock to the Karoo. Fortunately the motor car has largely eliminated the necessity for that as well. The motor car has brought the Karoo nearer to the farmstead and made it possible for the farmer to go and regularly inspect his livestock. The wives have also been unwilling lately to go on the trek to the Karoo. They all have such good houses today that they no longer really suffer during the Bokkeveld winters. These days they have also become increasingly averse to enduring the hardships of life in the Karoo, which the old-timers did not find so burdensome because they had fewer comforts in the Bokkeveld. Moreover, the women also have various interests that make their presence desirable throughout the year at the homestead. Many of them keep poultry or made butter to sell and they do not like to leave their farming untended.

Consequently, the majority of Bokkeveld farmers nowadays send their livestock to the Karoo with a son or a foreman. They only go every week or two to have a look at their stock. At the busiest days of lambing time they will stay for perhaps two weeks or a month on the Karoo farm. Occasionally the whole family went to the Karoo for a week or ten days, but then it became more of a vacation. Not more than 25 percent of the families of farmers who trek with their livestock still go regularly together to the Karoo and remain there for the entire winter.

The tent life of the good old days is today almost entirely dead and gone. It still often happens that trekboers who own no Karoo land pitch tents, but almost all of the land owners have small houses on their winter farms. After the farmers received ownership of the land towards the end of the nineteenth century, they began to build. The majority of farmers, however, did not think it worth the trouble to set up large and substantial houses in the Karoo, which had to remain boarded up for two-thirds of the year. Even today most winter residences in the Karoo are still simple flat-roofed houses with a couple of rooms and very few comforts. The family that treks in the winter to the Karoo well-understands that they are going to be camping there.

Many Karoo farms lie completely deserted in the summer. It does happen, however, that a farmer maintains a caretaker who looks after the farm while he is away. Usually it is just a poor sharecropper who gets the right to graze his few livestock on the small patch of land that remains after the owner goes away. After the winter the majority of farmers take all their livestock back to their homesteads. Those who have caretakers on their farms, however, sometimes leave a few livestock, usually goats, which remain in the Karoo right through the year.

It sometimes happens that a farmer hires out his Karoo farm in the summer to one of the farmers who remains there permanently, or perhaps to a poor fellow who has just a few livestock. Most farmers, however, do not like to do this. They find it is not worth the trouble for the sake of the £10 or £15 they can receive for the season to allow their land to be trampled.

In the old days it was the ideal of anyone who trekked to the Karoo to obtain a winter farm there. Today the farmers still prize Karoo land very highly. Almost all the farmers who regularly trek to the Karoo own land there. This means that, with a few exceptions, every farmer in the Cold Bokkeveld and Little Roggeveld, as well as the Sutherland farmers who live along the ridge of the Roggeveldsberg, own winter farms. The few stock farmers still in the Warm Bokkeveld nearly all own farms in the Karoo as well. In Calvinia-Roggeveld there are fewer farmers who own Karoo land than in Ceres and Sutherland, since there are not as many there who regularly trek to the Karoo.

Apart from these land owners, a handful of farmers trek there every winter—some from Laingsburg, Williston and other districts—who do not own land in the Karoo. In dry years even farmers from Beaufort, Fraserburg and Bushmanland trek to the Karoo. Occasionally they hire farms, but mostly they lease pasture and pay by the hundred head of livestock. The farmers who remain permanently in the Karoo usually have more pasture in the winter than they can manage. But they are already becoming reluctant these days to lease out pasture. There are many who would rather save their grazing land for the summer than earn a few pounds in rent. A point of view one still fortunately comes across, however, is "But if a man unburdens himself to you about his difficulties, you can hardly say 'no'."

Land owners who trek from the Roggeveld and Bokkeveld do not readily lease out their pasture in the winter. But particularly in good years some have more grazing land in the Karoo than they can use and they sometimes help trekboers as well. An old gentleman in Ceres told me that a trekboer from Laingsburg came to stay on his winter farm every winter for thirty-five years. In the Calvinia-Karoo, furthermore, there are still a few government farms (Volmoersfontein, Potkleiberg, Springbokvlakte, Luiperdskop, Papkuil, Grasberg-Noord and others) for which grazing licenses are granted.

3. The Trek Can Be Done Away With

In 1805 the Commission for Stock Raising and Agriculture stated that "One could not keep as many livestock in the Roggeveld as in the Cold Bokkeveld, without the privilege of making use of the Karoo during the winter seasons."[1] It appears from archival documents from the nineteenth century that this was the general opinion at that time.[2] Indeed, until about thirty years ago most farmers did not believe it possible to keep livestock on the mountains in the winter and to let lambs be born there.

In recent years, however, it has been repeatedly demonstrated that it is possible to remain in the Cold Bokkeveld if one took the necessary precautions. There is evidence that a farmer can provide effective shelter against the cold for his livestock at relatively low cost. It is actually only necessary to provide shelter to the lambing ewes. Barren stock is fairly resistant to the cold and damp. If Merino sheep have fleece of long wool and are in good condition, they will not just die from cold.

The question of grazing land in the Bokkeveld is likewise not an unsolvable problem. To keep the ewes in milk, the farmers make provision for fresh fodder. They usually sow winter grain such as oats, rye or barley, which the livestock then use as green pasture. Provision is also made for days when it is so wet that the livestock must be kept off the land, or when they cannot graze because of the cold and snow. The sheep are driven into barns and fed maize, oats, and dry alfalfa in troughs.

In this way it is not only possible to keep livestock healthy through the winter, but some farmers even claim that their season's fall of lambs is better in the Bokkeveld than in the Karoo, even when the Karoo is at its best. In spite of the cold, a farmer in the Bokkeveld who looks after his livestock gets nearly all his lambs through the winter alive, while in the Karoo he always loses one or two hundred.

It remains a fact, naturally, that the sour grass around Ceres does not contain all the nutriments that the livestock need. But it is doubtful whether the situation is really as serious as some farmers contend. The claim that livestock that are kept in the Bokkeveld permanently will degenerate physically, has still not been demonstrated empirically. The farmers who believe this have not yet spent a long period of time, year after year, in the Bokkeveld. What the natural pasture lacks can undoubtedly be added artificially. It is still not known precisely how the livestock should be treated. On that point the farmers have not yet troubled themselves too much, because up to now they have always trekked. The farmers who tried to feed their livestock salt and bone meal hold that a person can perhaps solve all their problems that way.

As to grazing land, the Roggeveld is much better off than the Bokkeveld. The livestock do not need any change of pasture. There are even farmers who think that the livestock do better in the winter in the Roggeveld than in the Karoo. They claim that livestock that have trekked may well be in a better condition just after the winter than livestock that remained behind, but the livestock that remained in the Roggeveld for the winter overtake them very quickly. If a farmer does not trek to the Karoo one year—they contend—he can sell his livestock more quickly. Admittedly it may happen that a heavy snowfall interrupts grazing for the livestock for eight or ten days, but this does not occur every winter and seldom happens twice in the same season. Even in cold years a farmer can easily get his livestock through the winter with forage.

The possibilities for growing feed in the Roggeveld are limited. Alfalfa does not do well there. Summers are dry and in parts of the Roggeveld the winters are very severe. But on the other hand a farmer would not need to provide feed every year. In cold years he would most likely need to make provision for feed for a few weeks. He need only concern himself mainly with the lambing ewes. If barren stock that are in good condition have to go for a few days in their pens without enough to feed on, it will not do them any harm. Most farmers who trek today to the Karoo will undoubtedly be able to make provision for the fodder that they need, if they want to spend the winter in the Roggeveld Mountains. The others will not need to purchase much.

The farmer who wants to stop making the winter trek will naturally be faced with the difficulty that his farm cannot then support all his livestock. This will not necessarily mean, however, that he will then have to purchase more ground in the Roggeveld. It is the considered opinion of various well-informed farmers that a farmer will be able to increase the carrying capacity of his farm to such an extent with jackal-proof fencing that it will amply make up for the loss of his Karoo land.

It also seems that the cold in the Roggeveld is not such an insurmountable problem as it was first thought. Farmers who have jackal-proof enclosures say that the herdsman is responsible for the death of the livestock, not the cold or snow. As soon as it begins to snow or rain, the herdsman drives the livestock to the farmyard or he drives them all together. This is fatal. If you want to kill sheep, you must chase them about until they are hot and then let them stand in the freezing weather and get cold. Sheep that are tended also often begin to run of their own accord when they get cold in the fields. Experience has shown, however, that when livestock have become accustomed to roaming about freely in jackal-proof enclosures, losses from the cold occur much less often. As soon as it begins to rain or snow, every sheep seeks shelter for itself. No one drives the livestock on and the danger that the herd will begin to run is very slight.

In the Little Roggeveld and in the Calvinia-Roggeveld it has been demonstrated experimentally that one can go through the winter with livestock without many problems or risk of loss. In that part of Sutherland that lies along the ridge of the Roggeveld Mountains conditions will be much more difficult because of the more severe cold. The general opinion of the farmers there is that it is too cold for lambing on the Roggeveld Mountains. One or two farmers have already tried to do so, but in general the outcomes of such experiments have not been satisfactory. But one must point out that stock farming in this region is still entirely geared towards the trek to the Karoo, and that the farmers are still not well-prepared to pass the winter on their farmsteads.

Where farmers have tried to prepare themselves properly for the winter, the results have been encouraging. In 1939 Bismarck Louw told me that two years before he had built for himself a barn for his sheep for £40. After that he managed to add 2,000 lambs to his stock and lost not one of them due to the cold. It is true that there are many farmers who have colder farms than he does, but in light of what has been done thus far, one is inclined to think that a farmer who takes the necessary precautions will be able to remain anywhere in the Roggeveld throughout the winter. During exceptionally cold weather even the farmer who is well-prepared will still always suffer some loss but, on the other hand, there are also risks connected with the trek to the Karoo.

Thus, it will undoubtedly be physically possible for the farmers of the Bokkeveld and Roggeveld to do away with their winter trek to the Karoo. The question is only whether this will be economically possible.

4. The Economic Effectiveness of the Trek System

In the old days the winter trek to the Karoo was a very inexpensive manner of farming. Until well into the nineteenth century the farmers of the surrounding mountain country made use of crown land in the Karoo free of charge. Later they were obliged to pay £1 per year for their winter farms. Even under the quitrent system the majority of farmers paid just a few pounds per year for the use of their Karoo land.

Today the farmers pay dearly for their winter grazing in the Karoo. If a farmer treks regularly and is dependent on the Karoo, it is expedient to have a Karoo farm. Before the war a person paid anywhere between £500 and £2,000 for one. I even know of a farmer whose Karoo land, plus the improvements on it, cost him £3,700 today. And this farm can only support 2,500 head of livestock for three to four months of the year and 100 goats during the rest of the year.

This is an exceptional case, but it remains a fact that the majority of farmers invested large sums of money in Karoo land, which they can use only a few months per year and cannot even rely upon every year. The interest on that capital plus the taxes represents a sizable yearly amount. In addition there are the expenses connected with the maintenance of the farm. It is true that on most Karoo farms there is not much to neglect, but all the same a farmer must maintain his house and pens, have his dams repaired and cleaned, or perhaps have his wire fences mended. The landowner has all these expenses, whether he treks to the Karoo for the year or not.

The leasing of pasture is also expensive in the Karoo these days. When today's old people were children one could pay 2s. 6d. per hundred head of sheep and goats per month—that is, if you were not assisted free of charge. Later the price climbed to 5s per hundred. Farmers in Elandsvlei today (1938) still lease pasture at "5s per hundred to fellow-Afrikaners and 10s per hundred to speculators" (the latter must always have first-class pasture); but these days one is very lucky to get good pasture at 10s per hundred in the Karoo. The average pasture lease is already about £1 per hundred. It has also happened that trekboers pay £2 10s per hundred.

Apart from this, for some farmers there are also large expenses connected with the trek. The majority of trek trails today are already horribly trampled. Valuable vegetation, which the livestock can eat, has already to a large extent disappeared, and poisonous plants that can kill the livestock have taken its place. Farmers who trek long distances are thus obliged in most cases to feed their livestock along the way, otherwise the animals will not survive the trek over the narrow and barren trek paths. Moreover, the livestock also readily eat the poisonous plants when they become hungry and then die. If the farmer transports his lambing ewes in trucks, he does not need to feed them along the way, and can prevent the losses from poisonous plants, but this also entails great expense. Before the war transporters asked about £5 to transport around fifty ewes with lambs over a distance of fifty miles. For a farmer who uses his own trucks, the cost is not so high. But if he has to travel any considerable distance, it in any case costs him at least 2s to transport a ewe with her lamb to or from the Karoo.

In most cases the trek to the Karoo increases the farmer's labor costs. A farmer whose farmstead is fenced in, but not his Karoo farm, needs many more people in the Karoo to tend to his livestock than he does on his farmstead. One such farmer told me that in the Karoo he needed at least three herders and three extra helpers during the lambing month. On his Bokkeveld farm, where the livestock wander freely in jackal-proof enclosures, he could get by with two workers. Apart from this, a farmer whose work on the farmstead continues through the winter needs special laborers for his livestock when he sends them to the Karoo.

Finally, the trek to the Karoo entails many traveling expenses for some farmers. A farmer today no longer risks trekking to the Karoo as a matter of course when the time comes to trek and all the little chores have been completed. He usually first goes to check whether it has rained enough on his land for him to trek. Sometimes he must go off and look a number of times before he can move the livestock onto the road. The cars from the Bokkeveld all have to travel through Karoopoort, with the result that such a journey for a Bokkeveld farmer is seldom under 100 miles, and in many cases it is over 200 miles. Furthermore, the farmer who does not accompany his livestock to the Karoo must go and check on his livestock at least every fourteen days. This again entails a number of trips.

Apart from the fact that trek farming has already become much more expensive today, there are other factors that undermine some farmers' confidence in the effectiveness of the system.

To begin with, the farmers who trek to the Karoo often suffer heavy losses. Many times along the trail livestock die from eating poisonous plants. The Roggeveld farmers also often suffer losses coming down from the mountain because of tribulosis.[*] They attribute this to the sudden change of the air, and it usually happens when the livestock descend from the mountain too quickly. It often happened that a farmer lost 100 or even 200 head of livestock from an outbreak of tribulosis. The livestock also frequently died from *skolsbos*[†] in the Karoo. One farmer in the Roggeveld told me that at one time he lost 250 head of livestock in four days to *skolsbos*. In the Roggeveld-Karoo the livestock also occasionally contract loco disease.[‡] Farmers, particularly those who keep a good class of sheep, have been afraid of late to run the risks that are connected with the trek to the Karoo.

It is also a fact that the Karoo is changeable. The farmers can really not rely on the Karoo at all. One year all goes well and another year it goes badly. For the farmer who has no Karoo land this is not such a serious matter. If one year the Karoo is bad, he feeds his livestock on his farm, or he makes another plan, and he has no capital invested in the Karoo that is not giving any return. If one year the Karoo is fine, he treks and leases pasture. The situation is different for the man who owns land in the Karoo. He has expenses related to his Karoo farm, whether he uses it in any given year or not. At the same time, he needs to manage the farmstead in such a way that he can spend the winter there if necessary.

Finally, there is also the realization that the winter trek in many cases leads to the maintenance of extensive farming methods where more intensive methods are warranted. The trek to the Karoo often gets in the way of making improvements to the farmstead. In some cases much capital has been invested in the Karoo that can surely be utilized more productively on the farmstead. There is often work on the farmstead that is neglected. Labor is also often drawn away from the farm. When the farmers are in the Karoo in the winter, work on the farmstead comes to a standstill, while there really is not much to do on the Karoo farm. Undoubtedly the farmers can make better use of their time in the winter on their farmsteads than in the Karoo. In the Roggeveld, for example, there are many opportunities to build catchments. This sort of work can only be done in the winter, when the ground is wet. But then the farmers are in the Karoo again. The trek to the Karoo thus contributes a great deal towards the situation whereby a farmer has two farms, both of which are untended.

---

[*]Trans. note: *Tribulosis* is known locally in Afrikaans as "dikkkop' (literally, 'thick head") or "geeldikkop" ("yellow thick head"). It is a disease affecting small animals, including sheep, brought about by the grazing of low shrubs, bushes, and pioneer grasses typically found in the Karoo, and the northwest Cape. Characterized by yellowing of the skin and mucus membranes due to severe liver damage, and a harsh reaction to sunlight, which can lead to the splitting of facial skin and the loss of ears, lips, and eyelids.

[†]Trans. note: The local Afrikaans term for one of many varieties of poisonous plants and shrubs in the Karoo.

[‡]Trans. note: A nervous disease of cattle, sheep, and horses characterized by paralysis, impaired vision, and weakness, caused by eating the locoweed. See also ch. IX, p. 117.

In these circumstances the question now arises of whether trek farming in the Roggeveld and Bokkeveld is still always the most economically effective manner of farming. The answer to this question is not simple, because everyone who treks is not in the same situation. Not all farmers derive equal benefit from their Karoo land and the costs are not the same for everyone to trek to the Karoo.

The farmers of the Bokkeveld, particularly those who live in the Friesland and Skotland areas, seem today to be the most anxious to avoid the winter trek. Indeed in this part of the mountain region the trek is associated with the most hardship and expense. Not only because of the remoteness of the Karoo, but also because the majority of farmers today can no longer accompany their livestock to the Karoo. Every year the winter trek is becoming a greater bother in the Bokkeveld.

In spite of these problems, the stock farmers of the Bokkeveld have still not really considered giving up the trek altogether. They now try to arrange things so that they can pass the winter on their farmsteads if they cannot trek at all. When the Karoo is good in a given year, no farmer will even consider staying over in the Bokkeveld. Even the individual farmer who has no Karoo land will not hesitate in good years to trek to the Karoo and lease pasture there, if the size of his livestock herds warrant this in any degree. And if he has too few livestock himself to trek, he will try to send his livestock together with those of another farmer. If it is in any way possible for a farmer to trek, he will not even try to spend the winter in the Bokkeveld. It has even happened that the Ceres farmers have loaded their livestock onto the train and sent them to Beaufort West or Carnarvon when they could not trek for the winter to the Karoo.

At the moment it is the decided opinion of the overwhelming majority of the Bokkeveld farmers that it is not economically possible to halt completely the trek to the Karoo. They accept the winter trek with all its hardships and expenses as an economic necessity.

The general view is that if a farmer wants to farm right through the year in the Bokkeveld, it will cost a great deal to provide effective protection against the cold for all his livestock and to build barns where they can be fed on days when they cannot go outside to graze. The greatest difficulty, however, is the question of grazing land. A farmer who wants to spend the winter in the Bokkeveld has to feed his livestock from the time of the first frost until the pasture begins to grow again after the winter. The majority of farms in the Bokkeveld are capable of producing a certain amount of fodder, but there are only a few farmers who will not need to purchase some feed. Alfalfa does not really do well in the Bokkeveld. One can grow it only on some farms. Some parts of the Bokkeveld are so wet and cold that it is very difficult to make provision for enough green pasture. Many farmers have used nearly all their usable arable land for growing fruit trees and do not have enough left over to produce fodder for all their livestock. Moreover, most farmers are inclined to figure that they can employ their arable better than by growing livestock fodder on it. And purchasing feed is completely out of the question. This would be too expensive for them.

The general view is that one can only spend the winter with livestock in the Bokkeveld if necessity drives you to do it. From this point of view, it is better to feed your livestock in the Bokkeveld than to let them die off in the Karoo or to lose the season's lambs. But when a farmer spends the winter in the Bokkeveld, he actually purchases his lambs[§] and after the winter is over he sits with a worn-out farm without any pasture. In this way he can at best avoid losses, but not farm at a profit.

The farmers' opinions are based on experience. They have all spent the winter in the Bokkeveld and know what it is like. I am also inclined to attach much value to the farmers' opinions. The Ceres farmers are well-informed people, who well know how the business aspects of farming affect them. On the other hand, however, one has to point out that the matter has perhaps not been thoroughly tested yet. Since the farmers have still always depended on the Karoo, they have not yet organized their farms with the intention of permanently farming in the Bokkeveld. Most have still only made provision for the situation that, in bad years when they really cannot trek, they should not be caught out too badly. They more or less just keep the backdoor open. There have thus not been altogether satisfactory experiments conducted to determine whether a stock farmer can farm permanently in the Bokkeveld at a profit. Perhaps the farmers' views have also been influenced by the fact that they have invested a good deal of capital in the Karoo: they now have the land and they have to use it.

I have met only two farmers in Ceres who figure that they can profitably stop trekking to the Karoo altogether, namely, Tippie du Toit from De Keur, and Frans van der Merwe from Moerasvlei. Frans thinks that the other Bokkeveld farmers could all do so as well. These two persons, however, are in a more fortunate position than the other farmers in their vicinity. Their farms have sweeter pastures, with the result that they have better winter grazing. Furthermore, their farms are also warmer and they therefore have a better opportunity to harvest fodder. Neither of them, however, had stopped making the winter trek entirely. Tippie du Toit has land in the Karoo, which he uses as often as possible. The van der Merwes do not have a farm in the Karoo and they are also not even very large stock farmers, but they also still trek more often to the Karoo than they remain in Ceres.

The future of trek farming in Ceres is not predictable. The general opinion today is that it will continue as long as there are large livestock farmers in the Bokkeveld. As long as a farmer has enough livestock to trek, it is cheaper to trek to the Karoo than to provide fodder in the Bokkeveld. There are people, however, who are concerned about the future of stock farming in the Bokkeveld. The farmers are very fond of their livestock and will not simply do away with their stock farming. But the Bokkeveld is really not a livestock district. The old pioneers only took up stock farming because they had no market for agricultural products. In recent times the farmers concentrated more and more on agriculture, market gardening, and fruit growing. The expansion of this form of farming, which still continues every day, occurs at the expense of stock farming. The best land is increasingly being ploughed and the livestock are shunted aside to the poorer plots of land. This leads to a reduction in livestock herds.

Where this development will finally end cannot be predicted, but if it proceeds in the same direction, it could happen that the Bokkeveld farmers' livestock herds will eventually become so

---

[§]Trans. note: That is, to remain in the Bokkeveld all winter, the farmer's expenses for constructing shelters and buying fodder are the purchasing price for the lambs that are born during this time.

small that it will no longer be worth their while to take them to the Karoo. It will then also no longer be so difficult to provide some shelter and fodder for a small number of animals.

In the Roggeveld today there are also already some farmers who believe that you will farm more economically effectively if you remain on your farmstead throughout the year and cultivate it. In the Calvinia-Roggeveld it has been experimentally demonstrated that a farmer can profitably do away with the winter trek. Various farmers who formerly trekked to the Karoo regularly have no longer been doing so in recent times, after they enclosed their farmsteads with jackal-proof fencing. In general they are very pleased with the result. They continue to have problems every now and then with the cold weather and with lambs that freeze to death, but these are negligible in comparison with the losses that farmers sometimes suffer on the trail or in the Karoo. It is risky to maintain that such farmers will not have to trek at all. There will perhaps be years when they can again trek profitably to the Karoo. but they feel that it is no longer necessary to trek regularly.

It can be expected that more farmers will abandon the trek system in the future. In the Roggeveld the winter trek is in great measure the legacy of the extensive farming system. As farming becomes more intensive, so the trekking will tail off. Particularly farmers who trek long distances will begin to balk at the expenses, worries, and losses that such travel brings with it. And the trek is really not an absolute necessity in all parts of the Roggeveld. Some farmers who still trek to the Karoo will undoubtedly do better if they sell their Karoo land and use the money to manage their farmsteads in such a way that it will no longer be necessary to trek.

At the moment, however, it can still not be predicted whether the trek to the Karoo will completely die out. In the coldest parts of the Roggeveld the winter trek is definitely advantageous. In addition, there is the fact that the trek to the Karoo in many cases is not accompanied by significant hardship or expense. Some of the farmers who live on the ridge of the Roggeveldsberg own Karoo land that borders on their farmsteads. In such cases a Karoo farm is a great advantage for farming. It means not only that such a farmer has more pasture land that lies at a convenient distance from his homestead, but also that he has a warm little corner for the winter on his property that is perfectly suited for lambing time. When it begins to get cold, or if the ewes had to begin lambing, he simply drives the livestock down the mountain. At the same time, he saves his farm land for as long as the pasture needs to grow out well. He also has no problems with trails or trekking over another man's land. Finally, he can easily keep watch over his livestock in the Karoo without having to trek there with them.

One of the Roggeveld farmers who is in such a lucky position assured me that he would have abandoned the winter trek long ago if he had to trek from fifty miles away, but that he saw no reason why he should do so as his Karoo land was so conveniently located.

One cannot exclude the possibility, however, that the subdivision of land in the future, even in such cases, could put an end to the winter trek. The Karoo farms that lie on the slope of the Roggeveld Mountains have constant pasture that is usable in the summer as well, and many of them are permanently inhabitable.

5. The Influence of the Winter Trek on the Karoo

In the old days people figured that the Karoo would never get permanent inhabitants. Indeed the greatest part of this region, which has been so harshly treated by nature, was always used only as periodical pasture land. In the course of time, however, people nevertheless settled in the Karoo.

The Calvinia-Karoo already has a large fixed population today. The greatest part of the land is owned by people who live there permanently. The majority of them have an extremely hard time maintaining their livestock on their land throughout the year. If a farmer owns any livestock at all, he has to give them fodder in the summer. Luckily though, it is possible here and there to grow forage. Some farmers trek in the summer into other districts such as Williston, Carnarvon and Beaufort West. Others move around in the Karoo. Small farmers, who own little livestock, remain on their land in the summer and lease out pasture in the winter to migrants coming in. If better provision is made there for water in the summer, the need to trek will decrease a great deal.

There are already people living in the Ceres- and Sutherland-Karoo today as well, but only a small number of the permanent inhabitants are land owners. The majority of farms today are still in the hands of farmers from the Bokkeveld and the Roggeveld, who use it only three to four months in the year. The greatest part of the permanent inhabitants in this part of the Karoo are renters, sharecroppers, or farm overseers. Coloureds live permanently on some farms. Most of these people possess only a few hundred cattle, from which they can hardly make a living, and which they can barely keep alive through the summer. They must continually dash around from one farm to another. Usually they do not leave the Karoo at all. It is not worth the trouble to trek far with so few livestock.

There are few farmers in the Karoo (the Calvinia-Karoo included) who are well off. Here and there one comes across someone who owns a lot of land and can make a respectable living. But the overwhelming majority of the permanent inhabitants of the Karoo are destitute. At times one wonders how some of them make a living from the small number of animals that they keep alive with so much difficulty. Livestock farming in the Karoo is very precarious and the people who live there have very little opportunity to get ahead, or become rich, by farming.

The old people were of the opinion that the Almighty intended the Karoo only as winter pasture for the farmers in the surrounding mountain country. There are still people today who are inclined to think that the Karoo should never have acquired permanent inhabitants. But the farmers who live there view the matter in a different light. They feel that the Karoo is capable of far greater development, but that the periodical trek has always prevented this.

There is much to say in support of this viewpoint. The greatest portion of the Karoo at the moment is not being used in a manner calculated to make it habitable throughout the year. Every winter the farmers come from the Bokkeveld and the Roggeveld with their large herds of cattle. They trampled the ground to dust and then depart again to their farmsteads. There is no pasture saved for the summer. This is why it is so difficult for those who remain behind on the winter farms to get through the summer.

In addition, the Karoo farms are also too small for anyone to survive on them right through the year. When the farms were originally surveyed and given out, the intention was to further the interests of those farmers who used the land only for a few months in the winter, when the pasture was at its best. For that purpose a Karoo farm of 4,000 to 5,000 morgen is quite large enough. But a farmer cannot exist on such a farm if he has to live on it permanently. If a farmer owns 50,000 or 70,000 morgen in the Karoo, however, he will be able to make a living on it, even if he has to wander about continually in the summer. The farmers of that region tell of an old baster who farmed in the old days with 2,000 head of livestock somewhere in the Karoo. He moved around a great deal, but he made a good living.

Another important fact is that most Karoo farms to date have been organized only as winter farms. The farmers make no provision for the summer, because they need the pasture only in the winter. The general opinion, however, is that the carrying capacity of the Karoo in the summer can be greatly increased if one makes the necessary provision.

In the first place the water supply of the Karoo can still be greatly improved. The topography and soil conditions of the region offer many possibilities for catching and storing rainwater in earthen dams. There is usually sufficient run-off and there is abundant pot-clay earth, which forms an ideal basin for catchment dams. In the old days the farmers did not bother too much about dams. In the winter there was usually enough rain water for their temporary needs.[3] Furthermore, it was very difficult to make dams before graders came into use at the end of the nineteenth century. At this time one saw only a little dam made with wheelbarrows here and there. During the past forty years, however, a good many scooped out dams[**] have been made. Recently the farmers have increasingly begun to realize the value of the dams. A large number of dams have been constructed particularly since the government scheme of dam subsidies came into effect a few years ago. But a great deal can still be done in this respect. One can easily construct a dam in the Karoo that holds water for six months or longer. There are even farms that are permanently occupied that are totally dependent for their water supply on storage dams.

Up to now the land owners of Ceres and Sutherland have gone in mainly for storage dams, with the intention of improving the water supply for the winter. Such dams are excellent for this purpose. When there has been so little rain that the dams have no water, then there is no grazing land as well, and the farmers cannot use the land. Over the summer, when water is most needed, the farmers are not worried, because then they do not need the pasture.

Water in the Karoo is not such an important issue as in some other regions south of the Orange. The underground water level is comparatively shallow. One can obtain water nearly everywhere in the Karoo if one is prepared to dig a well of 40 to 100 feet deep. The water is often brackish and not always suitable for drinking or irrigation. But the livestock usually drink it all the same. Wells and boreholes have been made here and there, but the underground water of the Karoo has still not been sufficiently exploited. The windmill has yet to take over in the Karoo.

[**]Trans. note: The word Dr. van der Merwe uses is "uitsleepdamme." These are water reservoirs, or "gorra," that the farmer scoops out by hand to provide water for himself and his livestock. For an extensive discussion of the methods used by the farmers to obtain water, with illustrations, see P.J. van der Merwe, *Reports from the Dorsland and other pioneering regions*, Compiled and translated by Margaretha Schäfer. Final edit by Franz Schäfer. (Stellenbosch: African Sun Media, 2020): 138-43. I am grateful to Mrs. Schäfer for this reference.

It would therefore not be difficult to provide more drinking places for livestock in the Karoo. This will greatly increase the carrying capacity of the land. It will allow the farmers to use the pasture land more systematically and lessen the traveling between the watering place and grazing area, which will protect the ground from being trampled.

The greatest difficulty in the permanent habitation of the Karoo is that its pasture land is so poor in the summer. A farm that can very easily support 2,000 head of livestock during the winter months, can support perhaps 200 during the rest of the year. This difficulty can be rectified in large measure, however, by enclosures. If the Karoo farms are fenced in and divided into enclosures, with water in every enclosure, the carrying capacity of the land will be increased during the summer. But most farmers today still question whether the results that can be obtained in this way justify the expense. There have been two experiments with jackal-proof fences in the Karoo, but these did not spur on the other farmers to follow the example. It is possible, however, that the value of the land. could justify fencing to protect their livestock.

The general feeling today is that one makes the best use of the Ceres- and Sutherland-Karoo if you "stock" the pasture densely in the winter and let it rest for the remainder of the year. Indeed, one also gets more usufruct from livestock pasture when you allow it to be eaten green than when you save it. They also claim that Karoo land is easily exhausted. If you keep your livestock on it for a few summers in a row, the pasture land is ruined and the vegetation deteriorates rapidly.

There is no doubt, however, that if ever the farmers from the mountain regions no longer have need of the Karoo, it will not lie worthless. The Karoo will acquire a permanent population, who will find a way of making a living there, even though they will have also to wage a constant battle against nature.

ENDNOTES

[1] Commission for Stock Raising and Agriculture, 20 November 1805, in Theal, *Belangrijke Historische Dokumenten over Zuid-Afrika* (Cape Town, 1896, 1911), III:354.

[2] 1/WOC 1/3, Minutes of the Landdrost and Heemraad, 6 October 1818, p. 392; 1/WOC 17/8, Letters Rec., Civil Commissioner for Worcester, P.J. Truter to Bell, 13 February 1817; 1/WOC 17/14, Letters Disp., Civil Commissioner for Worcester, P.J. Truter to Land Board, 2 September 1837. [Trans. note: The citation of 1/WOC 17/8 above, cited as Dr. van der Merwe had it, cannot be correct. There is 1) no letter for this date in this volume; 2) the volume should be Letters Disp. not Letters Rec.; 3) Truter did not become Civil Commissioner until September 1828. In 1/WOC 17/24, Letters Disp. for Worcester, March 1826 to October 1833, there are letters from Truter to Bell that may be the ones to which Dr. van der Merwe is referring.]

[3] C.O. 374, Letters Rec. from Land Board, Civil Commissioner Truter for Worcester to Land Board, 8 November 1830

CHAPTER XI

The Namaqualand Encampment System

1. General Practice

During the winter and spring months one would find very few Namaqualanders at home. As soon as they have finished plowing, the farmers shut up their "walled houses" and go with their livestock to "encamp," either in the outer pasturage of their farms or in areas with a milder climate. The plowing season is determined by the coming of the winter rains. They usually begin to fall in April or May, but can sometimes stay away till June. The Namaqualanders therefore trek between April and June, but most commonly in May, to their encampment sites. There they remain until they have finished harvesting in October or November. After that they trek again back to the "ordinance," as the homestead of a farm in that region is called.

Here and there one comes across a modern farmer in Namaqualand today who no longer goes to his encampment in the winter, or who perhaps leaves his livestock under the supervision of a herdsman. They claim that the trek is not essential for farming and that in any case the farmer does not need to accompany his livestock. They are, however, the rare exceptions. The overwhelming majority of the farmers still observe the old practice. The old sort of Namaqualander in particular treks every year, and he treks himself, with his entire family.

The Kamiesberge is the only part of Namaqualand where the farmers leave their farmsteads in the winter. Because of the altitude the winter is very severe. There is a heavy frost every night and the region is often covered under a blanket of snow. It then becomes unpleasant for people and also too cold for lambing. Consequently most farmers leave the Kamiesberge in the winter and seek shelter in regions with a milder climate. Some of them trek towards the west coast into the Sandveld. Others descend towards Bushmanland. This form of trek occurred in [John] Barrow's time.[1] Apparently it had already been in existence then for a long time. Presumably it developed when the first pioneers settled in the Kamiesberge. This is evident from [William] Paterson's account of his travels. In September 1778 he wrote, "As the dry season was now commencing, the greater part of the inhabitants were removed to their summer residence on the Camis Berg."[2]

In bygone days the farmers in other parts of Namaqualand also left their homes in the winter.[3] Old people say that the southern Sandveld farmers regularly trekked to the Hardeveld in the winter, or towards the Vanrhynsdorp area. This sort of trek died out about 1925. In 1938 only two or three Sandveld farmers trekked regularly. Furthermore, it is said that the Namaqualand farmers in the old days often owned two or more farms each, from among which one was used as a winter farm. Other farmers encamped on undistributed crown land. This type of farmer spent much of the encampment season moving around.

Currently the encampment system usually takes the form of a farmer spending the winter on the outer pasturage of his farmstead. This means that most of the farmers only trek a distance of between one and seven miles. This all depends naturally on the shape and size of the farm and the location of the "ordinance." It happens now and then that a farmer shifts his livestock post one or more times during the season. Most farmers these days, however, pass the entire winter at the same encampment. Farms have already become so small over time that there are not many opportunities for trekking left.

The winter station is selected for the sake of water that could be drawn for the house from a nearby small draw-well, stone pit, or little spring that flowed in the rainy season. It often happens, however, that the farmers have to convey drinking water in vats or large tanks to their encampment sites. In the Sandveld mobile casks pulled by donkeys were widely used. A small cross-plank was nailed into either side of the cask. Through each small plank there was a little bolt that had to serve as an axle. Hooked onto the small bolts were leather straps with rings on the end. One or two donkeys were then harnessed to the straps. The bilge of the cask that rolled over the ground was generally covered with a sheet of galvanized iron. In that way a cask lasts for years.

If water has to be conveyed in this way, there is not always enough to wash the crockery. Then the women scour their dirty crockery with sand and wipe it out with a dry cloth. "Water could not wash it any cleaner," one old pioneer assured me.

2. Origins of the Encampment System

In Namaqualand water is very scarce during the summer. The "ordinance" usually makes some type of provision for water right through the year, but very few farmers have a permanent water supply on their outer pasturage. This makes it very difficult for most of them to use the outer pasturage fully in the summer (or during a drought). And, even though they can get to it, this is generally associated with overgrazing and over straining of the livestock, if they want to let the pasturage be grazed all the way from the homestead. This was especially the case in the old days when farmers still had farms of 10,000 to 20,000 morgen and larger. Today the farms are much smaller but the homesteads are often very inconveniently located. This is particularly true of the Sandveld. In this arid region water is usually only to be had in the dry beds of the temporary streams throughout the year. Where this is the case, the farms have been cut up into pieces in such a way that each farmer gets a little piece of river bank. On either side of the river there is then a row of farms, with all the homesteads along the river. The water is therefore located on the outer reaches of the land and the outlying pasturage is unreachable from the homestead.

In the winter there is usually temporary water in pools or stone pits somewhere in the outlying pasturage. There are also trickling springs and small fountains everywhere that flow in the rainy season. In any event, the Namaqualand livestock do not really drink much in the winter. The pasture then is bright green and provides succulent young growth with so much moisture in its leaves and stems that the livestock have no need for water for months. Besides, the dew in Namaqualand is heavy, especially in the Sandveld nearby the coast. In the mornings the leaves of plants are overladen with glistening dewdrops. If you take only a few steps through the fields, your feet are soaked. The dew is also a source of water. In good years Namaqualand livestock could survive entirely without water from the middle of April to the middle of December. Even in arid years the livestock really do not need to drink for months. It often happens in Namaqualand that for the first six months of their lives lambs manage without water and then do not know how to drink when they are brought to the water in the summer.

The fact that the livestock do not need water in the winter then allows the farmers to trek to the outlying pasturage and to use pasture that cannot easily be reached from the homestead. This means that the pasture around the homestead, which is located near the water, can be saved for the summer, when the livestock have to drink.

Another reason that the farmers give for trekking to the encampments is that they want to keep their livestock off of the land. The Namaqualanders do not farm only livestock. They are usually also grain farmers and generally plant close to the homestead. The lands are not enclosed, however. And if the farmers remain on the farms while grain is growing in the fields, the livestock are all too eager to demolish the standing crop. For that reason all of the livestock on the "ordinance" are taken away as soon as the plowing is finished. Furthermore, until the harvest is over, the large animals that can travel far distances to graze are carefully watched. In the evenings they are often driven into the pens.

In the old days, when the population of Namaqualand was very mobile and fencing materials were not yet within the reach of everyone, this factor of grain farming was probably an important reason for trekking to the encampments. But this is undoubtedly not the most important factor for the preservation of the encampment system at present. There are certainly farmers in Namaqualand who cannot afford even the most trifling cash outlay. But on the other hand, many farmers, who can easily fence in their lands, regularly go to the encampments. In such cases one is putting the horse before the cart to claim that these specific farmers went to their encampments because their lands are not fenced in. Their lands are not fenced in because they still always go to their encampments.

In this connection one can point out that the Sandveld farmers also encamp, although many of them in fact sow in the outlying fields and others do not sow at all.

A factor that contributes a great deal to the continuation of the trek is the fact that the Namaqualander regards encamping with livestock as a sort of vacation. The people take pleasure in going to live for a few months every year in the fields in a reed hut, just as a city person finds pleasure in going for a hike with a rucksack over his shoulders, even though he could drive; or to give up city conveniences and go camping in the country, where he has to sleep on the ground and has to cook his own food. The encampment with livestock brings with it a change of life styles that breaks up the monotony of farm life. For that reason even the well-to-do farmers encamp— people who can hire enough laborers to look after their livestock and do not need to go along personally with their animals. One of the richest farmers in Namaqualand, who takes along his easy chair and radio when he encamps and always enjoys it very much, recently said to me: "the encampment is Namaqualand's vacation spot. There you can enjoy your peace. You live naturally and everything is abundant. When you return from the encampment, you are a totally new person."

3. The Family Treks Together

In other parts of the Union it also often happened that livestock are stabled in the outer pasturage of the farm. But then only the herdsman generally attends them. The question therefore now arises as to why whole families in Namaqualand trek with the livestock to the encampments.

This is connected in the first place with the fact that the trek to the encampment takes place during lambing time, when livestock farming requires much more care and attention than otherwise. There is also the fact that the Namaqualander, particularly the older sort, is very fond of farming with goats. Goats do very well in Namaqualand. In the mountainous areas the goats clamber about the craggy bluffs and cliffs much better than sheep can. In the Sandveld they also manage better than sheep, because they can stand up on their hind legs against trees and can eat leaves that no sheep can reach. Goat farming presents many more problems during lambing time, however, than sheep farming does. The goats have to be milked regularly, because the ewes have too much milk for the lambs and the farmers naturally also use the milk. Furthermore, the lambs have to be brought to the ewes regularly in the beginning. Kids are very stupid and often do not know their mothers. The ewes also often abandon their lambs. Then they must be tied up in the evenings, so that the lambs can suck. Moreover, numerous hand-fed lambs usually have to be cared for.

Under these circumstances a farmer generally prefers to be personally with his livestock at lambing time. He feels he cannot rely on a herdsman or on other farm-hands to do all this work conscientiously. The typical Namaqualander believes that the work will be neglected if he is not go with his livestock at lambing time. Another consideration is that the family itself willingly does the extra work that farming requires during lambing time in order to avoid extra expenses for the farmer. In recent years they have also often been compelled to work themselves, because there are not always enough laborers available.

A peculiar practice has developed in Namaqualand in connection with the encampment system that is typical of that region. This is that it has become the duty of the women and girls to work with the goats. The men concern themselves only with the large animals and the sheep. This interesting custom developed, in my view, in the following way: since the lands were not enclosed, the men had to look after the large animals. They drove them to the pasture in the mornings and in the evenings returned them to the pens. For other reasons too the men – in the old days more than today – were often obliged to be away from the house. They had to go out on commandos against the Bushmen; they had to go and search for lost livestock; they hunted, went to fetch wood, conveyed water, or went to town. The men therefore were often not at home. But if you want to work with kids, you always have to be at home. Every day lambs are born that need attention. You also need to know every lamb and every ewe, if you want to take good care of the lambs. And if you are away from the house for a day or two, you easily get confused by the little creatures that often look so alike. For this reason the women and girls, who were at home every day and all day, were the obvious members of the family to work with the kids. Perhaps a woman also has more patience than a man, so that it was more in their nature to do this sort of work.

4. Reed Huts

It is still an established practice in Namaqualand to live in reed huts during the encampment season. This custom developed in the time when there was still a lot of crown land and the farmers had large farms, so that in the winter there was a lot of wandering about. This created the need for a transportable house that could be easily dismantled and quickly set up again on another spot. The reed hut met this need superbly.

Nowadays the possibilities for trek have become so limited during the encampment season that it no longer necessary to have a transportable house. In spite of this, the farmers still do not build houses on their encampment sites. Only here and there will one perhaps come across a small galvanized iron house on a livestock post. During the times when the farmers wandered around a good deal they grew accustomed to the reed hut and now they remain attached to this practice. I once asked a woman whether she did not find the reed hut more uncomfortable than her walled house. Her answer was: "Yes, I like the walled house more, but you know it is now just the custom to live in a reed hut in the winter." In addition—the Namaqualanders say—you cannot hear the livestock in the night when you sleep in a walled house. When you camp out in a reed hut, you can hear every sheep bleat in the night, and if there is something wrong, you can get up and have a look.

A tent naturally meets this requirement as well. In addition a tent can be taken apart and transported more easily than a reed hut. But the Namaqualanders prefer reed huts. Here and there one finds a farmer who lives in a tent in the winter. Others make use of a tent as well as the reed hut. But the reed hut is still always used the most at the encampment sites. It is much airier than a tent and does not become so muggy in warm weather. It also does not remain clammy for so long after the rains as a tent does. It is thus healthier. Moreover, as a result of the humidity and the abundant rain in the winter, a tent never lasts long in Namaqualand. The canvas rots very easily from all the dampness.

Originally the reed hut took on the form of a perfect hemisphere. The diameter of the circular floor was about ten to twelve feet. The Namaqua Khoikhoi lived in such reed huts and the farmers adopted it in this shape from them.[4] Today, however, one finds only a few circular reed huts. The majority of reed huts that one comes across today in Namaqualand have an oval-shaped floor-plan and look roughly like half an eggshell cut through the length. The whites, however, not only produced a more economical shape for the reed hut. Since they had need of more space than the Khoikhoi, they soon make the reed hut larger as well. One finds reed huts of all sizes, but the most common will be twelve to fifteen feet at their widest and fifteen to twenty feet at their longest. The roof is around eight feet high at its highest point.

According to the testimony of old people the oval-shaped reed hut first made its appearance toward the end of the previous century and after that the round reed hut gradually disappeared. In recent times still another type of reed hut has made its appearance, which is generally called the "square house." As the name suggests, it had a rectangular floor. Furthermore it had vertical walls and a pitched roof like a frame tent. The house consisted of a rigid framework of poles and laths that were covered with reed panels. It had doors with frames and windows like a walled house. Such a house is stronger and more comfortable than a normal reed hut. But examined a little more closely, it is no longer a reed hut. It is a sort of wattle-and-daub hut covered with little panels. I have even seen a "square house" in Namaqualand that had walls made of reed panels and a roof of galvanized iron. Where will these new fashions end!

5. The Building of a Reed Hut

One can hardly imagine in this time of housing need and hard times for the building industry that there is a part of South Africa where building has not been disrupted at all by the war. There a man can build a house for himself without getting a permit from the building inspector. He can build it in just a few weeks, with only the help of his wife. The only building material that he needs is thirty poles, a few bundles of reeds and a few grain-bags. The main tools he requires are a light crowbar, a little reed awl, and a threading-hook. The result is a reed hut.

Namaqualand is the land of the reed hut. Nowadays the reed hut is principally used as winter housing on the encampment sites. In the summer one is scorched to death by the sun in a reed hut. Then the flies also become too much of a nuisance, because they can naturally crawl cheerfully through the walls and roof of the reed hut. Nevertheless, there were many Namaqualanders in the past who were born in reed huts and who also died in reed huts. Even today one still comes across people in that area who have never in their lives lived in a walled house. Someone who knows Namaqualand well assured me that between five and ten percent of the white population live permanently in reed huts.

There is no art to "building" a reed hut. And the only part of the work that is time-consuming and tedious is to "stitch" the little reeds together.

The first step is to get a hold of some reeds. The right material is a type of reed that grows in the Kamiesberge. Rushes also grow in the Sandveld that can be used as panels, but these are not as good as the ones from the Kamiesberge. The Sandveld reeds are shorter, harder and thinner. They also do not swell out as much when it rains. Consequently, the Sandveld reeds do not become so thick and your house leaks more easily.

One plucks the reeds only when they are ripe. Every clump provides two types of reeds. The seed-bearing reeds are longer and thicker than the other type. To make them even longer, the seed-bearing reeds are pulled out by hand. These are then used to form the walls of the reed hut. The ordinary reeds, which are used for the roof, are simply cut out with a reed pick. The reeds are first dried in the sun and after that they are left to soak. The seed-bearing reeds are left in the water for about twelve hours. The ordinary reeds are only well wetted and wrapped up in a wet sack. The water causes the reeds to swell and makes them soft so they can be stitched more easily. After the reeds have been prepared, they are sorted according to length.

While the man is busy with the reeds, the wife twists the tacking twine. Originally the white bark from young acacia tree shoots was used for this. The inner (white) layer of the bark is pulled off and dried. After that it is dampened again and beaten with the flat side of a rock on a wooden block to make it stringy. It is then fluffed, and, while still damp, twisted into tacking twine. This is how the Khoikhoi, as well as the first white pioneers in Namaqualand, went to work. Later the farmers used the threads from a rice sack, at times half and half with white bark when the rice sacks began to get scarce. Today threads from grain bags are mostly used.

The threads are carefully pulled out and then rolled into twine between the palm of the hand and the leg. It is a process that requires considerable practice before it goes without a hitch. Four or six threads are taken and are placed on the leg in two groups a little apart from each other. Then the threads are rolled back and forth between the palm of the hand and the leg. With the first movement the threads are twisted together into two separate strands. With the reverse movement the two strands are twisted over each other into a single strand. When the threads are used up, new threads are not tied onto those with which you have been working. The ends are rolled together with each other. In this way one can make twine just as long as you want to have it, without a single knot.

In recent times machine twine has also been used here and there in place of grain bag threads to twist into tacking twine. The advantage of machine twine is that you can cut off as long a length of tacking twine as you want. It is therefore not necessary to splice the pieces by rolling them together by hand. Usually a wagon or car wheel is used to twist the machine twine into tacking twine. The wheel is jacked up so that it can turn smoothly. Then two long pieces of twine are tied tightly to two opposing spokes an equal distance from the axle. The loose ends of the twine are then stuck through two holes in blocks. The twine is pulled tight, the wheel is turned, and at the same time the blocks are slowly pushed away from the wheel. In this way then an ever-lengthening piece of twine is twisted between the wheel and the blocks. This is a hundred times faster than doing it by hand.

The next step is to "stitch" the reeds together, that is, to tack them in such a way as to form a reed panel. For this purpose a reed-awl is needed. This is a long, flat awl with a strong wooden handle. The length commonly varies between fifteen and twenty inches. It is about one-eighth of an inch thick and three-eights of an inch wide. The Namaqualanders make such awls themselves. A old sickle or another piece of iron is beaten out and filed down until it is the right size. Then it is attached to a wooden handle and the point sharpened.

The reeds are then drawn together one by one and tacked with the awl about two to three inches from the ends. One cannot really pierce the reed with the awl any nearer to the tip of the reed, because then the reeds splits open. When there are about ten reeds in the awl, the awl is given a quarter-turn, so that it is on its side. This causes the reeds to be slightly torn open and at the same time the holes are stretched open. Now the tacking thread is stuck through the holes along the flat awl. After that the awl is pulled out. Generally just a common reed pen is used to tack the thread through the reeds. This pen does not have an eye. The thread is merely fastened to it. In the old days the farmers often made proper threading needles from ostrich bones. Nowadays they are mostly made merely from wire. An old umbrella spoke can also be used as a threading needle.

In this manner the various tacking threads are tacked one after another at fixed distances through the reeds. In the case of the roof panels the tacking threads are tacked through about five inches from each other; in the case of the wall panels, at a distance of about seven inches. The threads cannot be threaded too near to each other, because the reeds will then tear. But if the distance between the tacking threads is too great, the panel is not strong enough. The real art lies in tacking the threads in a perfectly straight line and parallel with each other through the reeds. Furthermore, care must also be taken that the reeds are pressed just tightly enough against one another. They must also be equally damp; otherwise the one shrinks more than the other. The test for a good reed panel is whether you can stick your finger between the reeds. If you can do this, then the panel has been badly made. To reinforce the panel, and particularly to prevent the reeds from tearing at their tips, the panel is given a seam above and below. The seam is placed as near as possible to the last tacking thread and entails the reeds being tightly bound together with a catch-stitch in bunches of twos or threes. When the panel is finished, the tips of the reeds are chopped or trimmed evenly just above the seam. It is usually the work of women to stitch the panels. It is not very difficult, but it is hard work. It is very hard on one's hands.

The reeds from which the panels are made usually taper off towards the tips. Allowance is made for this when one stitches panels. The panels that will be used for the wall of the house must be thinner above than below in order for it to fit the contour of the domed-shaped house better. For this reason the reeds are tacked with their thick ends together when one makes wall panels. The roof panels, however, must not be sloping. Hence, the reeds for the roof panels are tacked alternatively "head and foot." That is, every other thick end of a reed is at the bottom. In this way the long sides of the panel are of equal length.

The width of the panels is limited by the length of the reeds. These vary generally between four and six feet. The wider the panel is, the better. One would particularly like to have the wall panels as wide as possible. The length of the panel again depends on the size of the house that you want to build, but you can naturally make a panel as long as you want. The unit of length with which a Namaqualander measures the size of his panel, is the *faam*.* Panels are usually three and a half to four and a half *faam* long. But one even finds panels six *faam* long.

The majority of Namaqualanders make their own panels, or they have them made on their farms by their farmhands. One can also purchase panels in Namaqualand, however. Poor people often make panels to sell. Many laborers make a living by stitching panels. Thirty years ago one could purchase panels from the Coloureds on the Leliefontein reserve for one shilling. Today one pays around ten shillings per *faam* in stores.

The framework of the reed hut is made of poles (or rather, shoots). It has to satisfy three requirements: it must be thin, so that it is light and easily transportable; it must be flexible, and it must be strong. The framework of poles must not only be able to support the weight of the reed panels—it must also be strong enough to withstand the wind. Furthermore, the poles must be tough, so that they are not easily damaged when the house is taken apart and moved. The hook-thorn tree, which grows along the Orange River, provides the best poles for reed huts. In the absence of this sort of wood, common thorn tree shoots are used. Sometimes split bamboos are used in place of poles. In the old days bamboo was used much more widely for reed huts than today. The farmers in those days obtained bamboo poles from certain ravines in the Kamies Mountains. Today the Namaqualanders get their bamboo mostly from Clanwilliam and Robertson, and consequently it is now much more expensive than poles.

After the poles have been cut, they are buried for a few days in mud or under water. This makes the poles flexible and loosens the bark. The bark is then pulled off and the poles bent to fit the shape of the house. The shape that the poles must eventually assume is traced out on the ground. Stakes are then driven into the ground at short distances from each other all along the line. The poles are bent around these stakes, fastened to them and left for eight days. The poled dry on the stakes and maintain the shape that they have acquired. The bottom four feet of the pole remains straight because it has to support the wall panels. The rest of the pole is bent more or less into the form of a crescent moon.

The number of poles used for a reed hut depends on the size of the house. In the old days the Cape Copper Company allowed forty poles per reed hut for their people at Ookiep, but this was generously calculated. A house of twelve by fifteen feet requires about thirty poles. One can also build a reed house with twenty poles. You have to take into consideration, however, the fact

---

*Trans. note: The Namaqualander term for a fathom — the Dutch word is *vadem* or *vaam* — that has a standardized length of 6 feet. On p. 419 of *Reports from the Dorsland and other Pioneering Regions*, Dr. van der Merwe describes the mats as "normally 4 to 6 feet high and 2½ to 4½ fathoms long."

each year you will need four or five new poles per house, to replace old ones that broke when the houses were dismantled and moved.

The poles that one uses for a reed hut, however, are eight to sixteen feet long and usually one to two and a half inches thick. Thirty years ago one could purchase poles in Namaqualand for a shilling to 1s. 9d. a piece. Bennet and Webster, from Ookiep, in those days offered bundles of ten poles at 12s. 6d.

When the reeds and poles are ready, the site for the house is selected. This place has to be chosen carefully, because the reed hut is lived in during the rainy season. This is why one looks for a high place that the flood waters cannot reach. Preferably the house is built at the top of a small hill, so that the rain water can run down all sides. The ideal is to find such an appropriate site that it is not necessary to dig a drainage ditch around the house or to throw up a wall.

Once the site for the house has been chosen, the bushes are cut down and thrown onto a pile on one side. They are later used to build the cooking screen. After that the floor of the house is marked off. For this the direction of the prevailing wind must be taken into account. One has always to make sure that a reed hut stands with its nose into the wind. This makes the surface of the house against which the winds blows as small as possible. In addition, one then does not have the wind blowing right through the door openings, which are placed directly opposite each other in the middle of the long sides of the house. In Namaqualand it is mostly a southerly wind that blows in the winter. This is why the majority of reed huts generally stand north-south and the doors face east-west.

Once the floor of the house has been laid out, holes are dug with a pick along the line for the poles. The holes are about nine inches deep and eighteen inches to two feet apart. Then the poles are inserted in such a manner that the tips of the poles that are situated directly opposite each other lean towards each other. When all the poles have been inserted, they form a dome-shaped framework and they cross each other like the circles of latitude and longitude on a globe. The intersecting poles thus form squares of eighteen inches or two feet, and on every corner of the square, where two poles cross, they are fastened tightly to each other with thongs or binder twine. In this way a sturdy, uniform framework of poles is constructed.

From this point on it goes quickly. First the wall panels are placed around the frame, with the longest side on the bottom, so that they stand slightly tilted. Naturally there is a place left for the door. When the wall panel is high enough, the next row of panels comes along above the door, which is the ideal. This row lies tilted against the framework of the house and it sticks a bit over the top edge of the wall panel. The rain water can thus now run from one panel to the other without going through the joint. The rest of the house is covered according to the same principle. The last panel passes over the top of the house, so that is not a single joint that can leak. All the panels are fastened onto the poles as they are placed around the frame.

The reed hut does not have door frames or window sashes. There are only door openings left on opposite sides of the house. Two panels that can be rolled up like flaps serve as doors. During the day one of the door panels is usually rolled up and the other one rolled down. At night both panels are rolled down. The reed hut had no windows, since they were not needed. Between the reeds there are always open slits, so that the house remains airy. Even if the door flaps are closed, there is always air flowing through the house. Light also penetrates easily through the slits in the walls and the roof of the house. When the sun shines, the sunlight falls in thin strips on the floor. In spite of this, such a reed hut is practically watertight. When it begins to rain, the first few drops of rain will perhaps go through, but as soon as the reeds become wet, they swell. Within a few minutes the reeds press so tightly against each other that no water can come through between them. The reed hut is even comparatively windproof. If the wind blows outside, it whistles constantly through the reeds, but even if it storms, the candles in the reed hut remain burning.

The floor is simply made of clay. The earth is first made level and wetted down. After that a thick layer of clay, which has been well worked and well mixed, is applied. As soon as the clay is slightly dry, it is well tamped down. If cracks appear later, they are sealed with a light coat of mud. After that the floor is smeared with wet cow dung diluted with water.

The reed hut consists of only one room. Sometimes, however, partitions are made in the corners of the house that are only large enough for a bed. At an encampment site one often sees two reed huts or a large reed hut and a tent, plus perhaps still a smaller reed hut for the motor car. It also happens, however, that an entire family lives in one reed hut. The father, mother, and all the children live and sleep in the same room—the parents on the bed, the children on the floor. And if perhaps a stray traveler arrives, then a place is also made for him in the reed hut.

In the middle of the floor there is generally a fairly large table. In addition, the reed hut usually contains a bed, a few chairs and perhaps a food cupboard and a small table. This is usually the complete list of furniture, because there is no room for anything more.

As long as the family lives in the reed hut, the housewife has to make do without a kitchen. She has to manage with only a cooking screen and cook on an open fire. The cooking screen consists of a more or less circular little wall from three to four feet high that is made of stacked, wet *vyebos*† or *litjiesbos*‡ The diameter of the shed will be around twelve to fourteen feet. It also has no door. There is only an opening that faces the side of the reed hut. In the middle of the shed there is a fireplace. This consists of a small platform with a low little wall around it, just high enough to keep the coals together. Here the housewife cooks her food on a tripod or in long-legged pots.

The only purpose of the screen is to keep the wind away from the fire as far as possible. Rain is the cause of great misery for a housewife who works in a cooking screen. The rain constantly puts the fire out. If the sun is hot, she nearly scorches to death in the screen. For these reasons sometimes either poles and sacks or old panels are put up over the cooking screen as a sort of shelter. If the weather is fine, the family usually sits around the fire in the evenings.

As soon as the encampment season is over, or if the farmer perhaps wants to trek before it is time, the reed hut is dismantled. The reed panels are detached and rolled up. The poles are pulled

---

†Trans. note: A succulent plant — *Mesembryanthemum spp.* — of the large family Aizoaceae.
‡Trans. note: Another plant in the family Aizoaceae, which includes *Psilocaulon junceum spp.* and *Mesembryemum juncelum spp.* Also called *asbos* (Eng. ashbush) and *seepbos* (Eng. soapbush)

out and tied together in bundles. Then the articles are loaded onto the wagon and moved to the next outpost, or taken home and stored until the following winter.

The repeated dismantling, moving, and erecting again of the reed huts cause a great deal of wear and tear. Consequently, the reed huts that have been moved many times do not last as long as those that have remained standing in the same place. It is difficult to say how long a reed hut lasts. If one takes good care of a panel, it can easily last three to four years, sometimes longer. The poles break one after another. If a panel deteriorates, it is simply replaced by another one. If a pole breaks, a new one is set in its place. In this way a reed hut can sometimes last a long time. But then ultimately it becomes like the pocket-knife that the old farmer has used for fifty years and in that time it has gone through four new blades and three new handles.[5]

ENDNOTES

[1] J. Barrow, *Travels into the Interior of Southern Africa*, 2nd ed. (London, 1806), I:339 and II:63. See also, J. Backhouse, *A Narrative of a Visit to the Mauritius and South Africa* (London, 1844), p. 527; B.O. 105, Miscellaneous Letters, A.P. van Niekerk, et al, Petition of the Inhabitants of Namaqualand to Dundas, 20 November 1798, p. 307.

[2] Wm. Paterson, *A Narrative of Four Journeys into the Country of the Hottentots and Caffraria in the Years 1777, 1778 and 1779* (London, 1779), p. 68 and see also, p. 58.

[3] C.O. 2581, Letters Rec., Tulbagh, H. van de Graaff to Cradock, 29 June 1812, No. 20.

[4] Barrow, *Travels*, I:339, 342; B. Shaw, *Memorials of South Africa* (London, 1841), p. 23; R. Moffat, *Journey from Colesberg to Steinkopf, 1831-1835* (London, [1858]), pp. 11-13; G. Thompson, *Travels and Adventures in Southern Africa* (London, 1827), II:97.

[5] With regard to the building of a mat hut, I received the most information from Mr. Meiring, of Wallekraal, and Mr. Sybrand de Vries, of Koppieskraal.

CHAPTER XII

The Trek from Winter to Summer Rain Areas

1. The Distribution of the Rainfall

The Cape Northwest is comprised of a winter rainfall region and a summer rainfall region. The winter rainfall area receives most of its rain between April and September. In the summer rain area the rain falls in thundershowers—when it rains—between October and March, but usually more towards the summer time. The border between the two areas cannot be indicated precisely with a line on a map. The transition is gradual, and along the divide lies a band that receives winter and summer rains. It begins, however, somewhere between Goodhouse and Vioolsdrif on the Orange River and then goes only a little east of the broken chain of mountains that runs from northwest to southeast more or less parallel with the west coast through the Northwest: the Koperberge, the Kamiesberge, Langberg, Kobiskow, Spioenberg, the Hantamberg, the Roggeveldsberg, Komsberg and the mountains of the Klein-Roggeveld.

The Northwest is one of the oldest settlement areas in the interior. By the middle of the eighteenth century the entire winter rainfall area was nearly completely inhabited. The region was only colonized sparsely and sporadically, but by 1760 farms had already been allocated in the Kamiesberge, Kobiskow, the Hantam and the Roggeveld. [1] Expansion into the interior in a northwesterly direction came to a halt for more than a hundred years on the border of the summer rainfall area. The fact that the Cape government at the end of the eighteenth century established a northern border for the Cape colony that more or less followed the summer rainfall border through the Northwest did not have much to do with this. The pioneers of the Cape colony had never been influenced too much by frontier boundaries. In the Northwest, however, they run into an obstacle for which they had much more respect than for the government proclamations—a relentless waterless region.

That desert area was made inhabitable by later generations of pioneers, but it required a lot of work and capital—more than what the pioneers of the eighteenth century, under the extensive farming system of those days, were ready to expend on land. In addition, one also has to recognize that the forms of land ownership that were in use until the last years of the nineteenth century in the Northwest to a large extent countered permanent colonization of the summer rainfall area in the Northwest. [2] As long as the Northwest was still sparsely occupied, and the pressure of a surplus population had still not made further expansion necessary, the farmers of that area also continually opposed the colonization of the summer rainfall region, since they wanted to use that area periodically for grazing. [3]

Be that as it may, for more than a century the summer rainfall area in the Northwest awaited permanents inhabitants and it was used only as summer grazing land by the farmers of the adjoining winter rainfall region. Even after this grazing land became permanently settled, the regular seasonal migrations continued and they have still not died out up to the present day.

This part of the Northwest that was involved in this seasonal migration and is to a large extent still involved, lies along the west coast, just to the south of the Orange River, and is more

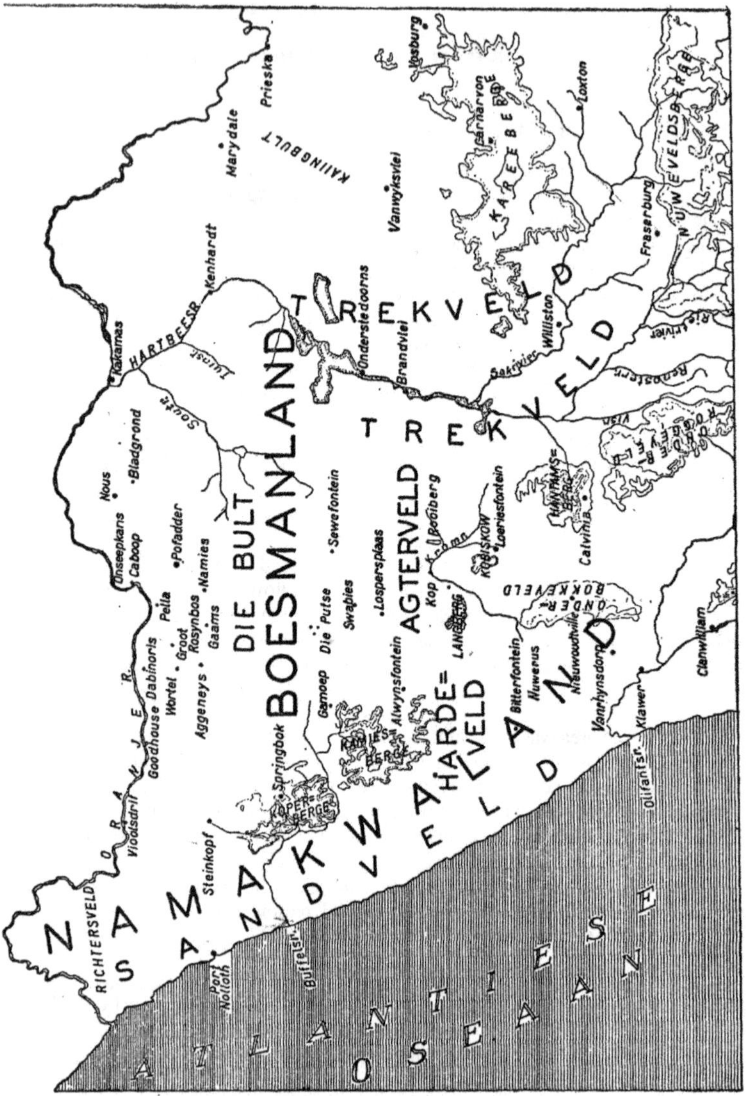

Map 2: The Trek between the Winter and Summer Rain Areas

or less encircled by a line that joins the following easily recognizable places on the map: Olifantsriviermond, Vanrhynsdorp, Sutherland, Fraserburg, Carnarvon, Onderstedoorns on the Sak River and Kakamas on the Orange River. As far as the seasonal migrations are concerned, those from the winter rainfall regions who participated can be divided into different areas. These areas form geographical and historical units and the inhabitants of each one had the use of a particular piece of the region into which they moved.

2. Namaqualand (Grazing Land: Bushmanland)

Along the cold west coast of the Cape colony, between the Orange River and the Olifants River, lies a relatively small strip of land that was called "Little Namaqualand" in the old days, but which today is generally known as Namaqualand. The name of this remote piece of the world became known early in our history because it had the honor at that time of being visited personally by Simon van der Stel. After that Namaqualand was forgotten, until it was noticed again in the second half of the nineteenth century because of the development of its rich copper mines. Today Namaqualand is famous mainly for its fabulous diamond wealth and beautiful spring flowers, and pretty much just as notorious for its droughts and the poverty of its farming population. The world still knows precious little, however, about the history of Namaqualand.

The northern section of Namaqualand was never actually colonized by whites. Shortly after the annexation of the area—and even before whites could trek there—it was reserved for Coloureds. Three reserves were established there—Concordia, Steinkopf and the Richtersveld—that prevented white expansion to the north. Steinkopf and Concordia are well known, because they lie just to the north of Springbok, along the main route to Port Nolloth. Even today most people still know very little about the Richtersveld. It is undoubtedly one of the most isolated and loneliest places in the Cape.

The Richtersveld is situated in the crescent-shaped bend that the Orange River makes just before it flows into the sea. Large parts of the area are an extremely harsh desert, rich in minerals but uninhabitable because of the scarcity of water and the scanty plant growth. On the periphery of the Richtersveld, just to the north of the main road between Steinkopf and Port Nolloth, a few whites trek around on unsurveyed crown land. A few farmers also live to the north of the Richtersveld, along the Orange River. Furthermore, a number of years ago an irrigated settlement for whites was established near Vioolsdrif. But people cannot survive there. The government will be doing a good thing if it takes them away from there to farm elsewhere.

For the rest, the population of the Richtersveld consists of about 500 physically degenerated Coloureds, who represent various degrees of interbreeding between Bushmen, Khoikhoi and whites. They are governed by a council that is located in the main city, Kuboes. In addition, there is also a school at Lekkersing. These people live in severe poverty on only meat and vegetables. Money is almost unheard of among them. When these folk sometimes do something for the whites, they prefer to receive sugar, tea, or meal as payment. For them these items are pure delicacies, not common commodities.

Sometimes the folk of the Richtersveld never see whites for months on end. Just before the gold war a herd of wild horses roamed in the Richtersveld. They were descended from tame horses that had broken away and could not be found again by their owners. And in that wilderness they had become as wild as the gemsbok, so inaccessible was this piece of rocky desert until recently. Even today the Richtersveld is still frightening to the prospector and succulent plant hunter. "If one comes across the trail of a man in some parts of the Richtersveld," a Namaqualander recently told me, "then you get frightened, because you fear that you will perhaps find him dead from thirst further along the path."

The part of Namaqualand where whites have settled lies more or less to the south of the railroad line between Ookiep and Port Nolloth. A large part of this area consists of mountains. Around Springbok, the main city of Namaqualand, lie the Koperberge. More to the south one finds the Kamiesberge, which climb imperceptibly step for step until they end in a peak more than 5,000 feet above sea level. The Kamiesberge is the best part of Namaqualand. Because the rainfall here is higher and the water supply better than in other parts of Namaqualand, the first colonists settled here. To the regret of the white farmers, Leliefontein, the crown of the Kamiesberge, belongs to the Coloureds.

The mountainous country of Namaqualand is very rocky and rugged. Many of the mountains consist of masses of rocks piled high, with here and there a little hill of bare granite as smooth and as round as an eggshell. Further to the south the landscape becomes less mountainous. In the vicinity of Bitterfontein and Nuwerus the ridges give way to rolling limestone hills. This part of Namaqualand is called the "Hardeveld." Along the west coast, between the sea on the one side and the Hardeveld and Bergveld on the other side, there is a band of low-lying land, whose width varies between around fifteen miles and forty miles. Because of the soft, sandy land formations it is called the "Sandveld."

Between Vanrhynsdorp, Nuwerus and the Bokveldsberg lies the poorest part of Namaqualand, the desolate Knechtsvlakte (also known as "Knersvlakte"). If one stands on the Bokveldsberg where people went to look at the eclipse of the sun in 1940, you see to the west one of the most spectacular scenes in the Northwest. From the foot of the mighty mountain a barren plain extends, with a light rust colour and perhaps here and there a dark patch or a shining pool of water, as far as the eye can see. The unsuspecting traveler who comes riding on level land from the direction of Calvinia gets a great surprise when he unexpectedly and without the least warning suddenly find himself on the rim of a precipice and he sees the earth fall away suddenly a few thousand feet before him.

The first pioneers of the Northwest steered clear of the Knechtsvlakte, because for the greatest part of the year it is an inhospitable desert. During the past forty years necessity has forced a few people to settle permanently on the Knechtsvlakte, but they were mostly farmers who did not own very much and they remained poor. The permanent inhabitants of the Knechtsvlakte to this day consist of a number of small farmers who possess about 150 to 300 animals and suffer bitterly through the stifling summer. Most of them cannot make a living on their little farms and therefore work a part of the year on the roads or wherever they can get other work. Knechtsvlakte land is worth 6d. to 2s. 6d. per morgen. A large part of this is still undistributed crown land futilely awaiting owners and that is leased in the winter under grazing licenses.

The part of the summer rainfall area that borders on Namaqualand is known as Bushmanland. The central section of Bushmanland consists of an endless plain as level as the sea. On this enormous expanse the traveler seeks in vain for a mountain to break the monotony of the landscape, or even for a little hill to use as a landmark for fixing his course. In all directions around him he sees only an unceasing low curvature. The land is so dead level that he looks straight at the edge of the earth's curve.

Towards the west coast the *Bult** as this area of Bushmanland is called, remains level until the odd granite hills and piled high masses of rocks of Namaqualand emerge slowly out of the plain. To the north the Bult extends out about 40 miles to the south of the Orange River. Then all at once there is a noticeable drop in the landscape and the plain changes over to a fantastical mountainous area, through which the lonely Orange River meanders to the sea. Even the highest peaks of these mountains are on a lower plane than the plains of the Bult, which extend in an easterly direction far beyond the borders of the grazing lands.

The rainfall of Bushmanland, however, is pitifully low and very erratic, but somewhere on that endless plain every year between September and April, but mostly toward the end of summer, thundershowers fall. And where there have been good rains, the pasture grows quickly and the grazing is excellent.

Bushmanland offers a large variety of species of grass, bushes, and shrubs, but the most valuable of these are Bushman grass and cauliflower. The livestock eat everything that grows there, and everything has nutritional value, green or dry. There are no poisonous plants there that will kill the livestock, so a livestock farmer does not have to be afraid to trek there. Livestock diseases are almost unheard of. Another advantage of Bushmanland is that the pasture is so stable. The shrub fields remain good for a long time and the bushman grass loses very little of its nutritional value when it becomes dry. It sometimes grows for three years. It then becomes brittle and soft and it takes on a bluish appearance. The farmers then refer to it as "blue-roof." At this stage the livestock eat it very eagerly and it has nearly as much nutritional value as green grass.

Bushmanland is subject to awful droughts. Parts of it sometimes never get rain for years. Then the pasture does not grow, and once the livestock have eaten up the dry forage, they die of hunger. In the old days, however, grazing land was not the problem in the migration areas. The limiting factor in finding grazing was water, which at that time was much scarcer than it is today. After the water was all gone, there were still usually large pieces of grazing land remaining that the trekboers could not use for grazing.

Before they began making deep wells and boreholes in Bushmanland about thirty-five years ago, trekboers were dependent on natural water supplies. Most of Bushmanland is poorly endowed in this respect, however, and in this connection the Bult is the worst off. On the extensive high plains of Bushmanland there are no springs and the underground water is so deep, often hundreds of feet under the ground, that no trekboer will try to dig a well on crown land. Fortunately the Bult drains very badly, since it is so level. The rainwater that falls in the summer does not run off to the sea, but collects in natural depressions, which the farmers of the Northwest call "marshes" if the water remains fresh, and "pans" if the water becomes salty. Luckily in most cases the water remains fresh. The smaller marshes often dry up within a few weeks, or at most a few months.

---

*Trans. note: *Bult*, English, the "Ridge" or "Rise."

Some of the larger marshes, however, easily hold water for six months to a year when there have been good rains, particularly if they later receive water again.

On the northern border of Bushmanland, in the mountainous world just to the south of the Orange River, the water supply is better. In the vicinity of Pella, which was made famous by the Catholic missionaries in later years, there are a number of strong, permanent springs. The best known of these are Pella, Little Pella, Namies, Pofadder, Agaab, Dabinoris and Caboop. At Aggeneys, Gaams, Great and Little Rosynbos, Wortel, Naroep and Hoogoor the water is shallow. Here in the old days the trekboers dug draw-wells that delivered a permanent water supply. Furthermore, at various other places in the mountains, there was temporary seepage water after rains, or draw-wells that were not permanent.

The western section of Bushmanland, which borders on Namaqualand, was completely without water until about thirty years ago. The last springs lay on the divide between the winter and the summer rainfall areas. From there on there was no permanent water in an easterly direction for about sixty or seventy miles. Then there were a number of salt pans lying nearby each other between low, barren sand dunes. On the edge of the pans the water was shallow. Around 1884, or perhaps even earlier, the Basters began digging draw-wells alongside the pans. Today there are several shallow pans lying near to one another and commonly called the Putse.[†] The best known of these are Bassonsputs, Bosluis, the Bitterputse (a group of four wells), Kleinputs and Galputs. As the names imply, the life-giving moisture that the desert generously provides here is so brackish that it is hardly usable. Livestock drink the water from it, and people can also get it down if they must, but it tastes like medicine and has the same effect as certain of the less pleasant kinds.

As long as the Namaqualanders were still few in number, they apparently trekked only up to the divide between the summer and winter rainfall areas and used the summer pastures that lay within the reach of the last water supplies. Of these, Eenriet, Kweekfontein, Ratelkraal, Dabeep, Gamoep, Goeinoep, Silwerfontein, Rietfontein and Alwynsfontein were the best known.

As these farms became permanently inhabited and the Namaqualand population increased, it became necessary to trek farther inland. And considering that there was no water in the area just this side of Bushmanland, they therefore just had to trek farther to obtain summer pasture.

The water closest to Namaqualand in the heart of the grazing land was the Putse. According to oral tradition, the Kamiesberg farmers often sent their cattle to the Putse under the watchful eye of farmhands. It also happened that the farmers of the Kamiesberg and the Hardeveld trekked with their families and sheep and goats to the Putse. But they were not keen to do this. The water was too poor and the area too ugly. In addition, there were usually always Basters at the *Putse,* with whom they then sometimes had to shake hands for the sake of getting water. The Namaqualanders usually did not migrate further in this direction than the Putse. Now and then in dry years, however, it happened that they migrated beyond the *Putse* to Swabies on the Calvinia route, or even further to Sewefontein and Rooiberg in the Calvinia grazing lands.

[†]Trans. note: Die Putse is a geographical site shown on Map 2, p. 162, and translates into English as "the wells."

The oldest evidence in archival sources for a migration in this direction to the Putse dates from 1826.[4] Most Namaqualanders, however, traveled for twelve hours by horse through a waterless desert to the water around Pella on the northern border of Bushmanland. Most of this water lay north of the main road between Springbok and Pofadder. Usually the Namaqualanders did not migrate further than Pofadder, but it sometimes happened that they pressed on to Caboop on the Orange River. In very dry years they even migrated into the region between Pofadder and Kenhardt, sometimes even as far as the Hartbees River.[5] This part of Bushmanland, however, lies beyond the border of the actual summer grazing area.

For the most part, the Namaqualanders who trekked to Bushmanland were drawn by the permanent water sites. When the marshes had water, however, they also went to the area just this side of Bushmanland and the northern part of the Bult. Once the Bult had permanent inhabitants and provision was made everywhere for water, they were led only by the rains. A Namaqualander who treks to Bushmanland today, does so only where he can find green pasture, unless he incidentally has land in Bushmanland.

As a rule, the farmers of the Sandveld did not take part in the summer trek to Bushmanland. They only trekked when a very severe drought drove them out of the Sandveld as happened, for example, in 1924. There was no question of a regular seasonal migration. The great distance from Sandveld to Bushmanland could have worked in some measure against the trek, but it could not have exercised too much influence, because it was not too far for the Bushmanlanders to trek to Sandveld. The Sandvelders' greatest difficulty was that the hoofs of their livestock, which were used to soft pasture, could not withstand the journey over the mountains and through the Hardeveld. Furthermore, livestock diseases also often led to problems if they trekked over the mountains in summer. The mountain pasture was then liable to cause loco disease and the Sandveld livestock, which were not accustomed to that part of the world, were very susceptible to it. It occasionally happened that the Sandvelders sent their cattle to Bushmanland in the summer, but generally left their smaller livestock and family behind in the Sandveld.

The Knechtsvlakte, which first became inhabited much later, also did not take part in the summer migration. The few permanent inhabitants that it has today own so few livestock that it is not worth the trouble for them to trek and the costs for the trek also cannot be justified. They simply struggle through the ferocious summers in the Knechtsvlakte.

The Namaqualanders usually finished their harvest first and then waited until the summer rains fell in Bushmanland before they trekked. They had to trek far through a waterless region before coming to the grazing land and could therefore not take any chances with the trek, particularly considering the return journey. For that reason they normally spent the winter in the encampments, with the result that they always had enough pasture around their homestead in the early summer. If it rained early in Bushmanland, they sometimes trekked by November. Other years they perhaps did not get away before February or even March. By April, or at the latest May, they came back again. Then Bushmanland often still had plentiful fodder and it was also still not really too cold. But by that time the plowing rains had already fallen in Namaqualand and it was time to sow.

The earliest references to the summer trek that I could find in the Cape Archives date from the first years of the nineteenth century. From the daily records of the deputy landdrost of Jan

Disselsvlei (later Clanwilliam) it appears that by 1814 the Namaqualanders had already trekked at least up to the zone between the winter and summer rainfall regions.[6] According to oral tradition the migration has taken place since the first pioneers settled in Namaqualand. There is no reason to doubt the correctness of this tradition. Indeed, the reasons behind the trek were present from the beginning and in earlier years there were far fewer obstacles to trek than there are today. Furthermore, life in the Northwest in the old days was also much more unstable than it is today, with the result that the farmers trekked more readily. The relative lack of archival information about the trek in the eighteenth century is not an indication that it did not take place then. This can be attributed to the general scarcity of reports about that remote and neglected frontier district, which was hardly ever visited by a government official at that time.

3. The Under-Bokkeveld (Grazing Land: the Agterveld)

If one leaves Bokveldsberg, between Vanrhynsdorp and Calvinia, by way of Vanrhyns Pass, you come upon a high plateau that drops nearly imperceptibly to the west. The region just above the Bokveldsberg, around the village of Nieuwoudtville, is called the "Bokveld," because such multitudes of springbok were found there in the old days.[7] This area, which is located in the Calvinia district, must not be confused with the Cold and Warm Bokkeveld in the Ceres district.

The real Bokveld is situated between the Doorn River (a tributary of the Olifants River) in the south and the Doorn River (a tributary of the Sout River) in the north. It is divided by the Oorlogskloof River into the North Bokveld and South Bokveld. The entire Bokveld at the beginning of the nineteenth century, however, was considered a part of the old frontier field-cornetcy of Under-Bokkeveld, which extends to the north up to the Langberg and Kobiskow, that is, up to the old northern border of the Cape Colony. Until well into the nineteenth century, however, the real Bokveld was the only part of the field-cornetcy of Under-Bokkeveld that was inhabited. The area between the old northern border and the Doorn River (a tributary of the Sout River) was in those days sometimes considered the "Agterveld" and used only as a summer grazing area.[8]

As soon as one comes out of the Bokveldsberg through Vanrhyns Pass, you find a region of sour pasture with undergrowth, bulrushes, and proteas. After about six miles this ends and one comes to mixed pasturage with grass and scrub. The pasture is much better than on the Knechtsvlakte, a few thousand feet lower. The rainfall on the mountain is much higher than that of the surrounding land and is also fairly regular. The soil, which was initially unusually fruitful, is very suitable for agriculture. Even the first generation of pioneers in the Under-Bokkeveld cultivated the land. They not only produced their own food grain, but also sold grain to neighboring field-cornetcies. Unfortunately, transportation problems at this time hindered the development of agriculture. The colonists were therefore obliged to concentrate mainly on stock-raising. The farmers kept large herds of cattle and sheep. In the old days the Under-Bokkeveld was also famous for its horses.[9] By 1805 there were 25 loan farms and a few registered farms in the Under-Bokkeveld. There were 20 landowners, and livestock in the district numbered 17,000 sheep, 2,000 cattle and 1,000 horses.[10] Very little of the land was worthless. By 1824 the entire area had been measured and distributed.[11]

According to the information that Commissioner [William] Hayward obtained in 1825, when the treks were already in full sway, the Under-Bokkevelders had regularly trekked in the summer with their livestock, from the time that the first two farmers had settled in that region.[12]

The Agterveld, which vaguely referred to the uninhabited area to the north, forms the southern part of Bushmanland. The Agterveld proper begins just north of Langberg and Kobiskow, although a large part of the world to the south of this line at the beginning of the nineteenth century was also still uninhabited.[13] In the documents from a century ago the terms "Agterveld" and "Grasveld" are sometimes used synonymously, but when examined closely, the two terms cannot be substituted for each other. The vast Bushmanland grass plains first begin only at Swabies, deep in the Agterveld, around 66 miles to the north of Loeriesfontein. More to the south one finds grassy plains and scrub bush and the landscape is also more broken.

The southern parts of Bushmanland are relatively well watered. Between Langberg, Kobiskow and Rooiberg there are, apart from temporary seepage springs, various permanent springs nearby to each other. Most of these lie along the Krom River, which twists and turns through the Agterveld. The river itself is mostly just a dry bed. Just after hard rains it flows a little. Here and there, however, the water rises to the surface of the bed even in the dry season, flows a mile or two, and then again disappears in the sand. The surface springs are often brackish, sometimes nearly undrinkable, but more or less always suitable for livestock.

To the north of Lospersplaas one does not really find more springs, but the underground water is close to the surface. Up to Sewefontein, which lies at 30° south latitude, one finds water at various places between ten and fifteen feet under the ground. During the second half of the nineteenth century trekboers in this region provided their livestock with water at draw-wells. At Sewefontein the Bult begins and the water suddenly becomes much deeper. From there to the north there were no surface springs in the old days. The farmers could therefore trek into this part of Bushmanland only when the marshes had water.

By the beginning of the nineteenth century the farmers of the Under-Bokkeveld usually trekked to the permanent water sources in the southern portion of the Agterveld, on the edge of Bushmanland. The springs that they regularly visited at this time were: Abikwasrivier, Brakfontein, Kopfontein, Klipfontein, Kluitjieskraal, Koppieskraal, Lospersplaas, Middelkraal, the Spruit, Rooibergsdrift, Rooiergsfontein and Zoutfontein. From the evidence that was given to Commissioner Hayward in 1825, it appears that the farmers were already familiar by this time with the southern marshes on the Bult, but that it was not yet the practice to trek so far to the north.[14]

When the trekboers in the Agterveld began to increase, and especially when the government began to distribute farms there, the Under-Bokkevelders had to trek farther. By the end of the nineteenth century it was a common practice to trek to the draw-wells between Lospersplaas and Sewefontein, and even to the marshes on the Bult. In dry years the farmers trekked to wherever they could find grass, even if it was to the Orange River. If the Agterveld offered no relief, it also happened now and then that the Onder-Bokkevelders fled to the Sak River area or in the direction of the *Putse*, but this was not their normal pasture land.[15]

The Onder-Bokkeveld farmers (and also the Hantammers who later begin to trek to the Agterveld) usually trekked earlier than the Namaqualanders. It was not so difficult for them to get to the grazing land, because there was enough water along the way, and in the grazing land there was usually dry fodder. They often did not even wait until the Bushmanland rains fell, but by the end of October or the beginning of November, when the winter pasture began to decline, they just moved away. By the end of April or the beginning of May they returned again. By the end of the nineteenth century there were many people in the "Binneveld" who trekked as regularly as clockwork back and forth between the winter rainfall area and the Agterveld. "As soon as October's Holy Communion was over, we trekked," explained an old pioneer to me. "On 15 May we came back, because on 1 June the ewes had to begin to lamb." And when the farmers did not trek in time, it often happened that the livestock strayed away. "No matter whether we were trekking out, or returning," an old trekboer said, "it was not necessary to drive the livestock. The herdsman walked in front, not behind."

If it had not rained at all in the Binneveld, and the Agterveld was still pretty, the farmers now and then remained in the grazing area for the winter. But these instances were the exception. Even farmers who did not have land did not normally remain behind in the Agterveld. They came to the Binneveld in search of green pasture and some had even come as sharecroppers on other men's land. In later years, however, it often happened that farmers without land did not return all the way to the Binneveld. After they had wandered around during the summer months on the Bult, they came to spend the winter on the border between the winter and summer rainfall areas in the neighborhood of Loeriesfontein.

4. The Hantam (Grazing Land: the Sak River and later also the Agterveld)

About 22 miles east of Nieuwoudtville, on the main road to Calvinia, the Onder-Bokkeveld changes to the Hantam. This area around the Hantam Mountains receives a little more rain than the surrounding regions and is well supplied with springs. The first colonists in that region settled here. The pasture is Karoo-like, with scrubs and succulent plants and good herbage in the winter. The Hantam is an excellent region for sheep, but is also very suitable for horses, which the farmers of the Northwest kept in large numbers in the days of the commandos against the Bushmen. When horse-sickness was prevalent there, the Hantam farmers went in search of safety for their horses on the mountain. The land on the mountain, which is free of horse-sickness, was reserved in the old days by the government for the common use of the farmers in the area.[16]

Until 1830 the Hantam area was divided into two field-cornetcies. The region north of the mountain, up to the old northern frontier of the colony, fell under the Agter-Hantam ward. South of the Hantam Mountains, up to the Karoo Mountains, lay the Voor-Hantam ward. In 1830 the two wards were merged and together formed the field-cornetcy of "Hantam."[17]

Until well into the nineteenth century the region to the north of the Hantamberg was uninhabited up to the old northern border. To be sure there in the Company period there was already an occupied loan farm on the slopes of the pretty Kobiskow, which also was inhabited in the nineteenth century. But this farm was actually situated in the grazing lands. For that reason the government hesitated until 1842 before actually distributing the land in perpetual quitrent to a man called Wiese. It also did this only once the applicant agreed to having a servitude, which assured trekboers the right to water and a resting place for their animals, written into the title-deed.[18] In 1823 [George] Thompson identified Slingerfontein as the northern-most farm of the Hantam.[19]

To the east of the Hantam lays an extensive summer rainfall area, which is really only a continuation of Bushmanland, but which in the documents of the nineteenth century is usually named after the Sak River. The rainfall of this region is generally better than that of central and western Bushmanland. The area also has plenty of water. According to tradition, when the first pioneers trekked into the Sak River area, there were many more springs than there are today. The farmers could also draw water right through the year in the Sak River (and also other temporary streams) almost as high up as Brandvlei. The river did not always flow, but when it was not running, there was standing water everywhere in the bed, in hippo-pools and holes. Furthermore, trekboers dug draw-wells of three to five feet everywhere in the dry bed. During droughts the water of the Sak River became salty. Even the water in the wells became brackish, so that it did not really help to dig deeper once the water level in the riverbed had sunk. At Brandvlei the farmers could still draw water after the rains in the marshes' water, but the water seldom remained fresh for longer than three months. After that the farmers who wanted to remain longer were dependent on the draw-wells in the riverbed.[20]

Opposite the Sak River, towards the Karee Mountains, there were also a considerable number of permanent springs and at various places the underground water was very near the surface. This part of the grazing land that lay to the east of the present-day Williston to beyond Carnarvon is usually called the "Kareeberge." Sometimes there a distinction is also made between the Karee Mountains, around Carnarvon, and the Karee mountain plains, between Williston and Carnarvon.

The topography of the eastern section of the areas used by the trekboers is not at all uniform. The area around present-day Williston and Carnarvon is fairly mountainous. To the northwest the land becomes much flatter. From the point where the Sak River turns north, it flows through a world that is so level that the river comes to a complete standstill in large pans. Only after heavy rains is the water of the Sak River pushed sluggishly on to the Hartbees River.

From the time that the first farmers settled there, the inhabitants of the Voor- and Agter-Hantam trekked during the summer in an easterly direction.[21] By 1825, during Hayward's investigation, the Sak River area was the recognized grazing land of the Hantam farmers. Under normal circumstances they would never trek to the Agterveld. This occurred only when there were exceptionally serious droughts, when a farmer naturally trekked wherever he could get pasture. The farmers chose, for completely understandable reasons, the Sak River beyond the Agterveld. In the first place, the summer pasture in this direction was nearer to their homes. The summer rains were of short duration to the east of the Hantam Mountains, around 20 miles east of Calvinia. Furthermore, the rainfall of the Sak River grazing land was a little better and it was also not so difficult to obtain water there for the livestock. The watering places in the Agterveld, which were located in a comparatively small spot, were more or less always occupied by the farmers of the Under Bokkeveld.[22]

Up to 1847 the farmers were not allowed to trek over the Sak River with their livestock, because it formed the border of the Cape colony at that time. There is, however, abundant evidence that early in the nineteenth century already farmers—occasionally with the permission of the government and sometimes on their own authority—trekked into the land to the east of the Sak River.[23] By 1856 the Hantam farmers had already trekked to the Karee Mountains in the present-day district of Carnarvon.[24] According to the statement of field-cornet J.B. Wiese of the Hantam, at this time around 100 farmers trekked yearly from his ward to the Karee Mountains.[25]

Other Hantam farmers, especially those of the Agter-Hantam, trekked in a north-easterly direction to the lower reaches of the Sak River. Usually they trekked no further than Onderstedoorns, where the districts of Calvinia, Fraserburg and Kenhardt join. It also happened, however, that the Hantam farmers trekked farther, up to the Hartbees River and even to the region across from the Hartbees River, where the best parts of the grazing land lay.[26] Old trekkers also say that they sometimes trekked along the Sak and the Hartbees Rivers until they reached Kakamas on the Orange River. But these were exceptional cases.

In the course of time the Hantam farmers also began to trek to the Agterveld, which they had scorned at first. This development had to have begun between 1825 and 1850. In 1854, on his journey from Colesberg to Steinkopf at the Krom River, [Robert, Jr.] Moffat[‡] met farmers from the Hantam. "They were just about to move to the northward, among the pans and vleys S.W. of Katkop." The writer also made mention of the large trek route from the Hantam to the great Saltpan, and later again of "the great trek road from the Hantam and Luries Fontein to the pans and vleys."[27] From this one can deduce that the trek to the Agterveld had already been going on for at least a number of years. By the end of the nineteenth century it was in full swing. Then the Hantam and the Under Bokkeveld farmers trekked any which way into the Agterveld, which they then usually begin to call "Bushmanland." Many old pioneers still alive today can testify to this phenomenon.

This did not mean that the Hantam farmers no longer trekked to the Sak River. Many of them still did. Everything simply depended on where the rains fell. But from the time that the government begin to distribute land around 1875 in the Sak River pasturage, opportunities for the Hantam farmers to trek in an easterly direction decreased more and more. After that the areas of the Sak River and the Karee Mountains quickly acquired permanent inhabitants. It was also not long before the farms begin to become smaller, and in time it became much more difficult to help the Hantam farmers. The same process was also occurring in the southern part of the Agterveld. But to the north land was not distributed due to a shortage of water. A large portion of central Bushmanland remained crown land on which the farmers could wander about at will. For that reason it was also named "Vrybult." From the end of the nineteenth century the majority of Hantam farmers trekked in the direction of Vrybult.

5. The Onder-Roggeveld (Grazing Land: the Sak River)

The last winter rainfall area that was important for the summer migrations was the Onder-Roggeveld. It consisted of the northern-most section of the Roggeveld, which today falls in the

---

‡Trans. note: See chapter XIII, p. 183, "Trans. note" for a 5 line biography of Robert Moffat, Jr., the son of the famous missionary.

district of Calvinia. It bordered on the Hantam and began just where the Ceres road descends the Bloukrans.

The old field-cornetcy of Onder-Roggeveld extended to the Sak River, that is, up to the old northern boundary. In 1830 the field-cornetcy was divided into two. The section between Renoster River and Sak River formed the new field-cornetcy of "Renoster River." The rest retained the old name.[28] In this chapter, however, we mean by the name "Onder-Roggeveld," only that part of the field-cornetcy that got winter rains, that is, a relatively small strip of land all along the ridge of the Roggeveldsberg.

From the time that the first colonists settled on the Roggeveld Mountains, they used the region to the northeast, which received summer rain, as periodical grazing land. This is evident from all the documents of the Company period.[29] The farmers of the middle Roggeveld trekked only in dry years.[30] There were no regular summer migrations. The only part of the Roggeveld that had truly great importance in the Sak River pasturage was the Onder-Roggeveld.[31] But evidently the Onder-Roggeveld was not as dependent on the Sak River as the Hantam farmers were. The Onder-Roggeveld had bountiful summer pastures just to the east of the Roggeveld Mountains, along the Fish, Riet and Renoster Rivers, where many farmers had summer farms. In addition, they trekked in the winter with their livestock to the Karoo, with the result that they had good pasture on their homesteads after the winter.[32] This is also why the Onder-Roggeveld farmers usually trekked later than the Hantam farmers. They usually only moved in January, or even later, to the pasturage.

According to a statement that J.E.P. Nel, field-cornet of the Onder-Roggeveld, made in 1856, all the farmers from his ward trekked a distance of about 200 miles in the summer with their livestock up into the Karee Mountains. There were 58 farms at this time in the field-cornetcy and on every one there were six to eight persons who were involved in farming.[33]

This statement was made for the purpose of defending the claim of the Onder-Roggeveld to the trek areas. It therefore perhaps gives an exaggerated representation of the extent of the summer trek. Otherwise the summer trek had declined quickly after 1856 because, according to the testimony of old pioneers, by the end of the nineteenth century the farmers of the Onder-Roggeveld did not make quite such general and regular use of the Sak River pasturage.

From the preceding discussion it is clear that the farmers who took part in the summer trek formed separate parties, each of which moved to a specific part of the migration area. The field-cornetcies that participated in the trek all lived along the long summer rainfall boundary, and every party trekked to that part of the migration area that he could most easily reach.

There had never been a formal division of the migration areas in the northwestern part of the summer rainfall area. Originally the Namaqualanders made use for practical reasons of the western and northern parts of Bushmanland, while the Onder-Bokkevelders trekked to the Agterveld. From the time when the Hantam farmers began to trek to the north, they and the Onder-Bokkevelders made joint use of the Agterveld. On the *Bult*, where the migration areas of Namaqualand and Calvinia border on each other, the Namaqualanders, Onder-Bokkevelders and Hantammers trekked pell-mell. Everything depended solely on which marsh had water.

In the nineteenth century, however, various attempts were made to divide the Sak River area among the farmers of the Agter-Hantam, Voor-Hantam and Onder-Roggeveld. The recognized trek pastures between Kichererskerk and Onderstedoorns were divided into three for that purpose. The Onder-Roggeveld would use the south-eastern part, the Agter-Hantam the northwestern part, and the Voor-Hantam the middle part. The attempts to maintain this arrangement, however, always came to naught because the fickle thunderstorms did not take it into consideration. The result was that the people from the Hantam and Roggeveld along the Sak River, and also later in the Karee Mountains, always more or less trekked willy-nilly.[34]

During droughts it often happened that one part of the trek areas received rain, while another part missed out altogether. Then the farmers simply went in search of relief where they could get it, and they often trekked to areas of the communal pasture that in the normal course of events they would never use.

6. The Causes of the Summer Trek

One must seek the causes of the summer trek in the first place in the geography of the Northwest. Inasmuch as the "Binneveld" and the trek areas received rain in different seasons, from the viewpoint of the livestock farmers the two bordering areas complemented each other perfectly.

During the summer the Binneveld did not receive sufficient rain for the pasture to grow. Consequently the pasture became dry and the nutritional value of the fodder declined. Every farmer naturally wanted to maintain his livestock in good condition throughout the year. For that reason he tried to find green pasture for them for as much of the year as was possible. For this reason the farmers of the winter rainfall region often moved to the migration areas, even though they still had enough dry fodder on their farms. The older group of trekboers in particular could not remain on their farms in peace if they knew that it had rained somewhere in the migration areas. "Here there is often still enough dry fodder to keep the livestock alive through the summer," an old trekboer assured me, "but if it rained in Bushmanland, there is ripe, young pasture. Why should we remain sitting here then? When a farmer hears of green pasture, then he treks there."

The value of the trek pasture increased still farther for the farmers of the Binneveld because the plant growth in a large part of the winter rainfall area was not permanent. This was especially true of Namaqualand. In the spring after good winter rains Namaqualand is a paradise. The entire region is covered with multi-colored flowers and the succulent winter herbage fattens the livestock within a few weeks. Unfortunately the abundance of nature is transient. The herbage remains only a few months. As soon as it becomes dry, the livestock trample it to dust, and it blows away in the wind. The scrub bush and large bushes remain good for longer, but by December the pasture land begins to decline quickly. From January to April, when it normally rains somewhere in Bushmanland and when there is always dry, nutritious fodder, the pasture in Namaqualand is bad.

As a result of the seasonal differences in rainfall and the inconstancy of the grazing land, Namaqualand cannot support the same number of livestock year round. In the spring one can easily keep one sheep per morgen. A few months later you need perhaps twenty morgen per sheep. In general, Namaqualand can easily support five to six times as much livestock between May and October as during the rest of the year. In the Onder-Bokkeveld, the Hantam and the Onder-Roggeveld the seasonal differences in the carrying strength of the pasturage are lower, but on average a farmer can also certainly feed at least twice as many livestock in the winter on his land as in the summer.

This means that the Binnevelder who initiates his farming in the scarce season cannot use all his grazing land in the plentiful season. If he initiates his farming in the rainy season, then his farm cannot support all his livestock in the "dry time." Apart from the quality of his pasture land, he has too little pasture for his livestock. In these circumstances it is understandable that so long as there were still abundant opportunities to trek and the summer rainfall area still did not have permanent inhabitants who could lease winter pasture, the Binnevelders manifested the inclination to keep more livestock than their farms could support in the summer, intending to trek for a portion of the year with their livestock.

Because in the old days the farmers of the winter rain areas counted on trekking to the summer rainfall areas, they made no effort to save pasture in the summer. It was also actually much more difficult to save pasture land before the farmers fenced their land. In the Hantam, Onder-Bokkeveld and Onder-Roggeveld it later emerged that through the implementation of prudent land management, it was possible to farm right through the year on the homestead. In Namaqualand, where wire fencing was rare and the seasonal differences in the carrying capacity of the pasture land are very great, the opinion of large livestock farmers even today is that they cannot subsist without trekking. They feel that one makes the best use of Namaqualand's herbage if you do not try to save it, but "stock" your land heavily in the winter and trek in the summer. If a farmer does not trek, he cannot keep much livestock. But then he can lease pasture in the winter. Since there are permanent inhabitants in Bushmanland, there are trekboers every year in the Binneveld who want to lease pasture there.

Another very important reason for the summer trek was that the water supply in the Binneveld was very poor in the old days. Before the wind pump and the water drill made their appearance at the end of the nineteenth century, the pioneers were exclusively dependent on natural water supplies. In the winter there were no problems with water. The temporary springs were strong, the periodic steams flowed, and across the lands there was surface water everywhere in marshes, pools and stone basins. Moreover, the livestock did not really drink in the winter, since the succulent herbage contained enough moisture. As soon as the days began to lengthen, the heat of the summer arrived, and the pasture lands began to dry up, the livestock needed water. But that was precisely when water became scarce. The surface water dried up, the springs became inadequate, the temporary little streams stopped flowing, and the water in the riverbeds became brackish. On the majority of farms in the Binneveld there was always a struggle for water in the summer. Some farms became altogether uninhabitable due to the shortage of water. Only a few had permanent springs that provided plenty of drinking water for people and livestock throughout the year.[35] In these circumstances then the farmers went in search of relief to the marshes on the Bult or to the permanent water sources in the grazing land.

One reason that is often advanced these days for the summer trek is that the Binneveld was unhealthy in the summer. One comes across this complaint everywhere in Namaqualand, the Onder-Bokkeveld and the Hantam. Around September-October loco disease makes its appearance in these parts. The farmers do not know precisely what causes this deadly sickness. Some feel that some or other poisonous plant is responsible for it. Others ascribe it to some or other condition of the pasture. Whatever the reason, nearly every summer the farmers of the Binneveld suffer heavy losses as a result or loco disease. In the migration area, which is exceptionally healthy, this illness hardly appears. Consequently in the summer many farmers try to prevent damage by fleeing to these communal pastures. What is more, generations of farmers have learned from experience that a change of pasture does the livestock good. It heals them of all sorts of illnesses and keeps them healthy.

Finally, it must be pointed out that in the old days there was much pleasure associated with the trek, and that, for this reason, it had a great attraction. The trekking life was free and sociable. At the watering places there were always lots of people who constantly came and went. One met relatives and friends there, and saw new faces. The trek therefore satisfied an important social need, particularly as long as the region was thinly populated and communications were poorly developed. In addition, the summer trek offered plenty of opportunities to hunt. The migration area was the last refuge for wild game south of the Orange River. The hunt not only provided sport and relaxation, but also enabled the farmers to make meat jerky for the winter and to obtain hides for leather and thongs. The result was that the trek to the summer rain areas was a wonderful adventure to which everyone eagerly looked forward.

7. The Summer Trek Declines

In the nineteenth century the farmers of the Binneveld repeatedly stated that they could not survive without the trek pastures. Without the prerogative of making use of it in the summer, they would not be able to subsist on their homesteads; they would all be ruined, and they would not be able to pay their taxes.[36]

From the archival documents of the nineteenth century it is also quite clear that the summer trek played a very important role in the Northwest at this time. It took the form of a regular seasonal migration in which nearly the entire population of Namaqualand (with the exception of the Sandveld), the Onder-Bokkeveld, the Hantam and the Onder-Roggeveld took part. The farmers would naturally have moved around more in some years than in others, depending on conditions, but it often happened—especially in dry years—that the entire field-cornetcy trekked away and that the farmers were spread out so far and wide in the migration areas that the field-cornet did not know where to find them.[37] Even by the end of the previous century—old people say—it was still a common practice in the summer among the Binneveld farmers to look for an escape in the communal pastures. Most farmers then also regularly participated in the trek. "We trekked so regularly, like the springboks that trekked in those days," an old pioneer assured me. Here and there were farmers who did not move with their families to the migration areas, but they usually sent their livestock, or at least their cattle and horses, there under the care of a son or servant, and went themselves now and then to inspect them. When transport riding for the copper industry was still a going concern in Namaqualand, the women trekked then with the livestock, while the men remained behind and rode transport.

There was not, however, an equal number of farmers who trekked each year. Much depended on the condition of the pasture. If the migration area was very dry, fewer farmers trekked. If it had not rained there, they returned much earlier. But, after all, dry pasture, a number of permanent water holes, and the hope of rain were always present. Consequently it was extremely rare that no one trekked in any year. If the migration area received soaking rains after a mild winter, then everyone was there.

From the beginning of this century—and particularly during the last twenty years—the summer trek has declined rapidly. Many of the Binneveld farmers, who had trekked more or less regularly before, now no longer trek at all. The overwhelming majority of those who still trek, no longer trek on a regular basis. If it is at all possible, they remain on their farms. They trek only when there is no other choice, perhaps once every two or three years. Only the few Binneveld farmers who have summer farms still trek quite regularly. They also trek in dry years since their farming has already been organized accordingly. Another type of farmer who also still regularly treks between winter pasture and summer pasture is the man who owns no land anywhere and lives a nomadic life. Until about twenty or thirty years ago there were still many such farmers in the Northwest, but today there are no longer many of them left.

The summer trek has therefore not only declined, but also changed character. Before it was a regular seasonal migration in which nearly everyone took part. Over the last few years it has increasingly developed into an incidental migration, in which only a portion of the Binneveld farmers is involved.

This process has advanced further in some parts of the Binneveld than in others. The seasonal migrations out of the Hantam and Under Roggeveld to the Sak River and the Karee Mountains have died out altogether. The Voor-Hantam farmers almost never trek to the Agterveld (or "Bushmanland," as it is usually called today). In the Agter-Hantam the trek has also diminished sharply. Only about five to ten percent of the Agter-Hantam's livestock still trek regularly to Bushmanland. A large percentage of Namaqualand's farmers still participate in the summer trek, probably nearly half of them, but most trek on a very irregular basis. In the South-Bokveld the trek has also nearly died out. The only part of the Binneveld where the summer trek has not declined significantly is the North-Bokveld. Around 80 to 90 percent of this region's livestock still trek regularly in the summer, although the family does not accompany the trek nearly as regularly as before.

ENDNOTES

[1] A.J.H. van der Walt, *Die Ausdehnung der Kolonie am Kap der Guten Hoffnung, 1700-1779* (Berlin, 1928), p. 69.

[2] I hope to return to this point later in another study.

[3] See, for example, the testimony given before Commissioner Hayward, in C.O. 8547, Commissioner Hayward, Clanwilliam Land Matters, 1825.

[4] C.O. 2696, Worcester, G. Nieuwhoudt (Hardeveld) to Secretary for Clanwilliam, 8 December 1826, and J. Cloete (Kamiesberg) to Secretary for Clanwilliam, 2 December 1826.

[5] C.O. 4414, Arrears, L. Anthing to Col. Secretary, 1 April 1862.

[6] 1/CWM, ADD 1/1, Logbook (Jan Disselsvlei), 9 July 1814. See also, C.O. 2696, Worcester, G. Nieuwhoudt (Hardeveld) to Secretary for Clanwilliam, 8 December 1826 and J. Cloete (Kamiesberg) to Secretary for Clanwilliam, 2 December 1826.

[7] F. Masson, "An Account of Three Journeys from Cape Town into the Southern Parts of Africa," in *Philosophical Transactions of the Royal Society* (London, 1776), 66:310; J. Barrow, *Travels into the Interior of Southern Africa*, 2nd ed. (London, 1806), II:62.

[8] C.O. 2867, Letters Rec., Clanwilliam, Civil Commissioner to Col. Secretary, 24 July 1850; C.O. 8547, Civil Commissioner Hayward, Clanwilliam Land Matters, 1825, R. Fryer to Hayward, 6 April 1825; C.O. 8547, Hayward's Report on Shaw's Memorial, 5 November 1825 and Petition of F. Kotzé, 20 April 1824. See also, Commission for Stock Raising and Agriculture, 20 November 1805, in George McCall Theal, *Belangrijke Historische Dokumenten over Zuid-Afrika* (Cape Town, 1896, 1911), III:391.

[9] Commission for Stock Raising and Agriculture, 20 November 1805, in Theal, *Belangrijke Historische Dokumenten*, III: 391-92; Barrow, Travels, II:61-2.

[10] Commission for Stock Raising and Agriculture, 20 November 1805, in Theal, *Belangrijke Historische Dokumenten*, III: 391-92.

[11] C.O. 8547, Civil Commissioner Hayward, Clanwilliam Land Matters (1825), Evidence of F. Kotzé, 28 October 1824.

[12] C.O. 8547, Civil Commissioner Hayward, Clanwilliam Land Matters (1825); See also, 1/WOC 11/7, Letters Rec. from Colonial Office, Hayward's Report, 22 September 1825, (Enclosure, Plasket to the Landdrost for Worcester, 6 October 1825).

[13] S.G.P., Letters from Civil Commissioners, H.C. Nieuwhoudt evidence for adjunct landdrost and heemraden of Clanwilliam, 9 September 1826. [Trans. note: This is the citation Dr. van der Merwe has for this footnote and although he cites this document four times – ch. 12, nos. 13, 19, and ch. 15, nos. 18, 32, I could find no such document for this date, 9 September 1826. There is a letter from Nieuwhoudt to Adjt. Landdrost and Heemraden for Clanwilliam, dated 9 July 1826, which deals with the topics of the Agterveld, Kobiskow, their past history and their identity. I believe this is the

document to which Dr. van der Merwe is referring. This document, containing essentially the same wording, may be found in SG 1/1/1/2 and C.O. 8430, both under the date 9 July 1826: SG 1/1/1/2, Letters from Civil Commissioners, Western Province, H.C. Nieuwhoudt to Adjt. Landdrost and Heemraden, 9 July 1826 and C.O. 8430, Inspector of Lands and Woods, Letters Rec., H.C. Nieuwhoudt to Adjt. Landdrost and Heemraden, 9 July 1826.]

[14] C.O. 8547, Commissioner Hayward, Clanwilliam Land Matters (1825), Enclosures: Petition from F. Kotzé, 30 April 1824; Evidence of F. Kotzé, 28 October 1824; F. Fryer to Hayward, 4 March 1825.

[15] 1/WOC 12/72, Letters Rec., Petition from I.J. van Zyl, et al, from the Hantam, 10 April 1826, enclosed with letter of 7 June 1826; 1/WOC 12/17, Letters Rec. from Officials, H.C. Nieuwhoudt (Over-Bokkeveld) to J. van Ryneveld, 17 February 1826, (enclosed with 1 March 1826): "And now that the thunderstorms have fallen in Bushmanland, most all the people have departed, some to the Zak and Fish rivers and some toward the great valleys. The people had moved on so far away that it was impossible for me to reach them. I am presently nearly alone on the Bokkeveld." See also, 1/WOC 12/19, Letters from Various Officials, J. van Ryneveld to Trappes, 6 April 1827; 1/WOC 17/14, Letters Disp., P.J. Truter to Civil Commissioner for Clanwilliam, 30 January 1836; 1/WOC 1/6, Minutes of the Landdrost and Heemraad, 3 January 1827; C.O. 8547, Civil Commissioner Hayward, Hayward's Report, 22 September 1825 and Evidence of J.A. Nel

[16] Commission for Stock Raising and Agriculture, 20 November 1805, in Theal, *Belangrijke Historische Dokumenten*, III: 377; Barrow, *Travels*, I:354-5 and II:62.

[17] C.O. 5829, Proclamations, Govt. Advertisement, 14 October 1830, p. 62.

[18] SG 2/1/1/2, General Letter Book, Mitchell, Report to Government on Memorial of Johannes Jacobus Wiese..., 23 May 1842, p. 333; C.O. 4917, Letter Book, Government to Surveyor-General, 30 May 1842, p. 45.

[19] G. Thompson, *Travels and Adventures in Southern Africa* (London, 1827), I:416; SG 1/1/1/2 and C.O. 8430 [Trans. note: see footnote 13 above.]; C.O. 8547, Civil Commissioner Hayward, Clanwilliam Land Matters, R. Fryer to Hayward, 6 April 1825.

[20] CCP 1/2/1/31, A21 of 1876, Report of the Hydraulic Engineer, 27 May 1876, p. 10; C.O. 8547, Civil Commissioner Hayward, Clanwilliam Land Matters, Evidence of J.C. Nieuwhoudt, 18 March 1825.

[21] 1/WOC 1/6, Minutes of the Landdrost and Heemraad, 3 January 1827; R. Moffat, Journey from Colesberg to Steinkopf, 1831-1835 (London, [1858]), p. 12.

[22] C.O. 8547, Civil Commissioner Hayward, Clanwilliam Land Matters, Report from 22 September 1825 and Evidence of M. Ras, D.C. Oosthuysen and J.C. Nieuwhoudt; 1/WOC 13/22, Letters Rec., A.E. de Waal to Trappes, 24 March 1828 and W.P. Burger to Trappes, 30 March 1828; 1/WOC 14/13, Private Letters Rec., W. Louw, et al, to Civil Commissioner for Worcester, 15 January 1833; 1/WOC 10/12, Logbook, 19 November 1827 [Trans. note: The entry in the Logbook for 24 November 1827 includes the Journal kept by the Landdrost on his way to the Eastern Frontier. The entry for 19 November 1827 cited here is in his journal]; 1/WOC 12/72, Letters Rec., Petition from I.J. van Zyl, et al, from the Hantam, 10 April 1826, enclosed with letter of 7 June 1826; C.O. 2723, Letters Rec., Worcester, Truter to Bell, 16 June 1830; C.O. 2680, Letters Rec., Worcester, C.A. van der Merwe and 11 others (Agter-Hantam), 18 January 1826, enclosed with No. 205; W. von Meyer, *Reisen in Süd-Afrika wärend der Jahre 1840 und 1841* (Hamburg, 1843), p. 150.

[23] 1/WOC 13/14, Letters Rec. from Field Cornets, J. Nel to van de Graaff, 4 June 1810; 1/WOC 13/20, Letters Rec. from Field-Cornets, J. Nel to Landdrost, 25 May 1826; 1/WOC 11/7, Letters Rec. from Colonial Office, Plasket to Landdrost for Worcester, 23 December 1825; 1/WOC 17/11, Letters Disp., Trappes to Maasdorp, 21 June 1826; C.O. 2679, Letters Rec., Worcester, Trappes to Plasket, 21 March 1826, No. 43; 1/WOC 10/8, Logbook, 17 August 1820, pp. 155-56 and 7 September 1820, p. 168.

[24] C.O. 4402, Arrears, J.B. Auret to Surveyor-General, 27 December 1856. See also, C.O. 4402, Arrears, Statement of Field Cornet J.B. Wiese, 10 November 1856, enclosed with J.B. Auret to Surveyor-General, 27 December 1856.

[25] C.O. 4402, Arrears, Statement of Field Cornet J.B. Wiese, 10 November 1856, enclosed with J.B. Auret to Surveyor-General, 27 December 1856.

[26] C.O. 2697, Worcester, Travel Account of Landdrost for Worcester, 9 November 1827, enclosed with Trappes to Plasket, 4 December 1827; S.G. 1/1/3/14, No. 211, Letters Rec. from Col. Secretary, Petition of J.A. Nieuwhoudt and 69 others (Calvinia), September 1849, to Sir H. Smith, enclosed with Col. Secretary to Surveyor-General, 21 November 1849; SG 1/1/3/15, Letters Rec. from Col. Secretary, W. van Ryneveld, Civil Commissioner for Clanwilliam, to Col. Secretary, 17 January 1850, with enclosed letter, Field Cornet W. Burger (Hantam) to van Ryneveld, 3 January 1850, under cover letter, Col. Secretary Montagu to Surveyor-General, 31 January 1850.

[27] Moffat, *Journey*, pp. 12, 13.

[28] C.O. 5829, Proclamations, Govt. Advertisement, 14 October 1830, p. 62.

[29] 1/STB 3/11, Criminal Evidence, Barend and Roman, 26 October 1769.

[30] Commission for Stock Raising and Agriculture, 20 November 1805, in Theal, *Belangrijke Historische Dokumenten*, III: 360; H. Lichtenstein, *Reisen im südlichen Africa in den Jahren 1803, 1804, 1805 und 1806* (Berlin, 1811-1812), I:167.

[31] 1/WOC 10/12, Logbook, 19 November 1827 [Trans. note: The entry in the Logbook for 24 November 1827 includes the Journal kept by the Landdrost on his way to the Eastern Frontier. The entry for 19 November 1827 cited here is in his journal]; C.O. 2679, Letters Rec., Worcester, Trappes to Plasket, 21 March 1826, No. 43; 1/WOC 12/27, Letters Rec. from Officials, J. van Ryneveld (Clanwilliam) to Civil Commissioner for Worcester, 14 December 1835; 1/WOC 12/28, Letters Rec. from Officials, J. van Ryneveld (Clanwilliam) to Civil Commissioner for Worcester, 12 March 1826; 1/WOC 11/15, Letters Rec. from Officials, J.N. Redelinghuys, et al, to Napier, 1 January 1844, enclosed with 29 March 1844; C.O. 2867, Letters Rec., Civil Commissioner to Col. Secretary, 24 July 1850; SG 2/1/1/10, General Letter book, Bell, Report to Government on Memorial of Inhabitants of Onder-Roggeveld, 22 May 1852, p. 394.

[32] 1/WOC 17/24, Letters Disp., P.J. Truter to Clanwilliam, 30 January 1836; Lichtenstein, Reisen, I:167.

[33] C.O. 4402, Arrears, Annexure B, No. 40, pp. 27-33, following J.B. Auret to Surveyor-General, 27 December 1856.

[34] 1/WOC 10/12, Logbook, 19 November 1827 [Trans. note: The entry in the Logbook for 24 November 1827 includes the Journal kept by the Landdrost on his way to the Eastern Frontier. The entry for 19 November 1827 cited here is in his journal]; C.O. 2697, Letters Rec., Worcester, C.

Trappes to Plasket, 14 December 1827, No. 61, p. 228; 1/WOC 14/13, Private Letters Rec., W. Louw, et al, to Civil Commissioner for Worcester, 15 January 1833; C.O. 4402, Arrears, Annexure B, No. 40, pp. 27-33, following J.B. Auret to Surveyor-General, 27 December 1856.

[35] 1/CWM, ADD 1/1, Logbook (Jan Disselsvlei), 9 July 1814; Commission for Stock Raising and Agriculture, 20 November 1805, in Theal, Belangrijke Historische Dokumenten, III: 372, 377-78; 1/WOC 11/4, Letters Rec., C. A. van der Merwe, et al, Petition from the Hantam, enclosed with Bird to Landdrost, 28 June 1816; C.O. 8547, Civil Commissioner Hayward, Clanwilliam Land Matters (1825), Evidence of F. Kotzé, 28 October 1824; C.O. 8547, Civil Commissioner Hayward, Clanwilliam Land Matters, Hayward's Report, 22 September 1825 and evidence of J.A. Nel; Lichtenstein, Reisen, I:144-45; Von Meyer, Reisen, p. 13; 1/WOC 12/72, Letters Rec., Answers by Deputy Landdrost and Heemraden of Clanwilliam on questions by the Inspector of Lands and Woods, 23 January 1826.

[36] C.O. 2697, Letters Rec., Worcester, Trappes to Plasket, 4 December 1827, with enclosure, travel journal of Landdrost of Worcester; C.O. 2679, Letters Rec., Worcester, Trappes to Plasket, 21 March 1826, No. 43; 1/WOC 10/12, Logbook, 19 November 1827 [Trans. note: The entry in the Logbook for 24 November 1827 includes the Journal kept by the Landdrost on his way to the Eastern Frontier. The entry for 19 November 1827 cited here is in his journal]; 1/WOC 14/13, Private Letters Rec., W. Louw, et al, to Civil Commissioner for Worcester, 15 January 1833; S.G. 1/1/3/14, No. 211, Letters Rec. from Col. Secretary, Petition of J.A. Nieuwhoudt and 69 others (Calvinia), September 1849, to Sir H. Smith, enclosed with Col. Secretary to Surveyor-General, 21 November 1849; SG 1/1/3/15, Letters Rec. from Col. Secretary, W. van Ryneveld, Civil Commissioner for Clanwilliam, to Col. Secretary, 17 January 1850, with enclosed letter, Field Cornet W. Burger (Hantam) to van Ryneveld, 3 January 1850, under cover letter, Col. Secretary Montagu to Surveyor-General, 31 January 1850; C.O. 2924, Civil Commissioners, Petition of 92 farmers from the Hantam, 3 May 1855, enclosure to No. 107, 27 November 1856.

[37] 1/WOC 12/17, Letters Rec. from Officials, H.C. Nieuwhoudt (Over-Bokkeveld) to J. van Ryneveld, 17 February 1826, (enclosed with 1 March 1826); 1/WOC 13/22, Letters Rec., W.P. Burgher to Trappes, 30 March 1828 and A.E. de Waal to Trappes, 24 March 1828; 1/WOC 12/72, Letters Rec., Answers by Deputy Landdrost and Heemraden of Clanwilliam on questions by the Inspector of Lands and Woods, 23 January 1826; 1/WOC 13/22, Letters Rec., J.J. Louw to Adjt. Landdrost, 7 March 1828.

CHAPTER XIII

The Trek from the Summer Rainfall Areas

1. The Occupation of the Trek Area

For more than a century after white expansion on the border of the winter rain area stopped, the trek area remained uninhabited. The farmers of the Binneveld trekked there every summer, but as soon as winter arrived, they fell back to inhabited areas. The trek area has only begun to get permanent inhabitants during the past sixty years. The occupation of this grazing land had begun by 1880 and continued very gradually thereafter until the last crown land was issued on the Vrybult in 1938.

Prior to the commencement of the permanent colonization of the trek area, stray whites had occasionally settled there. It is, for example, an interesting fact that a few farms had already been allocated in North Bushmanland in the days of the old Company. In 1776 the farm Jabiesiefontein on the Groot River was allocated to Jacobus Bierman by ordinance.[1] The following year Camasfontein, which had previously been inhabited by Coenraad Feyt, was also given to Bierman on loan.[2] These two farms have been identified by Dr. [Ernst] Mossop, our best scholar of the historical topography of the Northwest, as Klein-Pella and Pella, respectfully.[3]

These forerunners of civilization did not encourage others to settle in Bushmanland. So far as is known, the first farmer after Bierman and Coenraad Feyt to trek into Bushmanland was Coenraad Meyer, who settled at Groot Wilger in 1849. There he built a little hut, cultivated the land, and set up a horse-mill. From this it is clear that he must have stayed a while in Bushmanland. For how long, we do not know. According to a statement made by the Reverend [Ferdinand] Brecher in 1851, no other trekboers had settled on the Pella land before Meyer.[4] Any memory of the pioneering work of Bierman and Coenraad Feyt had thus not survived.

By the middle of the nineteenth century two foreigners also had settled in Bushmanland. In 1855 the surveyor [Robert, Jr.] Moffat* met a Dutchman at Gaams named Hollenbach, who had been living there since 1840. In his day he had been a sailor. Later he made a living as a schoolmaster among Witbooi's people. At Pella Moffat came across a Frenchman, who had already been living there for years, and before that was a lieutenant in Napoleon's army. His name was François P. Gabriel.[5] According to other reports, in 1851 he had gone to live at Pella, which at that time was a mission station. He built a small house there, made a little garden, ran a small farm, and married a young Baster woman.[6] Around 1855 an Irishman, John Hayes, settled at Aggeneys, but in 1868 he left this place and went to live in Namaqualand.[7]

The true pioneers of Bushmanland were the colonial Basters. Many of them had already immigrated there long before the expansion of the colonial border in 1847. Moffat says that in

---

*Trans. note: Robert Moffat, Jr. was the eldest son of the famous London Missionary Society missionary, Robert Moffat. He served for a while as Government Surveyor at the Cape. In 1854 a copper mining company hired him for two years to survey Little Namaqualand, although he eventually surveyed a much larger region. In 1858 he published an account of his travels and surveys, together with some of his maps, in the book cited by Dr. van der Merwe here.

1855 he met a Baster named Losper at Gaams, who had already lived there for 18 years.[8] In 1864 E.A. Judge, at that time civil commissioner for Springbok, established that various married Basters who lived at Pella were born there. Willem van Neel (75 years old) and his son Dirk had lived at Pella since 1824. Arie, Piet, Hans, Klaas and Paul Losper had been living at Gaams for more than a quarter of a century by the time of Judge's inquiry (1864).[9]

The Basters were also the people who uncovered the waters at Putse. The oldest Baster at Bosluis could not tell me precisely when they had dug these wells, but he declared that it was still "under the first kings." To the question as to which king it was, he answered: "the girl-king, Victorie." According to what all the Basters and old farmers say, however, one has to conclude that there were already Basters living permanently at Putse in the 1860s. The Farmers and the Cloetes appear to have been the first pioneers.

When the old people of today were children, there were still no farmers living in Bushmanland. Old pioneers still remember the time when the last inhabited farms of Namaqualand lay on the borders of the summer rainfall areas: Goegaap, Gamoep, Kamibees, Ratelkraal, Rietfontein, Silwerfontein and Alwynsfontein.

According to tradition, one of the first farmers who trekked into Bushmanland to live there was the old man, Jan Visser. As a Namaqualander he had always trekked in the summer into Bushmanland and returned again before it was winter. Over time, however, he became tired of the back and forth trek and in 1878 settled down for good at Namies-North. His son, Gert Visser, from Kykgat, is absolutely certain about this date. He says that his (now deceased) father trekked when Gert was two years old, and he was born in 1876. Furthermore, he informed me that his father trekked to Namies in a long-tent wagon, which his father bought from Gert Greeff just after Greeff had surveyed a number of farms in that part of Bushmanland in 1877. Research in the office of the Surveyor-General confirmed Mr. Visser's claim. Gert Greeff did indeed survey about 40 farms in the western portion of the Kenhardt District in 1877.

Arnoldus Maass settled at Namies-South shortly after Jan Visser. According to his children, it must have been by 1880. He dug a well and in 1882 built a walled house, which at that time was a rarity. The other farmers all still lived in tents then. Around the same time Alwyn Dippenaar, a brother-in-law of Jan Visser, also went to live at Namies-South, and the widow Neeltjie van den Heever went to settle at Gaams. Oral tradition also makes mention of other whites who were in that vicinity in the 1880s: Hollenbach, Machiel Hayes, Frikkie van Reenen and the Catholic missionaries at Pella; Herridge, Webster's foreman, and Bennet, from Springbok, at Aggeneys; a German with the name of Kleinhardt, at Naroep, and a Dutchman, who was apparently called "Korbo," at Pofadder. It is not known when these people came to live there.

From this time forward people trekked one after the other into Bushmanland. The first pioneers were almost all Namaqualanders. People later also came there from other places. The Burgers, of Aggeneys, came from Williston. Kruger, of Namies, came from Griqualand-West. Muller was a Transvaaler.

The first immigrants into the northern part of Bushmanland all settled at the well-known watering places in the vicinity of Pella, just to the south of the Orange River. Voor-Bushmanland, which borders on Namaqualand, as well as the Bult, had no permanent inhabitants at first. There was no permanent surface water, and the underground water was so deep that no one was prepared to dig a well there before he took ownership of the land.

When the first Namaqualanders begin to trek to the water in the vicinity of Pella, the southern portion of Bushmanland—known earlier as the Agterveld—was still without permanent inhabitants. Old pioneers say that there were still no farmers living to the north of Kobiskow by 1880. Between 1880 and 1890 a few farmers settled on freehold farms in the trekveld, but the real colonization of Calvinia-Bushmanland only began after the first farms were sold there, in the 1890s. In the years just before the Gold War, most of the well-known farms in the old Agterveld had owners. The majority of these owners had gone to live there straightaway. Some farms, however, were still used for years only as summer farms. Breekknie, along the Krom River, which had already been sold in 1892, only got permanent inhabitants in 1936. Even today a few farms are still used only as summer farms. The first pioneers to move to Calvinia-Bushmanland were farmers from the Hantam and Bokveld.

These farmers all settled in the southern part of Bushmanland, where there was plenty of water. Sewefontein, Katkop and Granaatboskolk were the farthest points that were permanently occupied in the nineteenth century. The Bult, which began about here, was used only as trek pasture.

The southeastern portion of the trek area already had a permanent population in the nineteenth century as well. The Karee Mountains must already have been inhabited fairly early on. According to a statement made by Willem Andries van der Berg, field-cornet of the Agter-Nuweveld ward in the Beaufort district, on 10 November 1856, there were already people moving around in the Karee Mountains at that time who had no land anywhere else.[10] Someone who was born in the Karee Mountains in 1860 assured me that there were already many farmers in the vicinity as early as he could remember. The population of that region, however, was still very mobile. Even landowners almost always moved around following the rains—the occupants of freehold farms and landless farmers as well.

According to oral tradition there were still no people living in the vicinity of Brandvlei by 1865. When the plots of land were sold there in 1877, however, there were already farmers settled on freehold farms everywhere along the Sak River. By the beginning of the 1880s there were several farmers all along the river who were applying irrigation.[11] By the end of the nineteenth century the Sak River area and the Karee mountains were already densely populated.

A considerable number of the pioneers who settled in this part of the trek area, however, were originally from the winter rainfall region: from the Bokveld, the Hantam and the Roggeveld. There were, however, also many people from other summer rainfall areas more to the east—such as Prieska, Victoria West, Beaufort West, etc.—who had trekked there. The Namaqualanders did not penetrate so far to the east. The farthest that they had come in this direction during the nineteenth century was the vicinity of Pofadder in the western part of Kenhardt. The Hartbees River area was colonized by people from Calvinia, Williston, Carnarvon and Prieska. The names and nature of the farmers along the Hartbees River differed a good deal from those from Namaqualand.

At the beginning of the twentieth century, therefore, the border areas of the old trek area, which even in pioneer conditions was inhabitable without any difficulty, already had permanent inhabitants. There was still a large piece of free land left over in the central part of Bushmanland, however, which lay completely uninhabited. It stretched from east to west, and was on average about 60 miles wide and 120 miles long. It included the northern part of the Calvinia district, the eastern part of Namaqualand, and the western part of Kenhardt.

The Vrybult, as this enormous expanse of crown land was called, offered healthy and good pasture land, but was not permanently inhabitable because of a shortage of constant surface water. Before a farmer could subsist on the Bult, he had to first tap into the underground water. And the water was so deep under the ground that no farmer would undertake digging for it before he took ownership of the land. It was too risky to dig a well of a few hundred feet on crown land. In a future leasing of the land, you could find yourself out of land and then all your troubles and expenses were in vain.

One of the reasons why the government delayed so long in the distribution of the crown land on the Bult was that it had still not been surveyed. This work was completed bit by bit between 1908 and 1926 and as this proceeded, farms were allocated one after the other on application. The last seven farms on the Bult were given out in 1938. With that the occupation of the trek area, which had begun about sixty years before, was complete.[12]

2. The Winter Trek to the Binneveld

Over time, as permanent occupants settled in the trek area—people who bought, leased, or just moved around there, but in any case considered the summer rainfall region as their permanent home—the practice developed of trekking in the winter with their livestock to the Binneveld. The winter trek developed spontaneously and unnoticed. The first occupants of the trek area were former Binnevelders, who were living there in order to trek back and forth between the winter and the summer rainfall regions. They merely continued with the same sort of trek. The only difference was that they later acquired vested interests in the trek area and viewed it as their land.

The farmers of the old trek area generally begin to trek from the beginning of May to the Binneveld. Sometimes, however, they trekked as early as April and occasionally as late as June: everything depended on conditions in the trek area and when the first rains fell in the Binneveld. They then stayed three or four months—at the most five—in the Binneveld. By September, or at the latest October, they trekked back again to their lands. Usually it had not yet rained there, but as soon as it began to get warm in the Binneveld, the pasture withered. As the herbage deteriorated, pasture became scarce and it became ever more difficult to manage. Furthermore, by October the Binneveld became unhealthy. Loco sickness began to make its appearance and livestock accustomed to pasture elsewhere did not do well there. If the farmers did not trek back in time, the livestock wandered away. As soon as summer came, the trekboers in the Binneveld also had more problems with water—particularly in Namaqualand. If the livestock begin to drink more and the open waters in the outfields dried up, the landowners fell back on the permanent water and the trekboers had to make tracks.

This trek still continues today. The farmers of the summer rainfall region generally do not maintain winter farms in the winter rainfall area. Some of them do own land today in the

Binneveld, but they are only a minimal percentage of the farmers who trek. They do sometimes lease land permanently in the Binneveld, but very seldom. There are very few farms that are for lease. Most are inhabited by the owners themselves. In the Sandveld, in the Knechtsvlakte and also in Calvinia there is still undistributed crown land, but the government seldom leases entire farms. The usual practice is to issue grazing licenses for the same farm to several farmers. The majority of farmers from the trek area therefore have to make arrangements anew every year for pasture land in the Binneveld.

Sometimes the farmers of the Binneveld and the trek area help each other reciprocally with pasture at no charge. Usually, however, the trekboers hire pasture land in the Binneveld by the month and pay per hundred head of livestock. The tariff is about the same as the going rate in other parts of the Northwest, namely 5s. to £1, and still more per month for a hundred sheep and goats, according to the circumstances. If a man is happy to use pasture that is assigned to him, he can get grazing land on the Steinkopf and the Leliefontein reserves for 4s. per hundred. If he is prepared to pay 7s. 6d. to 10s, he can trek wherever he wants. At this price he can generally also be assisted by white landowners. If pasture is scarce, however, he must often pay much higher prices for good pasture land.

3. The Causes of the Trek

The major cause of the winter trek from the old trek area to the Binneveld must undoubtedly be sought in the difference between the seasonal rainfall in the two areas. When the old trek area is dry in the winter, the Binneveld gets its rain and there is green pasture. In the old days this was enough for any farmer to trek. For the farmers of the old trek area the green pasture land of the Binneveld was even more attractive because the winter was their lambing time. It was too dry then in the trek area for lambing. What is more, it was bitterly cold. Under these circumstances farmers preferred to spend the lambing season in Namaqualand with its mild winter climate, or in other parts of the Binneveld where at least there was green pasture.

Naturally lambing was possible during the summer in the trek area, when there was green pasture. One never knew, however, when to expect the summer rains. In addition, it became very hot in the summer. In Bushmanland in the summer it became so hot that young lambs' hoofs would split open when they walked on the hot sand. Lambs also easily swelter to death in the sun. For these reasons the old pioneers chose to have lambing time in the winter.

There are already many farmers today who have lambing time in the summer in the old trek area, but the majority of them also lamb once more in the winter in the Binneveld. Usually they do not allow the same ewes to lamb at both times, but they divide the flock into two. The first ewes then have their lambs in February or March, only after the summer rains have fallen, on their farms. The rest of the ewes have their lambs in June or July in the Binneveld. By lambing twice a year, a farmer lessens the possibility of losing his entire season's fall of lambs. If the first lambing season was unsuccessful, he still always had the chance perhaps to have a better one later in the year.

In dry years the winter grazing in the old trek area was often so scarce that the farmers were obliged to go and look for pasture elsewhere. Apart from this, however, it was a common practice in the summer rainfall region to maintain more livestock than what your farm could support through the year, with the intention of trekking for part of the year. Such farmers then went in search of the additional grazing land that they needed in the Binneveld and left their livestock there to graze during the winter months, when there was green pasture. Even if the trek land received its rain late, however, so that there was plenty of good pasture in the winter, many farmers would still trek. The purpose of this was to save their own pasture for the summer, because during the summer there was no possibility of being helped in the Binneveld if they would perhaps run into problems with grazing land.

Another cause that is usually put forward for the winter trek is that the livestock needed the change of pasture. Many of the farmers held fast to the belief that they could not farm successfully if they had not been in the Binneveld for some part of the year. If the livestock just continually ate dry grass—the farmers said—they developed lumps in their stomachs and they were also inclined to get gall sickness.[†] The winter-rainveld of the Binneveld offered more healthy and varied *slaaiveld*[‡] and shrubland, allowing the animals to quickly recover from these digestive disorders. Sometimes the livestock would also not grow properly if one did not trek. In 1939 Niemüller, from Pofadder, told me: "My two farms are bright green, but I trekked. I could not get my livestock fat. They wanted to have a change."

In some instances the need for a change was because the respective farms only had pasture land, while sheep and goats actually do better on small shrubs. If a farmer had no shrub brush on his own farm, it was desirable for him to trek. Moreover, the pasture in some parts of the trek area was too "fresh." Livestock did not get all the salts and phosphates that their bodies needed from the plants that they ate. The Bushmanland farmers also did not feed their livestock salt and bonemeal, so there was a need for the grazing land of the Binneveld, which contained those substances. It was also sometimes said that Bushmanland was "too rich" for sheep and goats, especially if the region received a lot of rain in a given year. Then it was also desirable to trek.

Farmers also often trekked to the Binneveld because they wanted to fatten up their livestock for the market quickly. Namaqualand was particularly suitable for this purpose. If it was a good year for vegetation and flowers, one could not want better pasture for getting the livestock fat for market. If a farmer trekked to Namaqualand, he brought his livestock at the same time nearer to the railroad line that runs from Bitterfontein to Cape Town. There was thus no danger that the drive to the station would harm their condition.

Sometimes the Bushmanlanders just had their sheep sheared in Namaqualand, with the intention of lessening the transportation costs to the station. It also happened that a farmer would trek to the Binneveld simply because he had pasture due to him there that he wanted to use. He had perhaps helped someone from the winter rainfall area the preceding year for nothing, on the condition that this person would help him later—and now he trekked on account of the free pasture, even though he did not really need it.

[†]Trans. note: Afrikaans *galsiekte*. In this context, it is "dry" gall sickness, caused by eating too much dry fodder, which causes constipation or blockage in ruminants.

[‡]Trans. note: Afrikaans *slaaiveld* translates as "saladveld" in English. This is land where there are a variety of plants that make ideal fodder. These include *bloomkoolganna* (cauliflower ganna) and *koolganna* (cabbage ganna) (both of which are a variety of *Caroxylon tuberculatum*), *sandganna* (sand ganna - *Lebeckia plukenetiana*) and *tsamma*, which includes several plants in the family Cucurbvitaceae, such as *wilde waatlemoen* (wild watermelon), *soelwaatlemoen* (sweet watermelon) and *karkoer* (gourd).

4. No Winter Trek in the Eastern Part of the Trek Area

The greatest portion of the farmers who settled down permanently in the old trek area in the course of time took part in the winter trek to the Binneveld. But not everyone did. The farmers who lived to the east of the line connecting Kakamas, Onderstedoorns and Williston did not trek much "in country."

The eastern section of the old trek area had excellent sheep pasture. The farmers had no need to trek for the sake of a change of grazing land. Furthermore, the rainfall of the trek area also improves from west to east, which increases the inhabitability of the region. The farmers along the Hartbees River never needed to trek a great deal with livestock. It was not necessary anyway to trek regularly in the winter. It happened now and then that they had to resort to going to the winter rainfall region, but this occurred very seldom. When it did happen, they trekked to the Hantam side. Namaqualand was too far. The farmers between Williston, Fraserburg and Carnarvon trekked more regularly than the Hartbees River farmers did. But even in these cases it was by no means a regular winter trek. When the area to the east of the Sak River received its summer rains, the grazing land in the winter was perfectly satisfactory and the farmers did not trek. They trekked only in times of drought. If perhaps the drought caught them in the winter, they trekked to the Hantam, Roggeveld, or other winter rainfall areas. Otherwise not. By the end of the nineteenth century there were a few farmers in Fraserburg and Carnavon who more or less regularly trekked in country. But it was not a common practice at all and had died out early in this century already.

5. Sak River -- Hantam

In the old days the Sak River farmers, west of the line that connects Onderstedoorns and Williston, regularly trekked in the winter to the Hantam. Many older people can still remember this. Over the past forty years this trek declined rapidly, especially since 1930 when the Sak River farmers begin to fence off their land. The only Sak River farmer who, so far as I know, still regularly treks in the winter to the Hantam is Hugo van Niekerk (Hugo-Bokkie). And he treks because he owns a farm in the Hantam, which he maintains especially because he speculates a good deal in livestock and wants to be in a position to have fat livestock for market at any time of the year. Moreover, it is well known that the "Bokkies" had always loved the trek.

The other Sak River farmers trek these days only to Hantam when there is truly a pressing need and then they do so reluctantly. It is so difficult today with all the *gorrels*,§ particularly in times of drought, to trek to that part of the world that the Williston farmers usually just transport their livestock by train to Carnavon. That costs money and brings its own worries with it. In addition, the Sak River farmers are rather afraid of the livestock sicknesses of the Hantam and of the poisonous plants that their livestock do not know. These days it is also difficult to get grazing

§Trans. note: A *gorrel* (English, "gullet") is a fenced-off strip of land on either side of a trek road that serves as a passage for the livestock. It also keeps the animals off the established farmer's land to protect his grazing and water. Dr. van der Merwe discusses these *gorrels* in two articles beginning on pages 469 and 476 respectively in *Reports from the Dorsland and other pioneering regions*. He notes on page 479 that "These days [i.e., 1952] [the Bushmanlanders] also talk about a *passaat* [passage]." See also page 178 in *Reports*.

land in the Hantam. Therefore the Sak River farmers just try to set up their farms so that they have to trek, no matter where, as little as possible.

6. South Bushmanland (Agterveld) -- Hantam and Bokveld

The farmers of southern Bushmanland (the old Agterveld) who presently fall under the jurisdiction of the Calvinia magisterial district, in the old days usually trekked towards the Hantam and Bokveld when winter came. Most of them came from those parts, so they were quite familiar with it. They also had family and friends there who could help them with pasture. Many of the Bushmanlanders did not even trek as far as the Hantam and Bokveld. They only came up to border between the summer and winter rainfall areas, in the area between Loeriesfontein and the Kromrivier.

In the old days it was quite the exception for a Calvinia-Boesmanlander to trek to Namaqualand. Over the past forty years, however, it has become more difficult for the Calvinia-Boesmanlander to find winter pasture in his own district. The region is more densely populated, and especially since the farmers begin to fence their land, they have become much more unwilling to lease pasture. Consequently the winter trek from Bushmanland to the Hantam and Bokveld has gradually declined. Today there are still always Bushmanlanders who trek to the south, but in comparison with earlier times they are relatively few.

7. Bushmanland -- Namaqualand

The Calvinia-Bushmanlanders still all trek in the winter with their livestock, but for the last few years they have been trekking much more towards Namaqualand. Some spend the winter in the vicinity of Nuwerus and Bitterfontein, that part of Namaqualand that is commonly called the "Hardeveld." Others move down to the desolate Knechtsvlakte, which in the winter receives the little rain it is granted all at one time, and then as if by the touch of a magic wand changes into a flower garden. There they take out grazing licences on crown land or lease pasture from the landowners, who for a few months have the unheard of luxury of too much pasture land. The Calvinia-Bushmanlanders also sometimes trek past Vanrhynsdorp up to the Sandveld along the west coast, but they will never do this while the Knechtsvlakte is looking beautiful.

The farmers of the northern part of Bushmanland, what the Namaqualanders have always called "Bushmanland," still always trek in the winter to Namaqualand since that region became populated. We include in northern Bushmanland that part of Bushmanland that falls under the jurisdiction of the Namaqualand mageristerial district, as well as the western part of Kenhardt. The Bushmanland farmers trekked to Namaqualand up to about 60 miles to the west of Kenhardt.

They usually went in the direction of Springbok and Steinkopf. As long as Bushmanland still had few permanent inhabitants, they did not trek any farther. They could almost all be helped in the mountainous area of Namaqualand. As the population of Bushmanland grew, however, they had to trek farther. Since about 1910 they have begun to trek to the Sandveld. Before this time— old Sandvelders say—they never saw a Bushmanlander. But now they are a plague. They are as plentiful as partridges every winter and they come more regularly than the peacock.

If one wants to move down from the heights of Springbok to the Sandveld, there are only two possible routes by which you can travel, namely, over Spektakel or over Aninoes. Here the trekboers go down the mountains and then they usually travel until sunset to the sea. Then they turn southward and trek down along the coast of the Sandveld to the mouth of the Buffels River. There some of them turn around, travel back up the old route, and go through the mountains again at Spektakel and Aninoes. Others turn eastward by Kleinzee and travel through Garies or Bitterfontein back to Bushmanland. It sometimes happens that trekboers go down the Sandveld to the mouth of the Olifants River, but most travel no farther than the mouth of the Buffels River. Garies and Sandveld are too thickly overgrown, with the result that the farmers' livestock, which do not know this kind of terrain, can easily get lost.

Until recently the Bushmanlanders did not really go beyond the Kamies Mountains. They usually only came up to the slopes of the mountains. Since around 1933, however, it has become a common practice for them to trek into the Kamies Mountains. Some of them travel right over the Kamies Mountains to the sea. "And if it was possible to trek over the water," an old Namaqualander assured me, "they would have trekked still farther."

8. Extent of the Winter Trek in Bushmanland

The pioneers who had settled in the vicinity of Namies by 1880 did not regularly trek back to Namaqualand every winter. If it was at all possible, they spent the winter in Bushmanland. Only if the drought became serious, did they trek. And even then the old people usually remained at home and let the children trek with the livestock. At that time Bushmanland still lay, as it were, uninhabited, with the result that the farmers at Namies had plenty of opportunities to trek in their immediate vicinity. This lessened the necessity for trekking to Namaqualand.

In addition, at that time there was still no permanent water between Namies and Namaqualand. And the farmers did not trek willingly through a desert for twelve hours by horse unless it was necessary.

Since 1910, however, the population of Bushmanland has grown rapidly. This has increased the number of migrants, and at the same time lessened the number of opportunities for migration in Bushmanland. Furthermore, water became more available over time all along the trail, which facilitated the trek to Namaqualand. As a result, more Bushmanlanders went to spend the winter in Namaqualand every year. By the end of the 1920s the illegal diamond trade led to an unprecedented flourishing of the winter trek. In those few abundant diamond years the nearly forgotten Namaqualand was overrun by thousands of fortune-seekers. Among them were also farmers who brought their livestock with them, so as to provide a convincing motive for their presence in the diamond region. At that time people from far and wide, who had never trekked before, arrived with their livestock. After that the trek subsided a little, but it is still in full swing today.

The average Bushmanlander treks—to this day—very easily. He usually does not have a garden that can go to seed. It is therefore every easy for him to put the brakes on his windmill, to close up his house and to go trek with his family. The children of school-going age usually remain behind in boarding schools.

The winter trek out of Bushmanland still always assumes the form of a regular seasonal migration. Nearly every year there are Bushmanlanders in the Binneveld. Naturally not everyone treks there every year. In a year such as 1938, when the Binneveld had a dry winter and it coincidentally rained late in the last part of the summer in Bushmanland, very few farmers trekked. If Bushmanland is dry during the year, on the other hand, it has happened in many winters that one can ride from Loeriesfontein to Pofadder (a distance of about 150 miles) right through Bushmanland without seeing a living soul. This is what happened in 1933, for example, when the greatest part of Bushmanland was completely unpopulated. Every living being had trekked to the Binneveld. Not a man, dog or chicken was left behind.

It is very difficult to offer a statistical representation of the extent of the winter trek out of Bushmanland. In normal years more than half of Bushmanland's farmers trek to the Binneveld. What is more, I also get the impression that during the past thirty years (1909-1939) the majority of the Bushmanlanders have trekked more often to the Binneveld than they have spent the winter in Bushmanland.

Some of the Bushmanlanders trek every year. In 1938 Reverend J.H. Roos, who at that time was minister at Nuwerus, told me that many farmers from Brandvlei and Loeriesfontein trekked so regularly to the Hardeveld that he considered them as members of his congregation. Others trek one year perhaps and not the other year, but there are few Bushmanlanders who have never trekked to the Binneveld.

Some Bushmanlanders have recently begun to lose confidence in the winter trek. Here and there one comes across farmers who had previously often trekked to Namaqualand, but of late trek rarely or not at all. They claim that one can achieve success in one's farming without trekking, and they have also proven this experimentally.

A. Coetzee, of Namies-North, for example, informed me in 1939 that he had trekked seven times during the previous thirty years. The first thirteen years he trekked six times. The last seventeen years only once. Today he does not trek at all. He claims that he reduced the need to trek by 90 percent as soon as he fenced his land. He is of the opinion that other Bushmanlanders will also be able to survive on their land if they have enough fencing and water.

The most noteworthy evidence I received relating to this matter came from van der Heever, of Ariep. He was one of the first Bushmanlanders to fence in his land. In 1922 he followed Albertus Roux's example and in 1935 all of his farms were enclosed with jackal-proof wire. He farmed with 4,000 livestock on 37,000 morgen of land. In relation to his livestock he thus does not have too much land. The general view is that one needs ten morgen per sheep in Bushmanland.

In 1938 van der Heever informed me that his pasture has not been luxuriant since 1930. During the preceding seven years his land had not received proper rainfall. In the last four years it was terribly dry. Some rain fell now and then, but never enough to get the pasture growing. But he has farmed on his own land for the previous ten years and during the drought had even helped others. He saved pasture for bad times and trekked from one farm to another on his own land. Previously he had also trekked to the Binneveld, but often sustained great losses. "In Namaqualand it often does not go any better with the livestock and there I have to pay for them. Here they die for free."

Dixon, from Haramoep, also used to trek regularly to Namaqualand as well. Later, however, he bought an additional farm (Springputs), in order to be able to eliminate the need to trek, "because I did not see how it could continue." The two farms get rain at the same time of the year. This simply means then that he has more grazing land. It was his experience as well that a Bushmanlander could eliminate the migration to the Binneveld by saving pasture.

These examples are not exceptional. Particularly on Kenhardt's side one finds large areas where the farmers do not trek any longer at all. These farmers had also formerly trekked on a regular basis every winter to Namaqualand, but as soon as they had finished enclosing their property (around 1934) they no longer found this necessary. Many of them specially put up fences, because they no longer wished to trek.

There is not the slightest doubt about whether it is possible for a Bushmanlander to improve and expand his farm in such a way that it is no longer necessary to trek in the winter to the Binneveld. It can definitely be done. Most Bushmanlanders will not even have to purchase additional land. They have enough land. Their greatest problem is that they cannot use their land economically enough. This must be ascribed mainly to two causes. The first is that most farms in Bushmanland are still not fenced in. Very few of those that are in fact fenced have enough internal enclosures. This makes it very difficult for the farmers to save pasture land and to apply sensible land–management practices.

Another difficulty is that there are still not enough watering-places for livestock in Bushmanland. There are still many farms of 20,000 to 30,000 morgen and greater that have only one source of permanent water. Very few of the farmers have more than one watering-place per 10,000 morgen. And even then the water is very inconveniently situated, so that the outlying fields are 15 to 20 miles from the water. In such circumstances the farmers often cannot use their outlying fields properly, particularly during droughts, when they need to do so the most. There is often then good grazing land available that the livestock cannot reach. The scarcity of watering-places also means that the livestock have to walk a long distance to get to water. This leads to the trampling of fields and during droughts exhausts the already weak livestock even more.

The fact that farming in Bushmanland is still so extensive today must not be ascribed to backwardness on the part of the farmers. It is a young district. Most farmers have trekked there only since 1907, and many of them were dirt poor then. And it requires a lot of work, patience, courage and money to make a farm in Bushmanland inhabitable. On many sites the underground water is over 200 feet below the surface, without there being the least indication of where to dig. There are farmers who struggled twenty years and longer before they got water. One should rather be amazed that so much constructive work has been done in such a short time.

The struggle to get water goes on unceasingly, however, and most farmers today are convinced of the value of enclosures. As soon as fencing material can be obtained once more at reasonable prices, fencing will immediately begin again. And as the development of farms progresses, the necessity for a regular winter trek will gradually diminish, and will later disappear altogether. People who happen to have summer and winter farms will probably continue their treks. The common view, however, is that the winter treks to the Binneveld will decrease considerably in the near future and that over time—as a regular seasonal migration at least—will disappear altogether.

ENDNOTES

[1] RLR 24/2, Old Gamehunters Books, 21 November 1776, p. 437.

[2] RLR 25/1, Old Gamehunters Books, 22 October 1777, p. 261.

[3] E.E. Mossop, *The Journal of Hendrik Jacob Wikar (1779),... and the Journals of Jacobus Coetsé Jansz. (1760) and Willem van Reenen (1791)...* (Cape Town: Van Riebeeck Society, 1935), Series I, vol. 15, p. 34.

[4] S.G. 2/1/1/10, Surveyor General, General Letter Book, Surveyor General Bell, Report to Govt. on application of Revd. F. Brecher, Missionary of German Evangelical Church at Steinkopf and Pella, for land in Little Namaqualand for Native Locations, 25 September 1851, p. 125.

[5] R. Moffat, *Journey from Colesberg to Steinkopf, 1831-1835* (London, [1858]), p. 17.

[6] C.O. 3068, Letters Rec., Civil Commissioner for Namaqualand, E.A. Judge to Col. Secretary, 24 March 1864.

[7] 1/SBK 5/1/5, L. Boyes to Col. Secretary, 2 October 1873; 1/SBK 5/1/2, E.A. Judge to J. Hayes, 6 May 1863.

[8] Moffat, *Journey*, p. 16.

[9] C.O. 3068, Letters Rec., Civil Commissioner for Namaqualand, E.A. Judge to Col. Secretary, 24 March 1864.

[10] C.O. 4402, Arrears, Statement of Willem Andries van der Berg, Field-Cornet of the Agter-Nuweveld, 10 November 1856, enclosed with J.B. Auret to Surveyor-General, 27 December 1856, p. 3.

[11] CCP 1/2/1/31, A21 of 1876, Report of the Hydraulic Engineer, 27 May 1876, p. 11; S.G. 1/1/4/15, W.E. Mandy to Surveyor General W. de Smidt, 2 February 1882, p. 24.

[12] P.J. van der Merwe, *Pioniers van die Dorsland* (Cape Town, 1841), p. 36-53.

CHAPTER XIV

Incidental Migrations

In contrast with regular seasonal migrations, in the Cape (as in other parts of the Union) there was a form of migration with livestock that exhibited no regularity. It occurred sporadically, when and where the occasion arose, for reasons that cropped up unexpectedly and that were not repeated at regular intervals. This sort of migration we can call an incidental migration.

Incidental migrations appeared more or less often at one or another period in all parts of the Cape where the farmers kept livestock. They are as old as livestock farming itself in the Cape. They first began to play an important role only in the nineteenth century, however, when the dry parts of the Colony had become inhabited. During the past half century they have declined considerably.

1. The Company Period

We already find the first traces of incidental migrations in the time of Simon van der Stel, when livestock farming was gradually becoming a separate, independent occupation. Specifically, in 1688 it came to the governor's attention, much to his consternation, that the colonists were letting their livestock graze at uncharted and distant places. He viewed this innocent practice in a very serious light and set himself squarely against such "rowdiness." He issued a proclamation strictly forbidding "the grazing of any livestock at uncharted and distant places." There was also an order that all free burghers "settled, or with their livestock" outside the borders of the Colony must return to the Colony within six months.[1]

The livestock farmers, however, did not let themselves be intimidated by the strict punishments (fines, confiscation, and even flogging) that the proclamation threatened. Trekking with livestock continued. This is evident from the fact that a new proclamation forbidding the trek with livestock was found necessary in 1691. This one stated that farmers must return to their homes every evening with their livestock, after they have spent the day grazing in the fields. If anyone remained away from their homes for eight consecutive days, they could have their livestock confiscated.[2]

Simon van der Stel was succeeded in 1699 by someone who was more sympathetic to the livestock farmers and also had a better understanding of their needs. The new governor, Willem Adriaan van der Stel, did not worry too much about the trek with livestock. It is true that the legislation against roaming with livestock was actually not formally revoked. Indeed, it was even included again in the General Proclamation of 1705.[3] But there is no evidence to be found in contemporary documents that the governor ever tried to enforce the laws. And with his system of grazing licenses, he acted in direct opposition to the laws.

As a result of the lifting of the restriction against the cattle trade the colonists' livestock herds expanded quickly during the first years of the eighteenth century. This made the chronic question of grazing land acute. By 1705 there was a shortage of grazing land and water in the inhabited areas even in the rainy season. During the dry season there was sometimes no water or pasture to be had at all. Then the colonists were obliged to trek with their livestock into the interior.[4]

In order to provide for the temporary grazing needs of the settled livestock farmers, the governor began extending grazing licenses in 1703. It appears from the grazing licenses that were issued between 1703 and 1709 that some farmers trekked regularly a few months every summer, usually by November or December, with their livestock into the interior. Other license holders' names, however, appear only once or twice during the above-mentioned period in the Gamehunters Books.[5] From these it appears that they did not trek regularly, but only when the need was pressing. Unfortunately the Gamehunters Books do not shed much light on this practice, because very soon it became the custom to grant the grazing licenses for a full year. Thus, the grazing license system soon made way for the loan farm system. After that it is no longer possible to determine on the basis of grazing licenses between farmers who lived permanently on the loan farms and those who used them only as temporary livestock stations.

The loan farm inhabitants in the interior also trekked often with their livestock. In the western part of the Colony regular seasonal migrations came into existence. More to the east, where the farms were inhabitable right through the year, even under pioneer conditions, the farmers trekked only occasionally when it became necessary or when they had the desire to do so.

In the archives of the eighteenth century one repeatedly finds references to such incidental migrations. In 1770 a government commission reported, for example, that they had met several persons between the Gamtoos and the Fish rivers, "who were grazing considerable herds of cattle, and without possessing any farm thereabouts, or farms in loan from the Company among them; while others wandered about with their cattle many days' ride from their loan places."[6] The commission also found dung piles and the remains of grass houses at different sites, which led them to conclude that farmers kept livestock stations there.[7]

In these circumstances the landdrosts of Stellenbosch and Swellendam were instructed to keep an extremely careful watch to make sure that no one allowed his livestock to graze anywhere than on the farm or farms that he had received from the Company on loan, "much less wander about with them hither and yon, or on any other pretest, proceed from his place of residence deep into the interior."[8] Notwithstanding this prohibition the farmers of the eastern border districts still trekked with their livestock occasionally. If there were severe droughts or when the locusts were particularly troublesome, the farmers even trekked over the Fish River to Kafferland.[9]

2. Incidental Migrations Increase in the Nineteenth Century

From the sketchy and fragmentary evidence that is available about pioneer lives, it is not clear what role incidental migrations played in the seventeenth and the eighteenth centuries. The most one can say is that they occurred. This lack of positive evidence about incidental migrations can partially be ascribed to the scarcity of reports about the condition of the interior during this time period. Many things happened in our country about which we will never know the history because the sources are lacking. On the other hand, it would have been clearly evident from the available sources if this sort of migration had been quite extensive. Thus, one can surmise *a priori* that this was not the case. In the eastern part of the Colony it was not quite as necessary to trek with livestock. And in the drier, western part of the Colony the occasion for incidental migrations was much reduced because of the regular seasonal migrations.

From the beginning of the nineteenth century there are many more references in archival documents to incidental migrations with livestock and one also gets a much clearer understanding of the extent and importance of this type of migration.

The increase of incidental migrations in the nineteenth century must be ascribed to the fact that the colonists had trekked into the arid, central plateau of the Cape Colony, to the south of the Orange River, where it often became necessary to trek with livestock. In this area, however, there were not—as in other parts of the Cape Colony—local differences in the climate and in the seasonal distribution of rainfall, which led to the trek with livestock taking on the form of regular seasonal migrations.

3. The Expansion in the Nineteenth Century

Shortly after 1800 the pioneers began to trek into the Bo-Karoo to the north of the Sneeuberg and Nuweveldsberge. The trek was led by people who originally came from the vicinity of Graaff-Reinet. They followed more or less the course of the Seekoei River and quickly spread out in the area between the Seekoei River, Stormbergspruit and the Orange River. At the same time, farmers settled in thinly scattered sites to the west of the Seekoei River. The latter area, however, attracted more and more people after settlers had taken the best farms east of the Seekoei River. By the middle of the nineteenth century the area of the Bo-Karoo east of the line that connects Hopetown and Williston was fairly well populated, that is to say, more or less the areas that today comprise the magisterial districts of Albert, Britstown, Colesberg, Hanover, Maraisburg, Middelburg, Philipstown, Richmond, Steynsburg, Tarka, and Victoria West.[10]

The area of the arid Cape plateau to the west of the line connecting Hopetown and Williston first received permanent inhabitants during the second half of the nineteenth century. The present day districts of Hopetown, Prieska, Carnarvon, the eastern part of Kenhardt and the northern part of Fraserburg are mainly populated by immigrants from the eastern part of the Bo-Karoo. During the last quarter of the nineteenth century the farmers of the Hantam and Onder-Bokkeveld trekked into the dry area from the south and they settled in the Calvinia-Bushmanland. About the same time the farmers of Namaqualand trekked into Northern Bushmanland, i.e. the eastern part of Namaqualand and the western parts of Kenhardt. While the Bushmanland Bult remained temporarily uninhabited, during the last years of the nineteenth century an expansion to the area north of the Orange River also took place. Griqualand West had already been colonized before the gold war. Gordonia already had a few white inhabitants, but this region as well as Bechuanaland really only became densely populated during the twentieth century.

4. Scarcity of Water

The arid parts into which the farmers trekked during the nineteenth century were very short of water. Only the eastern edge of the Bo-Karoo, where the farmers had settled during the first twenty years of the nineteenth century, had a fairly ready supply of permanent natural water. After the best farms in these parts were inhabited, and particularly from the time when the farmers in the region to the west of the Seekoei River begin to trek there, they begin to experience ever greater difficulties with water. Farms in the Bo-Karoo that were inspected in the 1830s and 1840s, some of which had already been inhabited for many years, more often than not had water supplies for only a part of the year.

Some farmers lived by weak little springs, which easily dried up if rain did not fall for long periods. Others settled along little rivers in the Karoo, which flowed only now and then. When these river beds were dry the farmers were dependent on the standing water in hippo-pools and holes, which became brackish during droughts. Others were dependent on rain water that collected in pools, pans and earthen dams.

Under these circumstances there were often water shortages. If the rains remained away a little too long, the standing waters dried up. During droughts the springs weakened one after the other and stopped flowing. As soon as the water gave out, the farmers had to trek with their livestock, even though they still had a lot of pasture. Apart from this there were so few watering-holes for the livestock that the farmers could not completely use all of their grazing land. Even if the water lasted, during droughts there were often large patches of pasture land left over that the weak livestock could not graze because they were long distances from the watering holes.

During the last years of the nineteenth century many wells were dug in the arid parts—in spite of the uncertainty about rights to possession of land. This greatly improved the supply of water. But then it was still always very difficult getting the water out of the well. This situation led to many farmers trekking with their livestock as soon as there was someplace else that had open water, in order to free themselves from the sheer bother associated with drawing water.

5. Droughts and Lack of Grazing Land

Lack of grazing land also often obliged farmers to look elsewhere for relief for their livestock. The rainfall on the Cape plateau is pitifully low. The eastern edge of the region receives between 10 and 20 inches of rain per year, but the greatest part of that area gets less than 10 inches. This gradually diminishes from east to west. In a large part of Bushmanland rainfall is less than five inches per year. Many farmers are thankful if they get two inches every year. Apart from this, the rainfall is very erratic. Dr. [Johannes] Grosskopf points out that a place such as Prieska received an average of 9.63 inches of rain per year over a period of 48 years. The lowest number for a twelve-month period, however, was 1.37 inches (in 1903) and the highest 18.71 (in 1907).[11] Apart from this yearly variation, the distribution of the rainfall during the year is also important. Sometimes the total rainfall is quite enough for the specific year, but it falls so sporadically that the pasture cannot grow properly, or it falls so late that the pasture cannot ripen before the winter. Consequently, for a part of the year, sometimes for long periods of time, there is a lack of grazing land.

We do not have rainfall figures available to indicate the incidence of droughts during the nineteenth century. Elsewhere I have tried to offer, on the basis of numerous reports about the condition of the pasture land and water, a representation of the incidence of droughts in the Bo-Karoo during the first thirty years of the nineteenth century.[12] It is not necessary to repeat that evidence here, or to provide an account in the same manner of the droughts that have stricken the

Cape during the past hundred years. A few observations about the nature of droughts and the ways in which they prompted incidental migrations are sufficient for the purpose of this chapter.

6. Characteristics of Droughts

In the first place it must be pointed out that droughts are not a recent phenomenon. Droughts and losses from droughts were quite common in the nineteenth century and the farmers at that time undoubtedly suffered much more from this widespread problem than they do today. By that I do not at all want to suggest that rainfall in the nineteenth century was less than it is now, but only that the farmers at that time were subjected much more to the consequences of the scanty and erratic rainfall of our country than the farmers of our own time. This was the case because at this time there were far fewer watering-holes for livestock than today, and also because the farmers back then had enclosed their land in order that they could save pasture for times of drought. This obliged the farmers of the nineteenth century to trek much more than today's farmers. And if losses from drought back then were fewer than today—which I doubt—this can only be ascribed to the fact that there were many more chances for trekking than there are now.

The most important characteristic of droughts as a cause for incidental migrations is that their appearance and disappearance are always quite unexpected. A farmer can always be certain that the drought will come again. He can also count on it not lasting forever. But precisely when the drought will come and how long it will remain, no one can determine beforehand. If we study the nature of past droughts, it is clear that incidence of droughts displays no rhythmical pattern. Good and bad years follow one another without any recurring regularity. Sometimes a few good years follow on each other, occasionally a few bad years follow on one or more good ones. The duration of droughts also varies a good deal. Sometimes a drought lasts a few months, sometimes a few years. In Bushmanland there is a farm that—according to what people living there tell you— was uninhabitable for nine long years because of drought. In 1938 G.J. der Heever, of Taaiboschmond, told me of a farm that has not had rain since 1925. The area that is stricken by drought is also not always the same size. Now it affects only a few farms, then again it might be an entire district and sometimes several districts all at once. The appearance and disappearance of a drought is also not always linked to the sequence of the seasons. A drought can begin at any time of the year and end at any time of the year.

Consequently, treks with livestock that were the result of drought occurred quite irregularly. Sometimes a farmer was obliged to trek with his livestock every year for a couple of years in succession, or even two or three years on end. Sometimes he remained on his land for a year or a few years without ever having to leave it. In Bushmanland a farmer informed me that he once remained on his farm continuously for seven years. Then a great drought appeared that forced him to trek about for three years in a row. Other Bushmanlanders trekked one or more times virtually every year because of drought. Here and there one still even finds a farmer who lives in a canvas tent or caravan, spending only a few months each year on his own farm, and the rest of the year on one site after the other as he moves around the countryside. One year only a few farmers in a specific district trek. Another year the entire district or several districts empty out and trek. Sometimes a trekboer is helped out in his own region; sometimes he is obliged to trek hundreds of miles. One year perhaps he treks in the summer, the following year in the winter.[13]

7. Locusts and Migrating Antelope

A shortage of pasture land and water, that is to say, drought, was the most common cause of incidental migrations in the nineteenth century. But there were other causes as well. Just like today, the locusts visited the Colony periodically in the old days, without anyone being able to say beforehand when they would come or how long they would remain. Farmers were often troubled by locusts for two or three years in succession. Then the locusts would remain away for perhaps several years, but they always returned again. The devastation that locusts caused a century ago was much greater than today, because the modern means to eradicate them were not available at that time. Sometimes they so devoured the pasture that it looked as if it had been burned up by fire. The destruction caused by locusts often forced the farmers to trek. Just like droughts, the locust invasions resulted in a shortage of pasture at unexpected times. The locusts did not take any notice of the season or the condition of the pasture. Occasionally flying locusts, carried from far away by the wind, appeared in times of scarcity, and ate up what plant growth remained. Sometimes it happened that the rains, which brought an end to a severe drought, caused the locust eggs to hatch. The black wingless locusts and the hoppers then consumed all the green pasture, with the result that the farmers, perhaps a few months after good rains, had to trek again with their livestock.[14]

Another plague that the farmers of the northern parts of the Cape Colony often suffered in the old days was migrating antelope. Springbok did not perhaps make their appearance as regularly as locusts, but the devastation they caused was much greater. They sometimes gathered in such large herds that they laid waste to everything in their path. What they did not devour, they trampled to dust underfoot. If a large herd of migrating antelope, numbering in the hundreds of thousands according to some accounts, migrated through a district, the farmers had to flee. Until it rained again, the land over which they had migrated was completely worthless. Sometimes the migrating antelopes destroyed such a large area that many livestock died before they could be brought to grazing land again.[15]

8. Other Causes

Farmers also often trekked although there was no shortage of pasture and water whatsoever. In the arid northwestern areas of the Cape Colony, which had permanent inhabitants after 1850, the farmers trekked quite readily during the early years. They had grown up on migratory trails and were accustomed to trekking. Many of them lived in tents, so the trekking life did not bring with it exceptional hardships. What is more, on the farms there was nothing that required their presence. There was usually no water for irrigation. Moreover, a farmer did not like to build up and cultivate a freehold farm, because he could perhaps lose the lease in the following round of lease allocations. In these circumstances the custom developed of trekking as the rainfall shifted. When a farmer heard, or even only suspected, that there was green pasture somewhere else, he trekked there, although there was still plenty of dry food on his farm. His motive was not always simply to obtain better pasture, but also to save his own land for the times of scarcity that could come. Up to the present day there are still farmers in Bushmanland who put their livestock on the move as soon as it rains, in order to give their pasture a chance to grow out fresh and green, and to use the pasture along the migratory trail as long as it can be found.

Another situation also connected with the trek with livestock was the recognition from experience that a "change of pasture and climate" did the livestock good. In the opinion of the farmers the change kept the livestock healthy and it was the most effective remedy when the livestock had some or other sickness. Many farmers held fast to the belief that their livestock had to trek a good distance at least once per year.[16] When this trek took place naturally depended on the condition of the farmer's pasture and livestock, and the possibility of being helped somewhere else.

9. The Extent of Incidental Migrations

For all these reasons the farmers trekked very often with their livestock. About a century ago, for example, there were very few farmers in the present districts of Albert, Britstown, Colesbert, Middelburg, Molteno, Philipstown and Steynsburg who did not trek every year with their livestock/cattle to the southern Free State. Farmers who lived near the Orange River often trekked more than once a year across the river and then came back again.[17] In the districts of Carnarvon, Prieska, Kenhardt, the northern part of Fraserburg and the eastern part of Namaqualand, there were even more treks with livestock during the second half of the nineteenth century. When the first pioneers settled in these dry areas, it was an exception if a man lived twelve months in a row on his farm. It made no difference whether a farmer lived on freehold land, quitrent land, or just on crown land. There were years when the farmers could not trek, but generally a farmer trekked one or more times every year with his livestock. Some farmers trekked nearly continually along with the shifting rainfall and were seldom at their permanent homes.

Up until about 1920 this sort of trek was still practiced in Bushmanland, large areas of which had only been recently colonized at the time. As soon as a storm was brewing, the Bushmanlander with his telescope sat up on a hill (if there was one), or if not, on his house (if he already had one). As soon as the shower began, he sent someone by horse to go and see how much it had rained. If he received a report that the marsh was full, he immediately trekked. If the marsh was on crown land, then everyone had an equal right to it. If it was on a neighbor's land, he could count on his neighbor's helping him. And if perhaps it happened that his farm had received rain, then his neighbors would descend on him from all sides. If it rained today, then tomorrow ten people came in search of pasture. Perhaps some of them arrived even before the hail had melted.

There was therefore often just as much, or perhaps even more migration in districts where incidental migrations were the custom as in regions where regular seasonal migrations occurred. The incidental migration lacked only the regularity of seasonal migrations.

10. Areas Where Incidental Migration Took Place

The areas where incidental migrations were predominant, as well as the trek areas where the farmers went to seek relief, have continually shifted since the beginning of the nineteenth century. One observes that, as a general practice, irregular migration with livestock occurred most often during the pioneer period in regions of newer settlement, before more stable farming conditions, resulting from the improvement of farms over time there, were in place. It is also evident that during this period most of the migration was to uninhabited areas over the border or to undistributed crown land within the Colony.

Thus we see that incidental migrations during the first half of the nineteenth century chiefly occurred in the Bo-Karoo between the Sneeuberge and the Orange River, that is to say, the area that was colonized during that time. At the time, the trekboers usually turned their eyes northwards. That was the direction of expansion at the time. To the north lay a thinly inhabited region with plenty of free land between the farms. Still farther north the country was completely uninhabited. There one could happily trek, although the farmers initially still had problems with the Bushmen.

Until about 1820 the trekboers usually traveled around to the south of the Orange River, first between the inhabited areas and the old northern border, later between the northern border and the Orange. As a result of the growing population in the Bo-Karoo, and also on account of the areas used for treks to the south of the Orange River acquiring permanent inhabitants over time, the farmers were soon obliged to trek farther. From about 1821 they began to trek across the Orange River. Every year a greater number of colonial farmers pushed into the Trans-Orange and every year they traveled farther. By the time the Great Trek began, the area between the Orange, Vaal, Vet, and Caledon rivers was the area commonly used for treks by the farmers living in the northeastern corner of the Colony.[18]

As the number of permanent inhabitants in the Trans-Orange increased (from about 1828), so trekking opportunities for colonial farmers decreased there. In time more stable conditions also evolved in the Bo-Karoo. The farms were surveyed and distributed as loan farms, and the farmers improved their land more and more. The result was that incidental migrations in the eastern part of the Cape plateau gradually declined during the second half of the nineteenth century.

After 1850 the location of incidental migrations shifted more and more to the arid Northwestern Cape, where the pioneers of the Dorsland [Thirstland] entered into a long and bitter struggle to find water. In Prieska, Carnarvon, Kenhardt and the summer rainfall regions of Namaqualand, Calvinia and Fraserburg even farmers who had permanent homes lived for years in tents and roamed the country almost like nomads. To the north of the Orange (in Gordonia, Griqualand West and Bechuanaland) the first newcomers also trekked a great deal with livestock, but not on the same scale and also not for as long as those to the south of the Orange River. In the latter area the duration of incidental migrations was exceptionally long and drawn out, because there in the world of the salt pans on the Bushmanland plateau and on the Kaiingbult lay large pieces of free land for years that could not be inhabited because of a shortage of water, and which offered an ideal refuge for trekboers. During the past forty years, but particularly since 1920, incidental migrations everywhere in the Northwest—in one district more rapidly than in another—declined a great deal.

In the majority of livestock districts in the Cape Colony there are still occasional migrations with livestock to this day, but incidental migrations do not play such an important role at all in farming as before. In districts like Prieska, Carnarvon, Kenhardt, Victoria West, Beaufort West and Fraserburg, where thirty or forty years ago many farmers still trekked with livestock, today they seldom trek. In Griqualand West the farmers almost never trek anymore. Incidental migrations still occur most often in the Northwest, especially in Bushmanland, the newest settlement area to the south of the Orange, where the struggle for water is by no means over and many farms still lie completely open. In this connection, however, another phenomenon has to be noted. In all parts of the Northwest where there was regular migration between winter and summer rainfall areas, incidental migrations declined. That is to say, the farmers no longer trek so much all over the place.

At the same time, however, the seasonal migrations became increasingly irregular, because a new type of incidental migration had developed there, namely a sporadic, irregular migration between summer and winter rainfall areas.

A farmer who undertakes incidental migrations today travels here, there, and everywhere, now in one direction, then in another. Everything depends on where he can obtain pasture and water for his livestock. If he can find assistance somewhere in his neighborhood, he treks there. If not, he treks to where he can get relief. During droughts, which can ravage large areas, farmers sometimes have to trek quite far. The Ceres farmers have already sent all their livestock to Beaufort West and Carnarvon. People in Williston sometimes trek to Port Nolloth, Upington, Prieska, Hopetown and Kimberley; farmers from Calvinia, Carnarvon, Britstown and other areas in the Northwest occasionally seek relief in Humansdorp, Griqualand West, Bechuanaland, the Free State and even in the Western Transvaal.

Farmers who trek such distances are currently forced to load their livestock on the train.

ENDNOTES

[1] C 19, Resolutions, 26 February 1688, p. 222; C. 2271, Original Ordinance Book, 27 February 1688, pp. 54-55.

[2] C 21, Resolutions, 19 October 1791, p. 399; C 2271, Original Ordinance Book, 22 January 1692, p. 101.

[3] C 2274, Original Ordinance book, January 1705, p. 387.

[4] P.J. van der Merwe, *Die Trekboer in die Geskiedenis van die Kaapkolonie, 1657-1842* (Cape Town, 1938), p. 58.

[5] RLR 1, Old Gamehunters Books, October 1687 to October 1712.

[6] C 2285, Original Ordinance Book, 26 April 1774, p. 382.

[7] C 148, Resolutions, 13 February 1770, p. 50; 1/STB 20/2, Letters Rec., Landdrost Faber, Mintz, et al, to Tulbagh, 17 February 1770.

[8] C 2285, Original Ordinance Book, 26 April 1770, p. 384.

[9] C 563, Letters Rec., Woeke to Governor, November 1785, p. 684; 1/GR, 3/16, Judicial Declarations, P.M. Bester and Pieter Barendse Botha, 28 January 1791, Nos. 166 and 167.

[10] P.J. van der Merwe, *Die Noordwaartse Beweging van die Boere voor die Groot Trek (1770-1842)* (The Hague, 1937), p. 107-15.

[11] J.F.W. Grosskopf, *Plattelandsverarming en Plaasverlating* (Stellenbosch, 1932), p. 43.

[12] Van der Merwe, *Noordwaartse Beweging*, pp. 176-86, 204.

[13] Ibid., chapters VI, VII, and IX.

[14] Ibid., pp. 197-99.

[15] Ibid., pp. 199-203. Also chapters VI, VIII, and IX. [Trans. note: Dr. van der Merwe must have intended these chapters to be VI, VII, and IX, as in footnote 13. Chapter VII rather than VIII is the relevant chapter in *Noordwaartse Beweging* relating to plagues and grazing land.]

[16] H. Lichtenstein, *Reisen im südlichen Africa in den Jahren 1803, 1804, 1805 und 1806* (Berlin, 1811-1812), I:167; Commission for Stock Raising and Agriculture, 20 November 1805, in George McCall Theal, *Belangrijke Historische Dokumenten over Zuid-Afrika* (Cape Town, 1896, 1911), III:360; C.O. 4438, Papers of Col. Collins, Collins to Caledon, 6 August 1809; C.O. 3951, Memorials Rec., G.D. Joubert (Nu-Hantam), 15 August 1831, No. 148.

[17] Van der Merwe, *Noordwaartse Beweging*, p. 306.

---

[18] I have discussed these migrations in detail in *Noordwaartse Beweging*. See chapters IV, VI, VII, IX, and map no. 3, opposite p. 304. [Trans. note: Dr. van der Merwe is of course referring to the original Afrikaans edition here.]

CHAPTER XV

Nomadism

It is evident from the previous chapters that farmers who owned fixed homesteads often trekked with their livestock. This moving around took the form of temporary migrations. The trekkers left their homes for an undetermined time or during a specific season, depending on the circumstances, with the intention of returning later. There was also a type of livestock farmer in the Cape colony, however, who possessed no fixed abode and continually roamed around from one place to another with his livestock. In such cases the movement took on the form of a permanent migration. We shall use the word "nomadism" to describe this phenomenon.

1. Early References to Nomadism

One of the oldest explicit references to nomadic livestock farmers is found in the travel writings of [François] Le Vaillant, a Frenchman who journeyed throughout the Cape during the 1780s. Le Vaillant divided the rural population of the Cape into three classes. The first class were the rich landowners, who lived a few miles away from the Cape. The second were the simple, hospitable farmers of the interior. The third class "are those who are found living still farther away, on the outermost borders of the colony, among the Hottentots....This last class, poor and too lazy to obtain their livelihood from the soil, have no other means of existence than the breeding of a few livestock, which they feed as best they can. Like the Bedouin Arabs, it is quite something for them to take the trouble to drive their livestock from one pasturage to another, or from one area to another. This wandering life prevents them from building fixed dwellings. When their flocks compel them to remain for a time in a specific place, they hastily construct a rude hut, covered with mats, in the manner of the Hottentots, whose customs they have adopted, and from whom they differ only in complexion and facial features."[1]

Twenty years later [John] Barrow wrote: "The graziers, properly so called, are those of Graaff Reynet and other distant parts of the Colony. They are a class of men, of all the rest, the least advanced in civilization. Many of them, towards the borders of the settlement, are perfect Nomads, wander about from place to place without any fixed habitation, and live-in straw-huts, similar to those of the Hottentots."[2]

[Henry] Lichtenstein, who traveled around the colony a few years after Barrow, corroborates the information that Barrow provides: "Yes, there are families, who (although against the expressed will of the government) have no home, and with their family and livestock move from one place to another, living in their wagon or under canvas, and only hold up for as long as they need to give their oxen grass and water, and shoot some wild game for themselves."[3]

At the foot of the Swartberge [Heinrich] Lichtenstein came across just such a nomadic trekboer. His traveling party came to a house that he described as, "A human dwelling, although only a reed hut, where lived a fine-looking young man and a neatly dressed wife, surrounded by three or four small children. They revived us with fresh milk and regretted that they could not offer us any bread because they lived solely on mutton. These people belong to an indigent class of colonists who call themselves *trekfolk** because they have no fixed place of residence, but roam from one place to another with their herds. There are many such nomadic colonial families, particularly in these remote areas, and in general they do not belong to a very respectable class of society. They often render themselves liable to punishment for committing atrocities against the savages and disobedience to the government, from whose eyes they can often conceal their existence."[4]

2. The Attitude of the Batavian government

The Batavian government was fully aware of the condition of a class of colonists, "who are continually on the move,"[5] and were not at all pleased about it. The greatest objection to the nomadic livestock farmers was that they often left the pasture on outspan† places so completely grazed over that nothing remained for travelers, or for butchers' servants who bought livestock in the interior and drove them back to the Cape. This was seriously reprehensible at a time when everyone who traveled or transported goods was dependent on animal fodder, and slaughter animals could not be brought to market by train.[6]

Apart from this, nomadic farmers were also a nuisance for the settled population. Farmers constantly complained that "wandering folk" let their animals eat all the pasture, drink all the water and destroyed the land.[7] By wandering from one district to another, they also succeeded in keeping off the field cornets' lists and thereby they evaded having to pay taxes.[8]

To combat these evils, the following order was inserted into the "Ordinance Concerning the Governance of the Country Districts" (1805): "The field-cornets must be scrupulous in taking care that no roaming People without fixed abode sojourn with their families and live-stock in their jurisdiction. When they discover this, they must instantly inform the Landdrost thereof and order such Roamers to depart at once – The field-cornets will above all not allow the public Places for Outspanning to be occupied for longer than *twenty-four* hours, no matter by whom, except where the swelling of Rivers, or other unexpected accidents, may prevent the continuance of the Travellers' journey."[9]

The government was fully aware, however, that many farmers, as a result of circumstances beyond their control, were forced to lead a wandering existence. As a result of the soil conditions the farmers of certain regions were often obliged to trek with their livestock. Bushmen raids as well as repeated Xhosa incursions often drove farmers from their homes. In addition, it was one of the chief aims of the new government to keep the colonists happy. Under these circumstances the Batavian government was not inclined to use strong measures against the nomadic livestock farmers.[10]

---

*Trans. note: In the original German, *"...Trekmenschen*, Zugmenschen...."
†Trans. note: Common resting places along a route where the cattle were allowed to rest, water and graze. If there were wagons with draft animals, the animals (generally oxen) were unyoked or unharnessed, or "outspanned."

3. Shortage of Usable Land

The instructions issued by the Batavian government forbidding nomadism, apparently had little effect. From the beginning of the nineteenth century one finds an increasing number of references to nomadism in the sources of the time, which suggests that this aggravation increased rather than decreased.

This phenomenon can easily be explained. During the period of unrestricted expansion there was no great need for a livestock farmer to wander about for long with his animals before obtaining a fixed residence. Land was plentiful. Everyone could get a farm in the colony, or across the border, that was good enough to take by ordinance. Admittedly, farmers during the Company period often found it very hard‡ to pay even the small quitrent of 24 rixdollars per year for their loan farms, but on the other hand, the government was exceptionally accommodating with the collection of it. What is more, farmers without ground could settle on crown land as squatters, as long as inhabitable, unoccupied crown land still remained; and as long as the trek into the interior continued unimpeded, there was always unusable land available farther ahead.

By the end of the 1770s, however, the expansion into the interior, which up until that time had continued unchecked, was suddenly cut off in all directions. The facts are well known. In the northwest the farmers were stopped by a semi-desert with scanty rainfall and very little permanent water. On the eastern frontier the farmers came into conflict with the Bantu. Moreover, the Bushmen along the entire northern frontier prevented further expansion. The result was that from about 1779 no significant expansion took place. In the northeastern corner of the colony the Bushmen even repeatedly drove the farmers back temporarily.[11]

The colony's population, however, continually increased. The inevitable result was a growing shortage of usable land. By the beginning of the nineteenth century the shortage had become acute. In 1804 General Janssens wrote to [Dirk] Van Hogendorp: "At present there are no more good new farms to be found, and the worse are gladly occupied."[12] Many farmers had to be content with farms that were poorly supplied with water for a part of the year. "The shortage of farms is already so great," according to the governor, "that wherever a jet of water arises from a mountain, as long as it runs permanently, a farm on ordinance is taken. On my travels I have had about a hundred applications to take places, outside the limits of the settlement, as well as in such places within them, where they figure they can lay by cattle for a short time or sow their bread corn, and of the latter, namely those within the limits, there are only a few that would not harm the neighbors."[13]

In these circumstances it became all the more difficult for farmers without land to make a living as squatters on undistributed land. At the time there was naturally still a lot of undistributed land within the colonial boundaries, but it was not of such a quality that it could easily be permanently inhabited without the application of labor and capital. This compelled livestock farmers who wanted to make a living on unoccupied land with their livestock to wander about from one temporary watering-hole to another.

---

‡Trans. Note: Dr. Van der Merwe uses the Afrikaans word "maklik" or English "easy" here. From the context it seems the Afrikaans word should have been "moeilik" or English "hard," "difficult."

In 1807 landdrost [Hendrik] De Graaff wrote to Governor Caledon: "The increasing number of inhabitants and their livestock without sufficient places for their residence and nourishment causes these days many roaming inhabitants who trek or are driven now hither and then thither, forever complaining that some of their fellow-men are privileged with extensive lands, which can hold several adequate farms without them paying any fees for it, which they would most happily contribute to the country's coffers whensoever they are allowed to receive these places as loan farms."[14]

In his famous report to Caledon [in 1809], [Colonel Richard] Collins described the same phenomenon: "There are a great many persons, in almost every part of the Colony in want of places. Some reside with relations, some wander thro [sic] this and other disregarded tracts."[15] A year later Andries Stockenström, landdrost of Graaff-Reinet, reported "that there are 8 to 900 inhabitants, who have no farms, and therefore must wander around a few months by the one and then some months by another, then some months in the still unoccupied lands by fountains or water holes."[16] In that year 1,449 persons in the Graaff-Reinet district submitted tax returns. Among them were 968 married couples and 276 owners of loan farms.[17]

4. Nomadism in the Frontier Districts

From the preceding quotations it is clear that at the beginning of the nineteenth century – just as in the time of Le Vaillant—one came across nomadism predominantly in regions of newer settlement at the outer reaches of civilization, where there was little control over the unlawful use of undistributed land.[18] In this connection Stockenström wrote in 1821 to the colonial secretary: "You are doubtless well aware that the earlier disturbances in these parts, when law had very little force among the inhabitants, these being for the greatest part of the pastoral class, yielded without check to the propensity of moving from one part of the country to another and making the most unrestrained use of land to which they possessed no sort of title, but to which indeed they were often compelled to resort, to find food for the immense flocks they possessed. In process of time when tranquility was restored, when the magistrate could once more interfere, when many loan places were again granted, when the population increased, and thus the scope each had to roam about became limited, fixed residences became, to the most, unavoidable."[19]

As stable conditions in the regions of newer settlement evolved, many of the farmers without land were pushed out to uninhabited areas in the north. There one also came across the phenomenon that a part of the pioneer population wandered around as nomads on crown land. In 1839 [James] Backhouse met such a farmer in the Winterveld—at that time one of the field-cornetcies on the northern frontier. It must have been in the present-day district of Britstown. "Near to this place was the temporary station of a Vee Boer, or *cattle farmer*, with a large flock of sheep, and a considerable herd of cattle. This class of men travel from place to place, with their flocks and herds, as the pasturage is consumed, or the water fails; they dwell in wagons, with the addition of tents or temporary huts. Two wagons and a hut were occupied by this party."[20]

Ten years later the civil commissioner of Colesberg reported "that beyond the western boundary of this division, also the boundary of the Colony prior to the proclamation of 17th December 1847 there are located a number of colonists with their wives and families and flocks and extending about one hundred miles along the left bank of the Orange river to where it is joined by the Brak river. According to a list lately furnished me by Mr. Siebert Wiets the proprietor of Duvenaarsfontein, the most westerly farm along the river in this division, there are not less than sixty families so circumstanced possessing together above 60,000 sheep and about 6,000 head of cattle. From the general scarcity of water and especially of springs in that part, but a few of these have fixed residences, the generality it appears are in the habit of removing from one stagnant pool to another and from the present drought a large number have removed to government ground in the Middenveld and Winterveld."

According to the field-cornet's list, which the civil commissioner enclosed in his report, eleven of the farmers owned "fixed" residences while 62 were described as "persons wandering about." All of them possessed livestock, although some were evidently members of the same family.[21] These farmers must have wandered about principally in the districts of Hopetown, Philipstown and Britstown.

About the same time a number of nomadic livestock farmers made a living in the vicinity of the Kareeberge in the present district of Carnarvon. The Kareeberge were situated along the old northern frontier, which was extended to the Orange River only in 1847. In connection with the farmers who wandered about in the Kareeberge with their livestock, surveyor [Jeremias Benedictus] Auret wrote in 1856: "The migrating boers consist of two classes: those who have no farms, and lead a purely nomadic life, and again those who have farms of their own, which they occupy during the greater part of the year, migrating periodically and after the rains have fallen with their stock to the Kareebergen."[22]

Among the seasonal trekkers there were apparently also farmers without permanent residences, but the greatest part of the nomadic farmers evidently roamed about continuously in the vicinity of the Kareeberge. This is clear from a statement made by Willem Andries van der Berg, field-cornet of the ward of Agter-Nieuweveld in the district of Beaufort, which Auret enclosed: "The grounds are at present all in my ward. I know the country well and have trekked about for 30 years. Most of the migrating farmers in my ward have no places and live in the Kareebergen with their stock."[23] About the same time one could also find nomadic livestock farmers in distant Namaqualand and the southern parts of Bushmanland (the Agterveld of Clanwilliam).[24]

5. Nomadism in the Northwest

The regions where one came across most of the nomadic farmers by the middle of the nineteenth century also received more and more permanent inhabitants with the passage of time. And as more and more land was distributed in these areas, the landless farmers were pushed into the arid northwesterly parts of the Cape colony, to the south of the Orange River, between Prieska and the west coast. During the last three decades of the nineteenth century one found most of the nomadic livestock farmers in this water-poor region.[25] The eastern part of this area, which received summer rainfall, was known at the time as the "Northern Border." "The Northern border proper," wrote M.J. Jackson in 1878, "is a belt of country about four hundred miles in length, from Priesca in the east to within thirty miles of the copper mines at Springbokfontein in the west, bounded by the Oranje river on the north, and extending inward or southward on an average, a hundred and fifty miles....The population consists chiefly of a very low tipe [sic] of Dutch farmer and a people known as Bastards....Both boers and Bastards lead a nomadic life, dwelling in tents and waggons [sic] and moving from place to place in search of pasturage and water for their flocks."[26]

In 1895 the resident magistrate of the newly founded district of Kenhardt, which formed a part of the old "Northern Border," reported that in ward five of his district there was still 200,000 morgen of unsurveyed crown land, "and it is next to impossible to reach the squatters thereon as they lead a nomadic existence remaining at a spot only as long as there is a sufficiency of water for their stock."[27] Two days later he wrote to the under-secretary of agriculture: "It is impossible for the farmers in our district to comply with the demands of the scab act by reason of the scarcity of water and as three fourths of the farmers are 'rondtrekkers' [nomads] who are not owners of fixed property and who are not sure today where they will find water tomorrow for their sheep to drink."[28]

By the end of the nineteenth century the civil commissioner of Namaqualand, which included the western portion of the "Northern Border," repeatedly refers to nomadism as well. In 1883 he wrote: "A large number of the farming population have no fixed residence. Many possess little besides their flocks and herds (some a wagon and a mud hut.). These are constantly shifting their quarters between Namakwaland west and Bushmanland."[29] In 1901 he wrote again to the secretary of agriculture: "The lessees (under act 15 of 1887) live in mud houses or wagon tents and move about from place to place without any fixed abode."[30]

In the northern parts of Calvinia one found the same conditions. In 1896 inspector J.H. Hofmeyr reported: "In a large portion of the division circumstances are of such a nature that at present there seems to be no possibility of starting more schools. A large number of families is constantly on the move and has no fixed habitation. Whenever they 'trek' the children are required to tend the flocks, and during seasons of drought, which, alas! are very frequent, they are busy from morning to night hauling or carrying water for the flocks or houses. This I found to be the state of matters throughout the whole district north of the Hantam River, and west of Brandvlei. In the vast tract of country north of Loeriesfontein and west of Brandvlei there are only about half-a-dozen brick-built houses in all, and people are to a great extent not yet settled on the farms."[31]

6. Way of Life of the Nomadic Livestock Farmer

References in official documents to nomadism are fragmentary, vague and unsatisfactory. For that reason, it is very fortunate that it has been possible to supplement those reports with oral tradition. According to the information provided me by the old pioneers, one could find farmers wandering about without fixed residences between 1875 and 1900, particularly in the Northwest. The actual home of the nomadic livestock farmers, however, was the trek area between the Orange River and the line that connects Vanrhynsdorp, Sutherland, Victoria West and Prieska. It is possible to make a vague distinction between three groups of nomadic farmers in this area.

A small group of nomadic farmers roamed about in the Namaqualand Sandveld, between the mountains and the sea. They traveled around in a relatively small area and left the Sandveld only on rare occasions. "We who roamed about on the crown land there," one old pioneer informed me, "were more or less constantly on the move. We remained perhaps a few days or a few weeks at one place and then loaded the mat huts again onto the wagon and trekked further. Often we had not even settled long enough at the place to make a floor for the mat hut. Sometimes there would be fleas in the sand floor and when the fleas became too annoying, we trekked further. I have wandered about for months in this way, without seeing anyone else except my family. In the summer we visited one watering place after another. In the winter, if the livestock did not drink, we could move nearly wherever we wanted. We had loaded drinking water on the wagon or transported it in round casks. And when there was not enough water to wash the crockery, we scoured the plates and pots with dry sand and wiped them off with a dry cloth. Water cannot wash them cleaner. We only worked a little in the mornings and evenings with the livestock. Then we had to bring water of course, but we did not have to do any more than that. On crown land you were not supposed to build or work. When you could not stand the boredom any longer, you trekked or you went on a hunt, or dug up edible bulbs." Another old Sandvelder told me the following: "My parents were the children of landowners, but they themselves had never owned land. They constantly roamed about in the Sandveld. Sometimes we stayed a year at a place, sometimes a month, sometimes a week and occasionally we just traveled. My mama moved about in this way when I was young and when I later married, I continued the same life. The longest that I remained on the move without making a house was from April to September. That time I was literally continually on the move – nowhere in particular, just round and about in circles. After I bought a farm in 1905, I never again trekked. I used only my own land."

In the area where seasonal migrations were the practice—that is, between the Sandveld and the line connecting Kakamas to the Orange, Onderstedoorns to the Sakrivier, and Williston—the nomadic farmers trekked back and forth between the summer and winter rainfall areas. In the summer they were all in Bushmanland, together with the Binneveld farmers who had permanent residences there. There they wandered around among the permanent water pools and marshes. As soon as the winter approached they fell back to the Binneveld along with the landowners. Some of them traveled around Namaqualand. then dropped down to the Knechtsvlakte, the Bokveld and the Hantam. They did not spend the winter in Bushmanland, except when the Binneveld was very dry. Some of the Calvinia trekboers who had no land, however, did not trek up to the Hantam and Bokveld. After the water in the marshes on the Bult dried up, they went to spend the winter in the transition zone between the winter and summer rainfall areas. In the scrub land between Loeriesfontein, Langberg and Rooiberg there was still a good deal of undistributed crown land until the end of the nineteenth century. There were also several fountains and draw-wells where they could let their livestock drink.[32]

The nomadic farmers who wandered about in the part of the areas used for treks to the east of Kakamas, Onderstedoorns and Williston normally did not return to the winter rainfall area. Most of them roamed about throughout the year in the summer rainfall area (Fraserburg, Carnarvon, Prieska and the eastern part of Kenhardt). After good rains they trekked from one marsh, pool, or water hole to another. When the open waters were exhausted, the farmers dispersed in different directions. Some went to settle along the Orange or along the upper course of the Sak River, where there was more or less always water. Others gathered together at springs in the Kareeberge or draw-wells in the beds of the Hartbees River. If the need arose, some of them went in search of relief to landowners who had watering-holes. But they never remained long. As soon as surface water came available again somewhere on free land, they were off.

Even when they had had good rains, the nomadic trekboer often stopped over among landowners. He did not become a tenant, however. He only helped to graze off the best of the new grassland on the landowner's farm or, at most, remained as long as the pasture was still fine and green. As soon as the pasture was killed by frost, or began to dry up, he trekked. Then the master of the farm could even offer him pasture free of charge or beg him, but he would not remain longer.

The wagon trail was the nomadic livestock farmer's home and the rain his ruler. His ever-changing, roaming existence was determined only by one issue, namely, where he could obtain the best grazing land and water for his livestock. If the watering-holes at one of the temporary halting-sites began to wane, or the pasture began to dry up, then he shifted to another place. It sometimes happened that he lingered for a few months on one farm or at the same well or marsh. But he *camped* there, not lived. He had no intention of remaining there permanently. He knew beforehand that his stay there would only be temporary. It also happened that he was more or less constantly trekking for weeks and months and stayed at the same place for only a few days at the most. Several of the old pioneers told me that they sometimes trekked for three, four or five months at a time, without once putting up a tent during that period. They traveled leisurely in all directions, hither and thither, without a fixed course or destination. They knew perhaps where they would be tomorrow or following week, but not where they would be in six months. Once I asked an old pioneer of this type with reference to a particular event where he had lived at that time. His answer was: "Nowhere—at that time we didn't live anywhere, we trekked."

Sometimes a nomadic livestock farmer wandered about for a few months in a relatively small area; then he would suddenly cover enormous distances in a short time. I met people in the Northwest who had trekked down from Calvinia along the Sak and the Hartbees Rivers to Kakamas and back, and others who trekked down from Prieska along the Orange River to its mouth.

The nomadic trekboer thought only of grazing land and water. He was passionately attached to the area in which he roamed about, but he never developed an emotional or sentimental attachment to a specific piece of land in the way that a normal person cherishes his house or farm in a settled society. One specific place in the trek area held no more or no less meaning to him than any other. One of the things that struck me the most in the Northwest was that I repeatedly came across old pioneers who could not tell me where they were born. They perhaps knew that it must have been in the Hantam, in the Kareeberge or in Bushmanland, but their parents never told them where the ox-wagon stood that day. It is highly likely that the parents did not know either. Every group of nomadic livestock farmers wandered about in a specific area from one familiar place to another, but the borders of these areas were not clearly marked. And if there was a pressing need, they left the area. They did not trek in groups, however. They moved about on their own, although a farmer often traveled about temporarily together with a few others.

7. The Last Refuge South of the Orange

From about 1880, as crown land was gradually surveyed and distributed, nomadism quickly declined in the Northwest. By 1900 the best farms in Prieska, Carnarvon, Fraserburg, the eastern part of Kenhardt and the southern Agterveld of Calvinia were all in private hands. Many of the farmers who had previously roamed about as nomads, obtained farms in these parts and they settled on them. The rest were mostly forced out to the Vrybult, that is, the western part of Kenhardt, the eastern part of Namaqualand and the northern part of Calvinia. Here on the barren Bushmanland plains they, like generations of pioneers before them, led a nomadic existence. The greatest part of the year they wandered about on undistributed crown land on the Bult. In the winter most of them fled to Namaqualand or towards the Hantam and Bokveld. About thirty years ago there were still a number of nomadic trekboers in Bushmanland.

In 1910 there were still around 2,500 square miles of unsurveyed crown land in Kenhardt. "The persons residing there are mostly 'trekkers,' and should the pans and vleys have water they would be found at these spots."[33] In 1912 the resident magistrate of Kenhardt wrote in his annual report: "There are at the present moment many landless farmers, who are bound to travel about seeking pasturage for their flocks who are most anxious to obtain a permanent interest in the land."[34]

The same state of affairs also still prevailed in Namaqualand. "There must be quite two hundred white families living in this division in mat or canvas huts and they are forced to move about as the few farmers who have their own property cannot afford to keep them permanently on their farms and individual lessees are prohibited from backing them on their ground without consent,"[35] according to the civil commissioner of Namaqualand in 1906.

8. Nomadism Dies Out

Between 1910 and 1938 all the crown land that still remained on the Vrybult was distributed. During this time period the nomadic livestock farmers of the Northwest nearly died out altogether. When I visited the Northwest in 1938 and 1939 one could, however, still here and there come across a trekboer without land, living on the wagon trail.

One day in the Ceres-Karoo I accidentally came upon such a farmer on the road. The man was not by the wagon. The wife informed me that she had been married for sixteen years, but that she had never had a house. All that time she had lived in a wagon or in tents. They were continually trekking and had never remained longer than a few months in the same place. There were eight children, the oldest was fifteen, the youngest a suckling—all of them born on the trail.

These days in the Karoo, Laingsburg, the Roggeveld and Beaufort West, where this family usually wandered about, there are very few such trekboers. There are more in Namaqualand, Vanrhynsdorp, Calvinia and Kenhardt, but they make up only a minimal percentage of the population. There is still only a small spot in the Northwest where the greatest part of the nomadic farming population roam about on undistributed crown land, namely the ward of Port Nolloth in the Namaqualand Sandveld. In 1938 the livestock inspector of Port Nolloth told me that 75 percent of the farmers in his ward had no fixed abode. Although they move around in a relatively small area, they shift continually from one site to another. In one case that he specifically mentioned, the trekker had that year camped at ten different places at least. A police agent who participated in the conversation verified this piece of information. He said that he never knew beforehand where he would come across these people on his patrols.

9. Nomadism and Poverty

According to Le Vaillant and Lichtenstein the nomadic livestock farmers belonged to the poorest classes in the colony.[36] This testimony is supported by a letter from the civil commissioner of Tulbagh to the Land Board in 1830: "The wandering class consists of persons that have scarcely any property. A poor young man marries a poor young woman and if they can bring together a wagon with a team of oxen and a couple of hundred sheep or goats, they consider themselves independent and move on with their small flock from one part of the country to another.... This class is leading a most wretched life and generally in the utmost state of poverty, which they prefer above making themselves serviceable to the more opulent class."[37]

One must not imagine, however, that nomadism was always related directly to poverty. In the arid northern parts of the Cape Colony where the nomadic grazing of the land was actually dictated by nature, there were also—before the land was distributed—more prosperous livestock farmers who roamed about without having fixed homesteads. In 1830 [Andrew] Steedman met a man named Breda along the Brakrivier in the Winterveld (it must have been somewhere in the vicinity of Britstown), "an extensive grazier.... who was said to be one of the richest boors in the Winterveld, having a flock of ten thousand sheep besides other cattle, though dwelling with his wife and family in tents; and constantly migrating from one place to another for the sake of water."[38]

In 1849 the civil commissioner of Colesberg sent to the government a list of the possessions of 42 nomadic livestock farmers whom they had found in the vicinity of present-day Hopetown. The average possessions of these farmers were more than 900 sheep and goats and 60 cattle each. Seventeen of them had 1,000 or more sheep and goats, and nine of them owned 2,000 or more sheep and goats.[39] The following year the civil commissioner of Clanwilliam gave the possessions of 17 families, or "unsettled whites," who wandered about in the trek areas to the north of his district, as follows: 170 horses, 340 cattle and 17,000 sheep and goats.[40] Many of the nomadic trekboers who roamed about toward the end of the nineteenth century in Kenhardt and Namaqualand were well-off, according to the views of their time and place, although there certainly would have also been some poor people among them.[41] Some of these farmers traveled around as nomads not because they could obtain no land, but because they did not want to have land. As long as there were still many opportunities for trekking in the Northwest, this class of farmer was really no worse off than his friends who owned land. These latter also had to trek around almost constantly with their livestock.

The need to own land in the Northwest really only developed when the free land began to be scarce and the landowners started becoming unwilling to help trekboers. Then most nomadic farmers who could afford it tried to obtain farms. The indigent among them continued their wandering around. Consequently, most nomadic farmers one finds today in the Northwest are poor people. Some of them not only own little, but mentally also belong to the poor white type. One also still finds among the nomads, however, persons who possess solid farming enterprises and who can make a very much better livelihood than many small landowners and tenants. It is not rare to see a good motor car or truck alongside such a trekboer's tent. The more affluent class of nomadic trekboer is often also very well informed. He has acquired a knowledge of human nature and a worldly wisdom on the trail. In his dealings with other people he makes a favorable and intelligent impression. Often he also displays a great interest in public affairs and takes an active part in them.

The nomadic trekboer's days, however, are numbered. His possibilities for earning a livelihood diminish by the day. Nomadism will soon be a thing of the past.

10. A Temporary Phase

From the end of the eighteenth century—perhaps even earlier—there were always nomadic stock farmers in the Cape Colony. One should not venture to conclude from this, however, that a separate group of colonists maintained a continuous tradition of nomadism right through the pioneer period. On the basis of the evidence available to us, it appears that in most cases nomadism was only a temporary phase in the life history of certain individuals. A young farmer who could not get land in regions of older settlement, trekked into the interior in order to look for a farm, but there was no reason to be in a hurry. "Water and pasturage are his first objects. He encamps near some unoccupied fountain, pool or river, changing his station according as necessity or inclination may require, until he at length finds some eligible spot, where he thinks he can advantageously fix himself."[42] One might wander about longer than another, but eventually most of them would certainly have settled down somewhere as landowners, tenants, or squatters.

In the Northwest I met various farmers with permanent residences who had never lived in a house for the first thirty, forty, or even fifty years of their lives. They had roamed about entirely like nomads in tents or mat huts. I also heard of people who traveled around until their deaths without ever settling down anywhere, but this was apparently the exception.

The overwhelming majority of the farmers who roamed about as nomads in the past, were—so far as I could determine—the children of people with fixed abodes (farm owners, tenants, or servants). Some told me that their parents wandered about as nomads until their deaths, but that their grandparents had owned land. No cases came to my attention of families that led a nomadic existence for one generation after another. It is possible, even probable, that there were such families, but it will be difficult to prove this.

Furthermore, the nomadic way of life can be viewed as a typical characteristic of the pioneer life of a new district.[43] In point of fact, in every pioneer district nomadism appeared during the first stages of its development, but soon it disappeared again. In the development of a frontier district it was also only just a temporary phase, a transition period, before more settled conditions prevailed. Nomadism did not play an equally important role everywhere, however, and also did not always last for an equally long period. In regions where the land was inhabitable without too much trouble—as for example in the Tarka, the area between the Stormbergspruit and the Kraai River, and the eastern part of the Cape colony—the pioneers settled down very quickly and laid out farms, even though this was sometimes done without the permission of the government.[44]

Even in some of the drier parts of the Cape colony—like Bechuanaland, Griqualand West and Gordonia—nomadism did not play an important role. This region had permanent pasture, which meant that the areas around the few permanent watering-holes that there were, were permanently inhabited. And because temporary water was scarce, the grazing of the pasture land was dependent on the permanent water. Furthermore, it was possible for the farmers who moved in there to immediately purchase farms from the Basters (and later from the government). The result was that the permanent watering places relatively quickly got owners, who settled at the water, although initially they had often trekked with their livestock. And the farmers without land became tenants.

Nomadism is found in its most typical form in the Cape Northwest, to the south of the Orange River. Here it also lasted the longest. Different factors were responsible for this. In the first place the geographical nature of the land is important. The area used for the treks south of the Orange River consists of a summer rainfall region and a winter rainfall region, which receive rain during different seasons of the year and thus complement each other well. Permanent watering-holes were also scarce during the pioneer period, but the trekboer could always be assisted somewhere. In the winter there were plenty of temporary small watering-holes in the Binneveld, and besides, the juicy wild pasture provided nearly all the water that the livestock needed. During the summer the trekboer could let his livestock drink at the few permanent watering-holes and the many marshes in the Agterveld. This enabled the nomadic farmer to continue trekking. What is more, it must be pointed out that for many years the government postponed distributing land in the summer rainfall area in the Northwest. This deprived farmers without ground of the possibility of obtaining right of possession to the watering-holes in the areas used for treks. And it would have profited a farmer little to settle as a squatter alongside a permanent watering place in the Agterveld. He would simply not have been able to keep the seasonal trekkers away from there. This obliged the landless farmers to wander about with the seasonal trekkers.

ENDNOTES

[1] F. Le Vaillant, *Reize in de Binnenlanden van Afrika, langs de Kaap de Goede Hoop, in de jaaren 1780 tot 1785* (Leyden and Amsterdam, 1791-1792), I:37.

[2] J. Barrow, *Travels into the Interior of Southern Africa*, 2nd ed. (London, 1806), II:117.

[3] H. Lichtenstein, *Reisen im südlichen Africa in den Jahren 1803, 1804, 1805 und 1806* (Berlin, 1811-1812), I:34-35.

[4] Ibid., II:108-09.

[5] AR, Colonial Accessions 4365, J.W. Janssens to De Mist, 29 November 1803; B.R. 61, Resolutions, Minutes of a Conference held by General Janssens, 30 December 1804, p. 5, enclosed in entry for 3 January 1805.

[6] AR, Colonial Accessions 4365, J.W. Janssens to De Mist, 29 November 1803; 1/GR 16/55, Letter Book, Civil Commissioner to P.A. du Plessis, 12 January 1838, No. 5; 1/GR 13/4, Letters Rec. from Private Individuals, C.J. Papenfus to Van Ryneveld, 5 January 1838, pp. 406-07; Lichtenstein, *Reisen*, II:109.

[7] 1/WOC 13/1, Letters Rec. from Field Cornets, G. Maritz to van de Graaff, 4 February 1805, p. 25, and 12 November 1805, p. 157; 1/GR 11/20, Letters from Cradock, Harding to Stockenström, 4 February 1820; 1/GR 13/4, Letters Rec. from Private Individuals, C.J. Papenfus to van Ryneveld, 5 January 1838 and G.F. Meynard to van Ryneveld, 4 August 1829; 1/BFW 9/46, Letters Rec. from Field Cornets, P.D. Jacobs to Baird, 26 April 1822. See also Le Vaillant, *Reize*, III:45.

[8] B.O. 72, Letters Rec. from Graaff-Reinet, J.R. Bresler to Governor, 27 January 1798, pp. 68-77.

[9] B.R. 390, "Ordinance concerning the governance of the interior districts," Article 270, 23 October 1805, p. 58.

[10] AR, Accession, 1913, Van Hogendorp, p. 760: PSB Mss. Germ. Quarto 857, J.W. Janssens, Memorandum over Loan Farms, 30 January 1805; AR, Colonial Accession, 4365, J.W. Janssens to De Mist, 29 November 1803; Journal of the Journey of Commissioner General De Mist, in George McCall Theal, *Belangrijke Historische Dokumenten over Zuid-Afrika* ((Cape Town, 1896, 1911), III:179; Lichtenstein, Reisen, II:109; P.J. van der Merwe, *Die Noordwaartse Beweging van die Boere voor die Groot Trek (1770-1842)* (The Hague, 1937), pp. 10-12.

[11] Van der Merwe, *Noordwaartse Beweging*, pp. 10-12.

[12] RA, Accession, 1913, General Janssens to van Hogendorp, 10 December 1804.

[13] RA, Colonial Accession, 4373, Enclosures and Letters, Janssens to Van Hogendorp, 19 January 1804, pp. 264-65.

[14] C.O. 2560, Letters Rec., Tulbagh, H. van de Graaff to Caledon, 8 December 1807.

[15] C.O. 4438, Papers of Col. Collins, Collins to Caledon, 6 August 1809.

[16] C.O. 2580, Letters Rec., Graaff-Reinet, A. Stockenström to Col. Secretary, 20 September 1810.

[17] J 133, Tax rolls for Graaff-Reinet, 1810.

[18] See also, C.O. 2581, Letters Rec., Tulbagh, van de Graaff to Grey, 14 August 1811, No. 5; 1/GR 8/8, Letters Rec., Bird to Baird, Beaufort, 4 December 1818, pp. 181-90; S.G.P., Letters from Civil Commissioners (Western Province), H.C. Nieuwhoudt to adjunct landdrost Clanwilliam, 9 September 1826. [Trans. note: This is the citation Dr. van der Merwe has for this footnote and although he cites this document four times – ch. 12, nos. 13, 19, and ch. 15, nos. 18, 32, I could find no such document for this date, 9 September 1826. There is a letter from Nieuwhoudt to Adjt. Landdrost and Heemraden for Clanwilliam, dated 9 July 1826, which deals with the topics of the Agterveld, Kobiskow, their history and their identity. I believe this is the document to which Dr. van der Merwe is referring. This document, containing essentially the same wording, may be found in SG 1/1/1/2 and C.O. 8430, both under the date 9 July 1826: SG 1/1/1/2, Letters from Civil Commissioners, Western Province, H.C. Nieuwhoudt to Adjt. Landdrost and Heemraden, 9 July 1826 and C.O. 8430, Inspector of Lands and Woods, Letters Rec., H.C. Nieuwhoudt to Adjt. Landdrost and Heemraden, 9 July 1826.]; W. Mackenzie, *Sketches of Travel*, p. 302 (1824). [Trans. note: I have given here the citation Dr. van der Merwe used for the reference to Mackenzie. This actually comes from William Mackenzie, *Outlines of Education; or, Remarks on the Development of Mind, and Improvement of Manners* (Edinburgh: Archibald constable & Co., 1824), p. 304. In his Bibliography, Dr. van der Merwe has "Mackenzie, W.: Sketches of Travels in Southern Africa, Edinburgh, 1824. (In "Outlines of Education.")." In Mackenzie's book, *Outlines*, pp. 247-298 are titled "Sketches of Travels in Southern Africa," and pp. 299-314 are titled "Sketch of the Boor." This reference actually comes from the section, "Sketch of the Boor."]

[19] 1/GR 16/10, Letters Disp., Stockenström to Bird, 26 April 1821.

[20] J. Backhouse, *A Narrative of a Visit to the Mauritius and South Africa* (London, 1844), p. 481. See also, A. Steedman, *Wanderings and Adventures in the Interior of Southern Africa* (London, 1835), II:13-14.

[21] SG 1/1/3/14, No. 211, Letters Rec. from Colonial Secretary, Civil Commissioner for Colesburg to Col. Secretary, with enclosed list, under cover letter of 21 November 1849, Col. Secretary Montagu to Surveyor-General.

[22] C.O. 4402, Arrears, J.B. Auret to Surveyor-General, 27 December 1856, enclosed with No. 40, p. 3.

[23] Ibid.

[24] 1/SBK 5/1/1, Civil Commissioner Rivers to Col. Secretary, 8 October 1856, p. 89; also 1/SBK 5/1/1, Civil Commissioner Rivers, Report on Petition for land, 20 November 1857, p. 182; C.O. 2867, Letters Rec., Clanwilliam, Civil Commissioner to Col. Secretary, 24 July 1850.

[25] C.O. 4423, Miscellaneous, Jackson (Kenhardt) to Col. Secretary, 25 October 1870; CCP 1/2/1/31, A21 of 1876, Report of the Hydraulic Engineer, 27 May 1876, pp. 4, 9.

[26] C.O. 3286, Civil Commissioner for Richmond, M.J. Jackson, to Col. Secretary, 27 August 1878. See also, 1/NBC 13, Letters Disp., Special Commissioner for the Northern Border to Secretary of Native Affairs, 3 March 1880, p. 97; 1/NBM 7, Letters Disp., Special Magistrate for the Northern Border to Under Col. Secretary, 6 June 1889, pp. 377-81; CCP 1/2/1/72, G60 of 1888, Affairs of the Northern Border, P. Nightingale to Under Col. Secretary, 27 July 1887, p. 5-9.

[27] 1/KEN 5/1/1/6, Letters Disp., Kenhardt Resident Magistrate to Col. Secretary, 13 August 1895, p. 301.

[28] 1/KEN 5/1/1/6, Letters Disp., Kenhardt Resident Magistrate to Col. Secretary, 15 August 1895, p. 296. [Trans. note: The letter for 15 August 1895 is located on p. 296 before the letter for 13 August 1895 on p. 301 in 1/KEN 5/1/1/6.]

[29] 1/SBK 5/1/8, J.T. Eustace to J.A. Ellis, 10 March 1883.

[30] 1/SBK 5/3/5, Report of J.B. van Renen, 8 November 1901, p. 228.

[31] CCP 1/2/1/95, G2 of 1896, Report of Survey Officer J.H. Hofmeyer on Calvinia, Annexure, II, p. 48 (b).

[32] Cf. – SG 1/1/1/2 and C.O. 8430 – see Trans. note in note no. 18 above.

[33] 1/KEN 5/1/3/17, Letters Disp., Kenhardt Resident Magistrate to Director of Census, 27 December 1910, p. 29.

[34] Kenhardt Letter Book (D. 18), Annual Report for 1912, p. 19. [Trans. note: I was not able to locate this document in the Cape Archives.]

[35] 1/SBK 5/3/10, Civil Commissioner to Director of Agriculture, 26 October 1906, p. 259.

[36] Lichtenstein, *Reisen*, II:109. See also, Le Vaillant, *Reize*, I:44.

[37] C.O. 374, Letters Rec. from Land Board, Civil Commissioner Truter for Worcester to Land Board, 8 November 1830.

[38] Steedman, *Wanderings*, II:13-4. See also G. Thompson, *Travels and Adventures in Southern Africa* (London, 1827), I:103 and G.R. Cumming, *Five Years of a Hunters Life in the Far Interior of South Africa* (London, 1855), I:95.

[39] SG 1/1/3/14, No. 211, Letters Rec. from Col. Secretary, Civil Commissioner for Colesburg to Col. Secretary, with enclosed list, under cover letter of 21 November 1849, Col. Secretary Montagu to Surveyor-General.

[40] C.O. 2867, Letters Rec., Clanwilliam, Civil Commissioner to Col. Secretary, 24 July 1850.

[41] 1/SBK 5/1/8 J.T. Eustace to Commissioner of Crown Lands, 25 October 1881 and W.C. Scully to Commissioner of Crown Lands, 18 June 1892, p. 243; 1/NBM 7, Letters Disp., Special Magistrate for Northern Border to Under Col. Secretary, 6 June 1889, pp. 377-381.

[42] Thompson, Travels, II:134-38. See also, O. F. Mentzel, Vollständige und Zuverläszige Geographische und topographische Beschreibung des Berühmten und in aller Betrachtung merkwürdigen Afrikanischen Vorgebirges des Guten Hoffnung (Glogau, 1785, 1787), II:172; Barrow, Travels, I:401; [J. MacGilchrist], The Cape of Good Hope (By a Traveller) (Glasgow, Edinburgh, London, 1844), p. 30; OPB 1/3, Evidence of W. Gisborne, 27 April 1836, in Report of the Select Committee on Aborigines, Imperial Blue Book 538 (1836) (London: House of Commons, 1836), p. 361.

[43] In addition to the references that have already been provided, see also: CCP 1/2/1/95, G2 of 1896, Report of the Supt. General of Education for 1895, and Report of Educational Survey Officer G.

Hagen on the Division of Hay, 7 October 1895, p. 306, and pp. 3, 6, and 7 in Report of Education Survey Officer W. J. Hugh Wilson on the Division of Prieska, for Nomadism in Hay and Prieska.

[44] C.O. 2756, Letters Rec., Albany and Somerset, J.F. Ziervogel to D'Urban, 22 June 1835; C.O. 4438, Papers of Col. Collins, Report of July 1809; van der Merwe, *Noordwaartse Beweging*, p. 336.

CHAPTER XVI

The Trekking Life in the Summer Rainfall Area

1. Trekboer Types

Fifty or sixty years ago, in the summer rainfall area to the south of the Orange, between Prieska and Goodhouse, there still lay in one block around 40,000 square miles of undistributed crown land. It included the district of Kenhardt, the eastern part of Namaqualand, the western part of Prieska and the northern parts of Calvinia, Fraserburg and Carnarvon. This arid world was the paradise of the trekboer. There he, like generations of trekboers before him, roamed about free and unrestrained at the end of the nineteenth century.

From the viewpoint of population mobility, one can differentiate three classes of trekboers in this area. Some were seasonal trekkers, who had fixed homes in the winter rain area, and wandered about in the trek areas only during the summer months. Others had fixed homes in the summer rainfall area, but often took part in incidental migrations. Finally, there were the nomadic livestock farmers who roamed about constantly with their livestock. Some of the latter, together with the seasonal migrants, went into the Binneveld for the winter. The rest wandered about throughout the year in the summer rainfall area.

The different classes of trekboer, however, traveled about together and in mixed groups in the summer rainfall area. As long as they were on the move, one could not distinguish between the different types on the basis of their way of life.

The written tradition of the Cape Colony provides extremely scanty information about the trekking life in the Northwest. This chapter is based on the testimony of old pioneers who themselves participated in the trekking life.

2. Communal Grazing Land

The first manifestation that strikes one about the trekking life in the summer rainfall area is that the trekboers in this part of the Cape Colony made communal use of the grazing land and water. They never developed a system of winter farms and individual grazing rights, as was the case in the Karoo, for example.

The causes for the development of this custom are obvious. Until well into the nineteenth century life in the Agterveld was very unsafe due to the robberies and murders committed by the Bushmen and Korannas. A farmer could not risk settling on a winter farm on his own. Moreover, it was too dangerous for the community. The weapons and ammunition of a trekker who could not defend himself could very easily fall into the hand of the natives. For that reason the farmers deemed it wiser to keep together in groups, [1] which meant continually wandering about of necessity.

Much more important, however, was the fact that the rainfall of the Northwest was extremely variable. Thunderstorm rains fall usually along small strips. One year a specific piece of ground will receive rain in time. The following year the rains perhaps come too late or the rain skips the farm completely. This was particularly of great importance in the old days, when there were very few permanent watering-holes in the trek area and trekboers were dependent in very large measure on open, surface waters. A winter farm in the trek area was therefore by no means a solution for the farmer's problems, because he could use it perhaps only once every two or three years. In these circumstances the farmers of the Northwest considered it advantageous to use the trek area communally. This put them in the position of being able to trek wherever the rains fell.

So during the pioneer period a system of communal trek originated in the Northwest that was really quite unusual among our pioneers with their keenly developed sense of private ownership and individual farming. It was simply a spontaneous adaptation to the circumstances of the time. As the number of trekboers increased and the trek area grew smaller, the disadvantages of this system came ever more clearly to the fore. But as long as there was plenty of space, the farmers never doubted its effectiveness.

3. In Search of Surface Water

Grazing land was usually not a significant problem in the trek area. There was always somewhere after all that had dry fodder for the livestock. The greatest difficulty for the trekboers in the Agterveld was obtaining water for their livestock, upon which the grazing of the pasture was directly dependent. Permanent watering-holes were scarce. On the outstretched Bushmanland Bult and its extension, the Kaiingbult, which formed the largest part of the trek area, there were no springs or ground water near the surface. This part of the trek area the farmers could therefore only use if there was surface water after good rains.

Between Prieska and the Augrabies waterfalls the farmers could find water more or less everywhere along the Orange River. In the beds of the Hartbees River and Sak River there were small drainage wells and permanent water. What is more, there were, along the northern and southern fringes of Bushmanland a number of draw-wells and springs that provided a permanent supply of water. The grazing land along the rivers and in the vicinity of the permanent watering places, however, could not support the livestock of all the trekboers throughout the year. They were therefore obliged, as much as possible, to make use of the pasture land on the waterless high-lying Bult, and to save the pasture around the watering-holes for times when there was no surface water on the *Bult*.

As soon as the thunderstorms began to fall on the *Bult*, the farmers trekked there with their livestock. But they did not just trek blindly. That was too dangerous; one could easily get oneself into difficulties. They first inquired beforehand as to where there had been good rains and which marshes had water. Sometimes it happened that someone lied about the pasture land and water and slyly trekked alone so that he could use it all to himself, but usually the farmers did not keep such good news to themselves. Reports of rain generally spread quickly.

In addition, the farmers kept an eye on the lightening. If a farmer saw a thunderstorm somewhere, he sent someone by horse to go and see how much it had rained there, and whether there was surface water. The old trekkers knew the nature of that area well and they could estimate fairly confidently from the lightening where the rain had fallen. In Bushmanland they still talk today of an old farmer who always went to stand in front of the door with a hand full of stones when a storm was brewing. As soon as the lightening flashed, he begin to count the stones until he heard the thunder clap and could then say precisely how many hours away by horse the rain was falling and which marshes would get water.

When a marsh filled up with rain, it was not long before a crowd of trekboers were packed tightly around the water, everyone with their families and livestock. Even farmers whose own farms still could support their livestock, trekked just to save their own pasture. Sometimes forty or fifty trekking parties gathered alongside some of the larger marshes. Occasionally there were altogether 80,000 or 100,000 head of livestock drinking. In such cases it was very difficult to keep the different herds of livestock apart. The farmers did not trouble themselves with the large animals. They moved about freely together without a herdsman, because they could easily be rounded up with a horse and separated again. Various arrangements had to be made, however, in order to make it possible for the separate herds of goats and sheep to be put out to pasture together. Every man had a path from the pasture to the water. So long as his livestock were nearby the water and there was a chance that they might be mixed up with other herds, he had to keep more or less to the path. As soon as he was in the open pasture, he could let his livestock graze where he wanted. It often happened, however, that a man had to travel three miles from the water before he could safely let his livestock spread out and graze.

What is more, everyone received a turn at giving his livestock water. As soon as a herd was finished drinking, the farmers had to drive them immediately back to the pasture again, and then it was usually a day or two before they could come to drink again. Sometimes it was necessary for different herds of livestock to drink at the same time. Then the men and boys had to pull off their shoes, roll up their trousers, and stand in a chain in the water to keep the herds apart. In spite of all these precautionary measures, now and then two or three herds occasionally still got mixed together. Then it was an arduous chore to separate the livestock again in the open pasture.

Strangely enough, there was very seldom any quarreling in the trek area over pasture land and water. The old people say that when they were children, there was more love among people than there is today. Be that as it may, the trekboers were so used to a communal use of the grazing land and water, that every one of them accepted the sacrifices that this brought with it. They proceeded from the standpoint that everyone had an equal right to grazing land and water that belonged to no individual. If there were five farmers around a watering-hole and a sixth one arrived, then his livestock drank together with the others, and then everyone moved on. There was no such thing as trekboers who, already gathered around a marsh, would chase off a newcomer, or make him feel ill at easy. Everyone who came was welcomed. And if perhaps there was someone who felt there were already too many people for pasture or water, he just had to move on himself.

Such encampments of trekboers remained for anywhere from a few weeks to a few months around a marsh. If the marsh had plenty of water and there was a lot of livestock, the pasture quickly became overgrazed. Then the farmers had to move on, even though there was still water. Usually the water gave out, however, before the pasture. And as the water grew short, the farmers moved on, one after the other, until they later were all gathered at another marsh. If the farmers remained for a long time by a marsh, then after a while the water would become nearly undrinkably dirty, because the livestock drank in the marsh and messed in it. In order to get clean drinking water, the farmers had then to dig suction wells a short distance from the water.

With the wandering from marsh to marsh the trekboers generally did not congregate in large groups. People came together by chance at the marshes. If the pasture or water was used up, everyone went their own way. But the trekboers did not like to move around altogether on their own. For the sake of sociability and also perhaps because they might need one another's help in times of sickness and in emergencies, they preferred always to have friends nearby. It was a common practice that one man invited another to trek with him or to come and camp near him. If he refused, there was often a quarrel. The normal party of trekkers consisted of three to four families. It was an exception for anyone to travel around entirely alone. But it also happened that someone died while trekking and there were not enough pallbearers at the funeral.

Life at the marshes was very sociable. When the livestock were in the pasture, the men had no work. Then they could loaf about to their heart's content, drinking coffee and chatting. And if the conversation gave out, they played jukskei,* shot at targets, or went hunting. In the evenings the young people danced, or amused themselves with traditional games. The old people who took part in it say it was a merry, carefree existence. And what made them happiest—one old pioneer assured me—was luscious pasture land and fat livestock.

4. Drawing Water

When the rainy season was past and the surface water on the Bult had dried up, the trekboers fell back to the permanent watering-holes. Some went to camp along the Orange, the Hartbees, and the Sak Rivers. Others went in search of relief at the springs on the border of Bushmanland. Where the underground water was near the surface, they dug wells. The first wells that the farmers dug on the edge of Bushmanland were so shallow that they could scoop out the water with a bucket. Such draw-wells are still to be seen at various places today. They are large, round or oval-shaped, holes, about eight feet deep and fifteen to twenty feet in diameter, with a low surrounding wall to keep the livestock away from the water. On the side of the well there is a stone ledge that stuck out just above the water. The herdsman stood on this with a bucket, which had a three-foot-long rope attached to the handle. With this he scooped the water without having to bend over and poured it directly into the trough. In the old days the farmers usually built stone troughs. These days one sees many watering troughs at the draw-wells. Sometimes there are two troughs that lead off from the well in different directions.

When the number of trekboers in the Agterveld began to increase, they were obliged to dig wells at sites where the water was deep under the ground. This was quite difficult. The farmers did not always have good tools and there were no effective explosives. Blasting materials first came into use only around the 1880s for well digging. Before that time, a special sort of explosive powder was used. The powder was put in a salad-oil bottle, the fuse was stuck in the bottle opening, which was then smeared shut with wax. When not in use, the powder was sewn up in canvas sacks, which had been soaked in tallow. The fat made the canvas watertight, so that the powder remained

---

*Trans. note: "Jukskei" translates into English as "yoke-pin," and refers to a game that originated in South Africa in the mid-1700s. "Juk" refers to the wooden pins in the ox-drawn wagon yokes, and "skei" means divider. The game consists of throwing the yoke pins at a stick planted in the ground at a fixed distance, something like American horseshoes.

dry. The blasting powder was not very effective, however, with the result that farmers often had to cease digging when they came to a hard stratum of earth.

The deeper the well, the more difficult it was to get water into the trough. Various methods were employed to make the scooping of water easier. Sometimes the well was dug in such a way that it had steps going down to the water. The last step was just above the water level. Someone stood on every step. The man at the bottom scooped the water. The bucket was then passed up from hand to hand and the last man poured the water into the trough.

This process was cumbersome, and required too many men. The trekboers soon solved this problem by making use of a *wip*.[†] They took a long pole and let it rest on a bridge a short distance from the well. The deeper the well, the higher the bridge had to be. If the pole lay horizontally over the bridge, then one end of the pole had to be over the middle of the well. From this end a long rope was then attached and on the end of the rope came the bucket. On the other end of the pole a heavy weight was attached. It served to pull down the lever and to lift the full bucket out of the well. The person who scooped water worked with the rope, to which the bucket was attached, lowered it down into the well, and in this manner lifted the weight into the air. When the bucket was full, he let the line slide through his hands until the bucket was out of the well, and poured the water in the trough.

If the wells became too deep for a *wip*, the trekboers sometimes drew out water with a barrel-like roller or cylinder.[‡] If this did not work, they hauled out the water with a rope over a pulley-block. It was hard work and went very slowly, because one could not use too large a bucket. In time, however, the farmers began to draw water with a sack and used donkeys to pull the water up over the pulley. Then it went much easier. As soon as the sack was full in the well, two or four donkeys were hitched to the rope. They were then led away from the well, until the sack was at the top. The water was then poured into the trough. After that, the driver unhitched the donkeys, took the rope in his own hands, and led the draught-animals back to the well. In the meantime, the sack was lowered back into the well. As soon as it was full, the donkeys were hitched up again, and the same procedure repeated.

The canvas sacks used for drawing up water in this process were usually made by the farmers themselves. They each held ten to twenty gallons of water. The top of the sack had a round hoop to hold the mouth open, so it could scoop more efficiently. Occasionally it also had a hoop on the underside, so that it had a flat bottom like a bucket. Some were simply sewn up underneath like a grain sack. It was naturally very difficult to pour water out of such a sack without spilling it. To get around this problem a long canvas tube was inserted into the underside of the sack. Before the empty sacks were lowered in the well, the end of the tube was secured to the top hoop of the sack. When the full sack came up, the tube was released and let down so that the water flowed into the trough or dam.

Scooping sacks were sometime made of tanned leather instead of canvas. A leather sack was stronger than a canvas sack. It easily lasted six to eight months. After it was used, it was

---

[†]Trans. note: *Wip* here refers to the tipper pole to which is attached the bucket at one end and the weight on the other end. *Wip* may also be translated as "seesaw," reflecting the seesaw motion of the pole.

[‡]Trans. note: A handle was used to wind the long rope around the roller and draw the bucket out of the well.

generally left hanging in the well just a short distance about the water, to keep it cool and moist. One could not leave it lying in the water, because then it would rot. The commonest way such a sack broke was when it dropped down a well while it was full of water.

5. Taking Turns for Water

During droughts the trekboers sometimes crowded together in large numbers at a couple of watering-holes in the Agterveld. At a place like Namies, where there was enough water, there were occasionally 30 or 40 trekking parties, everyone around the water, which gave the site the appearance of a new small village. The farmers then not only let their livestock graze at the watering-hole, but also on the dry areas in the vicinity. With sheep and goats they could use the pasture up to a distance of 12 to 15 miles from the water. Every farmer's livestock grazed in a separate direction and each had a cattle post in the pasture. After the livestock were finished drinking in the morning, they went to the fields to graze leisurely, and at night returned again to the cattle post, six to seven miles from the water, where they slept. The following day they grazed six to seven miles farther into the grazing land, and in the evening came back to the yard. On the third day they came again to the watering-hole to drink.

Just like at the marshes, every farmer received a turn at watering his livestock. Sometimes there were so many people that they had to come day and night in order to let everyone have a turn. And if someone's livestock came late for their turn, then they had to skip it, because the following man's livestock were already there. If there was just one well or draw-well at a site, then not too many livestock could drink, because it was then not possible to give water to more than one herd at a time. Fortunately it was possible at several watering-holes to dig more than one well. On such places one often found a patch of land of a couple of morgen—called the *maag*[§]—where the water was near the surface. In such instances it was possible to dig several wells a good distance from each other, which made the distribution of water much easier.

At the existing wells at a watering-hole all the trekboers had equal rights. Everyone was obliged, however, to wait his turn. If he was not satisfied with that, he could dig a well for himself and then it belonged only to him.

The large animals grazed all mixed together and came to drink when they wanted. In dry years they usually wandered into the desert farther than the sheep. They sometimes remained away from the water for days at a time, and then came back grazing at their leisure. First they wandered slowly, but gradually they moved more quickly, until they finally walked without having to graze. For the last stretch they stormed down toward the water at a wild gallop. When they finally reached it, they were as thin as reeds. They then drank as much as they could and then went to lie down. After a few hours they drank again and after that lazily ambled into the fields for who knows how far in search of food.

[§]Trans. note: Literally "belly," but here referring to an elevated patch of land with water underneath.

6. Line Tents and Frame Tents

The trekboers who roamed about to the south of the Orange River did not live in houses. Around 1880 it was a rarity to find a wall house north of Loeriesfontein, Brandvlei and Carnarvon. The farmers were here today and there tomorrow and therefore did not consider it worth the effort to set up a permanent residence in the trek area. Many of the seasonal trekkers had houses in the Binneveld, but in the Agterveld they, like those who wandered about there throughout the year, made use of transportable homes.

The Namaqualander often took reed mat huts with them to Bushmanland. It was very inconvenient, however, to travel around with a mat hut. The poles and rolled-up reed mats took up too much space in the wagon. For use on the trail a tent was much more convenient than the mat hut. It was lighter and took up less space. It was also easier to pitch and to strike again. Consequently, the Namaqualanders developed the practice over time of traveling about Bushmanland with tents. The other farmers of the Agterveld were in any event dependent on tents because they did not have the materials to make reed mats and suitable poles at their disposal.

Even the farmers living on quitrent farms to the south of the Orange River usually lived in tents up to the end of the nineteenth century. They trekked about with their livestock so much that it would have been inconvenient to have a house. Moreover, they were not prepared to make undue improvements to their property, because the next lease allocation could send them packing.** In addition, any improvements to crown land had the tendency to drive up the rent. Among the unsorted documents in the Cape Archives there is a petition that sheds interesting light on the matter. It is dated 1888 and signed by 70 farmers in the Prieska constituency. Eleven of these farmers possessed more than 1,500 head of livestock. Only eight had less than 500. They all lived in tents on quitrent land and complained that they had been struck off the voters list because they did not live in houses.

As long as the family was on the move, they did not pitch a tent. Even when they stayed over at a place for a few days, they usually just lived in and under the wagon tent. When the trek temporarily came to a rest at a well or marsh, however, the tent was pitched and the family led a normal life.

The trekboers mostly used square tents with a steep roof. Round tents were completely unknown in the old days and even today are almost never used. They had too little space, especially for people who had to live in them year in and year out. The usual dimensions of the tents used in the Agterveld were twelve feet by twelve feet, or twelve by fifteen. The "walls" were usually four and a half to five feet high. From the top of the roof to the ground was usually nine to ten feet.

There were two sorts of tents in use: frame tents and line tents. The frame tent had a square framework on the ground made of wood that was staked into the ground with iron pegs. The canvas walls of the tents were attached to this. Where the roof began, the tent did not have another frame. It had only two cross-beams on the long sides. One of these was usually attached to the railing of the wagon. The other was fastened to poles that were implanted along the side of the tent. These

---

**Trans. note: that is, lose their lease.

cross-beams supported the tents walls and kept them taut. The canvas roof was supported by a ridgepole, which rested on two wooden poles.

Outwardly, the line tent looked just like the frame tent. The only difference was that it did not have the wooden frame on the ground and the cross-beams under the roof. On the ground the canvas walls were fastened with guy lines to pegs that were driven into the ground. Furthermore, where the roof began, the canvas walls on the one side of the tent were tied with rope to the wagon railings, and on the other side to poles. The canvas tent had eyelets everywhere they were needed for the rope. The guy line was passed through the hole, given a small, sole-leather washer, and then was knotted to prevent it from pulling through the hole. The line tent was more popular among the trekboers than the frame tent, because it required less wood and it could also be transported more easily.

The tent roof was lined with a light, loose piece of canvas to keep out the dust. Sometimes the tent walls were strengthened from the inside with stiff mats. Occasionally the tent was divided by means of a curtain into two small rooms, or the bed is partitioned off with a curtain. If the tent was to stand for long on the same site, a hard, earthen floor was added, which was smeared with dung. If not, the ground on which the tent stood was cleared and made nice and even.

Some trekboers had two tents, but many moved about only with one tent. It often happened in the trek area that an entire family, consisting of perhaps twelve or thirteen persons, all slept in one tent. Then only one large shakedown bed was prepared on which everyone slept together, every two or three persons under a separate skin-blanket. And if perhaps a stranger came who had need of lodging, then a place was also made for him. Poor families did not even have a tent, but just lived in and under the wagon tent.

Anyone who is used to a good house will not last long in a tent. At night it gets bitterly cold and by day it is sometimes unbearably warm; after rain everything is the tent is clammy. The housewife has no conveniences. There is no privacy, something one misses most in times of sickness or during childbirth. Furthermore, one little room of twelve by fifteen is too small, in the view of people today, for a married couple to live in and raise a dozen children. The trekboers of the older generation, however, did not feel the hardships of life in a tent. They were not familiar with the conveniences of a good house and as a result they did not miss them. The tent met all of their household needs.

In this connection people who came into contact with the old type of trekboers twenty or thirty years ago in Bushmanland have many interesting tales to tell. A minister told me that he once asked a trekboer's wife why she did not persuade her husband to build her a house. To this she replied firmly: "Sir, I was born in a wagon, and grew up in a tent. Why should I want to have a house built now?" In another case an old Bushmanlander wanted to build a house for his wife after thirty years of married life. He did have enough money, because he had loaned various other people money over the years so that they could build. His old wife did not want to hear anything of it, however. Her reason was that it is too stuffy in a house. The old man then just built a reed scaffold for the motor car.

They also told me of a rich Bushmanlander who owned 50,000 morgen of land, but lived in tents until he was fifty. In 1925 he finally built himself a house. He and his wife lived there for only two months, however. They just found the house too confining. They then gave the house to the schoolteacher and went to live in tents again. Then a prominent farmer along the Sak River told me that his deceased father, who also roamed about for years in tents, had a house built for himself in his old age, but absolutely refused to sleep in it. Until his dying day, he slept in his wagon tent year in and year out, so that he could hear what was happening with the livestock.

Many of the old Bushmanland pioneers who are still alive today spent the greatest part of their lives in tents. Uncle Gert Maass, of Wolfkop, a son of one of the first farmers to settle in Bushmanland, told me that he was married in 1893, but it was not until 1932, when he was 63 years old, that he first built a walled house for his wife. The old lady informed me that she did not find tent life at all uncomfortable, because she was born in a tent and given in marriage in a tent. She had brought eleven children into the world. They were all born in a tent, all grew up in a tent, and were all given in marriage in a tent.

The tent inhabitants of the Northwest have died off rapidly during the past forty or fifty years. Even in Bushmanland the majority of farmers today all have houses. In 1939, however, I had the privilege to meet one of the last true trekboers of Bushmanland, namely Uncle Paul van der Westhuisen (Old Man Paul), of Swabees. The old gentleman was then 77 years old, but up to that time had still never lived in a walled house. He trekked constantly around on his own land, from one farm to the other, and did not feel the need at all to build a house. In the nineteenth century there were many farmers to the south of the Orange River who lived their entire lives in tents.

Today the tent is usually only used to meet the temporary needs of a family on the trail. It also still happens in Bushmanland that a young married couple will begin their married life in a tent. In that arid world, where the people must constantly struggle against wild nature, there are many other things that mean more to the farmer than a house. I am not speaking now of poor people, but of self-sufficient farmers who own their own land, and who can build houses if they want, but choose first to improve their farms. In South Bushmanland I met a married couple in 1939 that began in this manner. Only three years before the man had inherited land, which his father had used as a summer farm for forty years. When he acquired it, there was only a stone livestock pen. He had dug a well on the farmstead and another in the field, and put windmills and galvanized iron dams on both, and he was also planning to enclose the land before he built a house. During my visit he and his wife still lived in a tent of twelve by fourteen feet. The tent was clean and neat, and furnished cosily. They had a double bed, a single bed, and a child's bed. There was also a wash table with accessories, a dressing-table, and an oval dining-room table with several good chairs. On the floor lay a pretty linoleum-block. Near to the tent the man had built a brick kitchen of nine by ten feet. It was furnished with tables and racks and cupboards that he himself had knocked together from planks.

Some people will perhaps consider this a humble beginning. But this type of farmer gave the Land Bank no trouble.

7. Living Conditions in the Trek Area

The old-time trekboer lived an even simpler life. He did not have much room on his wagon for furniture, because he also had to transport his tent, his life's necessities and his family, and he often owned only one wagon. A trekboer family seldom had more than one bed. It was intended for the parents' use. The children slept on shakedown beds. The bedstead commonly used on the trek consisted of a rigid framework of wood, four detachable leg-posts, and was matted with leather thongs. When the wagon had to be loaded, the legs of the bedstead were removed, and the frame shoved into the wagon tent. It was so constructed that it could fit neatly into the wagon, and rested on the side rails of the wagon. A mattress and a featherbed were then placed on the frame, and after the bed was made, it was covered with a jackal hide or springbok mat. In the evening the mat or hide was taken off and the bed was ready. When the day came that a tent could again be pitched, the frame was hauled out of the wagon, the legs were attached, and there was a bedstead that could be used in the tent.

Furthermore, there were one or two large chests, that were used to pack away clothes, and also served as benches and tables, a few field stools, and one or two leather-thong stools. Perhaps place could still also be found for a foldable cross-legged table with a little drawer for knives and forks, and a small food chest with a shelf above and small doors below. The crockery consisted of a few plates, dishes, bowls, and cups. On the step at the back of the wagon was a box with a cover attached in which the pots, pans, and gridirons were stored.

Often a few long planks were brought along on the floorboard of the wagon in order to make a coffin in case someone died along the way and had to be buried beside the trail.

The trekboer did not often have an opportunity to get to a store. Therefore, when he was in town, he had to purchase enough provisions to get by for six months or a year. Velvet, chintz, and other materials, with which the women made clothes, he bought by the roll; coffee, sugar and other foodstuffs he bought in bulk. When something was used up in the field, he had to do without until an itinerant trader came by. By the end of the nineteenth century it was common for itinerant traders from the Binneveld to load their wagons with clothing, merchandise, ammunition, etc., and travel into the Agterveld. They usually waited until the seasonal trekkers were also in the Agterveld and then moved around from one marsh and watering-hole to the other. When the itinerant trader arrived, everyone soon discovered that they needed something. The trekboer did not always have much money, but the livestock were plentiful and the trader was ready to accept this. Occasionally an itinerant trader stayed up to fourteen days at a site before he was done trading. Often he traveled into the Agterveld with one or two wagon loads of goods, and returned with a large herd of livestock and a large wad of hard cash. It was a lucrative business, especially in the ostrich feather season, because the trekboers were great hunters.

On the trail the farmers lived on meat and bread, every mealtime, every day, without potatoes, vegetables, or fruit. The seasonal trekkers from the Binneveld usually harvested their own grain. The farmers who continuously traveled around in the Agterveld had to buy what they needed. If they could not obtain grain from the seasonal trekkers through bartering, they now and then sent a wagon off to Namaqualand or Bokveld to fetch meal. Sometimes, however, it became so dry that they could not hitch up their animals. Then when the meal was used up, they had to make do without bread. Three times a day then they ate meat, which was occasionally so lean that you could bounce it off a wall. Sometimes the trekboer went for months at a time without coffee, tea, and sugar. Fortunately they had plenty of milk when the pastures were green. The clothes of the trekboers in the Agterveld differed little from those of pioneers in other parts of the Cape Colony during the first half of the nineteenth century.[2] Velvet trousers began to supplant leather trousers, however, after 1850. Furthermore, the Bushmanland women usually wore headscarves under their bonnets to protect their faces against the sun and wind. And the men liked to stick a showy ostrich feather in their hat bands.

Even rich farmers in the Agterveld lived in this way—people with large farms, thousands of head of livestock and perhaps a knapsack full of golden sovereigns.

There is a strong inclination among many old pioneers to idealize the past. They always think back with melancholy to the old days when there was still love among the people, and when the farmers lived in poverty but had no debt. Also, in thinking back to the trekking life they are inclined to forget the rough times that were associated with it and only remember the pleasant things. Psychologically this phenomenon has the same origin as the centuries-old lamentation about the "good old times" that one comes across in all countries among every generation that outlives its own time. This is clear from the naive explanation that one of the old pioneers gave me about this matter. "It was wonderful then," the old gentleman said in all sincerity. "It was a difficult pleasure. Today I know that it was a pleasure. At the time I did not know it."

There were indeed many pleasures associated with the trekking life. When the Dorsland ["thirstland"] received refreshing rains one year, it was a pleasure to farm. Then the trekboer traveled through all the places where the grass was greenest and the flowers the thickest. If the pasture began to whither a little, or become dry, he moved off to a place where the grazing was better. There was never any haste. Where the sun went down, there he unhitched his team and slept, and the next morning he traveled on farther. The rains attracted the wild game and he could shoot them for the pot, make meat jerky to his heart's content, and save his livestock. The lambs were frisky and his farming flourished. He came across cheerful people everywhere, who were happy to see each other. If he had a few good years in a row, he was soon a rich man.

But the trekboer's existence was uncertain and his life was sometimes full of hardships. Farming on the move was precarious. As soon as the drought made its appearance, the trekboer's miseries began. Then his greatest concern was to get water and pasture for his livestock, and keep his thin and exhausted animals alive. The trekboers congregated in large numbers around the few permanent watering places that there were, and within a couple of months their livestock had trampled the fields to dust. The weakened animals then had to go farther away from the water every day to graze, and occasionally days passed before they could drink again. They then literally walked to death going back and forth to the drinking-hole. At times the water grew weak or stopped altogether. Then the trekboers had to dig a well hastily. And if they perhaps found water, then it was often so brackish that no man or animal could drink it. And drawing the water was also hard work. The farmers often had to draw water for their livestock with a rope day and night over a pulley or wagon pole until their hands were bloody.

It also often happened that, because the grazing land and water were used up, a farmer absolutely had to trek without knowing where he could find relief. Sometimes he came to different crossroads and did not know which one to choose. All were equally strange. What is more, the watering-holes along the trail usually lay quite far from each other. Frequently the trekboer was obliged to travel with his weakened livestock a *dors*[††] of twelve hours by horse from one watering place to another, so that his livestock could drink again only on the fourth day. Many animals then never made it to the water. And the rest were so thirsty when they finally got to the water that some of them died even after they had finished drinking.

But such waterless journeys were also no joke for the people either. They carried along drinking water and, if the draught-animals could hold out, their lives were safe. But they constantly had to struggle with enfeebled livestock and they had to travel right through the night without resting, so that sometimes they were dazed from lack of sleep and exhaustion. Occasionally the people on the trail almost died of thirst. They perhaps took the wrong route, the water keg leaked, or the oxen simply gave out. Sometimes a man heard that there was water further on and trekked there; and when he got there he discovered there was no water. Then he had to trudge on without delay to the next place and only pray that he would reach it.

During such droughts the trekboers suffered enormous losses. Rich individuals were reduced to begging. Some lost all their livestock. Others had only fifty or sixty animals left over from a herd of 2,000. After the drought they had to begin again from scratch to build up a farm, knowing that the drought would come again.

The men endured many hardships on the trail, but the trekking life undoubtedly placed the heaviest burden on the women. The constant moving about was itself very difficult for the women. There was a prodigious amount of packing and unpacking, and every thing had to be neatly put in its place, so that on the trail you could immediately put your hand on an awl or pliers or anything else when you suddenly had need of it. When the men were looking for lost livestock, or chasing after Bushmen, the women often had to harness and unharness the team themselves and travel on with the wagons. A woman told me how she traveled on her own with the wagon. She fastened her oldest son, a three-year–old boy, behind her in the wagon tent. He had to hold his younger brother firmly. She herself sat in front on the wagon box with the whip. Her greatest concern was the children who had to be kept in the shade during the day, cried when they got cold, and could have an accident at any time.

It was also not an easy task for the housewife to care for and feed her family without the conveniences of a house or even a kitchen. She often had to do the washing in dirty marsh water and iron it on the wagon's box-seat. Sometimes she had to grind her coffee or corn between two stones. The greatest inconvenience while on the move, however, was cooking, because it had to be done every day, usually just alongside the wagon or under a tree—if there was one to be found—exposed to cold and heat, wind and rain.

If the trekkers remained a few weeks at one place, they usually built a small oven in order to bake bread. While traveling, however, the housewife had to make do without it. Now and then the woman shaped dry cauliflower into the form of an oven. A layer of clay was plastered over it and the clusters set on fire. By the time the cauliflower had burned away, the oven was ready and warm. If there was an anthill nearby, it was dug out and the baking done in it. Occasionally baking was done in a large, flat pot, with a fire under the pot and coals on the pot-lid. The usual method,

[††]Trans. Note: *Dors* is Afrikaans for "thirst." In this context, Dr. van der Merwe is using the word to refer to a period of twelve hours of travel, or trek, without water, a *dors-trek*.

however, was to bake bread in a hole in the ground. The evening before was for the leavening. The following evening the kneading was done, and then the bread laid out on a seasoned hide, which was reserved for this purpose. While the bread was rising, a square hole was dug in a hard spot in the ground and a good fire made in it. By bedtime, when the earth was thoroughly heated, the fire was stamped out, and the pan with the prepared dough was placed in the hole. A piece of galvanized iron was placed over the hole and the family went to sleep without troubling themselves about the oven any further during the night. When they got up the next morning, the bread was done.

Most of the trekboers' wives became so accustomed to this sort of existence over time that the daily routine did not cause them any special difficulties. Many of them were born on the trail, had grown up on the trail, and did not miss the comforts that a settled life made possible. Nevertheless, the women in general liked the trekking life less than the men. And those who now have houses have no longing for the old days.

If there was sickness on the trail, the women had an extremely difficult time. To care for a sick person in a tent or wagon tent was difficult work and it could easily be a matter of life or death. The same with confinements, which often occurred along the trail, the women had to endure danger and hardships. Sometime the wagon remained still just long enough for the child to be born and then it moved on. Sometimes there was not even an experienced midwife at hand and the father had to help bring the child into the world without any assistance There were no doctors, trained nurses, and well-appointed maternity wards. No wonder that in the world of the trekkers so many women died in childbirth. It was a conspicuous feature of life in the Northwest in the old days that many men married two, three, or even four times. And when one begins to question them about their previous wives, then it appears that a surprising number of the women lost their lives in childbirth.

In general, old people also did not like much about the trekking life. As long as a man was young and healthy, all went well, but the older he got, the more uncomfortable the trekking life became. Old people, with their aches and pains, would much prefer a peaceful existence.

8. Education in the Trek Area

One of the things most lacking in the trekking life was the education of the children. Because the farmers traveled about so much, it was very difficult to establish schools among them. The parents wanted to always have the children by them to look after the livestock and to help with fetching water. Consequently, the children traveled around wherever the parents went. Up to the end of the nineteenth century the government made no provision for the education of the children of the trekboers in the Agterveld. They had to make do without school. I met various old people in that part of the world who had not sat at a school desk for a single day. But that is not to say the children grew up altogether illiterate. It was very rare to find someone who could not read and write at all. Some children received perhaps a little instruction for a few months from an unqualified, itinerant teacher. Most, however, were taught by their own parents. In the evenings after the meal they had a lesson for a half-hour or so; during the day they had to learn while following the livestock.

By the end of the nineteenth century the Cape Department of Education decided to appoint an itinerant teacher to work under the supervision of Reverend J.C. Truter in the northern areas of Calvinia. The first teacher to serve in this migrant school was a Mr. J.A.R. Volsteedt, later Reverend Volsteedt, of Moorreesburg. He was the first government teacher in the Agterveld. According to information Reverend Volsteedt provided me, he traveled about with the trekboers there for about four or five years in the 1890s.

The school was under the supervision of a local school committee, of which Dik Albert Nel was a member. The committee kept a minutes book, but it was later used to make a paper floor. At the end of every school term the committee met to decide where the school should be the following school term. The man who could guarantee the most children got the school. Usually the school did not stay less than one school term at the same place. During the summer months the school was located round and about in the Agterveld (at Camdini, Kaboes, Bitterputs, Groot-Brandpens, Knakkies, Granaatboskolk, Kromag, Lemoendoring and other places). In the winter it shifted around together with the farmers to the Binneveld, mostly towards the Hantam and Bokveld sides. One year the school moved close to Vanrhynsdorp.

Attendance at the school was very irregular. The number of students fluctuated between about 12 and 40. At the beginning of the school term the school was usually full, but soon the parents began to move away, one after the other. By the end of the school term the teacher was left with perhaps less than half the children. Another difficulty was that the teacher never ended the school year with the same children he had at the beginning. Older pupils constantly left the school and new ones entered every few weeks. According to Inspector J.H. Hofmeyer's report for 1895— which by the way spoke very highly of Mr. Volsteedt's sacrifices in his work—the number of children at the school during that year had fluctuated between 12 and 25, but not fewer than 72 different children had attended the school at one period or another during the year.[3] The children's ages ranged from about seven to 18 years.

The equipment for the teacher was quite primitive. The classroom was a frame tent of twelve feet by fifteen feet. The only table in the school consisted of a couple of long planks that lay across three small trestles. The teacher and the children who had to write sat here. The other students sat on two benches along the "wall." These were also merely loose planks resting on small trestles. Sometimes storms flattened the tent. On one occasion Mr. Volsteedt found books that had been washed away five miles from the place where the school had stood. The teacher lived in a small tent and often had to travel 120 miles on horseback to Calvinia to fetch his salary.

The school had to comply with the department's requirements. The children learned to read and write English and Dutch, and to count. For the rest, they sang and received a little religious instruction. Standard IV was the highest that students in Mr. Volsteedt's time ever attained. Inspectors De Villiers and Roux visited the school.

When Mr. Volsteedt left Bushmanland, his school was still a migrant school. After him a Miss van der Merwe came for six months, and she was followed by Isak van der Merwe. The school was later established at Taaiboskolk.

9. Pastoral Service to the Trekboers

In matters relating to religion the trekboers also lived in great neglect. The majority of them seldom came into contact with a minister or the church. For the Bushmanlanders Bowesdorp and Calvinia were the nearest places of worship, which they tried to visit at least for the October Communion. It was a great event, much more than a mere church function. The farmers with their ox-wagons and families came from far and wide, some of them from beyond the Orange River. At such occasions there was often an encampment of 400 to 500 tents to be seen at Calvinia, and they easily collected £3,000 with a church bazaar. Monday morning they carried the silver coins to the bank in tin buckets. When the Communion was over, it was sometimes a year before the trekboers saw a minister again. Home visits were not possible, but by the end of the nineteenth century the minister often undertook journeys through the Agterveld, and preached at a couple of permanent homesteads for whomever happened to be there to listen. Happily the seed never fell on a barren acre, however. The minister could count on coming back again to the same spot, and his congregation would still remember the text about which he had preached on the previous occasion.

10. Civilized People

In spite of the appalling neglect in the spheres of church and education, the trekboers in the Agterveld were civilized people. Everyone who came into contact with them, speaks of them with the greatest respect. Reverend Volsteedt, who worked among the Calvinia-Bushmanlanders in his youth, testified as follows: "The trekboers were decent people. You never heard them swear. They faithfully held a worship service mornings and evenings. In all the years that I was among the trekkers, I never heard of a case of immorality." I had the privilege of getting to know many of the old pioneers who traveled about to the south of the Orange River forty or fifty years ago. As a class they made an exceedingly good impression on me. The trekking life certainly fostered an exceptional type of pioneer. There is no question that it did not lead to spiritual or moral decline.

ENDNOTES

[1] 1/WOC 14/13, Private Letters Rec., W. Louw, et al, to Civil Commissioner for Worcester, 15 January 1833.

[2] P.J. van der Merwe, *Die Trekboer in die Geskiedenis van die Kaapkolonie, 1657-1842* (Cape Town, 1938), pp. 234-39.

[3] CCP 1/2/1/95, G2 of 1896, Report of the Supt. General of Education for 1895, p. 48 (b), Report of Survey Officer J.H. Hofmeyer on Calvinia.

CHAPTER XVII

The Decline of the Trek System in the Northwest

From the preceding chapters it is clear that trekking with livestock has greatly diminished in the Northwest over the past half century. Regular seasonal migrations have simply become incidental migrations in some regions and in others they have died out altogether. Incidental migrations are found much less frequently today than previously, and nomadism has already become something of the past. The trek system is rapidly dying out. Some farmers anticipate that it will soon disappear.

The decline of the trek system is due in the first place to the fact that trekboers have found it increasingly more difficult over time to find places for their cattle to graze.

1. Inexpensive Trekking on Undistributed Land

During the pioneer period trekboers could always make do on undistributed, unowned, land. The Company never tried to enforce proclamations prohibiting the use of undistributed land. When the English took over the Cape, the trek system was already so deeply rooted that the new government could not prevent the farmers of the Northwest from making use of their winter farms and grazing lands.

Until well into the nineteenth century trekboers made free use of the undistributed land. After 1833 various systems were introduced according to which crown land could be leased to trekboers. Under the system of yearly licenses a farmer had to pay 15s. (later £1) for the privilege of making use of the communal pasture during the trekking season.[1] This system was chiefly in use in the Roggeveld and Bokkeveld Karoo, before the quit-rent system was introduced there. Not much use was made of the yearly licenses in the areas used for trekking to the south of the Orange River. In this area the grass license and the quit-rent system were dominant.

The system of grass licenses was introduced in 1848 in Clanwilliam.[2] It later also came into use in other parts of the Northwest and it is still in use up to the present day. According to this system, a farmer paid in proportion to the livestock that he owned for the privilege of letting them graze on crown land. Originally the tariff was six pennies per hundred per month for goats and sheep. Over time, however, the tariff was raised to a half-crown per hundred per month. These days grass licenses are usually issued for a specific piece of land, often to more than one person at the same time. In the old days when there were still large patches of undistributed crown land, the holder of a grass license was free to trek wherever he wanted.

For the trekboer who was only looking for temporary grazing land for his livestock, it was very easy to evade the payment for the grass license, especially in distant parts. The magistrate who issued the licenses never came into the trek area, and naturally the farmers would not inform against each other. In 1861 the Civil Commissioner of Calvinia said that less than half of the farmers from his district who made use of trek area, paid for it.[3] The police, who in time made their appearance in the trek area, were never rigorous in the enforcement of the law. When a police agent caught a trekboer on crown land without a grass license, he generally did not prosecute him.

He was completely satisfied if the farmer took out a license for a month or two. After that the farmer could again farm for nothing. There were other ways to get around paying as well. The police never bothered about people having grass licenses if they were passing through. This meant that the farmer who remained continually on the move could use the land for nothing. The trekboer who was a little shrewd knew this well. Thus, wherever he stayed over for a few days, he left his harnesses and other gear lying in front of the wagon. When a police agent came to his camp-site, he simply said that he was on his way to this or that place and he was just getting ready to hitch up his team.

Under the quit-rent system crown land was leased for periods of one to twenty-one years by public auction. This form of temporary land ownership, as it appeared on paper, did not meet the trekboers' needs as well as the system of grass licenses. A farmer did not know on the day when a leasehold was put up for auction, which farms were going to get rain. But farmers also knew how to get around this. Those who usually trekked to the same region formed a "quit-rent company." They appointed one or more designated renters to lease all the farms that they needed and arranged not to compete with him at the auction. The designated renter thus had no competition and usually leased the land at the starting price (anywhere from £1 to £5 per year). Each member of the "company" then received a "trekbriefie"* from the designated renter, for which he generally paid no more than 7s. 6d. or 10s. This gave him the right to roam about on the "company's" quit-rent farms for one year.

By the end of the nineteenth century there were several such quit-rent companies in the Hantam, the Bokveld, and Namaqualand that leased farms in Bushmanland for a short term, usually only for a year. There was a good relationship between the members of the company, which meant they did not undermine each other. The quit-rent laws officially enjoined that quit-rent farms could not be sublet, and the government knew that the farmers did not obey this condition, but patiently connived at it.

As long as there was still plenty of crown land, the trekboers could thus count on their being able to obtain places for their livestock to roam about for nothing or under reasonable conditions.

2. The Farmers Help Each Other

In the old days trekboers also experienced no problems in getting help from the landowners. As long as the trek system was in full swing, and the landowners themselves all also trekked, farmers helped each other without hesitation. They were dependent on each other. When a landowner's farm received rain, he helped others, so that he in turn could get help when he himself had to trek. Before long the moral norms of the pioneer community itself were also adapted to the practical necessities. The farmers considered it as their obligation to help each other.

One found this tradition of mutual aid in all parts of the country where there was much migration with livestock. It was nowhere as strongly developed, however, as in Bushmanland. Among Bushmanlanders it was an unwritten law that the one farmer had to give the other pasture

---

*Trans. note: "trek letter"

when he needed it. "If a trekboer came along whom I could help," an old Bushmanlander assured me, "I never allowed him to pass on by. He had to remain at my place until we both moved on." In this connection, Reverend Marais (previously of Pofadder) told me the following story about old man Jannie Kruger, from Samoep. On one fine day Samoep received rain. Before it was dark, farmers had already come there in search of pasture. By the following afternoon, there were twenty-two of them. Uncle Jannie, who knew his neighborhood well, called them all together and said: "Look, this is everyone; no more are going to come. I will help you all, but only bring your weakest livestock." They all came. Within two months the farm was grazed completely bare, and then they all had to move on—including the owner.

Once I asked an old Bushmanlander, whose land even today is still seldom without trekvee,[†] whether it was not unwise to allow his pasture to be eaten up by others, considering that perhaps it could require him to trek later himself. Here was his answer: "I always reasoned like this: if I show no mercy to my neighbor, how must I expect that the Lord will have mercy on me."

In thinly inhabited regions where it was a rarity to see a white man, the landowner was happy when a trekboer arrived at his farm. The trekboer often did not even have to ask if he could "overnight." The landowner often invited him, or begged him, to stay for a while, simply to have company. Sometimes there was even a quarrel if the man moved on again too soon.

Up to the 1880s farmers in the Northwest rarely let each other pay for pasture and water. In instances where this did occur, the landowner was satisfied with 1s. or 2s. 6d. per hundred per month. Furthermore, the landowners in general did not trouble themselves over the width of the trail. It was also an exception for a trekboer to pay for water.

3. Pasture Land More Difficult to Obtain

During the past fifty years, however, the places where trekboers might go for pasture and water for their livestock have rapidly diminished. As the government gradually gave out farms to individuals in the trek area, free land became all the more scarce, and a few years ago ran out altogether. Today every marsh in the old trek area has an owner. There are still a few pieces of crown land of inferior quality remaining in the Northwest, for which the government issues grass licenses. But these can provide for the needs of only a very limited number of trekboers. In any case, the farms are usually leased to the farmers of the respective districts who farm the land continuously.

The trekboer today is in the first place dependent on private landowners, who are no longer prepared to provide water and pasture land to others for nothing. Furthermore, the good old days when a farmer paid 2s. 6d. or 5s. per hundred for grazing land are now long past. The leasing of pasture differs from district to district and from season to season, but in general the farmer who can still obtain pasture at 10s. per hundred is very lucky—£1 the hundred is a more common price. And if pasture is scarce, one pays anywhere up to £3 10s. per hundred for good pasture land.

[†]Trans. note: That is, livestock who trek from place to place.

Recently I read in the paper of a farmer from Beaufort West who paid £5 per hundred, but such an exorbitant price is extremely rare.

Apart from increasing the cost of leasing pasture, the majority of landowners became all the more unwilling over time to help trekboers. Farms today are all so small already and in many instances so overstocked that most farmers do not have pasture for themselves. Even when a farmer has a little pasture free at a given time, he would rather save it for droughts then earn a few measly pounds by leasing it. Here and there one still finds farmers of the old school who believe it is their duty to help trekboers. These are usually people who had themselves trekked or still trek, and know what it means, but farmers who no longer trek do not in general lease out their pasture gladly. Many of them have incurred great expenses, especially so that they could be in the position of not having to trek. And if they now allow other animals to eat up their reserve pasture, then it means that in spite of all those expenses they would still be obliged to continue trekking. In areas where there are significant seasonal differences in the carrying capacity of the pasture and it is very changeable—as in Namaqualand, the Knechtsvlakte and the Karoo—it sometimes happens that during the migration season small farmers are eager to lease out their pasture. In the areas mentioned above, it is useless to save pasture because the grazing land is so undependable.

4. Trekking Paths and "Channels"

In another respect also the attitude of landowners has became more unsympathetic. The trekboer today has to remain near to the trail and not let his animals graze too far into the field. What is more, he has to remain on the move. One finds many farmers today who saddle up their horses and provide servants free of charge to help a trekboer cross over their land. Many have gone to the expense of fencing off their land from the migrant trail. This means not only that the trekker now has to keep to the trail, but that fencing off the trail has also led to a significant narrowing of the path.[‡] Before the fencing off of trails began, the farmers of the Northwest by law and custom claimed a right of way of 400 feet on each side of the road. If it was needed, they took the law into their own hands and used even more pasture. The farmers, however, narrowed the paths considerably when they fenced them off. The majority of "channels" were only some 100 feet wide and many were even narrower. The wire fences on each side of the trail make trekking in the area that is "channeled" nearly impossible. If a few trekboers have passed through a long "channel" one after the other, it is impossible for those who come later to get their livestock through there alive. In various regions the fencing off of the migratory trails has killed off trekking with livestock altogether.

Some of the older generation of pioneers, who cannot accommodate themselves well to modern times with its economic rationalism, consider wire fencing, and particularly the fencing off of migratory trails, as evil. They often accuse landowners who put up fences of not caring at all for others and that they are not allowing the trekboer his livelihood. This standpoint is altogether justified if we judge the matter on the basis of the norms of fifty or sixty years ago, when farming everywhere in the Northwest was based on the trek system and everyone trekked. In light of today's conditions, however, it is easy to understand the position of the landowner. The greater latitude for movement of the good old times, when land was still plentiful and there were many opportunities

---

‡Trans. note: These are the *gorrels* briefly discussed in Ch. XIII, p. 189.

for trekking, no longer exists today. In addition, farming has become much more intensive, and the burdens of farming all the greater. The landowner today needs every morgen of his land and, if he cannot protect himself against trekboers, he will not be able to make a living on his land.

This is particularly the case in districts where many people trek with livestock. In Bushmanland and Namaqualand it often happens that in four or five months during the migration season 150,000 head of outsider livestock trek over a man's land. And to top it all, several trails may perhaps criss-cross his farm. If he does not harden his heart in this, nothing will remain of his pasture land. As soon as the trekboers were gone, he would have to trek himself.

5. Difficulties with Trekboers

The majority of landowners do not begrudge other farmers the right to trek when circumstances over which they have no control force them to trek with their livestock. Progressive farmers, however, are now beginning to object to the class of trekboers who has made not the slightest effort to cultivate his land and seeks to solve all his problems by trekking—particularly against that class of landowner who treks in order to save his own pasture and does not mind letting his livestock trample another man's fields and eat up the pasture.

There are many trekboers of the Northwest who are eager to lease fields and to pay for this. But one does also find a type of trekker who does not want to lease fields, even though he can obtain good land cheaply. He lives on the trail and on the back of other farmers. As long as he can get free pasture, he will stay in one place. After that he moves on again. He constantly travels about leisurely, as if he is heading towards pasture that he has leased, but he never reaches it. Many of the seasonal trekkers in the Northwest pass the entire trekking season in this way without paying a penny for pasture or water. Cases have even come to my attention of farmers who lived a year or sixteen months on the trail without ever leasing pasture in all that time.
This type of trekker is usually very crafty. He knows every means of stalling for time and has mastered the technique of the trekking life down to the finest detail. He never displays unnecessary urgency to move on, except when he accidentally finds himself in an overgrazed "channel." He usually moves along with his livestock grazing leisurely, often only a mile or two per day. If he is not detected, he will even stay as long as he can. He seldom keeps to the trail. Often his livestock graze lazily far from the trail, perhaps deep in the farm owner's reserved pasture. If an eye is kept on him during the day so that he cannot steal pasture, then he lets his livestock graze at night. He never makes a sharp distinction between a regular trail and a migratory trail. There is not even the faintest path on which he will not travel. If he sees a few wagon tracks that lead into the fields, he will assume for convenience sake that it is a migratory trail and travel on it. He will deliberately travel on the wrong trail and turn around again without protest if he is blocked: this gives him the opportunity to travel back the same distance again. He moves about here and there, criss-crossing through a district as long as there is good pasture. In order to stall for time he also travels in circles and squares.

This type of trekboer is a great nuisance and annoyance for the landowner. He uses your reserved pasture and overgrazes your farm. His livestock come onto your lands and often drink up all your water, even though you do not have enough for yourself. And to top it all, he will not ask permission, but takes the matter into his own hands and grabs what is not his. If a Namaqualander has a farm of 25,000 morgen, he has to ride about all day on his horse during the migration season if he does not want to have his farm overgrazed.

Moreover, some trekboers often adopt an insolent and impudent attitude. They won't allow themselves to be stopped from trekking where they want to. Sometimes they are even more bad-tempered than the master of the farm. If the master has one word, they have ten. When they are dealing with simple people who do not have much experience and worldly knowledge, they will often try to frighten them and threaten them with the law. If the landowner threatens to impound their livestock, they will say: "Well then, take the herd of animals and do with them what you will. But if *one* dies in the drive, you will be responsible for it." Meanwhile the trekker knows all the while that there are other reasons the landowner will not impound his livestock. The nearest pound is who knows how far, and while the owner is away, other trekboers would trample over his land.

As a result of the behavior of some trekboers the landowners in certain regions are very unsympathetic toward all trekboers. Sometimes they are definitely prejudiced; sometimes even hostile. This is particularly the case in Namaqualand. Most Namaqualanders are inclined to harbor less friendly feelings toward the seasonal trekkers from Bushmanland, who trek there every winter. "We have a very rough time with the trekboers," one Namaqualand woman informed me. "They often make you just want to leave your farm. One has to cling firmly to your Bible to remain good." Some expressed themselves even more strongly. I have heard Namaqualanders describe the trekboers as a "scourge," or as a "plague, just like locusts."

One cannot help but also have sympathy for the trekboers, especially with those who are forced by pressing needs to trek. If I man is on the migratory trail with weak livestock during a drought, he is in deep trouble. He has to have pasture land and water for his livestock. If he cannot get these for money and fine words, he is obliged to steal water and pasture or to let his livestock perish. Furthermore, the expenses connected with the trekking life have become so high over time that the trekboer is obliged to evade as far as possible paying for leasing land and for water. Otherwise he simply could not survive. It is also a fact that the honest trekboer often draws resentment and insults that he does not deserve at all from people who, on the basis of previous experience, are quite fed-up with trekboers.

The tragedy of the trekboer is that he outlived his time. The possibility of being helped gets less by the day and will eventually disappear almost completely. Then the trekboer will be something of the past. And for those who have not read the writing on the wall in time, the transition must necessarily be distressing.

6. Trekking Regulations

Apart from the increasing difficulties that the trekboers have experienced in the last few years in obtaining water and grazing for their livestock, various regulations relating to mange have been passed over time that have also worked against trekking with livestock. These regulations distinguish between fully-protected, semi-protected and unprotected regions. If a farmer from an unprotected region wants to trek to a protected region, or from a semi-protected to a fully-protected region, he is required to dip his livestock twice at the border, whether they have mange or not. The dipping not only entails expenses, but also affects the condition of the livestock and can cause large losses if the livestock are weakened. For that reason, a farmer will often prefer not to trek than to have his livestock dipped twice in a row.

Furthermore, the permit system has been in place in certain parts of the Northwest since 1937. Under this system no one with livestock may trek unless he receives permission beforehand from the livestock inspector of his ward. And the livestock inspectors have instructions that they are forbidden to grant a permit to a prospective trekker, unless he provides written proof that he has at least thirty days worth of grazing land somewhere for his livestock. In the permit the trail is indicated along which the farmer must travel. And it is generally the shortest trail, unless exceptional circumstances make it impossible to take the shortest route. What is more, the length of time in which the move must be completed is indicated in the permit.

The permit system served the death-blow to trekking in the Northwest. It was aimed particularly at two classes: the man who treks unnecessarily, and the farmer who wants to live on the migratory trail without leasing pasture. But the permit system is a bother for other trekkers as well. Livestock inspectors may only issue permits to allow travel in their own wards. This means that the farmer sometimes has to obtain two or more permits before he can trek. By itself this worked against the inclination to undertake unnecessary treks.

7. The Necessity for Trekking Diminishes

An important reason for the decline of trekking with livestock, furthermore, is that the necessity for it diminished greatly through the introduction of intensive farming methods. In regions that were uninhabitable throughout the year in their natural condition because of cold, lack of permanent surface water and scanty rainfall, trek farming during the pioneer period was the cheapest and most efficient adaptation to this geographical environment. As the farmers made their farms permanently inhabitable, however, through the application of capital and labor, the necessity for trekking was removed. In this connection, however, it must be pointed out that an important stimulus for such improvement of farms was precisely that the trek system had become inefficient over time through a decline in trekking opportunities.

To begin with, the farmers did a lot to improve the water supply on their farms. Many farmers who had previously been dependent on temporary springs or surface water dug wells and in this manner made their supply of water permanent. In this connection the introduction of better methods of hauling underground water to the surface were of the greatest importance. The bucket pump made its appearance during the last years of the nineteenth century. It was considered at the time as a very great convenience. The bucket pump hauled out water quickly and eliminated a great deal of human labor. After the drought in 1903, the windmill came into use quickly, and with the arrival of the windmill all problems connected with the drawing of water vanished. The result was that surface water no longer had as much attraction as in the old days, when the farmers had to draw water by hand or with animals. The windmill also had another advantage. It could function on a borehole. Consequently, the search for water was eased a great deal and the depth from which water could be hauled up was increased.

In time the farmers also begin to make provision for water in the outer pasture. This enabled many farmers to use grazing land that they could previously only use after good rains. The increase in the number of watering-holes on a farm further protects the land against being trampled by decreasing the amount of walking between pasture and water. The water issue in the Northwest is still by no means settled. There are still too few watering-holes for livestock that enable land to be used in the most economical manner. This is especially felt during droughts, when weakened livestock are often forced to walk long distances between the pasture and water, which exhausts them still further. It also still often happens during severe droughts that water in wells and bore holes runs low or dries up altogether, which forces the farmers to trek. In comparison with earlier times, however, there are today very few farmers who are required to travel about because their farms are supplied with water for only a part of the year or only after good rains.

In time the farmers of the arid parts of the country also very largely succeeded in settling the pasture land issue. From around 1910 the farmers of Hay, Prieska, Carnarvon, Victoria West, Beaufort West, and Fraserburg began to fence their properties on a large scale. The farmers of the Onder-Roggeveld, Hantam and Calvinia-Bokveld only began to follow their example in 1930, but then immediately put up jackal-proof fencing. The fencing of farms and dividing them into various enclosures enabled the farmers to save pasture for the dry seasons and for droughts, and to have their pasture land grazed more systematically. Jackal-proof fence in particular appears to be of inestimable value. A farmer who encloses his farms with jackal-proof fencing no longer finds it necessary to have his livestock guarded by a herdsman who drives them around in herds. The livestock are allowed to roam freely in the enclosure and to sleep in the pasture at night. In this way, the driving of herds to and from the corral was eliminated. It protected the pasture against being trampled and the sheep against unnecessary exhaustion. There is experimental evidence to show that, where sheep are allowed to move about freely in jackal-proof fencing, the carrying capacity of the land is increased, the sheep are maintained in better condition, and that even the quality and weight of the wool improve. The jackal-proof fencing solved the drought issue to a very large extent, and greatly diminished the need to trek.

Jackal-proof enclosures also impeded trekking with livestock. To prevent the livestock from wandering away if travelers perhaps leave the gates open, the farmers were forced to fence in the trails across their land. The "channels" naturally also trap the farmers who had done the fencing, if they want to trek. Where large areas are entirely enclosed and "channeled," it is nearly impossible to trek with livestock, unless trucks and trains are used, which naturally pushes up the costs of the trek again. Apart from this, it is also very difficult to trek with livestock that have become accustomed to roaming freely in enclosures. It is not only difficult to keep them together during the day, but at night they also break free and get lost.

Consequently, farmers who have enclosed their land, particularly those who have fenced in their land with jackal-proof wire, no longer like to trek with their livestock. They try to build up their farms in such a way that they do not have to trek. If the droughts still overtake them, they prefer to give their livestock fodder rather than to take to the trail with the animals.

8. The Farmer Shuns Trekking

Another factor that worked against trekking with livestock in the Northwest was that the life styles of the pioneers became more settled over time. The development of farms not only lessened the need to trek, but also made the farmers less inclined to trek. A man who had a well-cultivated farm did not like just to leave it lie there and trek with his livestock. There was too much on the farm that could go untended in his absence. Furthermore, the farmers (and their wives) also began to notice the discomforts of the trekking life increasingly as their living conditions improved. People who had become accustomed to living in a comfortable house found it a great hardship to wander around living in a tent, or in and under a wagon cover. What is more, the children today go to school, and some parents do not want to leave their children behind in the care of others. For the sake of the children, who can now no longer go along on the trek, the parents prefer to remain at home.

Today there is also no longer any pleasure associated with the trek. The good old times when the farmers moved around, socializing and camping out together at the marshes, are now long gone. With the passage of time trekking has become a bother. Most farmers who still trek today do so only because they have no other choice, and do not like it.

Finally, one can point out that the decline and eventual disappearance of trekboers during the last years of the nineteenth century also reduced the uncertainty of the grazing land issue, and contributed towards a decrease in incidental migrations.

9. Reduction of Livestock Herds in Namaqualand

Apart from these general causes that contributed to the decline of the trek system, one can also point to a factor that was present only in Namaqualand, namely, the impoverishment of the rural population. This process has taken on alarming proportions during the past thirty years. A very large portion of the rural population in this region presently consists of small peasant farmers, who sow a little bit of grain and own so few livestock that the problems and costs associated with trekking are not justified. They therefore just remain on their land through the summer and lease pasture in the winter to Bushmanlanders who trek there. This factor has contributed a good deal to the decline of the summer migration to Bushmanland.

10. The Future of the Trek System

It is difficult to predict the future of trekking with livestock in the Northwest. The majority of farmers, however, expect that it will decline even more in the near future. Fencing has been temporarily halted since the beginning of the current war, because of the expense and unavailability of fence material. The experiments that have been conducted in this regard have been very successful, however. It is to be expected that the majority of the farmers who still have not enclosed their land will sooner or later follow the example of their more progressive neighbors. This will bring about an even further decline in trekking with livestock.

It is also expected that the farmers in the regions where today there is still a good deal of trekking with livestock will improve their water supplies and perhaps will also do more to cultivate fodder for their animals.

It will not be possible, however, to improve all the farms to the extent that trekking will no longer be necessary at all. Nature is such that droughts will always return again, like the one of 1933, which will force the farmers to feed their animals fodder or to trek. And if it ever happens in the future that all the migratory trails in the Northwest are "channeled," the farmers will not be able to trek, except for the lucky ones near the train tracks. The rest will have to resort to using fodder, or let their livestock die.

This argument is still sometimes used against enclosure, but it is really foolish to condemn enclosure on these grounds. In the past, when there were still no "channels," or wire fences, it repeatedly happened that virtually all of some farmers' livestock died during great droughts. If such great droughts come again—in which case it is often useless to trek—the farmer who encloses his land will in any case be able to cope much better.

ENDNOTES

[1] 1/WOC 11/12, Letters Rec. from Colonial Office, J.G. Brink to Civil Commissioner for Worcester, 15 November 1833.

[2] C.O. 4934, Letter Book, Col. Secretary to Civil Commissioner of Clanwilliam, 12 December 1848, p. 123.

[3] 1/FBG 4/1/8/1/1, Fraserburg, Miscellaneous Letters Rec., 1848-1869, Civil Commissioner for Calvinia to Civil Commissioner for Fraserburg, 18 September 1861.

CHAPTER XVIII

Irrational Causes of the Mobility

(The Trekking Spirit, Trekking Customs and The Trekking Tradition)

1. The Trekking Spirit

It is a well-known phenomenon that there are individual differences in the ease with which individuals leave their homes—temporarily or permanently. At the one extreme one finds persons who are exceptionally attached to their environment. Apparently nothing will persuade them to exchange their own homeland, native town, home, or house for another. They do not even like to go for a ride or to visit. Recently I read of an elderly lady of close to eighty who had spent her entire life in a Boland village: she left it only once for a visit to a neighboring town. On the other extreme one finds individuals who cannot remain at a specific place for very long. They will eagerly take advantage of any opportunity to travel about and will change residences at the slightest provocation. And there are all sorts between these two poles. Viewed in psychological terms, one person is thus more mobile than another.

A certain degree of mobility in the above sense one must consider as normal. No one is surprised when a person is ready to leave his residence temporarily or permanently for reasons that the ordinary person regards as satisfactory. As soon, however, as a person reacts more easily to urges to trek than the average person, as soon as he allows himself to be prompted to trek for reasons that the ordinary person would not respond to and trek, it arouses the suspicion that there must be in that person an inner impulse to trek. An additional sign of the existence of such a trekking impulse is the fact that one often comes across individuals who are conscious of this impulse themselves and offer it as a motive for their wandering about. This trekking impulse is generally described colloquially by the phrase *trekking spirit*.

Because this term is so deeply rooted in our language, I am not going to forgo using it. It is necessary, however, to state here explicitly what is understood by this term. I am going to use it in relation to individuals who display a higher degree of mobility psychologically than the ordinary person. The precise analysis of the trekking spirit must be left to psychologists. It is sufficient here to say that the trekking spirit usually manifests itself in the form of a conscious but inexplicable urge to trek. It is usually associated with a feeling of restlessness, discontent with the surroundings in which the individual finds himself, and the desire for change, new things, and adventure. Furthermore, it must be pointed out that I am going to limit myself in this chapter to the trekking spirit as it appears in normal people. I am going to leave out of my account altogether the psycho-pathological cases that fall outside the borders of mental or spiritual normality.[1]

In some instances the trekking spirit is an important cause of mobility. The presence of the trekking spirit, however, will not always lead to a departure from the residence. The inhibitive effect of social sanctions or of reason could prevent a person, who at a given moment feels a strong impulse to trek, from doing so. His wanderlust could also be kept in check by the lack of freedom of movement. On the other hand, a person who was never conscious of a trekking spirit could, because of his occupation or circumstances, be forced to travel around a good deal. The degree of mobility that an individual or group displays, is therefore not as a matter of course an indication of the degree or even presence of the trekking spirit.

Finally, it must be pointed out that the trekking spirit is a universal human quality that can be found all over the world and among all peoples. It is by no means a specifically Afrikaans characteristic.

There are differences of opinion over the role that the trekking spirit played in our pioneer history, but that it indeed did play a certain role would probably be readily conceded by the majority of students of our past. Our research on the mobility of the pioneer population has led us to the same conclusion.

It is impossible to determine quantitatively the influence of the trekking spirit during the pioneer period – not even to estimate it. To be able to do this it would be necessary to know all the causes that were responsible in every specific case for the departure from the places of residence throughout the pioneer period. Then we would need to measure the exact strength of every cause, and then finally to isolate the trekking spirit as one of the causes from the rest. This is naturally impossible. All that we can do is to establish the presence of the trekking spirit as a partial cause for the mobility of the pioneer population.

The influence of the trekking spirit is noticeable in all forms of population mobility. In a previous chapter there was reference to the phenomenon of pioneers who were conspicuous in the number of times they changed the places where they lived. There are also all sorts of causes suggested for the phenomenon, which will probably explain the majority of moves that occurred. When one examines the life histories of old pioneers, however, you now and then come across cases where the trek cannot be explained satisfactorily unless you accept the existence of the trekking spirit. One finds not only among tenants, but also among landowners, a type of pioneer who cannot live for a long time on the same farm. After a while he becomes unhappy with it, and purchases another. If he wants to buy another farm, and he is very happy with it, he can easily persuade anyone who will listen that it is an excellent farm. After a few years, however, he is tired of this farm and wants to sell it. Then he can again in just such a persuasive manner explain why he must get rid of this farm. He always knows of a better farm, but it remains better only until he has bought it. Then there is another farm that is better. And ultimately he ends up with a worse farm than the one on which he first began to farm. He makes a profit with every transaction, but he also does not become richer. One still comes across this mentality today, which undoubtedly reveals a trekking spirit.

Some of this wanderlust for trekking is satisfied by simply wandering about in the same region. Thus one finds landowners who trek from one farm to the other in the same district, or tenants who move around in a smaller area. They evidently do not like to break all ties with the past. The trekking spirit also manifests itself, however, in the form of an urgent desire to venture into the unknown—the wanderlust for trekking is not satisfied with mere change or variety, it wants to have something entirely new. This type will trek for greater distances and move to unknown areas.

I recently listened to a pioneer of this type. He was then 87 years old and lived in impoverished conditions with one of his children in a settlement along the Orange River. I came across the old gentleman confined to his bed, bent and misshapen from rheumatism and full of aches and pains, but he relished telling about everything that he had done in his life. He had farmed on many farms—one after the other—in different districts; he also rode transport and undertook long trading expeditions. He traveled along the east coast from the Cape to Durban; along the west coast to Alexander Bay; he had penetrated the interior to the north as far as Ovamboland. He went there several times to trade horses. At one time he lived in the Free State, then in the Cape, then in South West Africa.

After he finished, I asked him why he had done so much wandering about. "It was a way that I had," he answered with a smile, "I was in love with wandering from childhood."

The *oubaas** did not succeed in saving anything. He never occupied a high position in the community. According to normal human criteria, his life was a failure. This was in my thoughts when I asked him whether he would again roam about if he could live his life over again. The *oubaas* had clearly thought about this before. He also did not have the least doubt about the matter. He answered with the greatest decisiveness: "If I could now begin again, than I would really do things properly. I have now had a lot of experience, and so I would really trek all the more. There are still too many places that I have not seen. If the old Voortrekkers had been like me, they would not have trekked just as far as the Free State and Transvaal, they would have trekked right through Africa.... " The *oubaas* clearly perceived his life as a journey—not towards eternity, but all over the place here on earth—to all the places that he had still not seen.

The trekking spirit also undoubtedly played a certain role in the trek from older districts to uninhabited areas and regions of newer settlement. Some people arrive at this conclusion by way of abstract reasoning. They point out that people from an entire district never trekked until no one was left. In a group of people who were more or less in similar circumstances, some trekked and others remained behind. One tenant trekked and another did not. The one small-landowner purchases additional land; the other sells and then buys land farther into the interior where it is cheaper. From this they conclude that the one decisive factor is the mental make-up of the person. Those who trek away will be more mobile as a group than those who remain behind.

Such reasoning will undoubtedly be correct in some specific instances, but it is dangerous to base a general conclusion on it. Such a general conclusion would then have to rest on the supposition that the circumstances (economic, social, and personal) of those who trekked were exactly the same as for those who remained behind, as well as that the people in the groups were mentally identical, except that one group was more mobile or trekked more readily than the other. One cannot accept such a conclusion. The fact that one farmer trekked while the other remained behind can often be explained in various ways without accepting that the trekking spirit played a role in it. Moreover, the trek to undeveloped areas, in a country where every farmer's son also became a farmer, has to be considered as a normal, economic phenomenon. The trek away from the centers of civilization cannot be viewed as an unequivocal expression of the trekking spirit *per se*.

---

*Trans. note: An Afrikaans term for an old man or old gentleman that usually carries with it a degree of endearment and respect.

When one begins to investigate the reasons why various pioneers trekked into the interior, however, then it is clear that the trekking spirit was actively at work in some of them. Listen, for example, to the frank acknowledgement by four prominent members of the Dorsland trek who left the Transvaal in 1874 to go in search of a new fatherland somewhere in the north: "The authors of this document experienced in their hearts a roaming spirit for trekking. The reasons for this desire to trek were not to be fathomed. Their abode was safe and good; they had no complaint against the government of their country, nor against any taxes, nor even on account of their religious beliefs; but a drifting spirit for trekking was in their hearts. They themselves could not understand what the cause for this roaming spirit was. They decided to sell their farms, which they succeeded in very quickly, and thus they conceived of the plan to put into action their desire to seek out for themselves a land on which to live further northwards."[2]

Other members of this disastrous undertaking offered other reasons why *they* left the Transvaal. But such reasons could only lead people whose wagons were already packed to trek. It is understandable that many conservative Transvaalers would have been shocked by their president's liberal, religious opinions, but this is not enough of a reason for the average person to leave his fatherland and to trek off into the wilderness. The normal reaction would have been to challenge the president at the following election. It can also hardly be said that Transvaal at that time was overpopulated, even according to the perceptions of the period. The story of the Dorsland trek, which forms one of the saddest pages in the book of our nation's history, remains incomprehensible, unless we are ready to accept that the trekking spirit played an important role here.

In the history of the Cape Colony there are no examples of such treks into the interior, but there is no doubt that the trekking spirit played an important role in certain individual cases. W. von Meyer, for example, refers to the following case: on his journey he met a field-cornet named Du Toit, who owned three neighboring farms in the Roggeveld on the edge of the Karoo, in size about 15,000 morgen altogether. Two of these farms were cultivated. All three had related winter farms in the Karoo. The pasture was outstanding and there was enough ground water. Du Toit bought the farms dirt cheap three years before from a farmer who trekked to Natal. He offered to sell them, however, to Von Meyer. He said that his family had trekked to the Sneeuberge in the Graaff-Reinet district and that he intended to follow them as soon as he could get a buyer for his land.

Here we have a case of a farmer who obtained good land in one of the best parts of the Cape Colony and had an excellent chance to succeed in farming. But he was not satisfied and wanted to trek again. His motive could not have been to get away from English rule, because then he would not have been satisfied with moving all the way to the Sneeuberge. One would also be inclined to think that simply the desire to be with his family would not have been strong enough in such a case to justify the move. The case gives one the impression that the man just had a desire to trek and was looking for an argument to justify it. Von Meyer also felt that the reason in the first place was "his irresistible taste for a free and varied life."[3]

Once I asked an old pioneer of Griqualand West, whose father had trekked there from Namaqualand, about the reasons for this. His answer was: "There was just a trekking spirit among the people. They just had a desire to be on the move. They were not pushed out. They could easily have lived in Namaqualand. My father had land enough for all his children. I think the chief cause was wanderlust."

Another Griqualand pioneer, whose old father had trekked into Griqualand from Philipstown and shortly thereafter went farther into Bechuanaland, began his story as follows: "There is one respect in which I differed from my father. He had the trekking spirit. I was not a wanderer. If I had had the same opportunities as my father to remain on the same farm, I would have lived there until the day I died." After that he told me the story of his father's wanderings and from that it was clear that he was justified in his conclusions.

"My father was born in 1850 on the farm Bosberg in the district of Philipstown. The farm had belonged to my grandfather. He farmed there until 1874. Then we trekked to the district of Jacobsdal in the Free State. There my father bought a farm, but he failed there and went back again to Philipstown. We went to farming again at Bosberg until we were prosperous again. Then my father purchased a good farm, one of the best in the district (Dwaalhoek). There we farmed very well and became rather rich. Then my father sold Dwaalhoek and purchased a worthless little farm in order to live close by a nephew who was a good talker. It was the poorest farm in those parts. Soon thereafter my father sold the farm and bought a good farm on the Groot River in Hopetown. As a result of drought and stock disease his farming failed there and he then sold the land. After that he farmed for two years in the Hopetown district on leased land. Then in March 1889 we trekked into Griqualand West, and my father purchased the farm Kameelpoort, near to Niekerkshoop. It was crown land, which he bought from the government. After a year he sold Kameelpoort and lived for a while at Modderfontein. Then he leased Dammetjies. In 1892 he bought an unsubdivided half of Middelplaas and Doradale for £275. Two years later he sold it at a profit. Next he leased a couple of farms one after the other and in 1896 bought the farm Leeuvlei. The farm slipped out of his hands after the English war. In 1902 he trekked to Bechuanaland. This was just after the land there had been surveyed. Near De Ben he then bought a beautiful farm (Cobham) of 5,090 morgen for £375. After about two years he sold Cobham for a small profit and bought another farm from the government. On that one he remained for a year and also sold it for a profit. The he purchased a plot of land at Kuruman, which he also sold again after a year. Next he again bought a farm two and a half hours from Kuruman. Then he bought another plot at Kuruman. This was in 1907, when he was 57 years old. He has lived there ever since."

Here we clearly have a case of someone who could not sit still in the same place for a long time. He was born in a frontier district, where there were plenty of opportunities at the time to obtain cheap land, but he could never be satisfied there. He moved from one farm to another, from one district to another, always forward, along with the stream of the expansion into the interior. Each time he was ready on the slightest impulse to sell his land and trek further away.

In very recent times the trekking spirit among we Afrikaners could best be observed in the northern parts of South Africa, where there was still plenty of unoccupied land and consequently enough opportunities to trek. People who are acquainted with the pioneer history of Northern Transvaal, Southern and Northern Rhodesia and East Africa can tell many stories that can testify to this.

In this connection Reverend J.N. Geldenhuys, at the time from Niekerkshoop, told me some interesting anecdotes. He was a minister of our church in Southern Rhodesia from 1904 to 1912 and as such had the opportunity to get to know many of the first Afrikaners who trekked there.

He said that he once met an old gentleman named Prinsloo at Umtali. He originally came from the Free State and in 1895 came with the Steyn party to Melsetter. There he obtained one of the most beautiful farms. After a few years, however, he left the farm and traveled elsewhere. Reverend Geldenhuys then asked him why he was dissatisfied with his farm, why he then trekked farther into the country. His answer was: "No, Sir, I had nothing against the old farm. It is just too far east. I want to be more to the north."

About a year later the minister met a rich brother-in-law of the old pioneer, who lived in Johannesburg. He was very concerned about the lot of his sister. He then told Reverend Geldenhuys that he wrote to Prinsloo and offered him a place to farm near to Johannesburg, in order to save his sister from being neglected. He received no response to his letter, however, and was afraid that perhaps it had not reached it destination. He then asked Reverend Geldenhuys to make the offer again to his brother-in-law in his name if he chanced to come across him.

The minister found Prinsloo on the same farm. He intended to trek further northwards, but coastal fever had upset his plan. On further questioning it appeared that he had received the letter, but did not intend to accept the offer. When the minister wanted to know why, Prinsloo answered: "No, Sir, Never! Forward, not backward!"

One also finds the same mentality among some of the old hunters, who lived at the outposts of civilization and constantly traveled after wild game always farther into the interior. Various people who have come into contact with this type in the Northern Transvaal and Rhodesia are convinced that many of them did not travel around because they were hunters, but that they were hunters because they loved to roam about. The mobility of the hunter type can in point of fact not always be satisfactorily explained on the basis of *rational* considerations alone. While a more tranquil and settled form of life can easily be established by staying in one place, the dangers and hardships that accompany a wandering life are accepted without hesitation. Although the desire to improve your economic position by a change of place of residence is a primary cause for mobility in general, we also find among the ever onward-moving hunter an apparent lack of interest in economic advancement, sometimes a complete indifference to the raising of his living standards. Some of these old hunters were restless, unsettled spirits, who simply could not stand to remain in one place for long.

Occasionally the trekking spirit manifested itself as an impulse that was felt periodically, which makes one think of the migratory instinct of some birds. In regions where seasonal migrations with livestock took place, one often comes across this phenomenon.

The seasonal migrations were definitely not the result of the trekking spirit. We have already dealt with the conditions that made these treks necessary elsewhere. But when one begins to chat with the seasonal trekkers, you very quickly come to the conclusion that they were not all equally fond of the trek. Some of them did not like the traveling around at all. They trekked only when they had to. This class of farmer will do everything in his power to eliminate the trek entirely. Many of them have succeeded in doing so, to the great advantage of their farming.

One also finds farmers, however, who love to trek. "In the summer I am completely happy here in Bushmanland," an old pioneer told me once, "but when the winter comes, I am just like a springbok that has smelled rain. Then I trek to Namaqualand and nothing can hold me back." I have heard similar comments from many seasonal trekkers, and several other people have had the same experience. Mrs. (Reverend) Eksteen, of Pofadder, told me in 1938, "When we came here, we pitied the trekkers. Later we discovered that many of them were not happy unless they could trek. One day I said to a woman: 'I am sorry for you that you have to move again!' She pulled herself up straight and said: 'When it is time to trek, I feel I cannot stay at home—I have to move on.'"

The true migratory bird migrates every year, whether it is necessary or not. Even though his farm may be lushly green, the trek farmer will trek as soon as it becomes time to trek. In this connection a livestock inspector from Kenhardt, Mr. M.C. du Plessis, told me in 1939, "The farmers of Kenhardt often trek with their livestock. It has become an epidemic among the people. In June and July we received two inches of rain. In August 40 of the 104 farms in ward seven were abandoned so the inhabitants could trek. At the time there was fodder on those farms for four times the number of livestock that were taken away. I am not accustomed to such things in the region from which I come. I then questioned the people a little. Hendrik Lintvelt of Houmoed declared, "All the officials like to have a little vacation every year, therefore I am also going to have a little vacation!' I asked Geldenhuys, from Van Tittensvlei, "Why do you trek to Namaqualand; you have had such good rain?' He answered: "I was going to look at the flowers and am just taking my livestock along with me.'"

Reference has already been made to the Bushmanland farmers' practice of putting their livestock on the trail as soon as it has rained. Some of them do this to this day. The reason that was offered for this was that they wanted to give the pasture a good chance to grow green, and also that they wanted to save the pasture for the droughts that were sure to come again. Everybody will acknowledge that there is something to be said in favor of this point of view, but will at the same time also recognize that there is a difference in mentality between the farmer who says: "It has rained, now I can trek," and the one who says: "It has rained, now I don't have to trek."

Among the nomadic livestock farmers, who used to be a common sight in the Northwest, one also found clear signs of the trekking spirit. Most of these people were evidently driven to trek by circumstances, but there were also some of them who chose this lifestyle over a settled existence. Some of them, for example, could easily have obtained land, but they did not want to have farms because they preferred to trek. There were even people among them who sold their land so that they could trek at will. In Vanrhynsdorp an elderly lady told me, for example, how in those days her father sold his land and went roaming about in Bushmanland without land. "He trekked there," according to the old woman, "because he could only be happy in wide open spaces, where he could happily wander about. My father just carried on trekking for the sheer pleasure of it. I never did like it."

The trekboer without land was compelled to travel around constantly with his livestock, but he often trekked before it was really necessary. An old pioneer who roamed about nomadically in Bushmanland fifty or sixty years ago told me that there was often still enough water in the marshes and that it was beautiful there, but when news came that it had rained someplace else, then there were immediately farmers who packed up and moved. "There was a spirit for trekking among us." he said. In the Namaqualand Sandveld I came across an old gentleman who had roamed about like a nomad for years. In 1905, however, he bought a farm and since then he never again trekked. "Trekking was a wonderful thing," he assured me. "I never wore out my desire to trek."

2. Habitual Trekking

One occasionally hears the view that habit also had something to do with trekking among our farmers. In 1805 Governor J.W. Janssens expressed his views on this matter. After he pointed out that the soil conditions of the country promoted periodical migrations, he said, "Therefore a portion of the farmers had to wander about out of *necessity*, and once they had the custom to do it, they finally did so out of choice."[4]

A few years later the inspector of crown land and timber forests declared that, according to information he had received, many farmers roamed about with their livestock "from habit and disposition."[5]

Even today one repeatedly comes across the notion among people who have a right to express an opinion that trekking with livestock in the Northwest in great measure depends on habit. Occasionally it is said that trekking is a "deep-rooted habit" among farmers. Some people also explain in this way the phenomenon among the seasonal trekboers to trek in years when it is not at all necessary to trek.

An elderly lady living along the Renoster River told me the following in connection with the winter trek to the Binneveld: "Our custom was to make our trek to the Hantam in April, although it had still not rained there yet. The belief was so strong that it will rain, that it usually did rain. By the end of August or the beginning of September we trekked back here. Whether it had then already rained here or not made no difference. "I have heard many other similar declarations from people who trekked as regularly as clockwork back and forth between the winter and summer rain areas, without taking the least account of the rains. Here is a case that I heard second hand. An old pioneer at Loeriesfontein told me of a Tobias Mostert, who lived years ago at Kluitskraal in the Bokveldsberg: "He always said to me that he believed this: when it was the first day of November, then he trekked to Bushmanland, although it was still blanched there from the drought and although the Bokveld still had plenty of fodder. He said when it was the first of May, that he then trekked to Klipgat (below the Bokveldsberg in the Vanrhynsdorp Karoo) and there he then let his livestock lamb. At that time there were many people who trekked regularly like this between the Bokveld, the Agterveld and the Karoo." In such cases one is clearly dealing with an individual habit that was formed through repetition. On the face of it, it is only relative to the time in which the trek occurred, but undoubtedly such a custom can also serve as a cause of the trek.

It also happened that farmers who would otherwise not have trekked took part in seasonal migrations simply because they had already arranged their farming accordingly. In those days they had perhaps bought a summer or a winter farm, and therefore trekked only because they had the farm and wanted to use it. In the Roggeveld I heard farmers say that they trekked to the Karoo in the winter because they owned land in the Karoo and that they would not have trekked had that not been the case.

In connection with the encampment system in Namaqualand, one can also clearly detect the influence of this habit. As a result of the subdivision of land some of the farms have become so small that the necessity, even the possibility, to trek in the winter with livestock has almost entirely disappeared. Yet the farmers still go every winter to encamp with their livestock. In some cases the distance they travel from their walled houses was just a mile or half-mile. I even know of an old man who one winter went to live in a mat hut about 200 feet from his walled house. It was not even necessary to load his mat hut onto a wagon and haul it to his encampment site; he just had somebody carry it. In such cases the trek no longer advances a practical plan; we are clearly dealing with an individual habitual trek.

The individual habitual trek, however, can never be more than a secondary cause for the mobility. Inasmuch as a habit can be formed only through repetition, there have to be other causes that give rise to the repeated action. The habit thus formed can, however, contribute towards causing a farmer to trek in a year when the usual reasons for the trek are not present; or it can make him inclined to continue the treks after changing conditions have made it possible to eliminate the trek. At the same time, it must be pointed out that predisposition for the formation of such a habit is an indication that, viewed psychologically, the specific person is a mobile type.

3. Trekking Tradition

In connection with the irrational causes for the mobility one must also point out the formative influence that the social environment had on the individual.

During the pioneer period sons grew up in an environment in which many people trekked. Farmers often wandered about from farm to farm. Every day people from regions of older settlement moved to regions of newer settlement and uninhabited areas. There was also a lot of trekking with livestock. A portion of the pioneer population lived in wagons and tents and were constantly on the move without having permanent homes. Some regularly trekked between winter and summer farms. Others wandered about every summer for a few months in the trek areas. Many trekked any time of the year when they had the desire to do so or when the circumstances required it. This made people accustomed to trekking. The thought of trekking, traveling around, moving away, departing and returning, even continuous trekking, did not appear at all strange to the members of the mobile pioneer community. It also did not run counter to other societal views of their time. The result was that the norms and sanctions of the pioneer community did not exercise any inhibiting power on the impulse to trek, or the desire to trek on the basis of other causes.

In addition, the economic life of society was based in very great measure on the trek and the trekking life. Farmers without land were in many cases obliged to roam about on crown land. The surplus population, as a result of circumstances over which they had no control, was obviously well-nigh dependent on the occupation of still uninhabited land farther into the interior. For the farmer without land and the land owner with many sons, moving to the frontier districts was the easiest way out of economic difficulties. Sons grew up with the realization that the proper thing for a farmer without land to do was to trek into the interior or to travel about on undistributed crown land. This undoubtedly contributed to making it easier for this sort of trek to occur.

Farming methods during the pioneer period were also based on the trek with livestock. Over time the trek system developed into a common custom, which was maintained by the entire community. That custom was passed down as a tradition from generation to generation and the younger generations accepted it in many instances on the authority of their elders without themselves investigating its necessity, or doubting its effectiveness. Naturally such a tradition originally had nothing to do with the creation of the trek system, but for that reason it contributed to maintaining the already formed custom in place, even keeping the treks going when they were no longer needed.

The fact that such an historically conditioned custom of social migration exercised an influence on the mobility of the pioneer population, is clearly evident from some of the answers that I received from trekboers. To the question: "Why then did you trek so much at that time?" one answered, "All the people trekked like this at that time. It was the custom." Another declared: "It was the custom of the people then." Once I asked a Namaqualander why he trekked in the winter with his livestock. "I don't know," was his answer, "As I understand it, we all trekked like this. My father always trekked and now I trek as well." On another occasion I asked an old farmer in the Roggeveld why he trekked to the Karoo in the winter. "I don't know," was his answer, "it was said that the Roggeveld got too wet and too cold. My father always trekked. I inherited my father's homestead and also his land in the Karoo. Now I trek as well. The old people trekked, now the children trek."

These answers are the exception. The majority of farmers will immediately offer reasons for why they trekked. Most also hold fast to the belief that the treks were a benefit to farming. But if one talks to many of the seasonal trekboers, you cannot quite escape the notion that the trek system was based in certain measure on tradition.

In this connection one can also ask what influence the history of trekking in the Old Testament exercised on people who read almost nothing else but the Bible.

Just like the patriarchal figures who are described in the Old Testament, the farmers were pastoral stock herders. There were great similarities in their life styles. The geographical milieu of the Bible stories was nearly identical. Dr. Theal strikingly sketched the analogous living conditions of the Afrikaner livestock farmer and the Old Testament heroes. "He was living under the same skies as those under which Abraham lived, his occupation was the same, he understood the imagery of the Hebrew writers more perfectly than anyone in Europe would understand it, for it spoke to him of his daily life. He has heard the continuous roll of thunder which was as the voice of the Lord upon the waters, and had seen the affrighted antelopes drop their young as they fled before the storm, when the great trees came down with a crash, and the lightening divided like flames of fire. He knew, too, of skies like brass and of earth like iron, of little clouds seemingly no larger that a man's hand presaging a deluge of rain, and of swarms of locusts before whose track was the garden of the lord, while behind was a cracked desert."[6]

These striking similarities in the living conditions of the Israelites and the livestock farmers, the certain belief that "Jacob's God" was also the farmers' God of the Covenant, and the lack of knowledge about historical facts in general, formed fruitful ground for the development of muddled associations. In the district of Swellendam, east of the Duivenhoks River, the farmers name a particular strip of ground the "Land of Egypt."[7] On his journey to the eastern border, [Jacob] De Mist rode through a gorge, at the entrance to which a number of rock mounds were found. The farmers named it "Israelites Gorge," because, as the guide indicated, "people claim in accordance with tradition that during their wanderings through the wilderness of Africa, the children of Israel had passed through here and that the aforementioned rock mounds are what still remained of their graves."[8] A number of years later the Voortrekkers discovered a river that flowed to the north. They firmly believed that it was the Nile, and named the river "Nylstroom." Soon a group of them, who were called the "Jerusalem pilgrims," would absolutely insist on trekking along the river to Jerusalem.[9]

From this it is clear how easily the old pioneers formed associations with the history of the stock herders of the Old Testament. The following remarkable quotation will demonstrate how the history of migration in the Bible also related to their daily existence.

In 1834 [Donald] Moodie was sent by the government to go in search of the trekboers of the northeastern frontier districts, who annually trekked into the southern Free State. In a travel journal he kept Moodie gave the following account of a conversation that he had with them on the banks of the Orange River: "The father of Field Cornet Kruger, then 84 years of age, was asked when the farmers would cease trekking, and live like civilized men? He replied: 'When they reach the sea—let them trek, they must trek, as Abraham, Isaac, and Jacob did before them!'....On pointing out the totally different circumstances of the Israelites, in sanction— guidance—and destination, and pressing the old man (who was listened to as a high authority) to say *how far* the Boers were to trek? he raised his hand, so as to indicate a great distance northwards, and said, in a loud decisive tone, *'Tot ander kant uit'*—till out on the other side."[10]

Here is clearly expressed the belief that it was the fate and destiny of the farmers to wander about in the old days like God's people; that the farmers had to trek until a physical obstacle blocked the way. One has to take into account that the wise old patriarch was perhaps just trying to justify the farmers' trekking to a government agent, who wanted to stop it, by calling on a still higher authority as the motivating force. But even though the notion that the farmers were obliged to wander about due to a compulsion willed by God, perhaps to be led later to a promised land, was not always present in a conscious way, yet the migratory history of the Old Testament was still important. It contributed to the idea that the migration was nothing unusual. The man who felt the impulse inside himself to trek had no need to be ashamed. He could justify his behavior to himself and others by referring to the highest power that gave the pioneer society its norms.

ENDNOTES

[1] Such cases are described in K. Willmans, *Zur Psychopathologie des Landstreichers* (Leipzig, 1906).

[2] D. Postma, *Eenige schetzen voor eene Geschiedenis van de Trekboeren...te...Humpata...* (Amsterdam, 1897), p. 11.

[3] W. von Meyer, *Reisen in Süd-Afrika wärend der Jahre 1840 und 1841* (Hamburg, 1843), p. 175.

[4] PSB Mss. Germ. Quarto 857, J.W. Janssens, Memorandum over Loan Farms, 30 January 1805, p. 66.

[5] 1/ILW 14, Inspector of Government Lands and Woods, C. D'Escury to Bird, 12 October 1821, p. 100.

[6] George McCall Theal, *History of South Africa* (London: 1915), III:299.

[7] Wm. Paterson, *A Narrative of Four Journeys into the Country of the Hottentots and Caffraria in the Years 1777, 1778 and 1779* (London, 1779), p. 22.

[8] PSB, Mss. Germ. Fol. No. 879, Journey of J.A. de Mist, 1804, p. 280.

[9] S.P. Engelbrecht, *Geskiedenis van de Nederduits Hervormde Kerk van Afrika* (Cape Town, 1936), pp. 57-58.

[10] Cited by Donald Moodie, "Saxon Nomads," in *South African Annals* (Pietermaritzburg, 1855), p. 37.

BIBLIOGRAPHY

[Trans. note: At the beginning of the Bibliography for *The Migrant Farmer*, Dr. van der Merwe included a note saying that "because of space limitations, not all sources cited in the text have been included in this bibliography. In such cases the specific bibliographical citation is given in the footnote. Refer as well to the Bibliography in my *Noordwaartse Beweging*...." As I did with the Bibliography for *The Migrant Farmer*, for the reader's convenience, I have included in this Bibliography all of the sources cited in the text.

In this Bibliography I have also reworked all of the published sources to include every source that is mentioned in the book, to update the information about that source, and to put it into a modern format. I have also included a few more recent sources that were not available to Dr. van der Merwe, such as Van Riebeeck Society publications.

For all of the Archival Sources (Part III, *Archival Sources*) I have simply reproduced Professor van der Merwe's Bibliography, which includes all of the archival sources that he looked at, whether he used the source or not, and whether professional archivists had organized, and given call numbers to, the documents or not. I have included a few Translator's Notes where necessary to explain the source or the archive. The reader should also look at the Bibliography in the Afrikaans edition of TREK, and in those for the other two volumes in the trilogy.

Finally, for a specific bibliographical citation I would refer the reader, as Dr. van der Merwe did, to the footnotes in the text.]

I. LITERATURE

Albertyn, J.R. *Die Armblanke en die Maatskappy*. Stellenbosch, 1932.

Cory, Sir George. *The Rise of South Africa*. London, 1921 and 1926.

Davenport, C.B. *The Feebly Inhibited*. Washington, D.C., U.S.A., 1915.

Davenport, C.B. *Naval Officers: Their Heredity and Development*. Washington, D.C., U.S.A., 1919.

Dehérain, H. *Le Cap de Bonne-Espérance an xviie Siècle*. London, 1865.

Fouché, Leo. *Het Dagboek van Adam Tas, 1705-1706*. London, 1914.

Geyer, A.L. *Das Wirtschaftliche System der Niederländischen Ostindischen Kompanie am Kap der guten Hoffnung, 1785-1795*. Munich and Berlin, 1923.

Grosskopf, J.F.W. *Plattelandsverarming en Plaasverlating*. Stellenbosch, 1932.

Macmillan, W.M. *Bantu, Boer, and Briton*. London, 1929.

Postma, D. *Eenige schetzen voor eene Geschiedenis van de Trekboeren... te ... Humpata...* Amsterdam, 1897.

Roscher, W. and R. Jannasch. *Kolonien, Kolonialpolitik und Auswanderung*. 3rd. edition. Leipzig, 1885.

Sorokin, P. *Social Mobility*. New York: 1927.

Theal, George McCall. *History of South Africa*. 11 volumes. London: 1915.

van der Merwe, P.J. *Die Noordwaartse Beweging van die Boere voor die Groot Trek (1770-1842)*. The Hague, 1937.

van der Merwe, P.J. *Die Trekboer in die Geskiedenis van die Kaapkolonie, 1657-1842*. Cape Town, 1938.

van der Merwe, P.J. *Die Kaffer-oorlog van 1793*. Cape Town, 1940.

van der Merwe, P.J. *Pioniers van die Dorsland*. Cape Town, 1941.

van der Walt, A.J.H. *Die Ausdehnung der Kolonie am Kap der Guten Hoffnung, 1770-1779*. Berlin: 1928.

Walker, E.A. *The Frontier Tradition in South Africa*. Oxford, 1930.

Watermeyer, E.B. *Three Lectures on the Cape of Good Hope under the Government of the Dutch East India Company*. Cape Town, 1857.

Wilcocks, R.W. *Die Armblanke*. Stellenbosch, 1932.

Willmans, K. *Zur Psychopathologie des Landstreichers*. Leipzig, 1906.

II. LITERARY SOURCES

A. Country and Travel Descriptions

Anonymous. "Four Months in the Cape Colony." *Chambers' Miscellany of Useful and Entertaining Tracts*, XX (173) (1847): 1-32.

Backhouse, James. *A Narrative of a Visit to the Mauritius and South Africa*. London, 1844.

Barrow, J. *Travels into the Interior of Southern Africa*. 2 volumes. Second edition. London: 1806.

Bird, W.W. *State of the Cape of Good Hope in 1822*. London, 1823.

[Blount, Edward]. *Notes on the Cape of Good Hope made during an Excursion in that Colony in the year 1820*. London, 1821.

Bogaerts, A. *Historische Reizen door d'Oostersche Deelen van Azie*. Amsterdam, 1711.

Borcherds, P.B. *An Auto-Biographical Memoir*. Cape Town, 1861.

Burchell, W.J. *Travels in the Interior of Southern Africa*. 2 volumes. London, 1822 and 1824.

Chase, J.C. *The Cape of Good Hope and the Eastern Province of Algoa Bay*. London, 1843.

Cornell, F.C. *The Glamour of Prospecting*. London, 1920.

Cumming, R.G. *Five Years of a Hunter's Life in the Far Interior of South Africa. 2 volumes. London, 1850*.

[Curtis, C.G.]. *An Account of the Colony of the Cape of Good Hope, with a view to the information of Emigrants*. London, 1819.

de Mist, Augusta Uitenhage. "Dagverhaal van een Reis naar de Kaap de Goede Hoop en in de Binnenlanden van Afrika door Jonkvr. Augusta Uitenhage de Mist in 1802 en 1803," *Penélopé* (Amsterdam), VIII (1835), pp. 94.

Donnithorne, F.A. *Wonderful Africa*. London, 1925.

Dryson, A.W. *Tales of the Outspan*. Second edition. London, 1865.

Engelbrecht, S.P. *Geskiedenis van de Nederduits Hervormde Kerk van Afrika*. Cape Town, 1936.

Franken, J.L.M. "Hendrik Bibault of Die Opkoms van 'n Volk," in *Die Huisgenoot*, 21 September 1928, pp. 9, 11, 13.

Holman, J. *A Voyage round the World including Travels in Africa, etc. from 1827-1832*. London, 1834-35.

Howison, J. *European Colonies in Various parts of the World*. London, 1834.

Kolbe, P. *Nauwkeurige en Uitvoerigne Beschrijving van de Kaap de Goede Hoop*. Amsterdam, 1726.

Le Vaillant, F. *Reize in de Binnenlanden van Afrika, langs de Kaap de Goede Hoop, in de jaaren 1780 tot 1785*. Leyden and Amsterdam, 1791-1792.

Lichtenstein, H. *Reisen im südlichen Africa in den Jahren 1803, 1804, 1805 und 1806*. Berlin, 1811-1812.

[MacGilchrist, J.]. *The Cape of Good Hope (By a Traveller)* Glasgow, Edinburgh, London, 1844.

Mackenzie, William. *Outlines of Education; or, Remarks on the Development of Mind, and Improvement of Manners*. Edinburgh: Archibald Constable & Co., 1824.

Masson, F. "An Account of Three Journeys from Cape Town into the Southern Parts of Africa," in *Philosophical Transactions of the Royal Society*. London, 1776, 66:314.

Mentzel, O.F. *Lebens-Geschichte Heern Rudolph Siegfried Allemans*. Glogau, 1784.

Mentzel, O.F. *Vollständige und Zuverläszige Geographische und topographische Beschreibung des Berühmten und in aller Betrachtung merkwürdigen Afrikanischen Vorgebirges des Guten Hoffnung*. Glogau, 1785, 1787.

Moffat, R. *Journey from Colesberg to Steinkopf, 1831-1835*. London, [1858].

Moodie, Donald. "Saxon Nomads," in *South African Annals*. Pietermaritzburg, 1855.

Moodie, J.W.D. *Ten Years in Southern Africa*. London, 1835.

Mossop, E.E. ed. *The Journal of Hendrik Jacob Wikar (1779)... and the Journals of Jacobus*

Napier, Lt. Col. E.E. *Excursions in Southern Africa, including a History of the Cape Colony, an Account of the Native Tribes, etc*. London, 1849.

Nicholson, George. *The Cape and its Colonists with Hints to Settlers*. London, 1848.

Nicholson, George. *Fifty Years in South Africa: Being some Recollections and Reflections of a Veteran Pioneer.* London, 1898.

Paterson, William. *A Narrative of Four Journeys into the Country of the Hottentots and Caffraria in the Years 1777, 1778 and 1779.* London, 1779.

Philip, John. *Researches in South Africa.* 2 volumes. London, 1828.

Polson, N. *Subaltern's Sick Leave; or, Rough Notes on a visit in Search of Health to China and the Cape of Good Hope.* Calcutta, 1837.

Preller, G.S. *Talana. Die Drie Generaals-slag by Dundee.* Cape Town, 1942.

Preller, G.S. *Voortrekkermense.* Cape Town, 1920-25.

Pringle, Thomas. *African Sketches.* London, 1834.

Robertson, G.A. *Notes on Africa – to which is added an appendix, containing a Compendius Account of the Cape of Good Hope, its Productions and Resources with a variety of important information very necessary to be known by persons about to emigrate to that Colony.* London, 1819.

Shaw, Barnabus. *Memorials of South Africa.* London, 1841.

Sparrman, Anders. *Reize naar de Kaap de Goede Hoop, de Landen van den Zuid Pool, en rondom de Waereld.* Leiden, 1786.

Steedman, Andrew. *Wanderings and Adventures in the Interior of Southern Africa.* London, 1835.

Swellengrebel, Hendrik, Jr. *Briefwisseling van Hendrik Swellengrebel, J. oor Kaapse Sake, 1778-1792.* Edited by G.J. Schutte. English summary by A.J. Böeseken. Assisted by H.M. Robertson. Cape Town: The Van Riebeeck Society, 1982, Series II, vol. 13. [Trans. note: See also *Swellengrebel Family Archives* below.]

Swellengrebel, Hendrik, Jr., *Hendrik Swellengrebel in Afrika: Journalen van Drie Reizen in 1776-1777/Hendrik Swellengrebel in Africa: Journals of Three Journeys in 1776-1777,* Edited by G.J. Schutte. Cape Town: The Van Riebeeck Society, 1918, Series II, No. 49. [Trans. Note: See also *Swellengrebel Family Archives* below.]

Theunissen, J.B.N. *Aantekeningen van een reis door de Binnenlanden van Zuid-Afrika van Port Elizabeth naar de Kaapstad gedaan in 1823.* Oostende, 1824.

Thompson, George. *Travels and Adventures in Southern Africa.* London: 1827.

Thunberg, K.P. *Travels in Europe, Africa and Asia performed within the years 1770 and 1779.* London, 1793.

Van Reenen, Willem. *The Journal of Willem van Reenen (1791).* English translation by E.E. Mossop. Cape Town: The Van Riebeeck Society, 1935, Series 1, vol. 15, pp. 292-323.

Van Rennen, D.G. "Reisverhaal," p. 13 (MS).

von Meyer, W. *Reisen in Süd-Afrika wärend der Jahre 1840 und 1841.* Hamburg, 1843.

Wieringa, Pietronella Anna Catharina. *De Oudste Boeren Republieken. Graaff-Reinet en Zwellendam van 1775 tot 1806.* 's-Gravenhage: Martinus Nijhoff, 1921.

Wilmot, A. and J.C. Chase. *History of the Colony of the Cape of Good Hope from Its Discovery to the Year 1819.* Cape Town, 1869.

B. Periodical Publications

The Grahamstown Journal (up to 1842).

Het Nederduitsch Zuid-Afrikaansch Tydschrift (1824-1843).

Government Gazette (1802 to 1910).

III. ARCHIVAL SOURCES

A. Published

(a) General

Botha, C. G. *Collectanea.* Cape Town: Van Riebeeck Society. Series. 1, No. 5. 1922. See:

Godée-Molsbergen, E.C. *Reisen in Zuid-Afrika.* The Hague: M. Nijhoff. 4 volumes. 1916, 1922 and 1932.

Leibbrandt, H.C.V. *The Defence of W.A. v. d. Stel.* Cape Town, 1897.

Mossop, E.E. (Ed., and Translator). *The Journal of Hendrik Jacob Wikar* [1779] *with an English Translation by A.W. van der Horst; and the Journals of Jacobus Cotsé Jansz* [1760] *and Willem van Reenen* [1791]. Cape Town: Van Riebeeck Society. Series 1, No. 15, 1935.

Reports of De Chavonnes and His Council, and of Van Imhoff, on the Cape. Cape Town: Van Riebeeck Society, Series I, No. 1, 1918.

Theal, George McCall. *Belangrijke Historische Dokementen over Zuid-Afrika.* 3 volu172.mes. Cape Town: Government Printing Office, 1896-1911.

Theal, George McCall. *Chronicles of the Cape Commanders, Or an Abstract of Original Manuscripts in the Archives of the Cape Colony. Dating from 1651 to 1691.* Cape Town: Richards, 1882.

Theal, George McCall. *Records of the Cape Colony.* 36 volumes. Cape Town: Government Printing Office, 1897-1905.

(b) Bluebooks and other Government Publications.

Appendix to Votes and Proceedings of Parliament (1854-1910).

Ordonnantie Raakende het Bestier der Buiten Districten in de Nederlandsche Zuid-Afrikaansche Volksplanting aan de Kaap de Goede Hoop. Cape Town, 1805.

III. ARCHIVAL SOURCES

(a) Cape Archives Depot, Cape Town

1. Raad van Politie (1657-1795)

C 1 — C 109	Resolution	1637-1793
C 120 — C 213	Bijlagen tot de Resolutiën	1716-1793
C 291 — C 325	Memoriën en Rapporten	1710-1791
C 409 — C 477	Inkomende Brieven	1637-1795
C 493 — C 573	Uitgaande Brieven	1637-1793
C 560 — C 567	Dagregister van Stellenbosch en Drakenstein, en van Swellendam	1729-1784
C 668	Berigt door H. A. Wikör, nopens zijne omzwerving langs de Groote Rivier	1778
C 680 — C 687	Originele Placcaat Boek	1652-1793
C 689 — C 697	Brieven en Bijlagen van Ncderburg en Frykenius	1792-1793
C 700 — C 707	Memoriën en Instructiën	1637-1793
C 710	Instructiën hier gelaten door Gouverneur Gen. V. Imhoff, met bijlgen	1743
C 735	Rapport van Gouverneur van Plettenberg Over Burger Memorie	1781-1782

2. Raad van Justitie

C.J. 1596.— C.J. 1604 Criminele en Civiele Regts Rolle, 1652-1727.

3. First British Occupation (1795-1803)

B.O. 21 — 24	Letters from Stellenbosch (and Swellendam)	1793-1802
B.O. 26	Disturbances in the Interior of the Colony	1793-1802
B.O. 27 — 28	Letters from Graaff-Reinet	1796-1802
B.O. 30 & 40	Letters from Various Individuals	1795-1802
B.O. 49 — 55	Letters Despatched within the Colony	1796-1803
B.O. 61 — 62	Original Placcaat Book	1795-1802

4. Bataafse Republiek (1803-1806)

B.R. 1 — 14	Resolutiën	1803-1805
B.R. 34 — 74	Bijlagen	1803-1806
B.R. 80	Besluiten omtrent Landerijen	1803
B.R. 86	Kaapstad Rapport	1802
B.R. 87	Inkomendebrieven	1803
B.R. 88 —90	Uitgaande Brieven	1803-1806
B.R. 92	Uitgaande Brieven	1802-1804
BR. 93	Brieven van Goev. Janssens op zijn Landreizen geschreven	1803
B.R. 104 — 105	Brieven de Mist	1802-1804
B.R. 106	Brieven aan Com.-Gen. de Mist	1802
B.R. 107 — 112	Notulen van Com.-Gen. de Mist	1802-1803
B.R. 114	Instructiën	1802-1803
B.R. 115	Origineel Placcaat Boek	1803-1806
B.R. 116	Ordonnantie rakende het Bestuur der Buiten Districten	1805
B.R. 123	Van Ryneveld: Verbetering van het vee	1804
B. R. 131	Scheeps- en andere Journalen	1802-1806

5. Colonial Office

Letters from Land Board, Inspector of Lands and Woods, and Surveyor-General

(1806-1872):

C. O.	4, 8, 13, 18, 19, 27, 35, 43, 53, 64, 65, 73, 79, 88, 89, 97, 131, 154, 167,197, 199, 221, 274, 278, 344, 370, 374, 391, 403, 413, 425, 435, 445, 456, 467, 478, 487, 496, 508, 515, 538, 547, 563, 572, 579, 590, 600, 611, 650, 666, 687, 709, 731, 749, 750, 768, 769, 748, 803, 820, 833, 848, 864, 881, 895, 913, 930, 931, 948, 962, 963.

Letters from Sundry Committees (1807-1867):

C.O.	5, 9, 14, 20, 28, 32, 33, 36, 44, 54, 67, 68, 74, 80, 90, 98, 116, 138, 159, 180, 204, 226, 292, 324, 354, 361, 385, 424. 505, 506, 522, 534, 544, 560, 610, 614, 647, 664, 683, 706, 729, 748, 766, 783, 801, 818, 824, 839, 862,878.

Letters from Court of Justice (1806-1822):

C.O.	6, 11, 16, 25, 30, 32, 34, 41, 49, 60, 71, 78, 84, 95, 107, 126, 148, 149, 169, 170.

Letters from Private Individuals (1806-1826):

C.O.	2, 6, 11, 22, 29, 32, 33, 38, 46, 58, 75, 81, 92, 105, 123, 145, 166, 187, 211, 235, 293.

Miscellaneous Letters and Documents Received (1806-1908):

C.O.	4362, 4365, 4381, 4382. 4399, 4429, 4432, 4433-4436.

Arrear and Miscellaneous Correspondence (1805-1882):

C.O.	4362, 4365, 4368-4370, 4372, 4375, 4381-4383, 4385-4390, 4392-4430.

Letters from Divisional Councils (1856-1893):

C.O.	674, 692, 718, 740, 759, 776, 792, 811, 825, 840, 852, 871, 886, 900, 919, 938, 953, 966, 978, 998, 1037, 1057, 1079, 1120, 1144, 1186, 1222, 1273, 1340, 1374, 1402, 1423, 1456, 1482, 1517, 1564.

Letters from the Departments of Land and Agriculture (1892-1893):

C.O.	1525, 1573, 1574

Acting Secretary to Lieutenant-Governor (1837-47):

C.O.	2766, 2780, 2789, 2797, 2805, 2810, 2815, 2821, 2827, 2835.

Letters Received from Commissioner-General (1828-1832):

C.O.	336, 367, 373, 390, 402.

Sir R. Donkin's Collection of Missionary Complaints:

C.O.	4447

Letters Received from Landdrosts and Civil Commissioners — Albany and Somerset (1825-1839), Beaufort (1838-1853), Calvinia (1855-1894). Carnarvon (1877-1894), Ceres (1889-1894), Clanwilliam (1839-1855), Colesberg (1838-1853), Fraserburg (1860-1894), Hopetown (1856-1894), Graaff-Reinet (1806-1853), Kenhardt

(1890-1894), Namakwaland (1855-1894). Prieska (1884-1894), Tulbagh (1806-1822), Victoria-Wes (1856-1894), Worcester (1823-1889):

From Special Magistrate and Commandant, Northern Border (1868-1888):

C.O.	3140, 3163. 3179, 3193, 3205, 3219, 3234, 3247, 3262, 3277, 3299, 3320, 3321, 3345, 3346, 3347, 1175, 1245, 3475, 3588.

Letters Despatched:

C.O. 4821 — 4855	General Letter Book	1806-1826
C.O. 5474	Dutch Letter Book	1806-1807
C.O. 4884 — 4885	Heads of Departments	1826-1828
C.O. 4886, 4887	Country Districts	1827-1828
C.O. 4889, 4890	Detached Bodies and Officers	1826-1828
C.O. 4898 — 4948	Civil	1828-1854
C.O. 5025 — 5080	Civil Country	1854-1885
C.O. 4960 — 5014	Civil Capetown	1854-1885
C.O. 5129 — 5166	Civil, Military and Naval	1886-1898
C.O. 4895	Miscellaneous	1826-1828
C.O. 5302 — 5377	Miscellaneous	1828-1898
C.O. 5239 — 5276	Civil Commissioners, etc.	1886-1892
C.O. 5935 — 5953	Circulars	1854-1891
C.O. 6183 — 6189	Semi-official Letter Books	1876-1898
C.O. 5658 — 5664	Semi-official Letter Books	1899-1909
C.O. 5165 — 5166	Agriculture and Cattle	1887-1890
C.O. 5490	Census	1875-1876
C.O. 5482 — 5483	Parliamentary	1854-1882
C.O. 5754	Instructions Country Districts	1805-1809
C.O. 5802 — 5835	Proclamations	1806-1845
C.O. 5755 — 5756	Instruction Books	1806-1887
C.O. 4429	Miscellaneous Correspondence	1871-1882

Land Records (Transferred from the Office of the Surveyor-General during 1936):

C.O. 6367	Letters Received from Inspector of Govt. Lands and Woods, 1818-1826.

Letters Received on Land Matters from Landdrosts and Heemraden:

C.O. 6372	Graaff-Reinet	1817-1829
C.O. 6381 — 6383	Tulbagh and Worcester	1817-1828
C.O. 6375 — 6376	Swellendam	1818-1827
C.O. 6385 — 6398	Letters Received from Private Individuals	1817-1828
C.O. 6399 — 6400	Letters Received from Private Individuals and Officials	1854-1872
C.O. 6470 — 6474	Letters Despatched on Land Matters	1817-1828
C.O. 6483	Letters Received and other Documents in respect of Land Matters, Clanwilliam	1825
C.O. 6484	Letters Despatched	1824-1825
C.O. 6485	Letters Received from Commission of Inquiry in respect of Land Matters	1824-1827
C.O. 6486	Board of Agriculture	1814-1815
C.O. 6297	Copies of Correspondence on Land Tenure	1810-1811

6. Government House

G.H. 34/3	Miscellaneous Letter Book, 1807-1833.
G.H. 30/3	Letter Book (Miscellaneous), 1854-1855.
G.H. 8/1 — 8/15	Despatched from Lieutenant-Governor, Eastern Districts, 1836-1846.

7. Land Offices

Receiver of Land Revenue

R.L.R. 1—37	Oude Wildschutte Boeken, 1687-1793.
R.L.R. 44 — 67	Bylae tot die Wildschutte Boeken, 1749-1828.
R.L.R. 68 — 72	Aantekeningboeke, 1755-1804
R.L.R. 73	Lys van Leningsplase.
R.L.R. 77	Aantekeninge in verband met Landerye, 1793-1827.

R.L.R. 87 — 101	Inkomende Briewe, 1793-1828.

Inspector of Government Lands and Woods

I.L.W. 1— 3	Letters Received, 1806-1827.
I.L.W. 4 — 5	Letters Received and Despatched, 1814-1827.
I.L.W. 6 — 9	Copies of Memorials, 1806-27.
I.L.W. 10—16	Letters Despatched, 1808-1828.
I.L.W. 17 — 22	Copies of Notes on Reports on Lands Furnished by Commissioners of Inspection, 1814-1827.
I.L.W. 24 — 25	Memoranda, Notes and Correspondence on Land Tenure and other Land Matters, 1813-1826.
I.L.W. 53	Title Deeds, Transfers and Diagrams, 1670, 1700-1732.

Board of Commissioners for Land

L.B. 1 — 2	Minutes of Meetings	1828-1877
L.B. 3 — 6	Land Reports, Cape Division	1818-1845
L.B. 9 — 14	Stellenbosch	1814-1852
L.B. 21 — 22	Swellendam	1814-1826.
L.B. 29 — 30	Graaff-Reinet	1816-1830
L.B. 38	Tulbagh	1816-1827
L.B. 39 — 44	Worcester	1821-1827
L.B. 57	Beaufort	1822
L.B. 58	Various Districts	1818-1828
L.B. 77	Albert and Hopetown	1859-1864
L.B. 78	Albert, Beaufort, Colesberg, Middelburg and Graaff-Reinet	1848-1868.
L.B. 79	Victoria West	1866
L.B. 97 — 101	Letters Received	1828-1876.
L.B. 102 — 104	Letters Despatched	1828-1876

8. Argief van die Luitenant-Goewerneur

L.G. 13— 16	Letters Received from Colonial Secretary, 1826-1843.
L.G. 41	Letters Received from Surveyor-General, 1837-1841.
L.G. 67— 71	Letters Received from Surveyor-General, 1837-1845.
L.G. 72— 74	Letters Received from Civil Commissioner, Cradock, 1836-1844.
L.G. 80 — 82	Letters Received from Civil Commissioner, Graaff-Reinet, 1836-1847
L.G. 97— 99	Letters Received from Civil Commissioner, Somerset, 1836-1847.
L.G. 188 — 202	Miscellaneous Letters, 1822-1847.
L.G. 117	Letters Received from Various Civil Commissioners, 1837-1846.
L.G. 135	Field Cornets' Returns, 1824-1840.
L.G. 279	Field Cornets' Returns, 1824-1840.
L.G. 280	Letters Despatched, 1836-1837.

9. Stellenbosch-Argief

St. 1/1 — 1/21	Notule van Landdros en Heemrade	1691-1795
St. 1/132	Rapporte van Gecommitteerde Heemrade	1746-1784
St. 3/8 — 3/13	Verklarings in Kriminele Sake	1740-1796.
St. 10/2	Inkomende Briewe	1732-1748.
St. 10/4	Inkomende Briewe	1759-1785
St. 10/165	Ink. Br. van Veldwagtmeesters en Private Persone	1795-1798
St. 10/166 — 10/171	Ink. Br. van Private Persone	1775-1795
St. 10/162	Ink. Br. van Veldkornette (i.v.m. Rowery van Boesmans)	1773-93
St. 10/163	Ink. Br. van Veldkornette	1775-1795.
St. 11/24	Korrespondensie insake Leningsplase	1793-1795
St. 11/48	Briewe en Verklarings ten opsigte van plase, bakens, water, vee en die onwettige verblyf van sekere persone op kroongronde	1767-1850
St. 13/1 — 13/11	Notule van die Krygsraad	1688-1798

St. 13/13	Inkomende Brieven	1780-1797
St. 13/31	Alfabetiese Naamlyste van Persone wat op Veldtogte uitgegaan het	1736-1744
St. 13/43	Kommando Dokumente	1776-1846
St. 18/153 — 154 and St. 18/157 — 18/165	Notariële Verklarings	1686-1796
St. 119/1, 19/2 and 19/4	Instruksies, Proklamasies en Ordonnansies	1686-1824
St. 19/23	Biljette	1686-1822
St. 19/165	Dokumente betreffende Overbergse Sake	1744-1767
St. 20/1 — 20/5	Uitgaande Brieven van Landdros en Heemrade	1687-1793
St. 20/30	Uitgaande Briewe van Landdros	1795-1801

10. Graaff-Reinet-Argief

G.R. 1/1 — 1/4	Minutes of Landdrost and Heemraden, 1786-1827.
G.R. 3/16 — 3/28	Judicial Declarations, etc., 1786-1826.
G.R. 7/1 — 7/11	Journal, 1811-1825.
G.R. 8/1 — 8/26	Letters Received from Government, 1806-1836.
G.R. 9/5	Letters from Commissioner-General, 1828-1830.
G.R. 10/1 — 10/27	Miscellaneous Letters Received, 1804-1840.
G.R. 10/40	Miscellaneous, 1789-1904.
G.R. 11/2 — 11/17	Brieven uit Cradock, 1818-1842.
G.R. 11/19 — 11/20	Brieven uit Cradock, 1813-1820.
G.R. 12/1 — 12/17	Letters Received from Field Comets, etc., 1787-1841
G.R. 13/1 — 13/5	Letters Received from Private Individuals, 1781-1853
G.R. 16/1 — 16/17	Letters Despatched (Landdrost and Secretary), 1786-1827.
G.R. 16/13 — 16/55	Letters Despatched by Civil Commissioner, 1828-1842.
G.R. 1/9	Minutes and Annexures of Krygsraad, 1787-1795.

11. Swellendam-Argief

SW 1/1 — 1/4	Notule van Landdros en Heemrade, 1747-1827.
SW 1/5	Kladnotule van Landdros en Heemrade, 1789-1804.
SW 3/10 — 3/17	Algemene Verklarings, 1746-1795.
SW 10/1 — 10/2	Dagregisters, 1755-1787.
SW 11/1 — 11/5	Inkomende Brieven, 1743-1795.
SW 14/1	Uitgaande Briewe, 1745-1767.

12. Colesberg

Colesberg 20 — 21	Letters Received by Civil Commissioner, 1840-1842.
Colesberg 96 — 98	Circulars and Letters, 1839-1846.

13. Beaufort-Wes-Argief

B.W. 1/1 — 1/3	Minutes of Meetings, 1823-1827.
B.W. 9/1 — 9/3	Letters Received, Colonial Office, 1818-1847.
B.W. 9/29 — 9/34	Letters from Landdrost, Graaff-Reinet, 1818-1827.
B.W. 9/38	Letters from Civil Commissioner, Graaff-Reinet, 1836-1837.
B.W. 11/1 — 11/6	Letter Books, 1818-1826.
B.W. 9/45 — 9/50	Letters from Field Cornets, 1819-1828.
B.W. 9/58 — 9/60	Letters from Private Individuals, 1819-1833.
B.W. 9/66	Miscellaneous Letter Received, 1823-1827.

14. Worcester-Argief

W. 1/1 — 1/6	Notule van Landdros en Heemrade, 1804-1827.
W. 1/7 — 1/14	Kladnotule van Landdros en Heemrade, 1805-1827.
W. 1/15 — 1/18	Bylae tot Notule, 1815-1822.
W. 10/1 — 10/17	Dagregisters, 1804-1833.
W. 11/1 — 11/19	Inkomende Briewe van Koloniale Kantoor, 1805-1859.

W. 12/1 — 12/66	Inkomende Briewe van Amptenare, 1804-1902.
W. 12/67 — 12/84	Gemengde Inkomende Briewe, 1814-1851.
W. 13/1 — 13/30	Briewe Ontvang van Veldkornette, 1804-1871.
W. 14/1 — 14/18	Inkomende Briewe van Private Persone. 1804-1871.
W. 14/19	Verklarings (Veldkornette en Private Persone), 1803-1805.
W. 14/20 — 14/21	Verklarings (meestal Landsake), 1800-1812.
W. 14/22	Rekweste vir Leningsplase en Rapporte en Korrespondensie in verband daarmee, 1802-1808.
W. 14/23	Lys van Rekweste vir Land.
W. 14/24 — 14/30	Register van Memories, 1823-1849.
W. 15/40	Kaarte van Leningsplase in die Veldkornetskap van Klein-Roggeveld, 1834.
W. 15/43	Gemengde Dokumente oor Landerye, 1809-1888.
W. 17/1 — 17/46	Uitgaande Briewe, 1810-1881.
W. 19/1	Notule van Adjunk-Landdros en Heemrade, 1821-1822.
W. 19/2	Bylae en Notule, 1821-1822.
W. 19/5	Dagregister van Adjunk-Landdros, 1821-1822.
W. 19/7 — 19/11	Inkomende Briewe, 1820-1822.
W. 19/12	Uitgaande Briewe, 1819-1822.

15. Calvinia-Argief (ongeorden)[1]

Letters Received, Lands, 1911-1913.

Letters Received, Agriculture, 1901-1910 (2 Bande).

Letters Received, Surveyor-General, 1900-1913 (3 Bande).

Letters Received, Miscellaneous, 1899-1911.

---

[1]Trans. note: *Ongeorden* translates as "unarranged," meaning that when Dr. van der Merwe accessed these sources archivists had not yet gone through them, arranged them, and given them call numbers. That is, they were simply loose piles of documents. The reader will note that the next seven collections of documents were also *ongeorden*.

16. Ceres-Argief (ongeorden)

Miscellaneous Records.

Letters from Commissioner for Crown Lands. 1892-1894.

Letters from Secretary for Agriculture.

Letters from Department of Agriculture.

Miscellaneous Letters. 1911-1912.

Lease of Crown Lands, 1872-1883.

17. Fraserburg-Argief (ongeorden)

Letter Book, 1860-1890 (10 Bande).

Letters Received, 1861-1890 (16 Bande).

Land Sales Register, 1837-1859.

Land Sales Register, 1866-1872.

Land Rent Book, 1859-1874.

Crown Land Leases. 1865.

Quitrent Register, 1867-1877.

Land Sales under Act 19, 1864; purchased under Act 5, 1870.

18. Kenhardt-Argief (ongeorden)

Letters Received, 1879-1918 (32 Bande).

Letter Book, 1872-1914 (62 Bande).

19. Namakwaland-Argief (ongeorden)

Letter Book, 1855-1914 (78 Bande).

Letters Received by Resident Magistrate, 1889-1913 (49 Bande).

20. Prieska-Argief (ongeorden)

Letter Books, 1883-1899 (14 Bande).

Letters Received by C.C. and R.M., 1883-1899 (13 Bande).

21. Richmond-Argief (ongeorden)

Miscellaneous Letters Received, 1861-1862.

22. Victoria-Wes-Argief (ongeorden)

Letter Books, 1862-1890 (15 Bande).

(b) Argief van die Landmeter-Generaal. Parlementstraat

(Afkorting: S.G.P.)

Government Letters Received, 1829-1886 (91 Bande).

Letters from Civil Commissioners, Western Province, 1824-1902 (26 Bande).

Government Letter Book, 1854-1890 (57 Bande).

General Letter Book, 1840-1876 (40 Bande).

(c) Algemeen Rijksarchief, Den Haag

Aanwinsten, 1914 (Versameling van J. van Plettenberg)

No. 26 (a):	Journaal van een Reisje gedaan naar de Saldanha en St. Helena Baaijen, 1776.
No. 27:	Dagregister van een Tocht in de Kaap door Pieter Cloetcn, 1776.
No. 27 (a):	Journaal van een Reisje, gedaan naar het Heeren Logements Gebergte en de mond der Olifants Rivier in het Noorden der Colonie. 1777.
No. 28:	Dagregister van den Tocht tot aan de Plettenberg's en Groote Rivier door Olof Gotlieb de Wet, 1778.
No. 20-50:	Reisverhalen van zijn Tochten langs de Groote Rivier door Hendrik Jacob Wikar, 1778-1779

Aanwinsten, 1900 (No. XX)

Journaal en Verhaal eener Land Reijze in den jaar 1803 door J. W. Janssens.

Aanwinsten, Nederburg Versameling

No. 40	157, 168. 242, 548 (a).

Koloniaal Archief

No. 3969 — 4338	Brieven en Papieren van Cabo de Bonne Esperance Overgekomen, 1657-1794.

Raad der Aziatische Bezittingen en Establissementen

No. 292	Missives van den Commissaris-Generaal over de Kaap de Goede Hoop, Mr. J. A. de Mist, aan den Raad met Bijlagen, 1802-1805.
No. 293 — 303	Notulen en Handelingen van Commissaris-Generaal Over de Kaap de Goede Hoop, Mr. J. A. de Mist met Bijlagen, 1802-1805.
No. 309 — 310	Missives van den Gouverneur en Raad van de Kaap de Goede Hoop Aan den Raad met Bijlagen, 1803-1806.
No. 311	Missives van den Gouverneur en Generaal en Chev. aan de Kaap de Goede Hoop aan den Raad met Bijlagen, 1803-1806
No. 350	Missives van bijzondere Kaapsche Ambtenaren aan den Raad met Bjlagen, 1803.

(d) Public Records Office, London

C.O. 48/1—48/186	Secretary of State, Original Correspondence, 1807-1837.

(e) Pruisiese Staatsbiblioteek, Berlyn

I. Mss. Germ. Octav. (M. H. K. Lichtenstein)

No. 275[2]	J. A. de Mist: Memoranda van de Kaapsche Landreize, 1803.

---

[2]Trans. note: In all three volumes of Dr. van der Merwe's triology, the "Mss. germ. octav." number is given incorrectly as 257. It should be 275. The translator thanks Dr. Peter Jörg Becker, librarian at the Staatsbibliothek Preussischer Kulturbesitz, for his helpful research on the documents cited and for pointing out the error. The call numbers for this collection of manuscripts have not changed since Dr. van der Merwe researched them. He obtained his citations from the "Degering," short for the catalogue created by Hermann Degering, *Kurzes Verzeichnis der Germanischen Handschriften der Preussichen Staatsbibliothek*, 3 vols. (Leipzig: Karl W. Hiersemann, 1925, 1926, 1932). Personal correspondence, Becker to Translator, 19 May 1992.

II. MSS. GERM. QUARTO.

| No. 857 | Berichte des General-Gouverneurs der Kap-Kolonie, General Comissar J. A. de Mist über die inneren Verhältnisse der Kolonie, 1804-1805. |

III. MSS. GERM. FOL.

No. 879	Reize uit Nederland Naar de Kaap de Goede Hoopf en terug. En voorts het Dagverhaal van een Landreize in de Binnenlanden op de Zuidhoek van Afrika door J. A. de Mist in de Jaaren 1802, 1803, 1804 en 1805, gevolgd door een beschrijving en beschouwing van den tegenwoordigen toestand dier Volkplanting en derzelver naburige natiën.
No. 880	Journaal en Verhaal eener Landreise in den Jaare 1803 door den Gouverneur en Generaal deezer Colonie J. W. Janssens door de Binnenlanden van Zuijd Afrika gedaan.
No. 881	Kladjournaal der Reize gedaan door den Commissaris-Generaal J. A. de Mist en deszelfs gevolg in de Binnenlanden van Africa, 1803-4.
No. 883	Notul of Dagverhaal der Reis en Verrichtingen van Praesident en Gecommitteerde Leeden uit de Commissie van Veeteelt en Landbou in de beiden Roggevelden, den Hantam etc. (1805).
No. 887	Zusammengestellte Schrifstücke und Notizen aus der Kanzlei des General-Kommissars J. A. de Mist, 1795-1804.
No. 888	Berichte des General-Gouverneurs der Kap Kolonie J. W. Janssens an den General-Kommissar J. A. de Mist betr. die inneren Verhältnisse der Kolonie, 1803-4.
No. 890	Lichtenstein, M. H. K.: Geschichte der Kap Kolonie (materialen und Entwürfde); Geschichte der Entdeckung und Colonisation des Südlichen Afrikas (autograph).
No. 892	Een Generale Beschrijving van de Kolonie de Kaap de Goede Hoop en de vier distrikten, waaruit dezelve is zamengesteld, 1798.
No. 894 and 895	Memorie over de Kaap de Goede Hoop, I en II en III.
No. 896 and 897	Schriftwechsel zwischen den General-Gouverneur der Kap Kolonie J. W. Janssens und dem General-Kommissar J. A. de Mist, 1803-1805.

(f) VARIA

Die Swellengrebel Familie-argief (Nederland).[3]

Travel journal of Swellengrebel, 1776, pp. 2, 23, 28, 74, 85, 94, 98, etc. [sic]. [Trans. Note: I have listed here all the page numbers in the original journals cited for this source in the footnotes. I did not have access to this archive to check the sources. The journals were written by the son of the first and only Cape born Dutch East India Company governor of the Colony, Hendrik

---

[3][Trans. note: Dr. van der Merwe simply makes a one-line reference to this archive at the end of his Bibliography. I have added references to the three documents that Professor van der Merwe cites in TREK from the Swellengrebel collection.]

Swellengrebel (1700-1760, governor - April 1739-February 1751). The journals are accounts of Hendrik Swellengrebel, Jr.'s three journeys into the interior—18 July 1776 to 31 July 1776; 10 September 1776 to 26 December 1776; and, 12 December 1777 to 29 January 1777. In 2018 the Van Riebeeck Society published Swellengrebel's journals of these three trips, edited by Gerrit Schutte: Hendrik Swellengrebel, Jr., *Hendrik Swellengrebel in Afrika: Journalen van Drie Reizen in 1776-1777/Hendrik Swellengrebel in Africa: Journals of Three Journeys in 1776-1777*, Series II, No. 49 (Cape Town: Van Riebeeck Society, 2018.) This volume also contains the aqarelles made by Swellengrebel's artist, Johannes Schumacher.]

Van Plettenberg to Swellengrebel, 7 March 1780. [Trans. Note: This letter from J. A. Baron van Plettenberg to Swellengrebel may also be found in the collection of letters published by the Van Riebeeck Society, *Briefwisseling van Hendrik Swellengrebel Jr. oor Kaapse Sake, 1778-1792*, VRS, series II, vol. 13, pp. 119-22 in the original Dutch, with a shortened English summary, pp. 329-30.]

Hendrik Swellengrebel, Jr. to C. de Gyselaar, 26 June 1783. [Trans. Note: This letter from Swellengrebel to Gyselaar may also be found in the collection of letters published by the Van Riebeeck Society, *Briefwisseling van Hendrik Swellengrebel Jr. oor Kaapse Sake, 1778-1792*, VRS, series II, vol. 13, pp. 151-62 in the original Dutch with a shortened English summary, pp. 348-52]

INDEX